Editor's Foreword

Snared by Words? (Proverbs 6:2): On the Perils of Editing

ADELE REINHARTZ

> For last year's words belong to last year's language
> And next year's words await another voice.
> —T. S. Eliot, *Four Quartets*

Every year, the Oxford Dictionaries choose a word "that captures the ethos, mood, or preoccupations of that particular year."[1] On 17 November 2015, Oxford Dictionaries announced that its Word of the Year 2015 would be an emoji, not emoji(s)[2] in general but a particular emoji  commonly known as "Face with Tears of Joy."[3] Casper Grathwohl, the president of Oxford Dictionaries, commented that the increasing popularity of this symbol, and of emojis in general, reflects the failure of "traditional alphabet scripts … to meet the rapid-fire, visually focused demands of 21st Century communication."[4] As a pictographic script, he maintained, the emoji is flexible, immediate, and capable of conveying tone and emotion in a way that standard words are not.[5]

The choice of an emoji as the 2015 Word of the Year acknowledges and indeed celebrates the paralinguistic symbols that have developed for the purposes of electronic modes of communication such as texting and Facebook. But from my perch in the ivory tower, this choice also sounds like a cry of despair—or at least an expression of angst and frustration—over the increasingly fraught and contested nature of language today, whether in the public sphere or in the academy. In my

---

[1] See http://blog.oxforddictionaries.com/press-releases/announcing-the-oxford-dictionaries-word-of-the-year-2015/. My thanks to Paula Fredriksen for alerting me to this announcement.

[2] On the vexed question of whether the plural is emoji or emojis, see http://www.theatlantic.com/technology/archive/2016/01/whats-the-plural-of-emoji-emojis/422763/.

[3] See http://blog.oxforddictionaries.com/press-releases/announcing-the-oxford-dictionaries-word-of-the-year-2015/.

[4] Ibid.

[5] Ibid.

own work in "Early Judaism" and "Early Christianity,"[6] I have been training myself to eschew both *Judaism* and *Christianity*[7] in favor of *Jews* and *Christ-followers*[8] or *Christ-believers*.[9] I am wavering on how best to refer to those Greco-Romans variously known as "gentiles," "pagans," or "polytheists."[10] I have foresworn *hybridity* due to its historical role as a foundation for racist laws against mixing and miscegenation—an unsavory past that is as yet (in my view) not entirely redeemed by its reclamation in postcolonialist theory.[11] Though I have not given up entirely on *identity* and *community*, I may yet do so given the vagueness of the first and the assumptions that attend the second.[12] Thankfully, I rarely write about *religion*, and have therefore been able to stay out of the current fray on the existence or nonexistence of religion in the past and in the present.[13]

As scholars and writers, we must all make terminological and conceptual decisions in keeping with changing sensibilities and the new approaches and insights within our fields. Journal editors, however, face a different problem: what to do about articles that use terms or expressions that we ourselves would avoid? As editors, we have a dual responsibility: to our readers—to ensure, as best we can, that the articles published in our journals constitute contributions to the field—and

---

[6] These are the areas as currently defined in the graduate program in Religious Studies at McMaster University, where I earned my doctorate. See the list of fields at https://religiousstudies.mcmaster.ca/graduate-program.

[7] Daniel Boyarin, "Rethinking Jewish Christianity: An Argument for Dismantling a Dubious Category (to Which Is Appended a Correction of My Border Lines)," *JQR* 99 (2009): 8, 13, http://dx.doi.org/10.1353/jqr.0.0030.

[8] Mark T Finney, *Honour and Conflict in the Ancient World: 1 Corinthians in Its Greco-Roman Social Setting*, LNTS 460 (London: T&T Clark, 2012), 1.

[9] Mikael Tellbe, *Christ-believers in Ephesus: A Textual Analysis of Early Christian Identity Formation in a Local Perspective*, WUNT 242 (Tübingen: Mohr Siebeck, 2009).

[10] Christopher P. Jones, *Between Pagan and Christian* (Cambridge: Harvard University Press, 2014).

[11] See Homi K. Bhabha, *The Location of Culture* (London: Routledge, 1994). See discussion in John Hutnyk, "Hybridity," *Ethnic and Racial Studies* 28 (2005): 79–102, http://dx.doi.org/10.1080/0141987042000280021; Gary Reger, "Ethnic Identities, Borderlands, and Hybridity," in *A Companion to Ethnicity in the Ancient Mediterranean*, ed. Jeremy McInerney (Chichester: Wiley & Sons, 2014), 112–26, http://search.ebscohost.com/login.aspx?direct=true&scope=site&db=nlebk&db=nlabk&AN=798813; Robert J. C. Young, *Colonial Desire: Hybridity in Theory, Culture, and Race* (London: Routledge, 1995); Philipp Stockhammer, "Questioning Hybridity," in *Conceptualizing Cultural Hybridization: A Transdisciplinary Approach*, ed. Philipp Stockhammer (Heidelberg: Springer, 2012), 1–3, http://public.eblib.com/choice/publicfullrecord.aspx?p=885088.

[12] Stanley K. Stowers, "The Concept of 'Community' and the History of Early Christianity," *MTSR* 23 (2011): 238–56; Rogers Brubaker and Frederick Cooper, "Beyond 'Identity,'" *Theory and Society* 29 (2000): 1–47, http://dx.doi.org/10.1023/A:1007068714468.

[13] Brent Nongbri, *Before Religion: A History of a Modern Concept* (New Haven: Yale University Press, 2013); Boyarin, "Rethinking Jewish Christianity"; Tomoko Masuzawa, *The Invention of World Religions, Or, How European Universalism Was Preserved in the Language of Pluralism* (Chicago: University of Chicago Press, 2005).

to our authors—to provide a venue in which they can express their ideas in their own voices and words. While we must exercise judgment, based on the considered advice of esteemed colleagues in the field, when deciding which articles to accept and which to reject, we have some obligation to retain to the extent possible the formulations and language of those articles that will be published in our journals.

Most articles accepted for publication do not pose major terminological or other semantic problems when being edited for publication: a footnote here, a semicolon there, some minor formatting changes, and we're done. Occasionally, however, an article will use a term that gives me pause, either because it represents a word choice with which I disagree as a scholar, or because it may be misinterpreted by some of our readers.

This dilemma arose with regard to two articles that appeared in the most recent issue of the journal (*JBL* 135, no. 2 [2016]). Heidi Wendt's fine article "Galatians 3:1 as an Allusion to Textual Prophecy" used the terms *Judean* and *Judean writings* consistently throughout the article in contexts in which I would use *Jew* and *Jewish Scriptures* or perhaps *Septuagint*. Although some readers might view *Judean* and *Jew/Jewish* as interchangeable, the question of how best to translate the Greek term *ioudaios* is a matter of considerable controversy within the field of early Judaism and New Testament studies. My own strongly held and oft-expressed position is that the term *Jew* or *Jewish* should always be used except when *ioudaios* (or cognates) refers explicitly to Judea as a geographical location or political entity.[14] My arguments are semantic and historical, but they also reflect a concern about the erasure of *Jews* from our discussion of Second Temple and first-century sources. Nevertheless, I acknowledge that *Judean* has become an acceptable, if not universally accepted, term, and for that reason it was my responsibility as an editor to respect the author's word choice. To avoid confusion, particularly with regard to *Judean writings*, and at my request, the author added a detailed and helpful footnote.[15] The explanation helps those who are not familiar or who disagree with the usage nevertheless to appreciate the article.

A somewhat different dilemma was presented by Joshua Berman's article "Supersessionist or Complementary? Reassessing the Nature of Legal Revision in the Pentateuchal Law Collections." In this case I was concerned that the use of the term *supersessionist* in the title of the article might offend some readers due to the historical association of this term with the theological claim that Christians have replaced—superseded—Jews as God's covenant people.[16] To describe a scholar as

---

[14] See, e.g., Adele Reinhartz, "'Jews' and Jews in the Fourth Gospel," in *Anti-Judaism and the Fourth Gospel: Papers of the Leuven Colloquium, 2000*, ed. R Bieringer, Didier Pollefeyt, and F Vandecasteele-Vanneuville (Assen: Royal Van Gorcum, 2001), 341–56; Reinhartz, "The Vanishing Jews of Antiquity," *Marginalia: A Los Angeles Review of Books*, http://marginalia.lareviewofbooks.org/vanishing-jews-antiquity-adele-reinhartz/.

[15] Heidi Wendt, "Galatians 3:1 as an Allusion to Textual Prophecy," *JBL* 135 (2016): 370.

[16] For the record, I have used this term myself, in its Christian theological context. See, e.g.,

a supersessionist is a serious charge, just one breath short of calling them an anti-Semite; was it appropriate therefore for *JBL* to publish an article in which this term features so prominently?

My decision to allow the term to stand was based on three important considerations. First and foremost, the article concerned "the nature of legal revision in the Pentateuchal Law Collections" and did not in any way—remotely or by inference—touch on any aspect of Judaism and Christianity, let alone supersessionist claims in Christian theology. Second, although it argues in favor of the complementarian view over the supersessionist view of the process of legal revision in pentateuchal law collections, it treats "supersessionist" scholars—scholars who argue that one set of laws superseded or replaced an earlier set of laws—with respect. One such work, for example, is singled out as a "valuable sustained meditation" that "systematically set[s] the methodological claims of each camp in conversation with each other to measure and mediate[s] the validity of these respective approaches."[17] Third, the editorial board members who provided double-blind peer review of the article did not react to the term, thereby allaying any remaining concerns and supporting my decision to allow the term to stand.

Unlike the terms *racism* and *sexism*, which carry consistent meanings and connotations across a broad range of contexts, *supersessionist* or *supersessionism* carries its highly negative association only in the context of a specific set of claims made by some Christians with regard to the relationship between Christianity and Judaism. Outside of that context, it does not carry that same force and, in many cases, is simply descriptive. In political discourse, for example, *supersessionism* has been used to refer to the view that "liberalism simply supplanted civic republicanism."[18] In the field of religious studies, the term can describe the view that religious societies inevitably and rightly give way to secular societies, as, for example, in France or in Quebec.[19] Most interesting for our purposes, however, is the use of the term in legal discourse, in which it means "to take the place of, as by reason of superior worth or right."[20] In legal argumentation, a supersessionist position would

---

Adele Reinhartz, "Jesus in Film: Hollywood Perspectives on the Jewishness of Jesus," *Journal of Religion and Film* 2, no. 2 (1998): 34 paragraphs, https://www.unomaha.edu/jrf/JesusinFilmRein.htm.

[17] Joshua Berman, "Supersessionist or Complementary? Reassessing the Nature of Legal Revision in the Pentateuchal Law Collections," *JBL* 135 (2016): 202.

[18] Nomi Maya Stolzenberg, "Review: A Book of Laughter and Forgetting: Kalman's 'Strange Career' and the Marketing of Civic Republicanism," *Harvard Law Review* 111, no. 4 (1998): 1054.

[19] See http://www.firstthings.com/article/2003/05/three-meanings-of-secular.

[20] As defined in *West's Encyclopedia of American Law*, edition 2. Copyright 2008, The Gale Group, Inc. All rights reserved. Available on-line at http://legal-dictionary.thefreedictionary.com/supersede.

For an example of the legal usage, see https://www.law.cornell.edu/cfr/text/2/200.104; http://www.osborneclarke.com/connected-insights/blog/supersession-dilapidations-not-superseded-yet/; and https://www.citizensadvice.org.uk/benefits/benefits-introduction/problems-

argue that "recently-enacted statutes ... superseded the prior legislation."[21] Because the *JBL* article in question dealt with biblical law, its use of supersessionism and supersessionist is consistent with the use of the term in legal discourse.

JBL is intended first and foremost for trained biblical scholars and interested laypeople—careful readers who share the ability to understand that words, like biblical passages, cannot be understood in isolation from their contexts. On these grounds, I am confident that most readers, even if momentarily surprised by this terminology, understand from the article, the abstract, or even just from the title itself that, in this context, the use of *supersessionism* and *supersessionist* is unrelated to the use of these terms with regard to a particular Christian theological stance toward Judaism.

No doubt I, and future *JBL* editors, will continue to encounter the language dilemma periodically. Words often fall short not only because of our own imperfect articulations but also because of our tendency to infuse them with our own meanings independent of the intentions, conscious or otherwise, of their authors. For this and many other reasons, working with words, whether as writers or as editors, is challenging, exhilarating, and often frustrating or perplexing. Although the Bible (King James Version) has recently been translated into emoji,[22] I do not anticipate that the *Journal* will abandon words altogether in favor of emoji or other transcultural symbolic systems. But I do hope you will enjoy this issue of *JBL*, or in the spirit of the times:

I 🙏 (hope) you 😍 (enjoy).

---

with-benefits-and-tax-credits/challenging-a-benefit-decision/challenging-a-dwp-benefit-decision-on-or-after-28-october-2013/changing-a-benefit-decision-by-revision-and-supersession/changing-a-dwp-benefit-decision-by-supersession/.

[21] See http://legal-dictionary.thefreedictionary.com/supersede.

[22] See https://www.theguardian.com/technology/2016/may/30/emoji-bible-arrived-god-king-james.

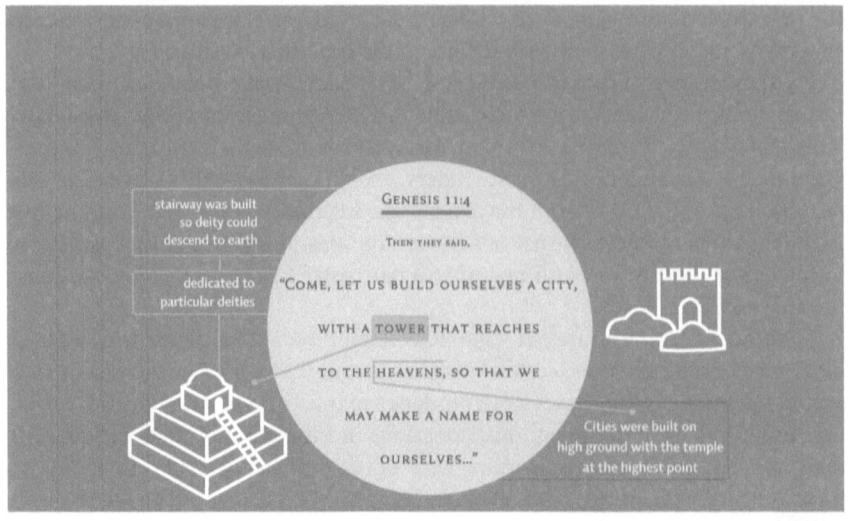

CONTEXT CHANGES EVERYTHING

The **NIV Cultural Backgrounds Study Bible**, with notes from Dr. Craig S. Keener and Dr. John H Walton, gives you insight on every page of the Bible. See the cultural background behind each story—even the ones you know by heart.

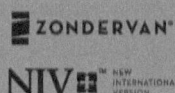

Dr. Craig S. Keener   Dr. John H Walton

Read the entire book of Genesis and Matthew for FREE
Text **"context7"** to **313131** and follow the directions.

Demons in the Hebrew Bible and the Ancient Near East

ANNE MARIE KITZ
anne.mariekitz@aol.com
New Berlin, WI 53151

Does the Hebrew Bible refer to demons? Remarkably, the standard answer to this question has remained rather stable: although there are indeed traces of demons, there is no evidence of the sophisticated type of demonology that is found in Akkadian texts. While this may be true, a more fundamental point remains unanswered. Did the ancient Near Easterners view demons in the same way as modern scholars do, as intrinsically evil beings who deliberately choose to engage in malicious activities contrary to the wishes of the governing deity? Here the answer must be negative. The present article examines the issue of demons in the Hebrew Bible through an evaluation of an Akkadian subordinate supernatural being called *rābiṣu*, the root of which is shared by רבץ (*rōbēṣ*) in Gen 4:7, which is routinely thought to denote a demon. Akkadian texts indicate that the *rābiṣu* is a neutral being that is nothing other than a current of wind dispatched by the deities to perform certain duties. This point not only informs the use of רבצה (*rābaṣâ*) in Deut 29:19 but also permits a connection with רוח אלהים ("spirit of God") and רוח יהוה ("spirit of YHWH"), both of which are occasionally qualified with רעה ("evil"). The evidence demonstrates that, like the evil associated with *rābiṣu*, the רעה attributed to a divine רוח actually references its mission and not its moral standing. Therefore, demons as inherently evil subordinate supernatural beings did not exist in the ancient Near East. They are, rather, divinely articulated verdicts handed down as judgments in response to human transgressions.

> Better to reign in Hell than serve in Heaven.
> —John Milton, *Paradise Lost*, 1.263

One of the most vexing problems of the Hebrew Bible concerns its references to subordinate supernatural beings that engage in destructive activities. Modern readers cannot help but react negatively when YHWH dispatches a company of מלאכי רעים ("messengers of evils") in Ps 78:49 that are expressions of divine "wrath, indignation, and distress" (עברה וזעם וצרה). In 2 Sam 24:16, when David is punished for taking a census, YHWH's מלאך is described as המשחית ("the one who destroys"), a name—if it may be called such—shared by המשחית in Exod 12:23, which YHWH prevents from entering the Israelites' homes. Even more disquieting is the fact that these מלאכים act according to the wishes of the Godhead. Do these particular beings have any relation to the רוח משחית ("destructive wind") of which YHWH states, according to Jer 51:1, "I am about to stir up [הנני מעיר] against Babylon"?

Theologians may find it difficult to accept that a deity who is all-good can nevertheless dispatch subordinate supernatural beings who wreak havoc. According to conventional views, even though these beings may act like demons, they cannot be identified as such because YHWH directs them to act. Scholars engaged in critical biblical scholarship may similarly ponder this paradox. On the other hand, Assyriologists are free of such limitations: all Akkadian-speaking societies that generated texts depicting the activities of subordinate supernatural beings were polytheistic. Their deities were evil and capricious with little to no shred of decency among them. It stands to reason, therefore, that such malicious deities would exploit a host of demons to achieve their equally malicious ends.

The aim of this essay is to demonstrate that the sharply antithetical perspective presented above is largely a construct that developed from a Judeo-Christian philosophical approach expounded by Thomas Aquinas (1225–1274) based on the works of Aristotle (384–322 BCE).[1] This perspective posits a deliberate moral choice behind all actions undertaken by mortal or immortal beings. Its foundation is the concept of free will. This somewhat "modern" perspective has been anachronistically incorporated into the interpretation of the Hebrew Bible and ancient Near Eastern religious texts. The goal here is to discern the ancient Near Eastern understanding of these supernatural beings apart from the Judeo-Christian presuppositions entailed by the idea of "demons."

I will address the issue of the existence, nature, and function of subordinate supernatural beings in the Hebrew Bible through an examination of the Akkadian entity known as *rābiṣu* and its Hebrew next of kin, *rōbēṣ*, a *hapax legomenon* that appears in Gen 4:7 and is typically understood to refer to a demon. After a review of the fundamental meaning of the Semitic root *rbṣ*, a survey of the activity, character, and manifestations of *rābiṣu*s will bring to the fore the unique relationship these beings have with the winds produced by a governing deity. While this point may not immediately explain *rōbēṣ*, it does inform the operation of רוח יהוה ("the spirit of YHWH"). My hypothesis is that the רוח אלהים רעה ("the evil spirit of God," 1 Sam 16:15) does not act in opposition to YHWH but, like the *rābiṣu*, is a supernatural being produced by YHWH's windy words that express his judgment against wayward human behavior. This means that the evil borne by the רוח אלהים רעה and the *rābiṣu lemnu* ("evil *rābiṣu*") refers to the character of the event articulated in the divine message and not the supernatural being itself.

---

[1] Thomas Aquinas, *Summa Theologiae* Ia. q. 83, a. 1; *De Veritate* 24.1–2.

I. A History of the Issue

The scholarly debate and the metamorphosis of the interpretation of *rābiṣu* and *rōbēṣ* are as interesting as, if not more engaging than, the actual issue at hand. The topic marks an early intersection between Assyriology and biblical studies, with Akkadian providing insight into the meaning of a Hebrew term. The path is paved with the names of some of the greatest scholars in each discipline, and their observations on the matter have contributed to the advancement of new perspectives but, at the same time, to the stagnation of established views.

The story begins in 1903, when the eminent cuneiformist R. Campbell Thompson published the seventeenth volume in the series *Cuneiform Texts from Babylonian Tablets, &c., in the British Museum*.[2] At the same time, he also published a two-volume work with the ponderously ominous title *Devils and Evil Spirits of Babylonia: Being Babylonian and Assyrian Incantations against the Demons, Ghouls, Vampires, Hobgoblins, Ghosts, and Kindred Evil Spirits, Which Attack Mankind*.[3] In this work Campbell Thompson transcribed and translated the now-infamous bilingual Sumerian-Akkadian exorcistic series UDUG ḪUL *Utukkū Lemnūtu*, which Assyriologists refer to as "Evil Demons." The work presented biblical scholars with the opportunity to examine the Neo-Assyrian version of the series in light of the Hebrew Bible.

A year later, Hans Duhm introduced his work entitled *Die bösen Geister im Alten Testament*.[4] In discussing Gen 4:7 and the meaning of *rōbēṣ*, he observed, "The interpretation of it as a predator, as Dillmann observes, is however inadmissible. As it seems to me the difficult point is clear at once, if one interprets רבץ as an evil demonic creature that is probably presented in animal form: it settles down, crouching at the door."[5] Duhm was the first scholar to identify *rōbēṣ* specifically as "ein böses dämonisches." His observation prompted many comments in both books and articles. In his book *Die Genesis*, Otto Procksch promptly agreed with Duhm: "It seems that sin was conceived as a covetous demon that clings to his victims."[6] Heinrich Kaupel agreed, going so far as to indicate a belief system that

---

[2] R. Campbell Thompson, *CT* 17 (London: Oxford University Press, 1903).
[3] R. Campbell Thompson, *Devils and Evil Spirits of Babylonia: Being Babylonian and Assyrian Incantations against the Demons, Ghouls, Vampires, Hobgoblins, Ghosts, and Kindred Evil Spirits, Which Attack Mankind; Translated from the Original Cuneiform Texts, with Transliterations, Vocabulary, Notes, Etc.*, 2 vols., Luzac's Semitic Text and Translation Series 14–15 (London: Luzac, 1903–1904). For a transcription and translation from an eclectic text of the entire series, see Markham J. Geller, *Evil Demons: Canonical* Utukkū Lemnūtu *Incantations; Introduction, Cuneiform Text, and Transliteration with a Translation and Glossary*, SAACT 5 (Helsinki: Neo-Assyrian Text Corpus Project, 2007).
[4] Hans Duhm, *Die bösen Geister im Alten Testament* (Tübingen: Mohr Siebeck, 1904).
[5] Ibid., 9.
[6] Otto Procksch, *Die Genesis*, KAT 1 (Leipzig: Deichert, 1913), 44–50, here 47.

included "doorstep demons."[7] The renowned Assyriologist Charles-François Jean approved and provided additional Akkadian evidence in support of the association.[8] Once Gustav E. Closen's article "Der 'Dämon Sünde'" appeared, the use of the term *demon*, whether appropriate or inappropriate, was established to such a degree that most future discussions on the subject began with a refutation or affirmation of the existence of these beings in Israel's belief system.[9]

This is not to say that everyone concurred with the assessment that *rōbēṣ* is a *rābiṣu* in Hebrew clothing. Those who disagreed, whether knowingly or not, reflected Hermann Gunkel's position: writing before Duhm offered his interpretation, Gunkel felt uncomfortable with the notion that sin could be compared with a wild animal lurking at the door. Certainly this activity was not normal.[10] Consequently many scholars have offered cogent arguments against the existence of a *rōbēṣ* demon. Most notable is Claus Westermann, who proposed that *rōbēṣ* refers to the languishing ghost of Cain's murdered brother, Abel.[11] Others develop their discussions based on a text-critical approach, since nothing has irked scholars more than the "incongruent" combination of the feminine חטאת with the preceding masculine term *rōbēṣ*. More recent studies completely dismiss the notion of a "sin demon."[12] As the term *rōbēṣ* is related to √*rbṣ*, an examination of the root's basic notion of "lie down, settle" is in order.

II. The Root RBṢ

Since the issue of demons in the Hebrew Bible began with *rōbēṣ* and its presumed relation to the Akkadian supernatural being *rābiṣu*, I begin with these two

---

[7] Heinrich Kaupel, *Die Dämonen im Alten Testament* (Augsburg: Benno Filser, 1930), 75–81, here 77.

[8] Charles-François Jean, "Le 'Démon de la Porte' dans un verset de la Genèse?," *RAp* 63 (1932): 113–17, esp. 115–16. His primary focus is on the function of *rōbēṣ* as "a demon *at* the door" and not "a demon *of* the door." The former is a role it shares with the Akkadian *rābiṣu*.

[9] Gustav E. Closen, "Der 'Dämon Sünde': Ein Deutungsversuch des massorethischen Textes von Gen 4, 7," *Bib* 16 (1935): 431–42, esp. 436–40. For a text-critical approach, see L. Ramaroson, "A propos de Gen 4:7," *Bib* 49 (1968): 233–37. C. L. Crouch advances the possibility that *ḥaṭṭāʾt* is a gloss ("חטאת as Interpolative Gloss: A Solution to Gen 4, 7," *ZAW* 123 [2011]: 250–58).

[10] Hermann Gunkel, *Genesis: Übersetzt und erklärt*, HKAT 1 (Göttingen: Vandenhoeck & Ruprecht, 1901), 38–39.

[11] Claus Westermann, *Genesis: A Commentary*, trans. John J. Scullion, 2 vols. (Minneapolis: Augsburg, 1984–1986), 1:300.

[12] Bernd Janowski, "Jenseits von Eden Gen 4, 1–16 und die nichtpriesterliche Urgeschichte," in *Die Dämonen: Die Dämonologie der israelitisch-jüdischen und frühchristlichen Literatur im Kontext ihrer Umwelt—Demons: The Demonology of Israelite-Jewish and Early Christian Literature in Context of Their Environment*, ed. Armin Lange, Hermann Lichtenberger, and K. F. Diethard Römheld (Tübingen: Mohr Siebeck, 2003), 137–59, here 147–49.

terms. A brief analysis of the root *rbṣ* may assist in the development of a more nuanced understanding of the activity associated with the *rōbēṣ* and the *rābiṣu*. Clearly no one would gainsay that the root *rbṣ* informs *rābiṣu* and *rōbēṣ*. Lexica affirm this relationship. According to all the major dictionaries of Akkadian and Biblical Hebrew, the basic notion of *rabāṣu* is "lie down."[13]

Additional insight into the meaning of *rbṣ* may be garnered from the fact that Arabic preserves two distinct roots *rbṣ* and *rbḍ*. While the former (*rbṣ*) reflects the Proto-Semitic *√rbṣ, the latter reflects the Proto-Semitic *√rbṣ́ (ṣ́ = emphatic *śîn*). Classical Arabic illustrates best the distinction in meanings. *Rabaṣa* means "expect," "await." It appears only in the fifth form of the verb, the reflexive, with the nuance "expect something to happen."[14] At no time is the root associated with "lying down." Modern Arabic also preserves *rabaṣa*, but the meaning has shifted a bit. The sense of expectation has receded, and the notion of visual activity is heightened. Thus, the first form of the verb means, "wait," "look," "watch," "be on the lookout." The fifth form now combines the preceding sense with the notion of "lie down" > "lie in wait," "lay an ambush."[15]

The Classical Arabic term *rabaḍa*, on the other hand, bears the fundamental meaning of "lie down." It is well attested and appears in the first, second (intensive) and fourth (causative) forms of the verb. The root *rbḍ* principally describes aspects of animals settling down to relax, specifically, "lying down on the breast."[16] When applied to human beings, it refers to a prone position. It also includes the sense "cover" and, by extension, "to offer lodging or refuge."[17] This, in turn, accounts for the noun *rabaḍun*, "a resting place for sheep or goats."[18]

The entry in the most up-to-date Ugaritic dictionary defines the G-stem verb formed from √*rbṣ* as "rest," "lie down," while the masculine noun *rbṣ* means "'inspector' (< the one on the watch)."[19] The former verbal definition displays an affinity with Arabic *rbḍ* < *√rbṣ́. The latter meaning suggests a connection with *rbṣ* < *√rbṣ.

Several observations can now be advanced. The three radicals that constitute the root could reflect two Proto-Semitic roots *√rbṣ and *√rbṣ́. The linguistic evidence suggests that ancient East and West Semitic did not distinguish the two roots in the same way as Classical and Modern Arabic do. Even so, the dominant and more commonly attested root is *√rbṣ.

---

[13] *AHw* 3:935; *CAD* 14:10–13; *HALOT* 3:1181–82.
[14] Lane, book 1, part 1, p. 1011, col. 2.
[15] Hans Wehr, *A Dictionary of Modern Written Arabic*, 3rd ed. (Ithaca, NY: Spoken Languages Services, 1976), 321.
[16] Lane, 1011, col. 3–1013, col. 3.
[17] Ibid., 1011, col. 3.
[18] Ibid., 1012, col. 1.
[19] Gregorio del Olmo Lete and Joaquín Sanmartín, *A Dictionary of the Ugaritic Language in the Alphabetic Tradition*, HdO 67.2 (Leiden: Brill, 2004), 731.

This root consistently retains the fundamental meaning "lie down," "settle down" (said of animals) in most ancient and modern Semitic languages, with the exception of Geʻez and Amharic. If the two roots ever existed independently in any of the ancient Semitic languages, they appear to have merged at a very early date, perhaps as early as the Ur III period, as this is the time when some texts coordinate certain officials by the Sumerian name MAŠKIM with the Akkadian term *rābiṣu*.[20]

The question now becomes: To which root are the Akkadian *rābiṣu* and the Hebrew *rōbēṣ* related? Long ago, Arno Poebel suggested that *rābiṣu* is founded on the Arabic *rabaṣa* (*rbṣ* < *√*rbṣ*), "'to wait for someone' (lit. 'look out for someone')."[21] A. L. Oppenheim rejected this proposal and preferred to see *rābiṣu*, an active participle, derive its meaning from *rbṣ*, which appears in Arabic as √*rbḍ*; we now know that both of these roots reflect *√*rbṣ*.[22] Oppenheimer's argument is that *rbṣ* describes "the typical activity of the demon—and of the official": they both lurk. He concludes that "the Akkadian *rābiṣu* official must have had—at least in the specific situation in which his name was coined—the hated function of spying on people in order to report them."[23]

Whatever the final determination may be, the data strongly suggest that the fundamental meaning of *rābiṣu* and *rōbēṣ* is related to the Proto-Semitic *√*rbṣ*. A nuanced understanding of the root needs to consider its foremost application—describing the action of quadrupedal, ruminant animals, that is, sheep, goats, cattle, and camels. The basic action associated with this root is one of settling down in order to stay and rest in one place for a period of time, that is, "linger." Nevertheless, this must not presuppose inactivity; rather, ruminants settle down to chew cud and digest food. Therefore, they have a specific task to fulfill before they move on to graze elsewhere. In other words, they roam about here and there; they linger in a wide variety of places for a period of time and then depart. One might consider this behavior continuously sporadic, sitting here, resting there, moving from one place to another.

---

[20] It is at this juncture that the Sumerian word MAŠKIM, a term that refers to an authorized government official, might be seen as relevant. Unfortunately, the exact relationship between MAŠKIM and *rābiṣu*, the Akkadian term that is commonly used to translate it, is not clear. The etymology of MAŠKIM is, at present, not known and so there is little guidance as to how the term is to be understood. Some data can be teased from the contexts in which MAŠKIM appears, but this too remains unsatisfyingly superficial. See Adam Falkenstein, *Die neusumerischen Gerichtsurkunden* (Munich: Bayerischen Akademie der Wissenschaften, 1956), 53 n. 3; A. L. Oppenheim, "The Eyes of the Lord," *JAOS* 88 (1968): 173–80, esp. 179; *AHw* 3:935; D. O. Edzard and Frans A. M. Wiggermann, "maškim (*rābiṣu*) 'Kommissar, Anwalt, Sachwalter,'" *RlA* 7:449–55.

[21] Arno Poebel, *Miscellaneous Studies*, AS 14 (Chicago: University of Chicago Press, 1947), 55–56.

[22] Oppenheim, "Eyes of the Lord," 179.

[23] Ibid.

III. The Supernatural Beings

The concept identified above provides the general foundation for the following examination of *rābiṣu* and *rōbēṣ*. In this section, I appraise *rābiṣu* and *rōbēṣ* based on three features: activity, character, and the manifestations generated by divine governance. As will become evident, the *rābiṣu*'s association with wind provides the key to linking *rōbēṣ* to רוח ("wind").

Rābiṣu

Behavior. On earth, the *rābiṣu* (MAŠKIM) is known to attack (*māḫaṣu*) people, the effects of which cause limpness in the limbs or on the sides of the body. Sometimes the individual will pass away. DIŠ(*šumma*) ... GIR₃-*šu*₂(*šēpšu*) *ša*₂ 15(*imitti*) *i-maš-šar* KA-*šu*₂(*pīšu*) *ṣu-dur, mi-šit-ti*[24] MAŠKIM(*rābiṣi*) GID₂-*ma*(*urrakma*) UŠ₂(*imât*),[25] "If he drags his right foot and his mouth twitches, (it is an) attack of the *rābiṣu*, he will linger and die." Other times the victim will recuperate: DIŠ(*šumma*) 15-*šu*₂(*imittašu*) *tab-kat*₂ *mi-šit-ti* MAŠKIM(*rābiṣi*) TIN(*iballuṭ*), "If his right (side) is limp, (it is) an attack of the *rābiṣu*, he will live."[26] We should note that neither one of these *rābiṣu*s is qualified as beneficent or maleficent; they are, for all intents and purposes, neutral. In that case, their character is determined according to the effect on the person attacked.

Character and effects. On some occasions the *rābiṣu* is qualified. An Old Babylonian letter prayer, written in Sumerian, is particularly revealing, because it specifically delineates the *rābiṣu* and attributes its release to divine wrath.

⁵ tukum-bi diĝir-mu-ra an-na-kam
⁶ ša₃-ib₂-ba-zu ga-ab-huĝ-e ur₅-zu he₂-bur₂-e
⁷ maškim-hul-ĝa₂-ĝa₂-da he₂-eb₂-si-il su-ma₃ he₂-[d]a-ab-dal[27]

⁵ If you are indeed a deity of the sky,
⁶ I would appease your angry inner (feelings), may your mood be dispelled.
⁷ May the evil MAŠKIM (*rābiṣu*) placed at (my) side, be ripped off,
    may he flee from my body.

---

[24] All of the transcriptions and translations of the Akkadian texts are my own. Text: René Labat, *Traité akkadien de diagnostics et pronostics médicaux*, 2 vols. (Leiden: Brill, 1951), vol. 2, plate 65, tablet [AO 3440], rev., line 63.

[25] Autograph copy: Sidney Smith, *CT* 37 (London: British Museum Publications, 1923), plate 44, tablet [K. 3826], rev., col. 4, lines 3b–4.

[26] Autograph copy: Labat, *Traité akkadien de diagnostics*, plate 48, tablet [AO 6680], line 9; R. Campbell Thompson, *Assyrian Medical Texts* (London: Oxford University Press, 1923), plate 77, tablet 1 [K. 2418 + 2465 + Rm 141], obv., col. 1, line 6.

[27] Autograph copy: Christopher B. F. Walker and Samuel N. Kramer, "Cuneiform Tablets in the Collection of Lord Binning," *Iraq* 44 (1982): 71–86, here 82, fig. 3, rev., lines 5–7; transcription: p. 80, rev., lines 5–7; translation: p. 81, rev., lines 5–7.

The language is telling. If an evil *rābiṣu* (MAŠKIM.ḪUL/*rābiṣu lemnu*) is to be SI-IL (Akk. *salātu*), that is, "split, ripped off," then it is strongly fastened to the person's SU (Akk. *zumru*, *šīru*), "body," in some way. The hope that it will DAL (Akk. *naparšudu*), "flee," probably indicates the *rābiṣu*'s ability to depart abruptly.

The *rābiṣu*'s capacity to come and go is well established. Especially informative are three lines from the bilingual, Middle Assyrian version of the *Utukkū Lemnūtu* incantation cycle. Aside from elucidating the *rābiṣu*'s capacity for movement, it provides additional particulars.

> [19] lu$_2$-u$_x$-lu pap-hal-la: *ša$_2$* LU$_2$ *mut-tal$_2$-li-ki*
> [20] maškim sa$_6$-ga-ni : *ra-bi-iš dum-qi-šu$_2$* ^{د}BIL.GI
> [21] ^{د}gil-gi-a hu-mu-un-da-ab-ĝen : *i-da-a-šu lil-lik*[28]
>
> [20] May Girru, his good *rābiṣu*, [21] go to the side [19] of the anxious man.

The passage identifies the fire deity, Girru (^{د}gil.gi/^{د}BIL.GI), as a *rābiṣu* of "goodness," a being who is free to attend to the misery of an afflicted person. In addition, there is a unique reflective character embedded in these lines based on the verb *alāku* ("to go"). The ailing individual is described as *muttalliki*, a Gt participle meaning "one who is restless" or "one who wanders around." He is agitated and anxious. He cannot settle down. Subsequently, we may presume with a positive outlook that the *rābiṣ dumqi* is able to counter this condition by going (*lillik*) to the victim to linger at his side. In this instance, the *rābiṣu* is acting in its capacity as an entity that brings well-being and eases suffering. But, like its negative counterpart, the favorable *rābiṣu* can also depart, should the circumstances require it: *iz-nu-u$_2$ ra-bi-*[*ṣu*] *šul-me e-lu-u* [*ana šu-puk šamê^e* ...], "the *rābiṣus* of well-being became angry and [went] up [to heaven]."[29]

In other cases, a clear distinction is drawn between two types of qualified MAŠKIM (*rābiṣu*). [98b] MAŠKIM SILIM (*šulmu*) KI LU$_2$ *ra-ki-is* [99b] MAŠKIM HUL-*ti* EGER LU$_2$ *ra-ki-is*,[30] "a *rābiṣu* of well-being is attached to [lit., with] the man; a *rābiṣu* of evil is attached behind the man." Even though one *rābiṣu* is good and the other evil, they both do the same thing. They "attach, tie" themselves (*rākasu*) to the victim's body, a capability that is born of the root meaning of their name *rābiṣu*. They are divine "lingerers."

References to the two strains of *rābiṣu*s appear together on some Neo-Assyrian apotropaic figurines. The inscription is terse and to the point; its meaning

---

[28] Autograph copy: Markham J. Geller, "A Middle Assyrian Tablet of Utukkū Lemnūtu, Tablet 12," *Iraq* 42 (1980): 23–51, here 43, fig. 1, tablet [BM 130660], obv., col. 2, lines 19–21; transcription: p. 28, lines 21′–22′, translation: p. 34, line 21. The transcription above follows the lines as they appear on the cuneiform text.

[29] Wilfred G. Lambert, "Enmeduranki and Related Matters," *JCS* 21 (1967): 126–38, here 128, line 19.

[30] Autograph copy: Cyril J. Gadd, *CT* 39 (London: British Museum Publications, 1926), plate 2, tablet 46 [KK 236 + 3548, reverse], lines 98b–99b.

is clear: [er]-ba? MAŠKIM s[IG₅ʔ]/ṣi-i MAŠKIM HUL-ti,³¹ "Come MAŠKIM (rābiṣu) of good; Depart MAŠKIM (rābiṣu) of evil."

Manifestations generated by divine governance. At no time do the above qualifications indicate these beings' ethical disposition to such a degree that a hostile MAŠKIM/rābiṣu is a demon. If a MAŠKIM/rābiṣu has evil or good intentions, it does not generate them itself. Rather its negative or positive aspects are determined by the nature of the assignment it receives from the deity who sends it forth. Subsequently the rābiṣus' purposes are derivative. An evil rābiṣu arises from the outward expression of the angered deity who produced it. Two lines from an incantation bear out this origin.

rev.1ʳ*ša-arˀ* KA HUL *i-di-p*[*an*] MAŠKIM HUL
rev.2ʳ*ša₂* ĜARˀ-*nam-ma* US₂.ˀUS₂ˀ-*an-ni*³²

rev.1(the) wind (of) an evil mouth has blown onto me; an evil rābiṣu,
rev.2who has been set on me, constantly pursues me.

The *rābiṣu lemnu*, here referred to by its Sumerian name, MAŠKIM HUL, is a term of specification and individuation. It distinguishes this *šāru* ("wind") from other permutations of air currents. The phrase *šār* KA HUL ("wind of an evil mouth") is introductory and serves an equally important purpose. It combines the manifestation of a MAŠKIM/*rābiṣu* in the physical presence of "wind" with its origin from KA HUL ("a mouth of evil"). Although we are not privy to the owner of this "mouth," it is likely that it belongs to one of the three beings mentioned earlier in the text, who, according to line 32, are *isbusū, šabāsu* ("angry") with the victim. This divine ire qualifies what has emitted from the KA ("mouth") as HUL ("evil"), a feature that is inherited by its offspring, the MAŠKIM/*rābiṣu*. The role of the *rābaṣu* is to transport that malevolence to the mortal realm, the presence of which is physically manifested in the wind.

It is, therefore, not surprising to find a text that sees Enlil (Sum. "lord wind") as the progenitor of a malevolent swarm of windy beings: ⁶⁷ᵇ*še-e-du nam-tar* ⁶⁸[*u₂-tuk-*]*ku ra-bi-ṣu lem-nu-te ši-pir* ᵈ*en-lil₂ šu-nu*, "the evil *šēdu, namtaru, utukku,* and *rābiṣu* (beings), they are the product of Enlil."³³ The *Utukkū Lemnūtu* exorcistic series confirms this relationship.

---

³¹ Anthony Green, "Neo-Assyrian Apotropaic Figures: Figurines, Rituals and Monumental Art, with Special Reference to the Figurines from the Excavations of the British School of Archaeology in Iraq at Nimrud," *Iraq* 45 (1983): 87–96, here 91 n. 40 [ND 7847]; plate 13, figurine *a* [ND 7847].
³² Autograph copy: Erich Ebeling, *Literarische Keilschrifttexte aus Assur* (Berlin: Akademie, 1953), plate 130, text 88, rev., lines 1–2.
³³ Autograph copy: Leonard W. King, *CT* 13 (London: Oxford University Press, 1901), plate 39, tablet [K 5418, *a*], obv., col. 2, lines 1–2; O. R. Gurney and J. J. Finkelstein, *The Sultantepe Tablets*, vol. 1, OPBIAA 3 (London: British Institute of Archaeology at Ankara, 1957), plate 37, text 30, tablet [SU 51/67A + 76 + 166], obv., col. 2, lines 68–69; O. R. Gurney, "The Sultantepe Tablets (Continued):

²⁴šu₂-nu ra-bi-ṣu lem-nu-ti šu₂-nu
²⁵iš-tu e-kur it-ta-ṣu-ni šu₂-nu
²⁷ana ᵈMIN EN ma-ta-a-(ti) DUMU šip-ri šu₂-nu³⁴

They are *rabiṣu*s, evil are they.
They have come from the Ekur temple.
They are the messengers of Enlil, lord of the land.

Here the function of the *rabiṣu*s is further specified; Enlil dispatches them as his messengers (*mārū šipri*). At the same time, the identity of the *rabiṣu*s has expanded. They are the *mārū šipri* (messengers) *lemnūti* (of evils) who, at the behest of the wind lord Enlil, *ittaṣūni* ("come forth").³⁵ The Ekur temple, the ziggurat that connects heaven to the earth, is the conduit. It provides the staircase the *rabiṣu*s use to descend to earth; they linger long enough to execute their mission and then move on.

Since *rabiṣu*s are often associated with windstorms and therefore, by extension, dust storms, they do not act alone. Quite often a *rābiṣu* is a constituent member of a "flock" of supernatural beings that coagulate to form a destructive front of hostile power. A bilingual text dating to the Neo-Assyrian period expresses their collective puissance. For ease of discussion, only the Akkadian segment is provided.

²[u]₄-mu la ṭa-a-bu DIŠ(ana) ma-a-ti u₂-ṣa-am-ma³⁶ ni-iš KUR e-liš u šap-liš id-luḫ³⁷
⁴be-en-nu mi-iq-tu ša³⁸ a-na ma-a-ti la i-nu-uḫ-ḫu da-um-ma-tu₂ i-šak-ka-nu³⁹
⁶še-e-du u₃-tuk-ku ra-bi-ṣu rab₂-bu-ti⁴⁰ ša₂ ni-ši AŠ(ina) re-ba-a-ti it-ta-na-aš₂-rab-bi-ṭu
⁸u₄-huš-gal-lu-u u₄-mu ra-bu-u ša₂ AŠ(ina) ṣe-ri₃ i-rat-su la ut-tar-ru ar₂-ki-šu₂ ⸢la⸣ ip-pal-la-su
¹⁰ᵈer₃-ra ra-ba-a ša₂ AŠ(ina) ⸢su⸣-qi₂ ni-ši u₂-šam-qa-tu₂ ṣe-eḫ-⸢ra⸣? ra-ba-a DIŠ(ana) ar-ki-šu₂ la iz-zi-bu⁴¹

IV. The Cuthaean Legend of Naram-Sin," *AnSt* 5 (1955): 93–110, transliteration: p. 102, lines 67b–68; translation: p. 103, lines 67–68.

³⁴ Autograph copy: R. Campbell Thompson, *CT* 16 (London: Oxford University Press, 1911), plate 1, text 3, tablet [K 38954], col. 1, lines 24–25, 27. The Akkadian text has been extracted from the Sumerian that also appears in this bilingual passage.

³⁵ Cf. Ps 78:49: מלאכי רעים, "messengers of evils."

³⁶ Autograph copy: R. Campbell Thompson, *CT* 17, plate 4, "Tablet of a Similar series, 'N,'" tablet [K 2859], obv., col. 1, line 3.

³⁷ Autograph copy: Oliver R. Gurney and Peter Hulin, *The Sultantepe Tablets*, vol. 2, OPBIAA 7 (London: British Institute of Archaeology at Ankara, 1964), plate 176, text 192, tablet [SU 52/113 + 158], obv., line 2b.

³⁸ Thompson, *CT* 17, plate 4, "Tablet of a Similar series, 'N,'" obv., col. 1, line 7.

³⁹ Gurney and Hulin, *Sultantepe Tablets*, vol. 2, plate 176, text 192, obv., line 4.

⁴⁰ Thompson, *CT* 17, plate 4, "Tablet of a Similar series, 'N,'" col. 1, line 11.

⁴¹ Gurney and Hulin, *Sultantepe Tablets*, vol. 2, plate 176, text 193, tablet [SU 51/186], obv., lines 6b, 8, 10.

² A disfavorable storm arose against the land. It disturbed the people of the upper and lower territory.
⁴ (It is) *bennu* (and) *miqtu*, who do not calm the land, (but) impose darkness.
⁶ (It is) *šēdu, utukku* and *rābiṣu*, the great (ones), who pursue people in the (town) squares;
⁸ (It is) the awful storm, the (great) storm, that will neither be returned to the steppe-land, nor look back,
¹⁰ the "Great Erra," who attacks people on the street, (who) leaves neither the small nor great behind.

The five beings that constitute this storm are *bennu, miqtu, šēdu, utukku,* and *rābiṣu*. Their presence is manifested in a *ūmu* ("gale") that brings darkness during the day. When compounded in this way they become a billowing expression of the deity who produced them. They are the ᵈ*Erra rabâ* ("Great Erra") that erupts from the *ṣēri* ("steppe-land"). Cities offer no protection, for such beings borne on the wind are able to penetrate the urban landscape. They pursue people. They invade dwellings and buildings. Knowing this, the great Esarhaddon called upon three members of this tribe in the curse section of his succession treaty: *še-e-du u₂-tuk-ku ra-bi-ṣu lim-nu* E₂.MEŠ *ku-nu li-ḫi-ru*, "May *šēdu, utukku* (and) *rābiṣu* fix on your houses."⁴²

The seventh tablet of the *Utukkū Lemnūtu* addresses a larger collective of six supernatural beings *utukku, alû, eṭemmu, gallû, ilu, rābiṣu*. The language underscores their pneumatic character.

²⁴ AŠ(*ina*) *tub-qa-a-ti la ta-at-ta-nam-za-zu*
²⁶ AŠ(*ina*) *ša₂-ḫa-a-ti la ta-at-ta-aš₂-ša₂-ab-šu₂*
²⁸ AŠ(*ina*) *l[i]b₃-[bi]* ⸢URU⸣ [*la tal*]-*ta-nam-meš*
³⁰ AŠ(*ina*) *a-ḫa-a-tu₂ la ta-sa-na-ḫur-šu₂*
³² [DIŠ(*ana*) *du-ru*]-*uš* KI-*ti₃* DIŠ(*ana*) *ek-le-ti-ka at-lak*⁴³

²⁴ You shall not repetitiously stay around (the person) in outer corners!
²⁶ You shall not repeatedly sit (next) to him in inner corners!
²⁸ You shall not incessantly whirl around him in the city!
³⁰ You shall not recurringly circulate along the bank!
³² Go to the bottom of the underworld into your darkness.

Like the other members of this corporate grouping, the *rābiṣūs*' airy quality enables them to settle in corners. Their presence is felt in the wind and seen in the deposits of dust, dirt, or sand, in exterior and interior nooks and crannies. These are the spaces where they linger and come into contact with anyone who may seek refuge from such penetrating gales. The number of the verbs, second person masculine singular, is, in this case, very compelling. The verbs address the

---

⁴² Autograph copy: Donald J. Wiseman, "The Vassal-Treaties of Esarhaddon," *Iraq* 20 (1958): plate 38, text 37, tablet [ND 37], col. 6, line 493.

⁴³ Autograph copy: Thompson, *CT* 16, Tablet "A," plate 26, tablet [No. 55473], rev., col. 4, Akkadian lines 24, 26, 28, 30, 32. The Akkadian text has been extracted from its bilingual context. The placement of this text in the overall ritual is Tablet 7.

supernatural beings as individual entities each of whom operates independently within a focused cluster. The Gtn Durative likewise stresses each one of the attributed actions as iterative. For example, *tattanamzaz* (*izuzzu*, "stand, stand ready") and *tattanaššab* (*wašābu*, "sit, dwell") are verbs of presence based on position that hint at a series of completed acts that are repeated, sometimes occurring intermittently. *Taltanamme* (*lawû/lamû*, "circle, surround") and *tassanaḫḫur* (*saḫāru*, "turn around") are verbs of motion based on surrounding someone. Here the action is an uninterrupted succession of each supernatural being's movements. They form a cloud of air currents that work to execute the wrath of the deity or deities who deployed them.

Rōbēṣ

While the term *rōbēṣ* is a *hapax legomenon*, the data on *rābiṣu* grant us some insight into the character of its Hebrew relative. The *rōbēṣ* that appears in Gen 4:7 is indeed a supernatural being who, like the *rābiṣu*, need not be presumed to be intrinsically evil in the modern sense of demon. Drawing on the Akkadian data, we might suppose that the *rōbēṣ* originates from YHWH's anger. It is a divine spirit born of a divine judgment. The *rōbēṣ*, as a reflection of a *rābiṣu*, would travel on divine currents of air, sweeping down from the realm of heaven above to the realm of earth below, bearing its commission for good or for evil. The task now is to prove or disprove this kind of supernatural operation.

It is not without relevance that the Hebrew Bible preserves one other, albeit oblique, glimpse of this being's manifestation as it descends to the earth. The passage, Deut 29:19 (Eng. 29:20), is especially informative because it not only bases its impact on the above image but also exploits a verb built on √*rbṣ*.

> YHWH will not be disposed to forgive him, for then the anger and jealousy of YHWH will exude smoke with fire against him. Every curse written in this book will linger on him and YHWH will blot out his name from under heaven.

All the components associated with the dispatch of a subordinate divine being are present. There is the spark of divine "anger" (אף), here expressed as a smoldering wrath that billows ever-expanding fumes. In his indignation, YHWH utters a host of curses. Even though האלה ("curse") is indeed singular, it is modified by כל ("every"), and therefore it is best to consider it a collective noun, as the passions of mortals and immortals are alike. When one is truly enraged, a torrent of maledictions erupts from the heat of such anger, not one. We may further envision the האלה riding the currents of the agitated smoke (יעשן) generated by YHWH's burning fire. They linger (רבצה) on the targeted, recalcitrant individual while surrounding him in a smoggy cloud. It can be said that this heated wind of maledictions bears YHWH's judgment to the earth. To qualify it as "evil" would not be inappropriate.

Rûaḥ YHWH

The above text provides only an indirect connection between *rōbēṣ* and wind, while the *rābiṣu* of Akkadian sources fashions a stronger bond. This relationship, coupled with the *rābiṣu*'s occasional qualification as "evil" and its inherent predilection for coming and going and lingering in one place after another, suggests an association with another Hebrew phenomenon, the רוח רעה ("the evil spirit"), which plays a significant role in the life of King Saul.

Very little has been written recently on the רוח רעה in relation to רוח יהוה ("the wind/spirit of YHWH"), both of which enjoy a unique, if not extraordinary, relationship with Israel's deity. The function of the רוח רעה in 1 Samuel has been described in various ways. It is an "objectification of Yahweh's abandonment of Saul."[44] It is indicative of God's oversight of human actions that are born of evil.[45] It expresses the notion "that *indirectly* it is Yahweh who brings about Saul's downfall," or it "maintains the ultimate causality of Yahweh with reference to evil."[46] It is the "spiritual dimension" of the struggle for the throne between the two contenders, Saul and David.[47] In addition, the רוח רעה is neither "personified nor does it demonstrate any belief in demons."[48] Rather the רוח רעה, especially in Judg 9, merely describes an "attitude of hostility."[49]

Behavior. The רוח רעה appears six times in 1 Samuel with slight variations (1 Sam 16:14, 15, 16, 23; 18:10; 19:9). In three cases, it is רוח אלהים רעה ("the evil spirit of God," 16:15, 16; 18:10). The remaining references are רוח רעה ... יהוה ("the evil spirit of YHWH," 16:14), רוח יהוה רעה ("the evil spirit of YHWH," 19:9) and רוח הרעה ("the evil spirit," 16:23). The verbs associated with this רוח רעה are revealing. It "departs, turns aside" (סרה, 16:23), "terrorizes" (בעתתו, 16:14, 15), "is present" (היה בהיות, 16:16, 23; תהי, 19:9), and "rushes upon" its target (תצלח, 18:10). In Judg 9:23 God "sends" (ישלח) the רוח רעה.

Additional details may be garnered from the prepositions that modify the verbs in five of the above verses. In 1 Sam 16:14, the evil spirit is מאת יהוה ("from with YHWH"), an expression that connotes a being that is dispatched from YHWH's presence to accomplish a specific commission. Saul's servants observe that "God's evil spirit is upon you" (היה בהיות עליך רוח אלהים רעה, 16:16). When David played his lyre, "the evil spirit departed from upon him [Saul]" סרה מעליו

---

[44] P. Kyle McCarter, "Evil Spirit of God," in *DDD* (1995), 602–4, here 603.

[45] Fredrik Lindström, *God and the Origin of Evil: A Contextual Analysis of Alleged Monistic Evidence in the Old Testament*, ConBOT 21 (Lund: Gleerup, 1983), 77.

[46] Edward Noort, "JHWH und das Böse," *OTS* 23 (1984): 120–36, here 127–28; Christoph Dohmen, "רעע," *TDOT* 13:560–87, here 578.

[47] Karel van der Toorn and Cees Houtman, "David and the Ark," *JBL* 113 (1994): 209–31, here 218.

[48] Lindström, *God and the Origin of Evil*, 77.

[49] McCarter, "Evil Spirit of God," 603.

רוח הרעה, 16:23). It is probable that על articulates two compatible notions: the spirit is at once "above and in contact with" as well as "at rest or on the surface of something." When these elements are taken together, the fundamental meaning of √$rbṣ$ is illuminated. The רוח רעה descends from above and settles down on the target. When the רוח רעה leaves, not only is there a separation (מן), but the רוח רעה is no longer resting on or near the target. Where the רוח רעה ultimately goes is unclear. In all probability it dissipates.

The evil spirit of God also gains entry "to/toward Saul" (אל שאול) in 1 Sam 18:10. Here אל is a preposition of motion, suggesting that the רוח is dispatched for a particular person and is specifically individualized for this purpose. In 19:9, the spirit of YHWH is evil "to/toward Saul" (אל שאול). The אל in this case is a preposition of position implying that the רוח is either facing Saul or turning around to him.[50] Since Judg 9:23 involved two parties, God sends the evil spirit "between" (בין ... ובין) Abimelech and the lords of Shechem. In this case, there are hints concerning the mission of the רוח רעה. בין is a preposition of separation; therefore, the רוח רעה is to cause a severance between two parties that were once united by a shared, evil goal.

Character and effects. Another feature the divine רוח shares with the *rābiṣu* is its positive or negative character. Both רוח יהוה and the רוח אלהים can be qualified with רעה:רוח יהוה רעה (1 Sam 19:9) and רוח אלהים רעה (16:16). Thus, the positive character of the רוח יהוה is heightened when it stands in contrast to its counterpart רוח יהוה רעה: "The spirit of YHWH departed from Saul and the evil spirit from Yahweh harassed him" (ורוח יהוה סרה מעם שאול ובעתתו רוח רעה מאת יהוה, 16:14). Like the *rābiṣu lemnu*, the רוח רעה comes and goes, as does its benevolent counterpart. Psalm 143:10 explicitly qualifies God's spirit as benevolent: "Teach me to do your will, for you are my God. Your spirit is good" (למדני לעשות רצונך כי אתה אלוהי רוחך טובה). The gift of the רוח יהוה on YHWH's servant in Isa 11:4 actually bestows a powerful weapon: "and with the breath of his lips he shall kill the wicked" (וברוח שפתיו ימית רשע).

The description of the רוח יהוה in 1 Sam 18:10 is perhaps the most interesting, not only because it links the רוח יהוה to רעה but also because it describes the effect the spirit has on wrongdoers. It reads: ויהי ממחרת ותצלח רוח אלהים רעה אל שאול ויתנבא בתוך הבית, "On the next day the evil spirit of God rushed (in)to Saul and he raged in the midst of the house." The third person feminine singular converted imperfect form of √$ṣlḥ$ confirms רוח as the subject. It underscores the powerful onrush of God's רוח and also recalls the description of the *rābiṣu* as "the wind (of) an evil mouth" that blows into a person. It overwhelms the individual, thereby affecting his behavior negatively. Since the רוח אלהים is רעה, it has an evil effect on Saul to such a degree that he reflects the divine rage. In this context, the use of יתנבא from √$nbʾ$ ("prophesy") is especially telling. It demonstrates that the integrity of

---

[50] Given the language found in the Akkadian texts, the latter sense is more likely.

prophesying is defined by the quality of the relationship between God and the person who functions as a prophet. Saul may be inspired by a divine רוח, but it is רעה only because Saul's bad behavior made it so, compelling God to take action and punish him.

Manifestations generated by divine governance. Saul's encounter with רוח אלהים רעה in 1 Samuel describes the effect it has on human beings who have engaged in activities that oppose YHWH. The incident takes place exclusively in the earthly realm and assumes that the רוח אלהים רעה reflects a divine response to earlier misdeeds. Subsequently, 1 Kgs 22:19–22 recounts an episode of the same phenomenon, but one generated from the perspective of the heavenly realm. 1 Kings 22:19–22 describes the events that take place in heaven prior to the dispatch of any רוח רעה, whether it is directed against Saul or Ahab. The fact that the passage is a vision of the prophet Micaiah is an important detail, since the רוח אלהים is clearly connected with prophecy and prophesying.

In this passage, the "entire host of heaven" (כל צבא השמים, v. 19) that surrounds YHWH is none other than an assembly of "the winds of heaven" (רוחות השמים, Zech 6:5). The scene depicts YHWH sitting enthroned in the midst of a windstorm the moment he pronounces the sentence of death on Ahab: the king will die at Ramoth-gilead. The only issue that remains is the actualization of the ruling. So God asks his assembled רוחות: "Who will deceive Ahab?" (מי יפתה את אחאב). One רוח steps forward in response to YHWH's invitation. Although a member of the צבא השמים, it is obviously an independent being, as it "came forth" (יצא) from the whirlwind "and stood before YHWH" (ויעמד לפני יהוה). It is a רוח יהוה who "speaks" (יאמר) of its own volition (v. 21). There is a sense that this is a particularly noble רוח, for out of all the other רוחות present, it alone offers its services to execute its king's request. It is also clever, for it presents YHWH with a viable strategy effectively to accomplish the proposed assignment, "I will go forth and become a lying רוח in the mouths of his [Ahab's] prophets" (אצא והייתי רוח שקר בפי כל נביאיו, v. 22). At this juncture the רוח is neutral; it is neither good nor bad. The change occurs when YHWH affirms the רוח's proposal, assigns the mission to it, and guarantees its success. The task—to mislead Ahab to his death—is where the evil resides, not in the רוח itself. Conversely, even though this רוח may be appropriately labeled רוח יהוה רעה, this does not mean that the evil originated with God. Rather, Ahab instigated it when he supposedly defied YHWH's will.

Other passages expand on YHWH's relationship with these רוחות. Psalm 104 describes YHWH's dominion over the heavens as one that allows him to use its features as modes of travel and forms of communication. YHWH journeys in a chariot he builds from clouds, YHWH is "the one who travels on the wings of the wind" (המהלך על כנפי רוח, Ps. 104:3b; cf. Ps 18:11). Here YHWH seems spontaneously to create subordinate supernatural beings from his central רוח, "(he is) the one who makes the winds his messengers" (עשה מלאכיו רוחות, Ps 104:4; cf. Ps 35:5). Thus, the רוחות are individual heralds that are spun forth from the single רוח of

YHWH's chariot cloud. Why does this happen? Jeremiah 4:12 provides the most explicit reason: "a wind belonging to me shall come forth; fuller than these. Now I will certainly pronounce *judgments* against them" (רוח מלא מאלה יבוא לי עתה גם אני אדבר משפטים אותם).

IV. The Ancient Near Eastern Concept of Subordinate Supernatural Beings

In light of the correspondences between Akkadian and biblical texts, can one justify the identification of the Hebrew *robēṣ* in Gen 4:7 as a demon? Probably not. If we did, we would be compelled to say that the רוח אלהים רעה was a demon too. As mentioned at the opening of this essay, this awkward dilemma pits ancient theology against medieval/modern theology. For us, it is particularly disquieting to envision God as the source of both good and evil. This, however, was not a problem for any of the ancient Near Eastern writers because they linked the activities of such subordinate supernatural beings to the execution of divine sentences pronounced by divine judges.

When the rationale supporting this judicial process is expressed according to ancient Near Eastern sensibilities, this is the result: (1) God's anger is externalized as a cloudy storm of רוחות, in the midst of which he hands down judgment involving punishment for an unjust deed (1 Kgs 22:19, Job 4:9b: מרוח אפו יכלו). (2) Since these רוחות have their origin in God, they are subordinate supernatural beings (1 Kgs 22:20, Judg 9:23a). In this way the רוחות and, of course, an individual רוח are created beings who belong to the deity who formed them (רוח יהוה, רוח אלהים; Ps 33:6). (3) The רוח is autonomous but derivative (1 Kgs 22:21). (4) It enjoys divine sanction (1 Kgs 22:22). (5) When the רוח becomes a רוח רעה of a deity, the evil does not indicate its origin. (6) Rather, evil describes its mission, which may be best defined as an evil event. Like any loyal, royal courtier, the רוח is assigned to execute divine judgment on behalf of the deity who produced it (Judg 9:24, 56; Jer 4:12; Job 4:8–9). This means that the רוח רעה constitutes YHWH's response to the evil first committed by wayward mortals.

The medieval/modern perspective is radically different. Certainly modern theology does not deny the existence of subordinate supernatural beings, and, much like ancient theology, it also distinguishes between evil supernatural beings and good supernatural beings. In contrast to the theology of the ancient Near East, however, modern theology identifies the evil and the good as expressions of dichotomous *moral* characters. This necessitates that one subordinate being become intrinsically evil and the other, intrinsically good. When placed in the context of a relationship with the divine in the Hebrew Bible, this conception of evil is understood to be incompatible with YHWH, while good remains compatible. The two must remain absolutely separate because they are oppositional.

It is this medieval/modern rationale that undergirds our notion of a demon when we apply it to ancient Near Eastern texts. We start with the *presumption* that a demon is an intrinsically evil supernatural being and an angel is an intrinsically good supernatural being, even though such philosophical concepts were not available during the period when these texts were composed.

V. Conclusion

The etymological relationship between *rābiṣu* and *rōbēṣ* led scholars to posit that Israelite religion included a belief in demons. The logic supporting this conclusion was straightforward: if *rābiṣu* refers to a demon in Akkadian, then *rōbēṣ* must reference a demon in Biblical Hebrew.

An analysis of √*rbṣ* < *√*rbṣ̂* demonstrates that the fundamental sense of the root is to settle down and linger in an area to perform a task. It marks a period of presence that is typically repeated in various places. The activities and behavior of the supernatural *rābiṣu* support this basic connotation. The *rābiṣu* is born of the divine wind that arises from divine utterances. Both the positive and negative *rābiṣu*s are currents of air that flow earthward to realize the supernatural articulation in the human sphere—the good *rābiṣu* to comfort and reward, and the evil *rābiṣu* to harass and punish.

The *rōbēṣ* in Gen 4:7 provides little insight into its nature, as it appears in a severely corrupted passage. Deuteronomy 29:19, however, is more enlightening. It relates the verb רבצה to many of the features associated with *rābiṣu*. The verse describes how YHWH's anger produces billows of smoke that develop from the breath YHWH produces when activating curses. The maledictions, armed with their task, descend (רבצה) to earth with one divinely expressed goal: to "blot out" unfaithful Israel.

The picture sharpens further when the nature of the רוח אלהים and רוח יהוה is factored into the equation. Both function in a manner that is extraordinarily similar to the *rābiṣu*. A רוח produced by YHWH is a subordinate supernatural being that operates under the authority of its progenitor. As in the case of the *rābiṣu*, the רוח develops from divine temperament and its subsequent oral expression. An individual רוח is a member of the host of heaven and, like any other faithful retainer, responds to YHWH's invitation to execute punishment. With the approval of YHWH, it can be tasked to be a "lying spirit."

Some רוחות are an elite group within in the heavenly council whose members are the four winds (Jer 49:36, Zech 6:5, Dan 7:2). On other occasions they are YHWH's messengers generated in the swirling wrath of a divine thunderstorm (Pss 35:5, 104:4). At no time do any of these entities operate in opposition to divine will. Consequently, to the ancient Near Easterners the evil רוח of a deity was a physical expression of the deity's *just* response to crimes against the Godhead.

Ancient Near Easterners did not attach a moral character to any subordinate supernatural being, whether a *rābiṣu, utukku, alû, eṭemmu, gallû, ilu*, or a רוח יהוה. The being is neither intrinsically good nor intrinsically evil. The ancients believed that every deity had the authority to judge mortal activities. In their world, the divine–human relationship was a dynamic one, founded on the notion that the deities issued their judgments on a regular basis. Texts demonstrate that these supernaturally generated beings were articulations of divine verdicts that were conveyed to the mortal world as events. It is the character of the assigned tasks of these רוחות that may be considered evil or good, not the רוחות themselves. This means that the cultures of the ancient Near East did not envision our understanding of either demons or angels.

Rereading 1 Kings 17:21 in Light of Ancient Medical Texts

ANDREW R. DAVIS
davisax@bc.edu
Boston College School of Theology and Ministry, Chestnut Hill, MA 02467

This article proposes a new reading of the verb וַיִּתְמֹדֵד in 1 Kgs 17:21 which, I argue, is not from מדד ("to measure") but from מיד ("to shake"). I begin by showing that the current understanding of the verb from מדד, which in this verse is usually translated "to stretch," is problematic. I suggest that the root מיד, which occurs in Hab 3:6, offers a viable alternative to this problematic reading. Finally, comparing this action to Mesopotamian protocols for diagnosing comas, I propose that Elijah shakes himself over the comatose boy in order to determine his condition. This diagnosis then informs Elijah's prayer for YHWH to return the boy's נפש, which is exactly what happens in the next verse. In this reading, Elijah's action is neither therapeutic nor magical; it is diagnostic and a necessary step that enables Elijah to formulate a prayer that is specific to the boy's predicament. His revival is not achieved through Elijah's self-measurement or sympathetic magic; rather it is the result of the prophetic word, which has the power to move YHWH to action.

I

First Kings 17:17–24 describes the (near-)death of the son of the widow of Zarephath and his revival through the efforts of Elijah. Just before Elijah beseeches YHWH to return life to the child, the narrator describes an action that the man of God performs three times over the recumbent boy. The verb for this action is וַיִּתְמֹדֵד, which seems to be a *hithpolel* of the root מדד ("to measure"). That is how the standard lexica understand the verb,[1] and this is the meaning that seems to underlie most translations. Indeed, with some minor variations, nearly all modern

---

I would like to thank Richard Clifford and Tod Linafelt for reading an earlier draft of this article and suggesting improvements. Any errors that remain are my responsibility alone.

[1] See *HALOT*, s.v. מדד; BDB, s.v. מדד.

465

Bibles translate 1 Kgs 17:21a as "he stretched himself upon the child three times."[2] Despite this agreement among translations, the precise nature of Elijah's action and its effect on the boy remain enigmatic. Many assume that the ritual involves some exchange of Elijah's health for the boy's sickness, with some emphasizing Elijah's transference of "life force" to the boy.[3] Others draw on Near Eastern parallels to argue that the point of the action is for Elijah to take on the boy's illness.[4] Adding to this wide range of interpretations is the LXX, which reads a different verb altogether. According to this version, which few interpreters have adopted, Elijah "breathes on" (ἐνεφύσησεν) the boy.[5]

Another complication of the story is the lack of agreement among scholars on the condition of the boy. Is he dead, almost dead, or just unconscious? In this essay, I suggest a new reading of the action performed by Elijah in 1 Kgs 17:21. I argue that Elijah himself is unsure if the boy is dead and that his action in verse 21 is an attempt to diagnose the boy's condition. This interpretation is based on a different reading of the verb ויתמדד, which, I suggest, is not from מדד ("to measure") but from מיד ("to shake"). Comparing this action to Mesopotamian protocols for diagnosing comas, I propose that Elijah shakes himself over the comatose boy in order to determine the boy's condition. This diagnosis then informs Elijah's prayer for YHWH to return the boy's נפש, which is exactly what happens in the next verse. In this reading, Elijah's action is neither therapeutic nor magical; it is diagnostic and a necessary step that enables Elijah to formulate a prayer that is specific to the boy's predicament. The boy's revival is not achieved through Elijah's self-measurement or sympathetic magic; rather, it is the result of the prophetic word, which has the power to move YHWH to action.[6]

---

[2] This is the translation of the KJV, RSV, and NRSV. The JPS, NAB, and NIV are basically the same, except for some variation in the preposition על ("out over," "out upon," and "out on," respectively). German and French translations show similar consistency: "Il s'étendit trois fois sur l'enfant" (*La Bible de Jérusalem, Segond 21*) and "er streckte sich dreimal [aus] über das Kind" (*Einheitsübersetzung*, [Neue Luther Bibel, 2009]).

[3] See Mordechai Cogan, *I Kings: A New Translation with Introduction and Commentary*, AB 10 (New York: Doubleday, 2000), 429; Ernst Würthwein, *Die Bücher der Könige*, 2 vols., ATD 11 (Göttingen: Vandenhoeck & Ruprecht, 1984), 2:223.

[4] John Gray, *I and II Kings: A Commentary*, 2nd rev. ed., OTL (Philadelphia: Westminster, 1976), 382. See also n. 11 below.

[5] The LXX reading is suggested by *BHK* and is followed by some (e.g., the NEB, and Armin Schmitt, "Die Totenerweckung in 1 Kön. XVII 17–24: Eine Form- und Gattungskritische Untersuchung," *VT* 27 [1977]: 457), but most commentators seem to regard ἐνεφύσησεν as a guess at translating the unusual Hebrew ויתמדד (see Cogan, *I Kings*, 21; Gwilym H. Jones, *1 and 2 Kings*, 2 vols., NCB [Grand Rapids: Eerdmans, 1984], 2:308).

[6] According to Richard D. Nelson, "Elijah's deed is more a matter of prayer (vv. 21b–22) than of magic" (*First and Second Kings*, IBC [Atlanta: John Knox, 1987], 111); see also Volkmar Fritz, *1 and 2 Kings: A Continental Commentary*, trans. Anselm Hagedorn, CC (Minneapolis: Fortress, 2003), 184–85; Martin Rehm, *Das erste Buch der Könige: Ein Kommentar* (Würzburg: Echter, 1979), 172.

II

Before advancing my argument for this new interpretation of ויתמדד in 1 Kgs 17:21, I will point out some problems with the current translation of this verb. As noted above, nearly every modern translation renders the verb "he stretched himself upon [the child]." The first sign of trouble with this translation is the variety of ways that interpreters have expanded this meaning of the verb. Stuart Lasine infers from the verb that "healers like Elijah actually *get into bed* with their patients," and Nobuyoshi Kiuchi, reading the gesture through the lens of purity laws, argues that "Elijah functions as an atoning or purifying agent for the dead child."[7] Hector Avalos takes the verb to mean that "Elijah simply leans over the youth three times."[8] Certainly, the most common expansion of the verb's meaning comes from commentators who import details from 2 Kgs 4:18–37, in which Elijah's disciple Elisha likewise restores life to a boy. This story explicitly describes Elisha lying on top of the child (וישכב על־הילד) mouth to mouth, eyes to eyes, and hands to hands (v. 34), and commentators often use this account to thicken their interpretation of ויתמדד in 1 Kgs 17:21. Of the two stories, most interpreters give priority to the Elisha story and presume that the Elijah story is dependent on it.[9] This presumed dependence has led scholars to treat 2 Kgs 4 as background material for 1 Kgs 17, providing material to fill in the gaps of the shorter, more opaque story. Some commentators recommend this approach in a general way,[10] while others simply import details from the Elisha story into their reading of the Elijah story, as when Marvin A. Sweeney writes that the latter's action involved "placing himself face-to-face with the boy."[11] At least two commentators have gone so far as to call the two stories "identical," thus collapsing them together completely.[12]

---

[7] Lasine, "Matters of Life and Death," 117 (emphasis original); see also p. 123; Nobuyoshi Kiuchi, "Elijah's Self-Offering: 1 Kings 17, 21," *Bib* 75 (1994): 78.

[8] Hector Avalos, *Illness and Healthcare in the Ancient Near East: The Role of the Temple in Greece, Mesopotamia, and Israel*, HSM 54 (Atlanta: Scholars Press, 1995), 268–69.

[9] See Georg Fohrer, *Elia*, ATANT 31 (Zurich: Zwingli, 1957), 34, 52; Stephanie M. Fischbach, *Totenerweckungen: Zur Geschichte einer Gattung*, FB 69 (Würzburg: Echter, 1992), 57–58; Schmitt, "Die Totenerweckung in 1 Kön. XVII 17–24," 454–55; Martin Beck, *Elia und die Monolatrie: Ein Beitrag zur religionsgeschichtlichen Rückfrage nach dem vorschriftprophetischen Jahwe-Glauben*, BZAW 281 (Berlin: de Gruyter, 1999), 117.

[10] See Würthwein, *Die Bücher der Könige*, 2:223; Gray, *I and II Kings*, 382; Cogan, *I Kings*, 429.

[11] Marvin A. Sweeney, *I and II Kings: A Commentary*, OTL (Louisville: Westminster John Knox, 2007), 215. Moreover, he cites the Mesopotamian parallels collected by Georg Hentschel (*Die Elijaerzählungen: Zum Verhältnis von historischem Geschehen und geschichtlicher Erfahrung*, ETS 33 [Leipzig: St. Benno, 1977], 193–94 n. 550), but these parallels correspond to 2 Kgs 4:34, not 1 Kgs 17:21, as Hentschel and Sweeney claim.

[12] James A. Montgomery, *A Critical and Exegetical Commentary on the Books of Kings*, ICC (Edinburgh: T&T Clark, 1951), 295–96; and Jones, *1 and 2 Kings*, 2:308.

This gap filling is not without its problems, however. For one thing, not everyone follows the consensus opinion that the Elijah story is dependent on the Elisha story. Indeed, some scholars have argued just the opposite, with a key counterargument coming from the verse that is the focus of this essay, namely, 1 Kgs 17:21 and its relation to 2 Kgs 4:34.[13] Rudolf Kilian asks why the Elijah story would omit the detailed account of Elisha's actions, especially those he performed on the boy (2 Kgs 4:34), if the Elijah story is secondary.[14] Indeed, if the Elisha story does such a fine job of interpreting Elijah's strange behavior, perhaps the story is just that: interpretive. To make an analogy from text criticism, where a gloss represents an attempt by a later scribe to explain an obscure word or phrase, the detailed description given in 2 Kgs 4:34 more likely represents a later writer's attempt to clarify Elijah's obscure action in 1 Kgs 17:21. This secondary status does not mean that 2 Kgs 4:34 should be disregarded—only that it should not be decisive for our interpretation of 1 Kgs 17:21. Elisha's action with the Shunammite's son is not identical to Elijah's with the son of the widow of Zarephath.

It is precisely this tendency to read the verses together that has led scholars to overlook fundamental problems with the usual interpretation of the verb ויתמדד. If we keep Elisha and 2 Kgs 4 at arm's length and look only at the verb, we find that its grammar and semantics do not support the translation "to stretch (upon)." Moreover, if this translation is dubious, then how much more so are the liberties that interpreters have taken with the verb's meaning? In the following analysis of ויתמדד as a *hithpolel* of מדד, I will show that a strict reading of the root in this stem undermines readings that see Elijah lying face-to-face with the lifeless child. Such readings are, in my opinion, a stretch.

Although every interpreter takes מדד ("to measure") as the underlying root of ויתמדד, we have seen that nearly all translations expand this etymology to mean "to stretch," as in "he stretched himself upon the child three times." This expanded meaning may seem to be a natural embellishment of the verb, but a closer look at other biblical examples of this root in factitive conjugations argues against such liberties. This argument begins with the *hithpolel* stem itself, which, along with the *polel* and the *polal*, belongs to a subset of the factitive conjugation group, with the *polel* corresponding to the *piel*, the *polal* to the *pual*, and the *hithpolel* to the *hithpael*. The subset consists primarily of hollow verbs, whose weak middle radical has resulted in a distinctive morphology, but it also includes some geminate roots, including מדד (as well as סבב and חנן).[15] Describing the *hithpael* stem and therefore

---

[13] See Rudolf Kilian, "Die Totenerweckungen Elia und Elias: Eine Motivwanderung?," *BZ* 10 (1966): 44–56; also Rehm, *Das erste Buch der Könige*, 172; Hentschel, *Die Elijaerzählungen*, 188–95. Moreover, Jürgen Werlitz acknowledges the parallels between the two stories but notes that the fuller account in 2 Kgs 4 does not mean that 1 Kgs 17 is secondary (*Die Bücher der Könige*, NSKAT 8 [Stuttgart: Katholisches Bibelwerk, 2002], 166).

[14] Kilian, "Die Totenerweckungen Elia und Elias," 49.

[15] See P. Kyle McCarter, "Hebrew," in *The Ancient Languages of Syria-Palestine and Arabia*,

also the *hithpolel*, Bruce Waltke and M. O'Connor write that it "is used primarily as the double-status (reflexive/reciprocal) counterpart of the *Piel* stem. The object of causation in the *Piel* is the subject of the *Hithpael* and transforms itself/is transformed into the effected state signified by the root."[16] The example they give is the root אזר, which in the *qal* means "to gird" (e.g., Job 38:3, 40:7) and in the *piel* "to make (someone else) girded" (Ps 18:33, 40), but in the *hithpael* it means "to make oneself girded" (Isa 8:9). In most cases, the *hithpael* has the same factitive meaning as the *piel*—someone (or thing) is put into an effected state. The only difference is the effected party: the object of the verb (*piel*) or the subject (*hithpael*).

To be sure, there are other uses of the *hithpael*, including evidence that originally separate *t*-stems merged with it,[17] but, to my knowledge, no scholar has analyzed ויתמדד in 1 Kgs 17:21 as anything but a *hithpolel* verb with a factitive-reflexive meaning. Thus, the following critique of the conventional understanding of ויתמדד through comparison with occurrences of מדד in the *piel* stem follows the interpretive framework of that analysis. What this comparison will show is the inaccuracy of "to stretch (upon)" as a translation of ויתמדד. The following examples demonstrate that מדד in the *piel* refers to precise measurements and sometimes involves the comparison of equal quantities. In none of the instances does מדד denote a vague action of stretching or extending. When this meaning of precise measurement is "translated" into the *hithpolel*, the verb functions as a reflexive but its semantic range is unchanged. The verb ויתמדד in 1 Kgs 17:21 can no more mean "to stretch (himself) over" than the following examples can be translated as he (or I) "stretched (something)." Moreover, considering how each example includes the comparison of equal quantities, we have reason to doubt that even the basic meaning "to measure" fits 1 Kgs 17:21.

The first two instances of מדד in the *piel* come in 2 Sam 8:2, in which David selects certain Moabite prisoners for execution by measuring them off by a line (וימדדם בחבל); two measured lines were put to death and one was spared. However we understand this method, which is unattested elsewhere in the Hebrew Bible, it is clear that this instance of מדד involves measuring the Moabites against set lengths of rope. David "makes them measured" (to translate the verb factitively) by comparing them against the rope, and when the length of the men equaled the length of a rope—"when the rope was full" (ומלא החבל)—the measuring was complete.

---

ed. Roger D. Woodard (Cambridge: Cambridge University Press, 2008), 72, http://dx.doi.org/10.1017/cbo9780511486890.006.

[16] *IBHS* §26.2a.

[17] See Mark Arnold, "Categorization of the Hitpaʿel of Classical Hebrew" (PhD diss., Harvard University, 2005), in which he asserts that "55% of the roots occurring as *hithpaʿēl* have no corresponding *piʿēl*" (48). See also Bruno Dombrowski, "Some Remarks on the Hebrew Hithpaʿel and Inversative -*t*- in the Semitic Languages," *JNES* 21 (1962): 220–23, http://dx.doi.org/10.1086/371696; Jeremy M. Hutton and Safwat Marzouk, "The Morphology of the tG-Stem in Hebrew and *Tirgaltî* in Hos 11:3," *JHS* 12 (2012): 1–41, http://dx.doi.org/10.5508/jhs.2012.v12.a9.

The equivalence between the rope and the men is underscored by the repetition of the verb מדד, used once with the Moabites as its object and then with the lengths of rope as its object.

The next verse in which we find מדד in the *piel* is Job 7:4, which most translate as "to stretch or drag on," sometimes even citing 1 Kgs 17:21 as support for the translation.[18] The JPS translation, for example, reads, "When I lie down, I think, 'When shall I rise?' Night drags on." While at first glance this usage of מדד might seem to support the standard translation of ויתמדד in 1 Kgs 17:21, a closer look at Job 7:3–4 reveals the same emphasis on the division and comparison of precise quantities that we saw in 2 Sam 8:2. This emphasis is clear when Job 7:4 is read with the preceding verse:

> Thus I am allotted [הנחלתי] months of emptiness,
> And nights of misery they have apportioned to me [מנו־לי].
> When I lie down, I think, "When will I rise?"
> But one has set [ומדד] the night and I am full of tossing [נדדים] until dawn.

Reading these verses together, we can see that ומדד is the last of three verbs that all denote apportionment. Of the other two verbs, the most significant is מנו, whose parallelism with מדד (both verbs are *piel* perfects that take "night" as their object) is instructive.[19] Though מנו is usually translated as a passive, several commentators observe that it is in fact an active verb with an impersonal subject ("they" or "one").[20] Few interpreters, however, note that the same is true of מדד: although most translations make ערב the subject of מדד (JPS: "Night drags on"), the active *piel* form requires that "night" be read as the object of the verb and that another impersonal subject be supplied. Job is not saying here that the night drags on indefinitely, as most translations imply, but that night is a fixed period of tossing that lasts until dawn (עדי־נשף). Translators will understandably take liberties, but it must be noted that "night" is not the subject of מדד in Job 7:4 and that the verb does not mean "to drag on, stretch on."[21] Rather, it denotes precise apportionment, which, as in 2 Sam 8:2, is measured against an equal portion. The counterpart of Job's fixed nights is his description in 7:1 of the workdays of a laborer. This verse begins with a reference to one's lifetime of hardship (צבא),[22] and the subsequent verses explain that this

---

[18] See David J. A. Clines, *Job 1–20*, WBC 17 (Waco, TX: Word, 1989), 163.

[19] The parallelism may even include certain homophonies between the two words, especially when they are read together with נדדים ("tossing"). The verbs מנו and מדד share the same first letter, and the remaining letters of each word are those that constitute נדדים. Thus, graphically speaking, Job's allotment is indeed made up of tossing.

[20] See Clines, *Job 1–20*, 163; Édouard Dhorme, *A Commentary on the Book of Job*, trans. Harold Knight (Nashville: Nelson, 1967; French original, 1926), 98.

[21] Dhorme noted the fallacy of this translation, but his alternative reading is equally problematic (*Commentary on the Book of Job*, 99).

[22] Reflecting on the word צבא, C. L. Seow comments that the word suggests a fixed period, bound on the one end by birth and the other by death: "mortality implies that the term of service

lifetime includes not just the drudgeries of the waking hours, plentiful as they are, but also the night, which brings an equal measure of suffering. What I want to emphasize in Job 7:1–4 is that the cluster of terms indicating precise measurement; צבא, הנחלתי, מנו, and מדד refer to specific allotments, not open-ended expansion or stretching. If our best evidence for the meaning of מדד in the *hithpolel* comes from its meaning in the *piel*, this is the denotation that should be brought to bear on 1 Kgs 17:21.

The last two occurrences come from identical lines in two different psalms: "God promised in his sanctuary: 'With exultation I will divide up [אחלקה] Shechem, and the Valley of Sukkot I will measure out [אמדד]'" (Pss 60:8, 108:8). In both psalms this verse is the beginning of a divine response (the same in both psalms) to a communal lament expressed in the preceding verses. After this initial announcement, YHWH goes on to name specific allotments, including Gilead, Manasseh, Ephraim, Judah, Moab, Edom, and Philistia. As numerous commentators have pointed out, YHWH is depicted in this oracle as the divine warrior who divides the conquered territory among his troops, and the territories mentioned represent portions of the promised land that biblical tradition associates with the united monarchy.[23] What is most significant for my purposes is the parallelism between the roots חלק and מדד, both in the *piel*. All agree that the former means "to divide into parts" (cf. Ezek 5:1–2), and the same is true for מדד in the *piel*. It would make little sense to translate אמדד as "to stretch forth," as if YHWH is extending the length of the Valley of Sukkot. Rather, it is clear that YHWH is describing here the precise apportionment of territories. More than the other examples, Pss 60:8 and 108:8 demonstrate the distinctive nuance of מדד in the *piel* and show even more starkly than Job 7:4 the misunderstanding that may result from imprecise translation.

These examples of מדד are vital to our understanding of ויתמדד in 1 Kgs 17:21, because their use of the root in the *piel* establishes a factitive meaning that is also operative in the *hithpolel* stem. The only difference between the two stems is the direction of the verb; in the *piel* the subject puts an object into the effected state, while in the *hithpolel* (and *hithpael*) the subject puts himself or herself into the effected state. What these examples show is that מדד in the *piel* does not denote vague stretching forth but precise measurement. This meaning is apparent from the verb's frequent pairing with other verbs of measurement and apportionment, and it is also implied in the process of measurement itself. To measure something requires a standard against which an item is compared, and each example of מדד in the *piel* features such comparison: men against a length of rope in 2 Sam 8:2,

---

is, for better or worse, limited: it is a term (Rashi, Ibn Ezra, Ralbag, KJV: 'appointed time')" (*Job 1–21: Interpretation and Commentary*, Illuminations [Grand Rapids: Eerdmans, 2013], 492).

[23] See Frank-Lothar Hossfeld and Erich Zenger, *Psalmen*, 3 vols., HTKAT (Freiburg im Breisgau: Herder, 2000), 2:162–63.

night against day in Job 7:4, and similar portions of land against each other in Pss 60:8 and 108:8.

When the fruits of this analysis are applied to ויתמדד in 1 Kgs 17:21, it becomes clear that the factitive meaning of מדד does not work in the verse. Expressing this meaning with the reflexive sense of the *hithpolel* stem, we are left with a translation that is confusing and almost comical: "He made himself measured over the child three times." How, for example, is Elijah's height (or width) related to his healing of the child? Why is it necessary that he measure himself three times? Most strangely, what does it mean for Elijah to measure himself "over the child"? All the other examples of מדד with a factitive meaning involved measurement through the comparison of like items, but Elijah and the child are hardly comparable. The prophet is a grown man, and the child is small enough to sit on his mother's lap (v. 19). In light of this asymmetry, how can we possibly understand Elijah measuring himself over against the child? As we have seen, translators might gloss over these problems by rendering the verb loosely, but any attempt to take seriously the factitive meaning of מדד with its emphasis on precise quantification leads to confusion. In light of these problems, it is time to consider other possibilities for the verb ויתמדד.

III

Having identified several problems with the conventional understanding of Elijah's action in 1 Kgs 17:21, I propose, in this section, an alternative interpretation of the verb, arguing that its root is not מדד but מיד, whose basic meaning is "to shake." Although the root is rare in the Hebrew Bible, occurring only in Hab 3:6, this biblical occurrence is supplemented by an Arabic cognate that sheds further light on the verb's meaning. As a middle-weak verb, the form of מיד in the *hithpolel* would be identical to the geminate מדד, so there is no need for emendation.

The advantages of this new reading are numerous. Not only does it avoid the vague looseness of the conventional interpretation of ויתמדד, but it also leads us to a new understanding of Elijah's actions in 1 Kgs 17:21. He is not "measuring himself" three times over the boy but shaking either the boy or himself (see below) three times in order to confirm the boy's lifeless condition.[24] This interpretation connects Elijah's action to the large corpus of medical texts from Mesopotamia, where we find examples of noxious stimuli used to diagnose a comatose patient. Although this corpus does not contain an exact parallel to Elijah's behavior, the

---

[24] Arnold ("Categorization of the Hitpaʿel of Classical Hebrew," 181, 201), building on Suzanne Kemmer's work on the middle voice in language (*The Middle Voice*, Typological Studies in Language 23 [Philadelphia: J. Benjamins, 1993]), discusses verbs of shaking as examples of "nontranslational motion" in the middle voice. See also Albert Bean, "A Phenomenological Study of the Hithpaʿel Verbal Stem in the Hebrew Old Testament" (PhD diss.; Southern Baptist Theological Seminary, 1975), 123.

variety of diagnostic practices found in it make this new interpretation plausible, though not certain, as we will see. A final advantage of this reading is that it focuses the reader's attention on Elijah's prayer and YHWH's response, not on some sort of sympathetic magic by the prophet, as the means of the boy's revival.

The best place to begin this argument is Hab 3:6, which contains the only other biblical occurrence of the root מיד. Habakkuk 3 is an archaic poem that exults in the victory of YHWH, the divine warrior who vanquishes his foes and saves his people. The first verses of this poem describe the coming of the divine warrior as he marches forth from Teman surrounded by a retinue of minor deities (vv. 3–6).[25] Verse 6 recounts his arrival in this way:

> He stood and made the earth shake [וימדד];
> He looked and made the nations recoil [ויתר].
> The ancient mountains were shattered;
> The eternal hills collapsed.
> His are the eternal pathways.

The second verb in this line is וימדד, which is a *polel* form derived most likely from the root מיד (or מוד).[26] This reading was first argued by G. R. Driver, who identified the Hebrew root as a cognate of the Classical Arabic verb ماد (*māda*), denoting violent agitation.[27] What makes this cognate convincing for Driver is the use of the verb to describe the convulsion of the earth.[28] This interpretation of וימדד finds support in the Targum (ואזיע), and, as James Barr has pointed out, it is reflected also in the LXX, which translates the line in the passive voice: "the earth was shaken" (ἐσαλεύθη ἡ γῆ).[29] Finally, an argument can be made from the poetry itself. All of the verbs in 3:6 indicate some sort of violent upheaval—tremble, shatter, collapse—so it is logical to assume a similar meaning for וימדד. Especially significant is the syntactic and grammatical parallelism between the first two lines. Both begin with a perfect third person masculine singular verb, followed by a third person masculine singular *vav*-consecutive verb in a factitive conjugation, and conclude with a direct object. There are some semantic changes between the two lines ("he stood" // "he saw," and "earth" // "nations"), so we should not expect וימדד to have the exact same meaning as ויתר. Still, the nations' recoiling in the second line suggests some sort of disruption of the mountains in the preceding line, especially when one

---

[25] The march of YHWH as divine warrior from the mountainous regions south of Israel is a common motif in archaic Hebrew poetry. See Richard J. Clifford, *The Cosmic Mountain in Canaan and the Old Testament*, HSM 4 (Cambridge: Harvard University Press, 1972), 114–20.

[26] See *HALOT*, s.v. מוד.

[27] G. R. Driver, "Hebrew Notes," *ZAW* 52 (1934): 54–55.

[28] See Lane, 7:2745–46, s.v. *mēd*. The use of this Arabic cognate meets the guidelines recommended by John Kaltner in *The Use of Arabic in Biblical Hebrew Lexicography*, CBQMS 28 (Washington, DC: Catholic Biblical Association of America, 1996), 98–102.

[29] James Barr, *Comparative Philology and the Text of the Old Testament* (Oxford: Clarendon, 1968), 252, 330.

considers the prevalence of this motif in other biblical theophanies. It is not at all uncommon, especially in ancient poetry, to find the natural world quaking at the arrival of YHWH (e.g., Judg 5:4–5, Pss 18:7, 68:9; see also Exod 19). Altogether this evidence suggests that וימדד in Hab 3:6 should be read as a *polel* form of the verb מיד, which denotes some sort of violent shaking.

Because of the antiquity and complexity of Hab 3, however, nearly every word of the poem has generated numerous interpretations. The verb וימדד is no exception, with scholars proposing a variety of readings and emendations. Such alternative readings include emending the verb to reflect different roots, such as נדד (Albright, Hiebert), מעד (Duhm), מטט (Driver), מגג (Wellhausen), and עמד (*BHS*, Tidiman).[30] Remarkably, a number of commentators take וימדד as a form of the root מדד and translate the first line of 3:6 "He stood and measured the mountains."[31] Those who argue for this reading sometimes even cite 1 Kgs 17:21 for support,[32] but more often appeal is made to the Vulgate, which translates the verb as *mensus est*. None of these proposals, however, improves on the reading that is based on the root מיד. Not only is this root attested in an Arabic cognate, but it requires no emendation and yields a translation that is consistent with Hebrew poetic style. Moreover, this translation finds support in the versions—not just the LXX but even some Latin sources. Although the Vulgate translates וימדד as *mensus est*, when Augustine quotes Hab 3 in *The City of God* (18.32), he reads verse 6 with the LXX: *stetit, et terra commota est*.

If one accepts this reading of Hab 3:6 and regards מיד as a root that is attested within the biblical lexicon, then there is no reason it should not also be considered in 1 Kgs 17:21. According to this interpretation, Elijah brings the lifeless boy to his room, lays him on the bed, and then thrice shakes the boy or shakes himself over the boy. This translation assumes that the verb can refer to mountains (Hab 3:6) as well as a human body (1 Kgs 17:21), but such semantic range would not be unique to מיד. In fact, several of the verbs meaning "to shake" demonstrate this range. The Arabic verb ماد (*māda*), for example, can be used to describe the earth's shaking, as

---

[30] See, respectively, W. F. Albright, "The Psalm of Habakkuk," in *Studies in Old Testament Prophecy Presented to Professor Theodore H. Robinson by the Society for Old Testament Study on His Sixty-Fifth Birthday, August 9th, 1946*, ed. H. H. Rowley (Edinburgh: T&T Clark, 1950), 14; Theodore Hiebert, *God of My Victory: The Ancient Hymn in Habakkuk 3*, HSM 38 (Atlanta: Scholars Press, 1986), 19–20; Bernhard Duhm, *Das Buch Habakuk: Text, Übersetzung und Erklärung* (Tübingen: Mohr Siebeck, 1906), 80; S. R. Driver, *The Minor Prophets*, 2 vols. (New York: Henry Frowde, 1906), 2:89; Julius Wellhausen, *Die Kleinen Propheten: Übersetzt und Erklärt*, 3rd ed. (Berlin: Reimer, 1898), 171; Brian Tidiman, *Nahoum, Habaquq, Sophonie*, Commentaires évangéliques de la Bible 27 (Vaux-sur-Seine: Edifac, 2009), 212.

[31] See RSV, KJV, and BDB, s.v. מדד ; also Francis I. Andersen, *Habakkuk: A New Translation with Introduction and Commentary*, AB 25 (New York: Doubleday, 2001), 308; Robert D. Haak, *Habakkuk*, VTSup 44 (Leiden: Brill, 1992), 83.

[32] E.g., Andersen, *Habakkuk*, 308.

already noted, but also the heaving of one's stomach or the bending of one's body.³³ Similarly, the Greek verb (σαλεύω) used in Hab 3:6 to indicate that "the earth was shaken" occurs in the preceding chapter to describe unsteady drunkenness (2:16).³⁴ Finally, the Aramaic verb that translates וימדד in Hab 3:6 can denote the shaking of mountains as well as human limbs.³⁵ These various verbs for shaking, one of which is a cognate of מיד, suggest that the Hebrew verb also may refer to both the natural world and the human body. The same verb can describe the mountains shaking at the arrival of YHWH in Hab 3:6 and Elijah's shaking in 1 Kgs 17:21.

But why would Elijah vigorously shake the lifeless boy or himself three times? The answer, I suggest, has to do with how unconscious patients were evaluated in antiquity. The best Near Eastern sources for this approach are Mesopotamian medical texts, including the Diagnostic and Prognostic Series (DPS), which has traditionally been attributed to Esagil-kīn-apli, the court physician of the Babylonian king Adad-apla-iddina (1068–1047 BCE).³⁶ The entries of this handbook have recently been published by JoAnn Scurlock and Burton R. Andersen, who have organized these and other medical texts into chapters according to subject matter.³⁷ The subject that seems most pertinent to 1 Kgs 17:17–24 is Scurlock and Andersen's chapter on neurology and its texts relating to comas. Of course, we do not know the precise condition of the boy in the biblical story, but certain clues from the text—there is no breath in the boy (v. 17); his mother regards him as near death (v. 18); and Elijah surmises that the boy's life has left him (v. 21)—suggest that he is comatose. According to an oft-cited definition, coma "is a state of unresponsiveness in which the patient lies with eyes closed and cannot be aroused to respond appropriately to stimuli even with vigorous stimulation."³⁸ Certainly, the

---

³³ See Lane, 7:2746, s.v. *mēd*.

³⁴ Here Gr. διασαλεύθητι translates Heb. והרעל (reading with 1QpHab XI, 9 against MT's והערל).

³⁵ See Michael Sokoloff, *A Dictionary of Jewish Babylonian Aramaic of the Talmudic and Geonic Periods,* Dictionaries of Talmud, Midrash, and Targum 3 (Ramat-Gan: Bar Ilan University Press, 2002), s.v. זוע.

³⁶ Translations of the DPS include the complete translation by René Labat (*Traité akkadien de diagnostics et pronostics médicaux,* 2 vols., Collection de travaux de l'Académie internationale d'historie des sciences 7 [Paris: Académie internationale d'histoire des sciences, 1951]) and selected tablets by Nils Heeßel (*Babylonisch-assyrische Diagnostik,* AOAT 43 [Münster: Ugarit-Verlag, 2000]).

³⁷ JoAnn Scurlock and Burton R. Andersen, *Diagnoses in Assyrian and Babylonian Medicine: Ancient Sources, Translations, and Modern Medical Analyses* (Urbana: University of Illinois Press, 2005). See also Scurlock, *Sourcebook for Ancient Mesopotamian Medicine,* WAW 36 (Atlanta: Society of Biblical Literature, 2014).

³⁸ Jerome B. Posner et al., *Plum and Posner's Diagnosis of Stupor and Coma,* 4th ed. (Oxford: Oxford University Press, 2007), 7. This definition (albeit from an earlier edition of the book) is cited by Joseph Giacino and John Whyte, "The Vegetative and Minimally Conscious States: Current Knowledge and Remaining Questions," *Journal of Head Trauma Rehabilitation* 20 (2005): 32, http://dx.doi.org/10.1097/00001199-200501000-00005.

statements by the mother and Elijah indicate the boy's unresponsiveness, and his lack of breath is also significant, since respiratory abnormalities, including apnea, are symptomatic of comas.[39] Without applying this modern medical designation too strictly, I think the description of the lifeless boy in 1 Kgs 17:17–24 is consistent with the signs and symptoms of coma.

Turning from modern medical sources to ancient ones, we find that the Mesopotamians were familiar with comas and had developed methods for diagnosing them. The term that most commonly denotes coma is the Sumerian word ù.sá, which can be translated into Akkadian *šittu* ("sleep") but in medical texts is best rendered *kūru* ("stupor").[40] In their collection of references to this medical condition, Scurlock and Andersen distinguish four stages of coma:

I. The patient can be roused for brief periods. This is referred to as a stupor.
II. The patient cannot be roused, even with painful stimuli, although she or he may moan and make semipurposeful avoidance movements.
III. Painful stimuli fail to produce a response or they lead to decerebrate posturing (extension and pronation of arms).
IV. The patient is no longer breathing, and his or her muscles are flaccid; the patient is brain dead. Stage IV can be indicated by bilateral fixed, dilated pupils, which usually indicate irreversible brain stem damage if they last longer than five minutes.[41]

Mesopotamian doctors attributed the less severe cases to the "hand of an evil demon [*alû*],"[42] and in all cases they undertook careful observation of patients' movements, noting tension in limbs, responsiveness of pupils, and abnormal breathing patterns.[43] This last symptom is especially relevant to the story of Elijah and the widow's son, whose condition was likewise characterized by respiratory

---

[39] Posner et al., *Plum and Posner's Diagnosis of Stupor and Coma*, 46–53.

[40] See Heeßel, *Babylonisch-assyrische Diagnostik*, 305.

[41] Scurlock and Andersen, *Diagnoses in Assyrian and Babylonian Medicine*, 339. This four-stage scale differs from current clinical approaches, which would not regard all four stages as coma. For example, Scurlock and Andersen's stage I corresponds to what is now called a minimally conscious state, and their stage II corresponds to what is called a vegetative state (cf. Posner et al., *Plum and Posner's Diagnosis of Stupor and Coma*, 357–62; Giacino and Whyte, "Vegetative and Minimally Conscious States," 32–34). I am grateful for the information and bibliography that my colleague Dr. Andrea Vicini provided me on this subject.

[42] The demon is referred to with the Sumerogram a-lá, a designation that may be related to the Sumerian verb lá, "which is frequently used in medical texts to describe a confusional state 'coming over' a patient" (Scurlock and Andersen, *Diagnoses in Assyrian and Babylonian Medicine*, 505). Scurlock and Andersen suggest that the medical condition evolved into an eponymous demon.

[43] Ibid., 339–41.

difficulties. One medical text describes rapid breathing, and two others seem to describe "gasping," which is not uncommon in comatose patients.[44]

This comparison of ancient and modern treatments of coma provides the backdrop for a closer look at a clinical practice that is a fixture of both eras, namely, the use of noxious stimuli to diagnose an apparently comatose patient. As already noted, the very definition of coma includes the use of external stimulation; patients' (lack of) response to such stimulation provides crucial information about their condition. In modern medical practice, physicians, after they have stabilized a patient and performed a physical examination, are instructed to

> conduct a formal coma evaluation. In assessing the level of consciousness of the patient, it is necessary to determine the intensity of stimulation necessary to arouse a response and the quality of the response that is achieved. When the patient does not respond to voice or vigorous shaking, the examiner next provides a source of pain to arouse the patient.[45]

Another set of recommendations advises that "a broad range of eliciting stimuli (eg, auditory, visual, affective) should be utilized to prompt behavioral response," and it mentions further that special care and modifications are required when administering these stimuli to children under the age of three.[46] External stimulation plays an indispensable role in the diagnosis of comatose patients; without it, physicians would lack vital data as they develop a plan of treatment.

Similar stimulatory practices are attested in the medical texts from ancient Mesopotamia. Scurlock and Andersen provide three examples of noxious stimuli.[47] The first comes from the DPS and describes water thrown on a patient's face:

> If he has been sick for six days and he does not get a respite [pa.an-$uš^{48}$] on the seventh, they throw water on his face and if he does not open his eyes, he will

---

[44] Ibid., 340–41. For a discussion of gasping in current medical literature, see Posner et al., *Plum and Posner's Diagnosis of Stupor and Coma*, 52.

[45] Posner et al., *Plum and Posner's Diagnosis of Stupor and Coma*, 40.

[46] Giacino and Whyte, "Vegetative and Minimally Conscious States," 39.

[47] Scurlock and Andersen, *Diagnoses in Assyrian and Babylonian Medicine*, 342–43.

[48] This verb (Akk. *napāšu*) is cognate with Heb. נפש, a significant word in 1 Kgs 17:17–24. Another possible translation, besides Scurlock and Andersen's "to get a respite," is "to breathe freely" (see Heeßel, *Babylonisch-assyrische Diagnostik*, 184, 191; also *CAD* 11.1:288–89). If we follow the latter translation, this text may be another reference to the respiratory difficulty that can accompany coma. Moreover, this Akkadian verb may cast new light on the meaning of נפש in 1 Kgs 17:21–22, in which Elijah prays for the return of the boy's נפש and the נפש returns. Typically, the word is taken to mean the boy's life, but in some cases נפש can refer to breath (Num 21:4, Judg 10:16, 16:16, Zech 11:8). After all, the root meaning of נפש pertains to the neck area, where vital signs of life (e.g., pulse, breath) are apparent. By metonymy, the word comes to mean life itself, but human breath is implied in this meaning. In this way, it is possible to suppose that the boy's missing breath (cf. 1 Kgs 17:17) is what Elijah prays for and the boy receives.

die. If he opens and closes his eyes at the water that they throw over him (and) wails, he will get well.⁴⁹

The other two examples involve auditory stimulus. The first of these two comes from a corpus of literary tablets found in Susa. This particular excerpt is part of a medical text that lists eighteen maladies according to their symptoms, diagnosis, and sometimes treatment:

> If the patient's eyes are dilated, you call out to him and he does not hear you, (and) whatever you hold before him he does not recognize, "hand" of the taciturn one.⁵⁰

The second example of auditory stimulus comes from Tablet II of *Ludlul bēl nēmeqi*, the Babylonian poem sometimes called "The Poem of the Righteous Sufferer," in which the speaker recounts a litany of illnesses that he has suffered:

> My body has donned an *alû*-demon as one would a garment; he covered me with sleep [*šittu*] as with a net. My eyes are dilated and do not see; my ears are open but do not hear. Paralysis has gripped my whole body.... Death has ˹drawn˺ (the curtain); it has covered my face. He ˹listens˺ to me, but I do not answer the one who questions me.⁵¹

To these Mesopotamian examples, I would add one from Josephus, who wrote from a different part of the ancient world several centuries later. In his account of King Herod's final days, he mentions a bath treatment after which the king passes out:

> [Herod's] eyes failed him, and he came and went as if he were dying, and as a tumult was then made by his servants, at their voice he revived again. (*J.W.* 1.33.5 §§656–658; cf. *Ant.* 17.6.5 §§168–179)⁵²

As in the previous examples, this text describes an unconscious patient to whom a noxious stimulus is administered. In all four cases, the patient's (lack of) response provides crucial information for determining his condition and, sometimes, prognosis.

In my opinion, this survey of clinical approaches to coma in ancient and modern contexts provides a plausible explanation for Elijah's action in 1 Kgs 17:21. According to this interpretation, the widow's son falls ill (חלה), and his condition worsens until he has no breath left in him. As already noted, it is not at all clear if

---

⁴⁹ DPS XVI: 63´–64´.

⁵⁰ René Labat and D. O. Edzard, *Textes littéraires de Suse*, Mémoires de la Délégation archéologique en Iran 57 (Paris: Geuthner, 1974), 11 v 15´–18´ (pp. 235–51).

⁵¹ This text is an excerpt from the *Ludlul bēl nēmeqi* (Tablet II, lines 71–74). See Amar Annus and Alan Lenzi, Ludlul bēl nēmeqi: *The Standard Babylonian Poem of the Righteous Sufferer*, SAACT 7 (Helsinki: Neo-Assyrian Text Corpus Project, 2010), 21, 36. In the lines that follow this excerpt (75–76), the speaker goes on to describe his condition as one of numbness (Akk. *rimûtu*) and paralysis (Akk. *mišittu*).

⁵² See Samuel S. Kottek, *Medicine and Hygiene in the Works of Flavius Josephus*, Studies in Ancient Medicine 9 (Leiden: Brill, 1994), 64, 186–90.

the boy is truly dead; the boy's symptoms could just as readily describe one who is comatose. Significantly, the two references to the boy's death occur in questions rather than statements of his condition. The first comes from the mother, as she brings the lifeless boy to Elijah's attention: "What do you have against me, man of God, that you have come to recall my sin and to cause my son to die?" (1 Kgs 17:18). Because she uses an infinitive to describe the boy's death, it is not clear if she regards his death as a fact or an imminent possibility. The second question is one that Elijah directs to YHWH after he has laid the boy on his bed: "YHWH, my God, have you brought calamity even on the widow with whom I am sojourning by causing her son to die?" (1 Kgs 17:20). His reference to the son's death is almost identical to the mother's: both are infinitive constructs that leave the boy's condition ambiguous. Moreover, we should take seriously the fact that both references occur in questions, the mother's to Elijah and Elijah's to YHWH.

If we restore this ambiguity to the passage, then it makes sense that Elijah would attempt to determine the boy's condition before he prays for his recovery. Elijah does so in the same way that we have seen ancient and modern doctors diagnose unconscious patients—by administering a noxious stimulus, which in this case involves repeated shaking by the prophet (ויתמדד). Although 1 Kgs 17:21 offers no adverb to describe the shaking, perhaps we can infer from Hab 3:6, where the verb מיד is used of mountains trembling in the presence of YHWH, that his shaking was vigorous. Presumably, it is from this diagnostic test that Elijah concludes that the boy's נפש is gone, since that is what he asks of YHWH immediately after the test. The narrator confirms the accuracy of this diagnosis by reporting that YHWH heard the prayer and that the boy's נפש returned.

Although this interpretation stands on strong linguistic and comparative evidence, one aspect of it remains elusive, namely, whether the object of Elijah's shaking is the lifeless boy or Elijah himself. Throughout this article, I have avoided committing to one view or the other because each reading has advantages and disadvantages and neither is certain. On the one hand, there is good reason to regard the boy as the object of Elijah's shaking. After all, the "vigorous shaking" mentioned in the medical protocol cited above involves the physician shaking the patient, not herself, and if we put ourselves in Elijah's position, our own instinct would likely be to shake the boy instead of ourselves. Moreover, this reading of ויתמדד is not without some philological support. I noted above that the *hithpael* seems to contain originally separate *t*-stems with different functions from the *hithpael*'s standard usage.[53] One of these seems to have had a durative-iterative meaning,[54] and it is intriguing to consider this iterative meaning for ויתמדד, especially since we know that Elijah performed the action three times. According to this analysis, Elijah shakes the boy in order to determine his condition.

---

[53] See n. 17 above.
[54] See E. A. Speiser, "The Durative Hithpaʿel: A *tan* Form," *JAOS* 75 (1955): 118–21, http://dx.doi.org/10.2307/595014; see also *IBHS* §26.1.2.

Yet this reading faces two obstacles, one minor and the other more serious. The minor obstacle is the prepositional phrase עַל־הַיֶּלֶד, which in this interpretation must function as the object of וַיִּתְמֹדֵד. Although the preposition עַל most often indicates location, it is sometimes used of objects that are physically acted upon (see Judg 18:9, 27; 2 Sam 18:32), and Waltke and O'Connor provide examples in which the preposition indicates the advantage or disadvantage of its object.[55] In this way, one could justifiably translate וַיִּתְמֹדֵד עַל־הַיֶּלֶד שָׁלֹשׁ פְּעָמִים as "he shook on the boy three times." The more serious obstacle to this translation has to do with the iterative meaning. One of the reasons for positing this iterative stem in the first place was that certain *hithpael* verbs lacked counterparts in other factitive stems, such as the *piel*. This distribution is still a defining characteristic of *t*-stem verbs with an iterative meaning, as all the examples of such verbs occur in the *qal* stem but not the *piel* stem.[56] According to this criterion, the root מדד is an unlikely candidate for this iterative meaning because it occurs in the *piel* in Hab 3:6, its only other biblical occurrence. Thus, although the image of Elijah shaking the lifeless boy is consistent with medical practice and, perhaps, our common sense, the advantages of this reading are vitiated by certain grammatical obstacles.

The other possibility involves Elijah shaking himself over the boy as a means of diagnosis. The advantages of this interpretation lie in the strength of the philological case that can be made for it. Elijah's self-agitation is consistent with the factitive-reflexive meaning of the *hithpael* (and *hithpolel*) found in most instances of the stem, and it also provides a better reading of the prepositional phrase עַל־הַיֶּלֶד, which, according to this analysis, indicates where Elijah shook himself (over the boy). The main drawback of this interpretation is the unusual picture it produces; if the point of Elijah's action is to diagnose the condition of the boy, shaking himself may not seem to be the most effective approach. This drawback is somewhat mitigated by the fact that none of the ancient examples of coma diagnosis involve physical contact between the physician and the patient. Of the four examples, only the water method entails any physical stimulus, and even this stimulus involves no interpersonal contact. The other three examples describe auditory stimuli. Given the extreme aversion to corpses in ancient Israel (see Num 19), one might speculate that Elijah purposely avoided direct contact with the lifeless boy, though this aversion seems not to have been widespread in the ancient Near East.[57]

---

[55] *IBHS* §11.2.13c.

[56] See ibid., §26.1.2d.

[57] The Late Bronze Age city of Ugarit is a good example of a contrasting perspective. Wayne T. Pitard writes, "We may reasonably propose that cultures such as that at Ugarit, in which the dead were buried in tombs beneath houses—tombs that were fairly accessible from the living quarters—did not have major concerns about the impurity of the dead and the potential for ritual pollution from the proximity of a corpse that characterizes much of the Israelite legislation concerning the dead" ("Tombs and Offerings: Archaeological Data and Comparative Methodology in the Study

Finally, it is worth noting that modern medical protocol recommends special care in pediatric cases, so perhaps Elijah's hands-off approach is an example of such care.

These challenges demonstrate that, although the root מיד represents a viable, even plausible, alternative to the conventional interpretation of ויתמדד, it is not without difficulties of its own. Without further data, there is no way of knowing the precise significance of this verb, but that does not mean that we should stop looking for new explanations. If this argument for reading ויתמדד as some sort of shaking by which Elijah diagnoses the comatose boy is, in the end, unconvincing, I have at least demonstrated that the conventional reading is equally unconvincing, perhaps more so. In that case, this article may open up a space for even further possibilities. If one finds the argument compelling, however, then this reading has important literary and theological implications. Literarily, the reading restores dramatic tension to the story. The boy's death is by no means certain in the eyes of his mother, Elijah, or even the reader. If we view Elijah's action as diagnostic, then the ambiguity of the boy's condition infuses the story with new urgency. This reading also avoids an awkward element in the story. That is, if we follow the conventional interpretation of 1 Kgs 17:21, whereby Elijah transfers his life force to the boy through contractual magic, then Elijah's prayer for the return of the boy's נפש is superfluous. This redundancy is avoided if we regard his action as a diagnostic test that informs the prayer that he addresses to YHWH.

This point leads to the main theological effect of this new reading, which is the emphasis on the efficaciousness of Elijah's prayer. Perhaps somewhat ironically, by reinterpreting Elijah's action as a diagnostic test instead of therapeutic magic, we have diminished the action's importance to the overall story. According to the reading proposed here, Elijah's action in 1 Kgs 17:21 does not contribute to the boy's revival; it is merely a preliminary, albeit necessary, test that he performs before he prays for YHWH's intervention. This understanding of 1 Kgs 17:21 agrees, then, with those interpreters who have on other grounds argued that Elijah's prayer is the centerpiece of the story.[58] Furthermore, it is consistent with the main theme of the Elijah cycle (1 Kgs 17–19): YHWH has the exclusive power to give and take away life, and Elijah is uniquely able to mediate this power.

---

of Death in Israel," in *Sacred Time, Sacred Place: Archaeology and the Religion of Israel*, ed. Barry M. Gittlen [Winona Lake, IN: Eisenbrauns, 2002], 150).

[58] See n. 6 above. See also Burke O. Long, who demonstrates how the ring structure of 1 Kgs 17:17–24 has at its center "the action between Elijah and Yahweh" (*1 Kings with an Introduction to Historical Literature*, FOTL 9 (Grand Rapids: Eerdmans, 1984], 185).

New from
BAKER ACADEMIC

Being Human in God's World
An Old Testament Theology of Humanity
J. Gordon McConville
978-0-8010-4896-8 • 240 pp. • $27.99c

"A richly textured account of our humanity as the Hebrew Bible portrays it.... Explores variously the material, political, gendered and sexual, as well as prayerful dimensions of human living 'in the image of God.'"
—**Ellen F. Davis**, Duke Divinity School

Jesus according to Scripture, 2nd Edition
Restoring the Portrait from the Gospels
Darrell L. Bock with Benjamin I. Simpson
978-0-8010-9808-6 • 752 pp. • $49.99c

Offering up-to-date interaction with the latest discussions about Jesus, this second edition has been substantially revised and updated throughout and includes three new chapters on how we got the Gospels.

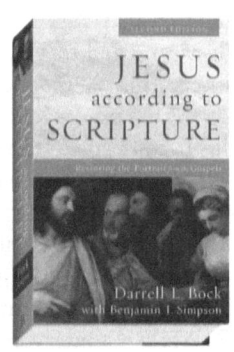

Philippians and Philemon
James W. Thompson and Bruce W. Longenecker
978-0-8010-3339-1 • 240 pp. • $30.00p

"A first-rate commentary.... I recommend it enthusiastically for students and ministers who are serious about the biblical text."
—**Gregory E. Sterling**, Yale Divinity School

bakeracademic.com
Available in bookstores or by calling 800.877.2665
Visit our blog: blog.bakeracademic.com

The "God of the Fathers" in Chronicles

TROY D. CUDWORTH
troy.d.cudworth@gmail.com
Washington, DC 20008

The Chronicler has a penchant for developing paradigmatic vocabulary throughout his narrative. Many scholars have noted the Chronicler's extensive use of the divine epithet "God of the fathers" throughout the books of Chronicles (twenty-seven times), yet few have investigated its meaning there. Sara Japhet has suggested that it emphasizes the continuous relationship between YHWH and the people. I propose that the epithet goes beyond this simple connotation in Chronicles by evoking YHWH's promise of land to the patriarchs with phraseology found most heavily in Deuteronomy. Occurrences of the appellation in the speeches of David and Jehoshaphat specifically include mention of the patriarchs in the immediate context. Several other instances show how the Israelites would either strengthen or weaken their position in the land based on their faithfulness or unfaithfulness to the "God of their fathers." With the few remaining occurrences, the broader context can accommodate the meaning from Deuteronomy.

The Chronicler has a penchant for developing paradigmatic vocabulary throughout his narrative.[1] His repeated use of both positive (e.g., דרש ["he sought"], כנע ["he humbled himself"]) and negative (e.g., עזב ["he abandoned"], מעל ["he acted unfaithfully"]) words in critical places of his history allows him to characterize the different kings and express his own theology succinctly.[2]

---

[1] As with the majority of recent scholars, I use the term "the Chronicler" to refer to a postexilic author who used various traditions found mostly in the books of Samuel and Kings (though not necessarily the version in the MT) as well as others (e.g., Psalms and Genesis) to retell Israel's history. A. Graeme Auld has disagreed with this near consensus and argued at length that the authors of Samuel–Kings and Chronicles shared a common source (*Kings without Privilege: David and Moses in the Story of the Bible's Kings* [Edinburgh: T&T Clark, 1994]). I also follow the arguments of Sara Japhet, H. G. M. Williamson, and others who hold Chronicles to be a separate work from Ezra-Nehemiah. See Japhet, "Supposed Common Authorship of Chronicles and Ezra-Nehemia Investigated Anew," *VT* 18 (1968): 330–71, http://dx.doi.org/10.1163/156853368X00258; Williamson, *Israel in the Books of Chronicles* (Cambridge: Cambridge University Press, 1977), http://dx.doi.org/10.1017/CBO9780511557453.

[2] Brian E. Kelly surveys many of these terms in *Retribution and Eschatology in Chronicles*,

Along these lines, scholars have long noticed the Chronicler's extensive use of the divine epithet "God of the fathers," which occurs twenty-seven times in his narrative with different variations, none having a parallel in Samuel–Kings.³ Gerhard von Rad notes that the same title occurs in Deuteronomy eight times and maintains that the Chronicler takes on that particular tradition with it. Von Rad asserts, however, that the appellation has only the general sense of holding on to the ancient faith.⁴ Sara Japhet disagrees with von Rad's position, arguing that no relationship exists between the usage of the epithet in Chronicles and that in Deuteronomy. She further contends that the Chronicler was not influenced by any other specific literary source for this term⁵ and then suggests that the Chronicler takes the epithet from the general linguistic pool and uses it freely to express his own conception of Israel's God, one that emphasizes a continuous relationship between YHWH and his people.⁶

By contrast, in this article I show how the Chronicler employs the epithet with a more specific referent than these other scholars have suggested. As in Deuteronomy, this divine title in Chronicles repeatedly evokes YHWH's promise to the patriarchs that he would provide their descendants (i.e., Israel) with a secure place in the land as long as they remain faithful to him.⁷ The Chronicler often makes acts

---

JSOTSup 211 (Sheffield: Sheffield Academic, 1996), 51–63. See also David A. Glatt-Gilad, "The Root *knᶜ* and Historiographic Periodization in Chronicles," *CBQ* 64 (2002): 248–57.

³ This title includes the variations "God of your/their/his/our fathers" (/אלהי אבותיכם/ אבותיהם/אבותיו/אבותינו).

⁴ Gerhard von Rad, *Das Geschichtsbild des chronistischen Werkes*, BWANT 54 (Stuttgart: Kohlhammer, 1930), 7.

⁵ Sara Japhet, *The Ideology of the Book of Chronicles and Its Place in Biblical Thought*, trans. Anna Barber, BEATAJ 9 (Frankfurt am Main: Lang, 1989), 18. It occurs only nineteen other times in the Hebrew Bible, with no clear concentration in any one place apart from Deuteronomy.

⁶ Ibid., 19. See also Gary N. Knoppers, *I Chronicles 10–29: A New Translation with Introduction and Commentary*, AB 12A (New York: Doubleday, 2004), 564; P. B. Dirksen, *1 Chronicles*, trans. Anthony P. Runia, HCOT (Leuven: Peeters, 2005), 92. Leslie Allen and Steven Tuell have included occurrences with the singular "father" in their discussion of the divine title, but this has not enabled them to go beyond Japhet's explanation for the Chronicler's usage of it. Moreover, their broader investigation does not capture the distinct use of the epithet with the plural. See Allen, "Aspects of Generational Commitment and Challenge in Chronicles," in *The Chronicler as Theologian: Essays in Honor of Ralph W. Klein*, ed. M. Patrick Graham, Steven L. McKenzie, and Gary N. Knoppers, JSOTSup 371 (Sheffield: Sheffield Academic, 2003), 123–32; Tuell, *1 and 2 Chronicles*, IBC (Louisville: John Knox, 2001), 33–34. Steven L. McKenzie and Ralph W. Klein both identify the epithet as the Chronicler's favorite title for Israel's God, but neither discusses his intent with it. See McKenzie, *1–2 Chronicles*, AOTC (Nashville: Abingdon, 2004), 128; Klein, *1 Chronicles: A Commentary*, Hermeneia (Minneapolis: Fortress, 2006), 170.

⁷ Thomas Römer avers that many (though not all) of the Chronicler's uses of the divine name follow the conception in Deuteronomy (*Israels Väter: Untersuchungen zur Väterthematik im Deuteronomium und in der deuteronomistischen Tradition*, OBO 99 [Göttingen: Vandenhoeck & Ruprecht, 1990], 344–52). He seldom discusses, however, how the usage illustrates consequences involving Israel's security in the land.

toward the temple (as opposed to the Mosaic law in Deuteronomy) the object of this faith, but the consequences always pertain to Israel's stability in the land.[8] To demonstrate this correspondence, the following analysis examines the background for the divine name in Deuteronomy, then the most illustrative examples for this meaning in Chronicles, and lastly how the remaining occurrences can accommodate such a connotation.

I. "God of the Fathers" in Deuteronomy

The background for each occurrence of the epithet in Deuteronomy comes from YHWH's recurring promise of land to the patriarchs found throughout Genesis (Gen 13:14–17, 15:12–21, 17:8, 26:4–5, 28:13–14). The first alludes to their prosperity in the land, the promise of numerous offspring: "May YHWH, the God of your fathers, increase you a thousand times more and bless you as he promised you" (Deut 1:11). The second regards the provision of land: "See, YHWH your God has placed the land before you. Go up, take possession, as YHWH, the God of your fathers, has promised you" (1:21). For both of these verses, the beginning of the passage makes the reference to the "fathers" explicitly to the patriarchs: "See, I have set the land before you. Go in and take possession of the land that YHWH swore to your fathers, to Abraham, to Isaac, and to Jacob, to give to them and to their offspring after them" (1:8).[9] On four other occasions also, Deuteronomy defines the "fathers" by specifying the actual names of the patriarchs (6:10, 9:5, 29:13, 30:20).

The remaining six occurrences of this divine epithet in Deuteronomy refer specifically to Israel's ability to possess the land. Four times Israel is reminded that YHWH has made the blessings of these promises contingent on obedience to the law (4:1, 6:3, 12:1, 27:3). Similarly, the passage in Deut 26 instructs the Israelites to acknowledge the God of their fathers with their firstfruits when they eventually settle in the land to honor him who brought them out of Egypt and led them there (v. 7; cf. vv. 3–9). Lastly, the occurrence in 29:24 explains how YHWH will destroy the land and uproot the Israelites from it if they abandon their covenant with the God of their fathers (29:21–27).[10]

The link to the patriarchal promises becomes even stronger if we consider

---

[8] The one occurrence of this divine title in the books of Kings (the books of Samuel have none) does not touch on this theme of the Chronicler, which perhaps reveals the reason why he does not include it (cf. 2 Kgs 21:22). For more discussion on the relation between Israel's faithfulness and their ability to stay in the land, see Troy D. Cudworth, *War in Chronicles: Temple Faithfulness and Israel's Place in the Land*, LHBOTS 627 (London: Bloomsbury T&T Clark, 2016).

[9] This theme reappears with different wording at the end of Deuteronomy in YHWH's words to Moses: "This is the land that I swore to Abraham, Isaac, and Jacob" (34:4).

[10] The covenant here refers to the law given to the exodus generation at Sinai, which still includes the promise of land to the patriarchs. All references throughout this article follow the versification in *BHS*.

Deuteronomy's many uses of the simpler term *fathers* (אבות, fifty-one times). Even though some occurrences of this word obviously do not pertain to the theme (e.g., 5:9, 24:16), the vast majority do. They use the same vocabulary as the well-defined first occurrence of the word in 1:8 (see above). For example, twenty-four occurrences have YHWH's oath to the patriarchs explicitly in the context ("as YHWH swore [שבע, *niphal*] to your fathers").[11] Along these same lines, four more occurrences speak of YHWH's promise (דבר, *piel*) to the fathers.[12] The land serves as another common theme from 1:8 (ארץ, but also the synonym אדמה), which appears in the immediate context of twenty-eight occurrences of the word *fathers*, five of which do not overlap with the above instances.[13] Lastly, we may count five additional occurrences that also have the patriarchal promises in view by other means,[14] giving a total of (at least) thirty-eight occurrences of the word *fathers* in Deuteronomy that refer to YHWH's promise to the patriarchs.

The consistent meaning, therefore, of the title "God of the fathers" in Deuteronomy, together with the frequent use of "fathers" in the context of the patriarchal land promises, provides ample justification for the Chronicler to use the divine name in the same way. The following survey of the many occurrences in Chronicles will demonstrate that he did.

II. "God of the Fathers" in Chronicles

A. *The Patriarchal Promise of Land Explicit in the Context*

Two passages in Chronicles make a particularly strong connection between the divine epithet and YHWH's promise of land to the patriarchs. The first comes at the end of David's reign, when he recites a prayer in front of the large assembly that he had rallied to support Solomon in the construction of the temple (1 Chr 29:10–19). Earlier passages describe how David gave to the temple fund from the great wealth he had accumulated over the course of his reign (22:3–5, 29:1–5a) and exhorted the people to contribute also (22:17–19, 29:5b–9). David then voices the plea, "O YHWH, the God of Abraham, Isaac, and Israel, our fathers, keep this forever in the intentions of the heart of your people and direct their heart toward you" (29:18). In response, the entire assembly blesses "YHWH, the God of their fathers" (v. 20).

---

[11] See Deut 1:8, 35; 4:31; 6:10, 18, 23; 7:8, 12, 13; 8:1, 18; 9:5; 10:11; 11:9, 21; 13:17; 19:8; 26:3, 15; 28:11; 29:13; 30:20; 31:7, 20.

[12] See Deut 1:11, 6:3, 19:8, 27:3.

[13] See Deut 1:21, 4:1, 12:1, 30:5 (2x). The word *land* appears in 31:16, but it is not obvious that *fathers* here refers to the patriarchs.

[14] The occurrences in 4:37 and 10:15 refer to the election of the fathers' offspring, which would indicate the promise to the patriarchs. As for 26:7 and 29:25, these both refer to the divine title "God of the fathers" discussed above. Lastly, the use of the word *fathers* in 30:9 likely has the same referent as the two occurrences in v. 5.

The Chronicler evokes the promise of land earlier in the same prayer. Although David and the assembly had given a large quantity of materials to the temple project, he acknowledged that they could give this much only because YHWH had blessed them abundantly (1 Chr 29:14). He explains, "For we are sojourners before you, and transients as all our fathers. Our days on the earth are like a shadow and there is no hope" (v. 15). This statement cannot have a literal meaning in light of David's earlier assertion that he had completely subdued the land (22:18).[15] Rather, it serves as a reminder to the people that, even with David's great success on the battlefield, their position in the land will remain as precarious as that of their transient patriarchs if not for the support of their God. With this in mind, David's request in 29:18 seeks to stir the people's faith in YHWH so that they can strengthen themselves in the land.[16]

The second key text comes from a prayer by Jehoshaphat when he hears the news that a southeastern coalition of armies has come to attack Judah (2 Chr 20). The Chronicler emphasizes Jehoshaphat's initial fear and desperation such that he proclaims a fast throughout all Judah as a result of the grave situation. In his prayer, he identifies two factors that bolstered his faith in the face of this massive oncoming threat. He begins with the first, "O YHWH, God of our fathers.... Did you not, our God, drive out the inhabitants of this land before your people Israel and give it to the descendants of Abraham your friend?" (20:6–7). Jehoshaphat, like David, uses this divine title to remind YHWH of his land promise to the patriarchs.

Jehoshaphat next mentions the completed and functioning temple in his reasoned plea, using language that strongly alludes to YHWH's response to Solomon in the temple dedication (2 Chr 7:12–22).[17] In that scene, YHWH promises to keep his eyes open and ears attentive to the temple so that his people can pray to him there in times of crisis (7:13–16). In light of this provision, Jehoshaphat affirms that Israel has established and maintained YHWH's sanctuary (20:8), that such a crisis has arisen (vv. 10–11), and that now their eyes are on YHWH to preserve their place in the land according to his word (v. 12). In other words, Judah's hope for divine protection from the invaders ultimately rests on YHWH's promise to the patriarchs.

---

[15] See also Daniel J. Estes, "Metaphorical Sojourning in 1 Chronicles 29:15," *CBQ* 53 (1991): 45–49.

[16] Many have noted the similarities between David's prayer in 29:10–19 and the medley of psalms in 1 Chr 16:8–36 (see H. G. M. Williamson, *1 and 2 Chronicles*, NCB [London: Marshall, Morgan & Scott, 1982], 185–86). The Chronicler urges Israel, "Remember his [YHWH's] covenant forever ... the covenant that he made with Abraham, his sworn promise to Isaac, which he confirmed as a statute to Jacob, as an everlasting covenant to Israel" (16:15–17). The following verses relate the promise specifically to Israel's claim on the land (vv. 18–22).

[17] For the critical function of the temple in this episode, see Gary N. Knoppers, "Jerusalem at War in Chronicles," in *Zion, City of Our God*, ed. Richard S. Hess and Gordon J. Wenham (Grand Rapids: Eerdmans, 1999), 57–76.

B. The Promise of Land in Close Context

Although the remaining occurrences of the divine epithet in Chronicles do not explicitly refer to the patriarchs, many allude to the land consequences for Israel due to their (un)faithfulness.[18] Two clear examples of this appear in relation to their exile. First, in the genealogical section, the Chronicler states that YHWH sent Tiglath-pileser against the Transjordanian tribes and exiled them to Assyria since they broke faith (מעל) with the God of their fathers (1 Chr 5:25–26). Second, at the end of his narrative, he explains that Babylon eventually exiled Judah from the land because they polluted the temple and did not turn from their wickedness despite the many warnings from the God of their fathers (2 Chr 36:14–17).

The exile looms over two other contexts in which the Chronicler inserts the divine name into a passage he borrows from the books of Kings. At the end of the temple dedication ceremony, he alters YHWH's warning to Solomon that he would remove Israel from the land if the people turned to idolatry (cf. 1 Kgs 9:6–9). He fittingly places the title "God of their fathers" into the context to relate their unfaithfulness to the loss of the land (2 Chr 7:22; see also vv. 19–20).[19] The Chronicler later associates this divine title with Josiah's reforms, which delayed Judah's exile from the land for a brief period of time (2 Kgs 22:16–20 // 2 Chr 34:24–28). The covenant Josiah made with YHWH in 2 Kgs 23:3 now in Chronicles aims to lead the people to faith in the God of their fathers so that they can maintain their position in the land (2 Chr 34:32–33).

In the contrasting reigns of Ahaz and Hezekiah, the Chronicler uses the divine name seven times to illustrate the land benefits of faithfulness to YHWH. The former king's unrestrained idolatry provoked YHWH to send five different assailants against Judah (Aram [2 Chr 28:5a], Israel [vv. 5b–8], Edom [v. 17], Philistia [v. 18], and Assyria [v. 20]). Ironically, where the books of Kings say that the Assyrians exiled the northern kingdom from their land (2 Kgs 17), the Chronicler claims that the latter carried off many from the southern kingdom because Judah had forsaken (עזב) the God of their fathers (2 Chr 28:6, 9; cf. v. 8).[20] To make matters worse, even after the five assailants had come and gone, the Chronicler avers that Ahaz continued to provoke the God of his fathers by making high places in all of

---

[18] Of course, the Chronicler does not mention the patriarchs every time he uses the title, since that would defeat the purpose of using the concise shorthand phrase. That is to say, he intended the name to be evocative in most cases.

[19] Compare 2 Chr 7:22, "Because they abandoned YHWH, *the God of their fathers* who brought *them* out of the land of Egypt," with the parallel in 1 Kgs 9:9, "Because they abandoned YHWH *their God* who brought *their fathers* out of the land of Egypt.…" This verse does not make "fathers" refer to the exodus generation. Although it alludes to the covenantal stipulations that YHWH gave to Israel at Sinai, the hope of land still rested on his promise to the patriarchs. See the discussion above on Deut 29:24, which has similar wording.

[20] Römer helpfully points out the Chronicler's aim to highlight the common ground (*Gemeinsamkeit*) between the northern and southern kingdoms with the occurrence of the epithet in 28:9 and also 13:12 and 30:7 (*Israels Väter*, 347–48).

Judah's cities (28:25). In the context of the two earlier uses of the divine name in Ahaz's reign (28:6, 9), Judah's position in the land could not have become any weaker after all that Ahaz had done.

Ahaz's son Hezekiah attempted to reverse the miserable condition in which his father had put Judah. In his first speech, delivered to the Levites, Hezekiah explains how YHWH had punished Ahaz's generation with the sword and captivity (2 Chr 29:8-9) because they neglected the temple (vv. 6-7). For this reason, he implores them to consecrate themselves and the temple of YHWH, the God of their fathers, in order to turn away this divine wrath (v. 5; cf. v. 10).[21] In a later phase of the reforms, Hezekiah exhorts all Israel and Judah to turn toward the God of their fathers from their faithless behavior, which had made the previous generation a desolation (30:7). If, on the other hand, they were to turn (שוב) to YHWH, he would return those family members who had been captured back to the land (30:9). Two more occurrences of the divine name confirm that the people responded positively to Hezekiah's call (30:19, 22). These verses reveal how the Chronicler makes the title "God of the fathers" the focal point of Hezekiah's reforms throughout 2 Chr 29-31. In 32:1-23, he then shows how the reforms strengthened the nation to the point that they could overcome a formidable Assyrian attack.

The divine name serves this purpose to a lesser degree in the reigns of several other kings. Soon after the division of the kingdom, a contingent of northerners came down to Judah to offer sacrifices to the God of their fathers; their faithfulness strengthened (חזק) the kingdom after it had shrunk to include only Judah and Benjamin (2 Chr 11:16-17; cf. v. 12b). After this, Abijah warned the idolatrous northerners that they should not even try to fight against his army, since the southern kingdom had kept faith with the God of their fathers (2 Chr 13:12). The Chronicler attributes Abijah's victory specifically to the Israelites' reliance on the God of their fathers (13:18).

The southern kingdom continued to have rest (שקט) because Abijah's son Asa instituted reforms and commanded Judah to seek (דרש) the God of their fathers (2 Chr 14:2-4). The root שקט is frequently used in the Hebrew Bible to apply to the situation after a long period of strife when the land finally enjoyed quiet and relief.[22] Later in his reign, Asa led the people into a covenant with the God of their fathers as a response to Azariah's admonishment that Israel never had peace unless they turned (שוב) and sought (בקש) YHWH (15:12; cf. vv. 2-7, esp. v. 4). Manasseh appears as a final example in this regard. Although YHWH had punished him with an individualized exile from Judah to Babylon for his great idolatry (2 Chr 33:11),[23]

---

[21] To be clear, the reference to the temple does not mean that the Chronicler equates the "fathers" with David and Solomon. Rather, he emphasizes the blessing of stability in the land, which looks back to the patriarchal promises.

[22] Note the occurrence of שקט in Josh 11:23 at the end of the conquest, or the several occurrences in the book of Judges (3:11, 30; 5:31; 8:28).

[23] See Rudolf Mosis, *Untersuchungen zur Theologie des chronistischen Geschichtswerkes*, FThSt 92 (Freiburg: Herder, 1973), 193; Williamson, *1 and 2 Chronicles*, 393.

he then brought him back to Jerusalem because the king had humbled himself (כנע) before the God of his fathers (33:12–13).

In other instances, the Chronicler uses the divine title to show how unfaithful kings squandered their domain. For example, he explains how both Edom and Libnah revolted from Jehoram's rule "because he had forsaken [עזב] YHWH, the God of his fathers" (2 Chr 21:10). Later, Joash and his leaders turned away from the God of their fathers to serve the Asherim and idols (24:18). The same divine title appears again to describe how YHWH in turn gave them into the hand of the much smaller Aramaean army as punishment (24:24).

C. The Promise of Land in Broad Context

These last occurrences of the divine epithet do not have the land promise directly in view, but they can still accommodate this connotation. For example, the Chronicler uses the divine name at the earliest recorded moment for his account of David, who first started to gather "all Israel" while hiding in the stronghold (1 Chr 12:17–19).[24] The band of men that approached him from the tribes of Benjamin and Judah would certainly have caused concern for David's camp, so he told them, "If you have come to me in peace to help me, my heart will be united with you; but if you betray me to my adversaries even though there is no wrong in my hands, may the God of our fathers see and rebuke you" (1 Chr 12:16). Not only does this particular group join David's cause (v. 19), but he continues to accumulate the rest of the people's support until he has gained the backing of all Israel due to his faith in this God (cf. 11:1, 4; 13:5).

Since the Chronicler's David aimed to rally all Israel to the worship of YHWH, his God continually gave him victory on the battlefield. Both David's conquest of Jerusalem (1 Chr 11:4–9) and his victory over the Philistines (14:8–17) mention his rule over all Israel at the beginning of the account and conclude with his victory as a blessing from YHWH. Thus, his early plea to the band from Benjamin and Judah to join his cause lays a foundation for his later conquests and Israel's security in the land.

The remaining two occurrences appear in the reign of Jehoshaphat. The first in 2 Chr 19:4 illustrates the king's desire to secure the broad scope of his rule after a devastating blunder. Jehoshaphat had prospered early in his reign on account of his devotion to YHWH (17:3–9). This piety resulted in many building projects (17:1–2, 12–13a), a vast accumulation of military forces (17:13b–19), and fear of YHWH coming on all the surrounding nations (17:10–11). Unfortunately, Jehoshaphat put himself and Judah in great danger through his alliance and joint military campaign with the wicked northern king Ahab and only narrowly escaped

---

[24] Sara Japhet demonstrates how the material in 1 Chr 11–12 illustrates the unity of Israel by the time of David's enthronement in 11:1–3 through a "flashback" technique (*I and II Chronicles: A Commentary*, OTL [London: SCM, 1993], 232–33).

(18:1–19:3).²⁵ As an act of repentance, Jehoshaphat brought the people back to the God of their fathers with the aim (presumably) of strengthening Judah's security in the land once again (19:4).²⁶ Similarly, when the southeastern coalition came to threaten this position soon afterwards, Jehoshaphat prayed to YHWH, the God of his fathers, who then saved Judah (20:6; see above).

The second occurrence of the divine epithet, in 2 Chr 20:33, has very little in the immediate context to illuminate the term's meaning. Following a spectacular display of faith by both Jehoshaphat and the people in the preceding verses (20:1–30), this verse offers a concession.²⁷ Not only did the king fail to remove some high places (but see 17:6); the people still did not set their hearts completely on YHWH, the God of their fathers. Although the verse presents an abrupt addendum to an otherwise happy ending, the divine title likely has the same connotation as the nearby occurrences in 19:4 and 20:6. Despite YHWH's faithfulness to fight for his people and provide national security, the Chronicler asserts that they still did not embrace their God as they should have. The Chronicler does not spell out the land consequences for Judah in this instance, but perhaps he adumbrates their dissipating territory in the reign of Jehoshaphat's son, Jehoram (see 21:8–10, 16–17).

III. Conclusion

Recent scholarship, mostly following the lead of Japhet, has contended that the Chronicler used the divine epithet "God of the fathers" to emphasize the continuous relationship between Israel and its God. Beyond this basic explanation, I have argued that the book of Deuteronomy's consistent use of the same title serves as the most likely source for the Chronicler's usage of the divine name. In both Deuteronomy and Chronicles, the epithet evokes YHWH's promise to the patriarchs that he would provide them with the land that Israel eventually possessed. The Chronicler adopted it into his own set of paradigmatic vocabulary to spur his audience to remain faithful to their God.

---

²⁵ See Gary N. Knoppers, "'Yhwh Is Not with Israel': Alliances as a Topos in Chronicles," *CBQ* 58 (1996): 601–26, esp. 612–16.

²⁶ Gary N. Knoppers argues convincingly that Jehoshaphat returns to the consolidation efforts that he pursued in the earlier part of his reign ("Reform and Regression: The Chronicler's Presentation of Jehoshaphat," *Bib* 72 [1991]: 500–524, esp. 514–15).

²⁷ As several scholars have noted, the Chronicler presents many contrasting, divergent episodes for Jehoshaphat to show his ambivalence toward the king. See Knoppers, "Reform and Regression," 522–24; Steven L. McKenzie, "The Trouble with King Jehoshaphat," in *Reflection and Refraction: Studies in Biblical Historiography in Honour of A. Graeme Auld*, ed. Robert Rezetko, Timothy H. Lim, and W. Brian Aucker, VTSup 113 (Leiden: Brill, 2007), 299–314, esp. 313–14; Ralph W. Klein, *2 Chronicles: A Commentary*, Hermeneia (Minneapolis: Fortress, 2012), 297.

New from
BAKER ACADEMIC

Intermediate Greek Grammar
Syntax for Students of the New Testament
David L. Mathewson and Elodie Ballantine Emig
978-0-8010-3072-7 • 336 pp. • $32.99c

"Provides students with the solid food necessary to read Greek at a more mature level. I will use this book."
—**George L. Parsenios,** Princeton Theological Seminary

The Synoptic Problem
Four Views
Stanley E. Porter and Bryan R. Dyer, editors
978-0-8010-4950-7 • 208 pp. • $22.99p

"This volume is particularly well done.... Students can consider this 'one-stop shopping' for scholarship on this important topic."—**Craig L. Blomberg,** Denver Seminary

The Mind of the Spirit
Paul's Approach to Transformed Thinking
Craig S. Keener
978-0-8010-9776-8 • 448 pp. • $32.99c

"An important book for anyone interested in the relationship of Pauline theology to its cultural context."
—**Harold Attridge,** Yale Divinity School

Baker Academic
bakeracademic.com
Available in bookstores or by calling 800.877.2665
Visit our blog: blog.bakeracademic.com

Where Art Thou, O Hezekiah's Tunnel? A Biblical Scholar Considers the Archaeological and Biblical Evidence concerning the Waterworks in 2 Chronicles 32:3–4, 30 and 2 Kings 20:20

MARY KATHERINE YEM HING HOM
marykatherinehom777@gmail.com
Wolfson College, University of Cambridge, Cambridge CB3 9BB, UK

The increase of Iron Age archaeological discoveries in the City of David in recent years has precipitated debates regarding the identification of the tunnel that Hezekiah built, as described in 2 Chr 32:30 (cf. 2 Kgs 20:20). While the linguistic and textual evidence is usually presented by biblical scholars and, likewise, the archaeological evidence is predominantly discussed by archaeologists, this article is a biblical scholar's attempt to address the question of the identification of Hezekiah's tunnel with both archaeological and biblical findings simultaneously, rigorously, and critically in view. Along the way, I explore related issues regarding the waterworks extant in Hezekiah's day and propose fresh resolutions to such matters as the assessment of archaeological proposals regarding the location of the springs and the stream in 2 Chr 32:3–4 with various aspects of Channel II; the diverse nuances of usage for terms involving עיר ("city") in 2 Chr 32; and the formulation of a solid logical explanation for how Channel II (or its runoff in the Kidron Valley) would qualify as flowing through the land while the springs are described as outside the city.

This article is a biblical scholar's contribution to the current debate regarding the identification of the "real" Hezekiah's tunnel, as described in 2 Chr 32:30 (cf. 2 Kgs 20:20) and, relatedly, the identification of the "springs and the stream that flowed through the land" in 2 Chr 32:3–4. The possibility of Channel II instead of

I am sincerely grateful to the anonymous *JBL* reviewer, to Mark Altaweel, and to the Archaeology Study Group that convened at the Annual Tyndale Fellowship Conference on 7–8 July 2015 in Cambridge, UK, for helpful comments and discussion on various matters throughout this article.

Tunnel VIII (see fig. 1)[1] as the actual conduit that Hezekiah built in response to the approaching Assyrian threat has gained increasing attention since Asher Grossberg's proposal,[2] and new discoveries in the past fifteen years have both answered questions and raised new ones. When the biblical text is considered in the context of its ancient Near Eastern literary milieu, several recent questions may be resolved.[3]

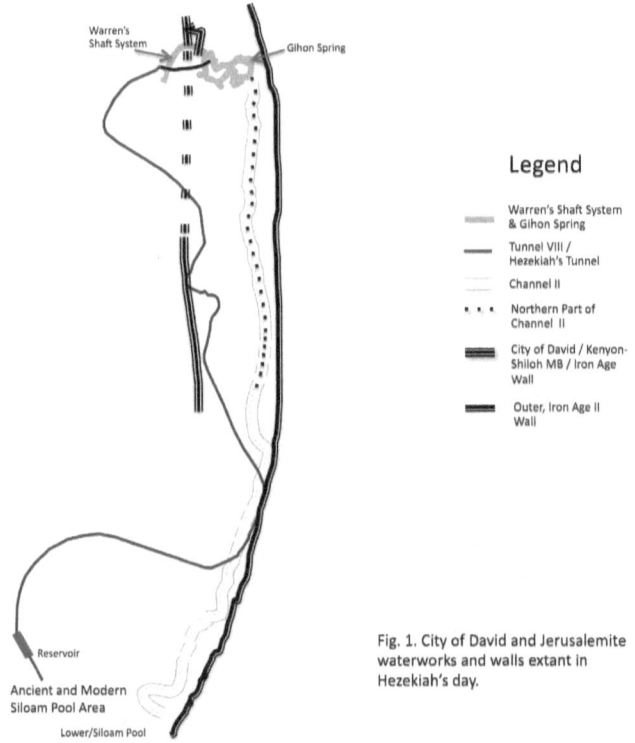

Fig. 1. City of David and Jerusalemite waterworks and walls extant in Hezekiah's day.

---

[1] This figure is based on Ronny Reich and Eli Shukron, "The Excavations at the Gihon Spring and Warren's Shaft System in the City of David," in *Ancient Jerusalem Revealed*, ed. Hillel Geva (Jerusalem: Israel Exploration Society, 1994), 329–30; Amihai Sneh, Ram Weinberger, and Eyal Shalev, "The Why, How, and When of the Siloam Tunnel Reevaluated," *BASOR* 359 (2010): 58; and Asher Grossberg, "A New Perspective on the Southern Part of Channel II in the City of David," *IEJ* 63 (2013): 206.

[2] See Asher Grossberg, "How Did Hezekiah Prepare for Sennacherib's Siege?," in *New Studies on Jerusalem: Proceedings of the 11th Conference* [in Hebrew], ed. Eyal Baruch, Tsevi Greenhut, and Avraham Faust (Ramat Gan: Bar-Ilan University Press, 2006), 113–28 (English summary, 35–36), for further details regarding his proposal that the southern part of Channel II was the tunnel that Hezekiah built in anticipation of Sennacherib's attack, while Tunnel VIII was built after the Assyrian encounter in order to improve the city's water supply security.

[3] For a good overview of the debates and issues regarding the identification of Tunnel VIII as the tunnel that Hezekiah built, see Hershel Shanks, "Will King Hezekiah Be Dislodged from His Tunnel?," *BAR* 39.5 (2013): 52–61, 73.

I begin with the issue of which tunnel is really Hezekiah's tunnel. In the biblical record, King Hezekiah is credited by multiple sources as the one who built a conduit and channeled the waters of the Gihon Spring to the west side and inside the City of David (2 Kgs 20:20, 2 Chr 30:30; cf. Isa 22:9). Further, according to the biblical account, Hezekiah made one tunnel and one pool by which he brought water into the city (in 2 Kgs 20:20, ברכה ["pool"] and תעלה ["tunnel"] are singular, and both are preceded by ה, as if to say *"the* pool and *the* tunnel"). While it is possible that Hezekiah made more than one tunnel or pool for redirecting the water, as far as the biblical account is concerned, there was only one of each worth noting and apparently recognized as such by early biblical audiences.

What then exactly is this exceptional conduit built by King Hezekiah? There are really only two options, because there are only two conduits dating from approximately Hezekiah's time that convey water from the Gihon to distant pools in a remarkable manner (there are also much shorter tunnels that are best accounted for as preparatory tunnels for Tunnel VIII).[4] Those two conduits are Tunnel VIII (popularly known as Hezekiah's Tunnel or the Siloam Tunnel) and Channel II (occasionally known as the Siloam Channel). There is only one tunnel, however, that actually transports water from the Gihon to the west side of the City of David (see 2 Chr 32:30),[5] and that is Tunnel VIII. Furthermore, while Tunnel VIII and the southern part of Channel II were cut during the Iron Age II, the northern part of Channel II was made during the Middle Bronze Age II.[6] The completion of

---

[4] Regarding the network of small tunnels near the Gihon Spring and Warren's Shaft, see Ronny Reich and Eli Shukron, "The History of the Gihon Spring in Jerusalem," *Levant* 36 (2004): 211–23, esp. 216–17, http://dx.doi.org/10.1179/lev.2004.36.1.211.

[5] Note that this is referring not to the wider city of Jerusalem but to the particular area of the City of David.

[6] For a recent scientific contribution regarding the date of Tunnel VIII, see Amos Frumkin, Aryeh Shimron, and Jeff Rosenbaum, "Radiometric Dating of the Siloam Tunnel, Jerusalem," *Nature* 425 (2003): 169–71, http://dx.doi.org/10.1038/nature01875; similarly, Amos Frumkin and Aryeh Shimron, "Tunnel Engineering in the Iron Age: Geoarchaeology of the Siloam Tunnel, Jerusalem," *JArS* 33 (2006): 227–37, http://dx.doi.org/10.1016/j.jas.2005.07.018. A date of ca. 700 BCE or slightly earlier was confirmed for Tunnel VIII by Frumkin, Shimron, and Rosenbaum by way of radiometric dating of the ancient original plaster, speleothems, and flowstone in Tunnel VIII. The results are compelling, and Shanks's assertion ("Will King Hezekiah Be Dislodged?," 73) that the study "is not precise enough to distinguish between the reigns of Hezekiah and Yehoash" is debatable. For example, the short-lived plant in the ancient plaster is carbon-dated with a 95 percent probability as having lived between 800 and 510 BCE (Frumkin, Shimron, and Rosenbaum, "Radiometric Dating," 171), placing its incorporation into the plaster sometime after Jehoash's death or in the very last few years of his reign, depending on one's chronology. Moreover, from the perspective of the biblical accounts, if someone earlier than Hezekiah had built Tunnel VIII, then what conduit did Hezekiah build, and why did the authors of Kings and Chronicles not record such a remarkable feat during the reign of Jehoash (or of any other king during that period, for that matter)?

Regarding the date of Channel II, see Ronny Reich and Eli Shukron, "Channel II in the City of David, Jerusalem: Some of Its Technical Features and Their Chronology," in *Cura Aquarium in*

Channel II during the Iron Age II *might* be considered to be the construction of a new tunnel, but it is an average accomplishment at best and cannot compare to the truly exceptional feat of cutting Tunnel VIII.[7] The seminal accomplishment of Tunnel VIII for its time is geologically evident—Amos Frumkin and Aryeh Shimron assert that the "ST [Siloam Tunnel] represents a major advance in tunneling techniques, being a long (533 m) tunnel without man-made intermediate shafts present"[8]—and was historically acknowledged by its contemporaries, as seen in the Siloam Inscription. Although it is apparently not a royal inscription, nonetheless "this is not a simple graffito," and the inscription was still impressive by the standards of those who engineered it: "the wall was carefully prepared and the letters are elegantly carved in a cursive style into the hard limestone.... The inscription is the work of engineers, craftsmen and labourers whose aim was to commemorate their accomplishment."[9] Clearly, the only tunnel that fits the distinctive attributes—of date, beginning and ending location, and significance—in the biblical accounts in 2 Kgs 20:20 and 2 Chr 30:30 is Tunnel VIII. Thus, we may confidently continue to identify Tunnel VIII as "Hezekiah's Tunnel."

A related but less-heated debate regarding the waterworks of Jerusalem in the eighth century BCE concerns the blocking of "the springs outside the city" and "the springs and the stream that flowed through the land" in 2 Chr 32:3–4. The proposal of Channel II (or, at least, part of it) as both the "stream" and the conduit for the "springs" is a now-familiar suggestion on the part of archaeologists.[10] The northern

---

Israel: In Memoriam Dr. Ya'akov Eren; Proceedings of the 11th International Conference on the History of Water Management and Hydraulic Engineering in the Mediterranean Region, Israel, 7–12 May, 2001, ed. Christoph Ohlig, Yehuda Peleg, and Tsvika Tsuk (Siegburg: Deutschen Wasserhistorischen Gesellschaft, 2002), 3–5.

[7] Frumkin and Shimron, "Tunnel Engineering," sect. 1.1; 5; 6. See also Avraham Faust, "Water Systems in Bronze and Iron Age Israel," in *Encyclopaedia of the History of Science, Technology, Medicine in Non-Western Cultures*, ed. Helaine Selin, 2nd ed., 2 vols. (Berlin: Springer, 2008), 2:2233, http://dx.doi.org/10.1007/978-1-4020-4425-0_9473: "The most sophisticated Iron Age water system is Hezekiah's tunnel, which was dug in Jerusalem during the late eighth century BCE." In the midst of a wider revolution at that time in urban water transportation technology in the ancient Near East (see Frumkin and Shimron, "Tunnel Engineering," sect. 5; cf. Larry W. Mays, "A Brief History of Water Technology during Antiquity: Before the Romans," in *Ancient Water Technologies*, ed. Larry W. Mays [Dordrecht: Springer, 2010], 18, http://dx.doi.org/10.1007/978-90-481-8632-7_1), Tunnel VIII remains a remarkable highlight.

[8] Frumkin and Shimron, "Tunnel Engineering," sect. 1.1; similarly, sect. 5: "ST is the oldest accurately-dated long tunnel constructed without using intermediate shafts for the excavation work proper" and "it may be concluded that ST was an innovative project which advanced the ancient tunneling practice in several ways."

[9] Gary A. Rendsburg and William M. Schniedewind, "The Siloam Tunnel Inscription: Historical and Linguistic Perspectives," *IEJ* 60 (2010): 191.

[10] See Louis-Hugues Vincent, *Jérusalem de l'Ancien Testament: Recherches d'Archéologie et d'Histoire*, 3 vols. (Paris: Gabalda, 1954–1956), 1:266; cf. 1:283. Grossberg supports the view that the northern part of Channel II was the stream ("New Perspective," 205–18). See also Hershel

part of Channel II was cut as an open channel from the rock surface in the Middle Bronze Age II and was then covered over with large, rough boulders.[11] As Louis-Hugues Vincent put it:

> Il devint évident qu'elle était primitivement, en partie du moins, à ciel ouvert; mais au lieu d'une couverture en dalles, ainsi qu'on aurait pu l'imaginer, on s'aperçut qu'elle était fermée par des quartiers de roche bruts et d'énormes blocs d'appareil jetés en travers de la tranchée, empilés au hasard de leurs arêtes avec une hâte visible et la préoccupation manifeste de décourager toute tentative de rouvrir la galerie qu'on prenait tant de peine à dissimuler.[12]

This unusual condition of Channel II fits well the situation in 2 Chr 32:3-4, in which "a great many people" (NRSV) were needed to block and hide the springs and stream. Reinforcing this historical-literary connection between Channel II and 2 Chr 32:3-4 is the approximate date of the blocking:

> Le trait saillant et le plus inexplicable en apparence, commun à ces canaux [channels I and II] est qu'ils ont été bloqués avec le plus grand soin à une époque assez exactement déterminée, puisqu'elle n'est pas postérieure au début de VIIe siècle avant notre ère et ne saurait être antérieure au milieu du VIIIe, au témoignage précis de la céramique.... le canal II, demeuré ouvert plus haut sur ce bassin, a été remblayé laborieusement et dissimulé en outre sur une longueur considérable par d'énormes blocs de pierre.[13]

If it is true that the northern part of Channel II is the stream, one may ask if the southern part of Channel II is also included in that. Two points diminish the strength of that association: (1) The southern part was constructed in the late Iron Age II, with features that "are typical of the cutting of Hezekiah's Tunnel in the late 8th century BCE," which indicates that it was most likely cut during Hezekiah's reign but before Tunnel VIII.[14] That is, the southern part of Channel II was quite short-lived for Hezekiah's Jerusalem and thus would not have gained the legendary status that the centuries-old northern part probably did. (2) The southern part was

---

Shanks, "Is the Siloam Channel Referred to in Chronicles and Isaiah?," *BAR* 7.4 (1981): 38; similarly, Yigal Shiloh, "Jerusalem's Water Supply During Siege—The Rediscovery of Warren's Shaft," *BAR* 7.4 (1981): 24–39.

[11] Reich and Shukron, "Channel II," 3.

[12] Vincent, *Jérusalem de l'Ancien Testament*, 1:265–66.

[13] Ibid., 1:283. Channel I, apparently created in the same period as Channel II, also follows the eastern slope of the hill, but lower down. Because of the difference in levels between Channel I and Channel II, Channel I could not be used simultaneously with Channel II (1:279). The two channels were also blocked off within the same time period, but Channel I was simply obstructed at its opening into the pool of the spring, while Channel II received more unusual blockages and further usage for a short time (1:283).

[14] Reich and Shukron, "Channel II," 5. Note that the completion and use of Tunnel VIII significantly reduced the normal functionality of Channel II, since Tunnel VIII is lower than Channel II.

tunneled underground and thus did not appear so much to be a stream (let alone appear at all to the general public apart from its apertures' flow, which adds to the likelihood that it did not gain much attention in ancient times).[15]

Meanwhile, it has also been convincingly proposed that the stream is the collection of rivulets at the bottom of the Kidron Valley that descended down the slope from Channel II (the northern part) and its apertures.[16] In supporting the likelihood of this hypothesis as reality, Jan Jozef Simons notes that, "as the text speaks of the *naḥal* we are not allowed to think of any place but the Kedron valley."[17] Allen P. Ross's definition of a נחל reinforces this:

> The word נחל applies most readily to a temporary river that flows with great force in the winter or rainy season but leaves only dry channels or deep ravines in the summer. Thus, the word can refer to either a fast flowing stream or torrent, or to the dry river bed.... The literal meaning of נחל applies to a rushing torrent or a flowing stream, rather than to a deeper, steadier river. It would be a wonderful, but temporary, provision of fresh water.... These fast flowing torrents were short-lived. In the dry season people would be disappoint[ed] to find water in them.[18]

Both the geographical location and the occasional nature of the rivulet collection in the Kidron Valley comport with the descriptor of the נחל in 32:4. With regard to the term נחל and the association of it with the waters of Channel II in general, L. A. Snijders asserts that elsewhere, in Ps 110:7, "the *naḥal* is probably the spring of Gihon."[19] If that is the case in 2 Chr 32:4, then either proposal above could be valid by way of reference to the extension of the waters of the Gihon.

Thus, the identity of the stream as being the northern part of Channel II or directly connected with Channel II is attractive.[20] Whether the stream is the humanmade channel or the more natural flow in the Kidron of rivulets from that

---

[15] Though it is beyond the boundaries of this article, an interesting question is, what was the purpose of the southern part of Channel II, especially if it was so short-lived? One likely possibility is that the expansion of Channel II simply served to supply water to further parts of the city and the valley before the more secure Tunnel VIII was complete. Christopher Davey suggests that the continuation of Channel II as a water conduit during the construction of Tunnel VIII provided a helpful source of water for maintaining vertical control in the creation of Tunnel VIII (personal communication; similarly, Frumkin and Shimron, "Tunnel Engineering," sect. 4.2; 6).

[16] See Jan Jozef Simons, *Jerusalem in the Old Testament: Researches and Theories*, SFSMD 1 (Leiden: Brill, 1952), 177, followed by H. G. M. Williamson, *2 Chronicles*, NCB (London: Marshall, Morgan & Scott, 1982), 381; and Shanks, "Is the Siloam Channel Referred to?," 38. In a similar vein, Vincent supposed that Channel II began in Solomon's day and that "le surplus des eaux que n'absorbait pas l'alimentation de la ville se perdait à peu près inutilisé par le lit du Cédron" (*Jérusalem de l'Ancien Testament*, 1:283).

[17] Simons, *Jerusalem in the Old Testament*, 177 n. 4.

[18] Allen P. Ross, "נחל," *NIDOTTE* 3:47. Similarly, Heinz-Josef Fabry and L. A. Snijders, "נחל," *TDOT* 9:335.

[19] Fabry and Snijders, *TDOT* 9:340.

[20] Though Channel I was rendered obsolete before Channel II, in the absence of further information concerning Channel I there is the possibility that Channel I was also identified with

channel remains an open question. The explanation involving rivulets does appear to fit the descriptor נחל slightly better, but we must remind our modern eyes that this is only *slightly* better. For the ancient Near East, constructed channels and natural rivers were sometimes considered the same (especially so if a humanmade channel simply followed and supported a natural watercourse). Several terms in Sumerian and Akkadian, for example, are used to describe both natural rivers and manufactured canals.[21] The particular Akkadian cognate for נחל, however, refers only to naturally flowing waters or geographical characteristics.[22] Yet another factor to consider, which is in favor of interpreting the stream as the naturally flowing collection of rivulets, is that the text focuses on the springs twice (vv. 3–4) before it attends to the stream (v. 4). That is, the issue is not blocking off the stream and hence the springs, but first the springs and thus both the springs and the stream. It is the springs, therefore, that are the source of the stream, and not vice versa. This fits perfectly with the explanation that the springs are the apertures of Channel II, which ran down the slope and sometimes—depending on irrigation needs and supply—collected into a free-flowing stream at the bottom of the Kidron.

That the springs of 2 Chr 32:3–4 are the apertures of Channel II is rarely contested. These apertures (or "windows") have been observed to be spaced along the eastern wall of the channel at an average height of 2.75 m, allowing for an easy outflow of water through any aperture by way of even "le plus élémentaire barrage momentané" raising the water level.[23] Vincent insisted that this aspect of Channel II can be explained only by the hypothesis of an irrigation channel.[24] Simons stated, "we feel justified in recognizing in 'all the fountains' [KJV] besides the exit from Gihon itself the 'windows' of this canal."[25] In view of the lack of natural springs in the Jerusalem area,[26] these explanations remain the most sensible and self-evident. While the diachronic purpose of the aperture blocks is currently debatable (that is, which of the apertures in Channel II were blocked off earlier to preserve the water flow and which were blocked off later to hide the water-carrying nature of the conduit), the fact remains that at some point the openings were intentionally

---

the springs and the stream. This remains purely conjectural, however, without further archaeological data.

[21] For a couple Akkadian examples, see "*nārtu*," CAD 11.1:362–63 and "*nāru*," CAD 11.1:368–76. For Sumerian watercourse terminology, see *id* and *nari* in Simon G. Fitzwilliam-Hall, "Sumerian Water Management and Irrigation Terminology," http://tinyurl.com/jbl1353a.

Function more than natural/unnatural composition appears to be the determining factor among various terms for waterways in ancient Mesopotamia.

[22] See "*naḫallu* (*naḫlu*)," CAD 11.1:124–25. Sumerian equivalents denote "cave, mine (a hole in the ground)," and therefore "it is possible" that uses of *naḫallu* not associated with water could refer to a "pitfall, ambush, or cave" (125c), but this has yet to be proven or convincingly supported.

[23] Vincent, *Jérusalem de l'Ancien Testament*, 1:266.
[24] Ibid.
[25] Simons, *Jerusalem in the Old Testament*, 177.
[26] Vincent, *Jérusalem de l'Ancien Testament*, 1:260.

made and not left as purely natural.²⁷ Moreover, we should not be surprised that all the apertures were eventually blocked off by the late Iron Age II—that is, after all, exactly what verses 3–4 record. In addition, that a wall was later built outside of Channel II (v. 5) presents no difficulty or contradiction, especially considering that Hezekiah's defensive preparations would necessarily have occurred in stages and would likely have taken at least four years, if not considerably longer.²⁸ Finally, supporting the popular "window" theory, it should be observed that עין, which has the basic meanings of both "eye" and "spring," can also denote water rising in a well, which was naturally connected to an underground watercourse.²⁹ If the water rising from the fresh source of an underground watercourse was considered an עין, it probably would have been even more natural to consider the water spurts flowing out of the apertures in the natural-rock sides of Channel II and connected to the fresh source of the Gihon Spring (which was effectively *the* spring for Jerusalem)³⁰ as העינות.

Regarding concerns that the biblical text describes the springs as "*outside* the city" and the stream as flowing "*through* the land" (2 Chr 32:3–4) while Channel II is now understood to be *within* the fortified city,³¹ a closer look at the biblical account indicates that there is no contradiction. First, we must bear in mind that there actually were two city walls of Jerusalem during the late Iron Age II (eighth

---

²⁷ For further discussion, consider Donald T. Ariel and Alon De Groot, "Iron Age Extramural Occupation at the City of David and Additional Observations on the Siloam Channel," in *Extramural Areas*, ed. Donald T. Ariel, vol. 5 of *Excavations at the City of David: 1978–1985; Directed by Yigal Shilot*, Qedem 40 (Jerusalem: Institute of Archaeology, Hebrew University of Jerusalem, 2000), 165–66; Grossberg, "New Perspective," 208–9; cf. Reich's editorial side note in *The City of David: Revisiting Early Excavations; English Translations of Reports by Raymond Weill and L.-H. Vincent*, notes and comments by Ronny Reich, ed. Hershel Shanks (Washington, DC: Biblical Archaeology Society, 2004), 204.

²⁸ Shanks ("Will King Hezekiah Be Dislodged?," 57) cites Maeir and Chadwick, who defend the view that the Assyrian records show that Hezekiah actually had four years to prepare. Vincent, in discussing various arguments about the time required to build Hezekiah's Tunnel and the time Hezekiah had to prepare defense against an approaching Assyrian attack, asserts, "Il n'est cependant pas besoin d'alléguer cette double campagne insuffisamment prouvée pour se convaincre que les transes d'Ézéchias furent beaucoup plus prolongées que ne l'exigea la réalisation des défenses envisagées à Jérusalem. Dès le début de son règne, toute sa politique fut manifestement inspirée par la préoccupation de se soustraire à l'emprise assyrienne, de plus en plus menaçante depuis la chute du royaume du Nord. On le voit en effet lier partie avec tous les ennemis de Sennachérib: Babyloniens, Araméens, Égyptiens et Arabes. Rien n'est donc plus naturel que la pensée d'augmenter sa propre sécurité en travaillant à fortifier sa capitale bien longtemps avant que l'Assyrien soit aux portes" (*Jérusalem de l'Ancien Testament*, 1:284).

²⁹ J. Schreiner, "עין," *TDOT* 11:46.

³⁰ See, e.g., Vincent, *Jérusalem de l'Ancien Testament*, 1:260; and Fabry and Snijders, *TDOT* 9:340.

³¹ See Reich and Shukron, "History of the Gihon," 217; and Grossberg, "New Perspective," 213.

century BCE).³² That another city wall was discovered outside of the wall of the City of David should not be surprising—2 Chr 32:5 records that Hezekiah built another wall outside of the already established one. Second, 2 Chr 32 makes frequent reference to terms involving עיר ("city"): העיר ("the city," vv. 3, 6, 18); עיר דויד ("the City of David," vv. 5, 30), and ערים ("cities," vv. 1, 29). While there is no clearcut formula regarding the use of these specific terms, there is a general tendency in biblical literature for העיר ("the city"), if not further qualified, to refer to Jerusalem or the specific area of the City of David. That appears to be the case in 2 Chr 32, where contextually העיר can only represent Jerusalem or the City of David.

Therefore, a key question is whether העיר in verse 3 refers to the City of David or greater Jerusalem with its expanded walls. If the former is the case, then there is no contradiction between the biblical record and the archaeological record, because the springs of Channel II were indeed outside the City of David. If the latter is the case, then springs refers to a source that was farther away and other than Channel II (i.e., on the other side of the second city wall). In evaluating these two possibilities, the former is convincingly the case by way of chronology and some reasoning. The biblical account indicates that the second, outer wall was built sometime later, after the springs and stream had been blocked and the previous wall had been repaired and given towers (vv. 3–5; cf. Isa 22:9a, possibly also 22:10b). Further, it would be sensible to stop a water flow before commencing a significant construction project that could be affected by irrigation streams from above. Therefore, when the springs were blocked but before the second wall had been built, Channel II would still have been technically outside the city (i.e., outside the city walls of that time).

Though this should be enough to conclude the matter, a couple additional minor points are also worth considering. One is that העיר in verse 3 is not modified by √בצר ("to make inaccessible [esp. by fortifying]"),³³ as in 32:1 (cf. 2 Kgs 18:8, 13; 19:25),³⁴ which we might expect if a freshly fortified Jerusalem were intended. Similarly, the Chronicler does not write ירושלם here, so wider Jerusalem is not so much in view as the defining characteristic of an עיר—that is, its wall.³⁵ By the same token, however, העיר is not modified by דויד (see 32:5, 30); therefore, neither was specifying the royal area a concern for the Chronicler here. Again, the point is not area but the wall. I would argue that, for Jerusalem in the late eighth–early seventh century BCE, there was only one wall that was *the* wall, and *the* wall was the established wall for the City of David. Notice that in 32:5, there is החומה הפרוצה (lit., "the wall the broken") and then there is לחוצה החומה אחרת ("to the outside the wall other"). Slightly later, when Manasseh builds or rebuilds a wall in 2 Chr 33:14, it

---

³² Reich and Shukron, "Excavations at the Gihon Spring," 329, 337–39.

³³ BDB, s.v. בצר.

³⁴ The vocabulary and emphases for Jerusalem and the entity of the city in the books of Kings have some significant differences from those of Chronicles; consequently, the point should not be overly pressed.

³⁵ In agreement with James D. Price, "עיר," *NIDOTTE* 3:395.

does not supplant the established City of David wall but is חומה חיצונה ("wall the outer"). In the same way that there was *the* established wall for the City of David, and then an outside, other wall (or two!), I would argue that, in Hezekiah's day, there was *the* city, which coincided with the area within the walls of the City of David (i.e., *the* wall), and then there was greater fortified Jerusalem, which corresponded to the area within the outer wall(s).[36] At a time when the population of Jerusalem was quickly expanding, *the* city and its wall were already established and gave a sense of permanence and continuity in the midst of changing boundaries and new walls. Further, Price states, "At times עיר is used of a fortress or other construction within the walls of another city." In other words, עיר may designate a fortified area or construction within a city, somewhat like a mini-city-within-a-city.[37]

In addition to all this, it is helpful to take into consideration the ancient Near Eastern literary structure of the passage. 2 Chronicles 31:20–32:33 is a demonstrable narratival chiasmus (or mirror structure).[38] Verses 3 and 30 are strongly paired by way of their structural placement within the chiasmus, a shared rare root (סתם, "to stop"), and a shared theme of the manipulation of the waters of springs related to Jerusalem.[39] Quite possibly, then, the strong relationship between the two verses suggests that the reference in verse 3 to העיר ("the city") is the same as that of verse 30, which is clearly qualified as עיר דויד ("the City *of David*").

Relatedly, the biblical text does not necessarily contradict the currently popular archaeological hypothesis that part of Channel II is the "stream that flowed through the land" (2 Chr 32:4). Grossberg states that "2 Chron. 32:3–4 locates both the springs and the stream outside the city," but this is incorrect. Verse 3 locates the springs outside "the city" (the details of which I have discussed above), while verse 4 describes the stream as "flowing through the land." Only the springs, therefore, are described as outside the city, but the stream was השוטף ("flowing"—note that this is singular, not plural, so the reference is only to the stream and not also the springs) through the land. "The land" could designate any location and any expanse of area; the capital city of Jerusalem (in whichever sense) was not excluded

---

[36] This is in the context of discussing Jerusalem exclusively. When the focus is wider and Jerusalem is compared to other cities, it appears that העיר refers to Jerusalem. Agreeing with E. Otto, "עיר," *TDOT* 11:58; and Price, *NIDOTTE* 3:395. Consider also Reich and Shukron, "Excavations at the Gihon Spring," 339; and Dan Bahat, "The Wall of Manasseh in Jerusalem," *IEJ* 31 (1981): 235–36. Though the details of their hypotheses vary, they agree that there were multiple walls for Jerusalem—and particularly for the eastern part of the City of David—during the time of Hezekiah and Manasseh.

[37] Price, *NIDOTTE* 3:396.

[38] While one should not overdo perceiving chiasmuses, the fact of the frequent presence of the structure in ancient literature should be neither denied nor discredited. See Mary Katherine Y. H. Hom, "Chiasmus in Chronicles: Investigating the Structures of 2 Chronicles 28:16–21; 33:1–20; and 31:20–32:33," *AUSS* 47 (2009): 172–74.

[39] Ibid., 173–74.

from this concept. From the perspective of a Jerusalemite in the last fortified city standing (cf. 2 Kgs 18:13), the capital was probably more than ever an essential part of what constituted "the land." That a stream flowed partly through or alongside Jerusalem still qualified it as "flowing through the land."[40] Moreover, as discussed above, the order in which the springs and stream were blocked and the second, outer wall was constructed would have placed Channel II outside (and not inside) the city during the stoppage; consequently, there is doubly no difficulty resolving this with the possibility that Channel II was the stream of 2 Chr 32:4. Of course, if the stream is the rivulets from Channel II that collected at the bottom of the Kidron, there is clearly no contradiction. As Williamson put it, "This natural explanation does full justice to the demands of the context."[41]

In this article, we have looked at the various conundrums and issues concerning the identification of waterworks in 2 Chr 32:3–4, 30 and 2 Kgs 20:20. Some long-standing views, such as the identification of the actual Hezekiah's tunnel, have been further supported, while newer hypotheses, such as the nature of the "stream" in 2 Chr 32:4, have been rigorously evaluated with fresh considerations with regard to the biblical text. Seemingly contradictory details between the text and the archaeological data have been critically discussed and, for the most part, have been been resolved through close, reasoned engagement with the text, with attention to the archaeological witness. In all this, I have dealt with both archaeological and biblical data to construct the most plausible historical explanations, appreciating along the way that insights from one field may inform the other, that text and object—when intelligently and carefully evaluated—may be even more informative witnesses of the past together than apart.

---

[40] Interestingly, the LXX describes the river as running διὰ τῆς πόλεως ("through the *city*"), in which case Channel II (or part of it) might possibly have been in mind for that version. Alternative explanations, however, include those of Leslie C. Allen, who suggests that the *Vorlage* was assimilated to 2 Kgs 20:20 (*The Translator's Craft*, vol. 1 of *Greek Chronicles: The Relation of the Septuagint of I and II Chronicles to the Massoretic Text*, VTSup 25 [Leiden: Brill, 1974], 211) and Ralph W. Klein, who proposes that the change is simply "a correction for the difficult word 'land'" (*2 Chronicles: A Commentary*, Hermeneia [Minneapolis: Fortress, 2012], 456). It is unclear, however, why "land" was necessarily a difficult word for either the literary or material context.

[41] Williamson, *2 Chronicles*, 381.

New Titles from EERDMANS

THE APOCALYPTIC IMAGINATION
An Introduction to Jewish Apocalyptic Literature
THIRD EDITION
John J. Collins

One of the most widely praised studies of Jewish apocalyptic literature ever written, *The Apocalyptic Imagination* has served for over thirty years as a comprehensive survey of the apocalyptic literary genre. This updated third edition brings to bear the recent profusion of studies germane to ancient Jewish apocalypticism.

ISBN 978-0-8028-7279-1 • 456 pages • paperback • $38.00

THE OFFERING OF THE GENTILES
Paul's Collection for Jerusalem in Its Chronological, Cultural, and Cultic Contexts
David J. Downs
Foreword by **Beverly Roberts Gaventa**

"Erudite and convincing, this book is the new touchpoint for future research on Paul's collection for the Jerusalem church."
— **Richard S. Ascough**
in *Religious Studies Review*

ISBN 978-0-8028-7313-2 • 222 pages • paperback • $35.00

TODAY WHEN YOU HEAR HIS VOICE
Scripture, the Covenants, and the People Of God
Gregory W. Lee

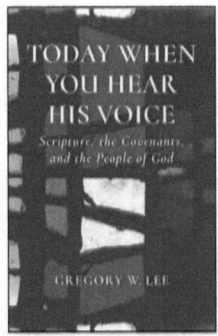

"Greg Lee here makes a significant integrative contribution to discussions about the theological interpretation of Scripture by comparing and contrasting three Christian readings of the Old Testament: Augustine, Calvin, and the Epistle to the Hebrews. The result is an important proposal about biblical authority and interpretation that carries considerable ecumenical and interdisciplinary promise."
— **Kevin Vanhoozer**

ISBN 978-0-8028-7327-9 • 324 pages • $30.00

At your bookstore, or call 800-253-7521
www.eerdmans.com

Wm. B. EERDMANS PUBLISHING CO.
2140 Oak Industrial Dr NE
Grand Rapids MI 49505

The Destruction of the Samaritan Temple by John Hyrcanus: A Reconsideration

JONATHAN BOURGEL
jbourgel@gmail.com
Martin-Luther-Universität Halle-Wittenberg, D-06099 Halle, Germany

The destruction of the Samaritan temple on Mount Gerizim by John Hyrcanus (ca. 112/111 BCE) is often regarded as the decisive cause of the final breach between Jews and Samaritans. This action is usually interpreted as one of hatred and contempt directed against the Samaritan community as a whole; it has even been maintained that Hyrcanus's real intention was to exclude the Samaritans from Judaism. Yet comparative analysis of John Hyrcanus's treatment of the people he subdued may lead to the opposite conclusion. I propose that John Hyrcanus's policy toward the Samaritans was aimed at forcing their integration into the Hasmonean state, which would lead to their exclusive dedication to the Jerusalem temple and its high priest.

The emergence of the Samaritan community as a self-contained entity is generally considered to have been the outcome of a process of mutual estrangement between Jews and Samaritans. Much has been written in an attempt to delineate the moment of the final separation between the two groups, and many divergent views have been expressed on this matter. It has become common in current scholarship to place the "parting of the ways" in the second century BCE.[1] In particular, the destruction of the Samaritan temple on Mount Gerizim by John Hyrcanus is often regarded as the decisive cause of the final breach between Jews and Samaritans.[2] Hyrcanus's action is usually interpreted as demonstrating his hatred and

---

Research for this paper was supported by a grant from the Alexander von Humboldt Foundation. I am also very grateful to Prof. Dr. Stefan Schorch and Prof. Reinhard Pummer for their valuable comments.

[1] See Stefan Schorch, "The Origin of the Samaritan Community," *Linguistic and Oriental Studies from Poznan* 7 (2005): 7–16, esp. 10; Ingrid Hjelm, "What Do Samaritans and Jews Have in Common? Recent Trends in Samaritan Studies," *CurBR* 3 (2004): 9–59, esp. 29.

[2] See, among others, Frank M. Cross Jr., "Aspects of Samaritan and Jewish History in Late Persian and Hellenistic Times," *HTR* 59 (1966): 201–11, esp. 210–11; James D. Purvis, "The Samaritan Problem: A Case Study in Jewish Sectarianism in the Roman Era," in *Traditions in Transformation: Turning Points in Biblical Faith*, ed. Baruch Halpern and Jon D. Levenson

contempt for the whole Samaritan community; it has even been maintained that his real intention was to exclude the Samaritans from Judaism.³

Comparative analysis of the different ways in which John Hyrcanus treated the various peoples he subdued, however, may lead to the opposite conclusion. In this article, I propose that his policy toward the Samaritans aimed not at their exclusion but, on the contrary, at their assimilation into the Hasmonean state.

I. John Hyrcanus's Military Conquests and His Treatment of Subdued Peoples

According to Josephus's *Jewish War* (1.62), Hyrcanus launched a military campaign against the cities of Syria during the expedition of the Syrian ruler Antiochus VII Sidetes against the Medes (130 BCE). In *Antiquities* (13.254), however, Josephus reports that Hyrcanus began his campaign immediately upon learning of the death of Sidetes (129 BCE). Taking advantage of the weakening of the Seleucids, he first took the Transjordanian cities of Madaba and Samaga (together with neighboring places) and then attacked Shechem and Gerizim, subduing "the nation of the Cutheans" (*J.W.* 1.63; *Ant.* 13.255). After this, he turned southward to Idumea and captured Adora, Marisa, and other cities. Finally, he conquered the city of Samaria (*J.W.* 1.64–65; *Ant.* 13.275–281). Josephus's dating of Hyrcanus's military expeditions has been revised in the light of recent archaeological discoveries: the results of the excavations at sites such as Marisa (Maresha), Tel Beer-Sheva, Mount Gerizim, Shechem (Tell-Balâtha), and Samaria appear to indicate that Hyrcanus's territorial expeditions occurred toward the end of his reign, between the years 112/111 and 108/107 BCE.⁴ In what follows, I will concentrate more specifically on the fate of the inhabitants of the areas conquered by Hyrcanus.

(Winona Lake, IN: Eisenbrauns, 1981), 323–50, esp. 348–49; Menahem Mor, "The Persian, Hellenistic and Hasmonean Period," in *The Samaritans*, ed. Alan D. Crown (Tübingen: Mohr Siebeck, 1989), 1–18, esp. 18; Sean Freyne, "Behind the Names: Galileans, Samaritans, *Ioudaioi*," in *Galilee through the Centuries: Confluence of Cultures*, ed. Eric M. Meyers, Duke Judaic Studies 1 (Winona Lake, IN: Eisenbrauns, 1999), 39–55, esp. 52; Robert T. Anderson and Terry Giles, *The Keepers: An Introduction to the History and Culture of the Samaritans* (Peabody, MA: Hendrickson, 2002), 30.

³ See, e.g., Mor, "Persian, Hellenistic and Hasmonean Period," 16; Anderson and Giles, *Keepers*, 28–29; and Vanmelitharayil J. Samkutty, *The Samaritan Mission in Acts*, LNTS 328 (London: T&T Clark, 2006), 75.

⁴ See Dan Barag, "New Evidence on the Foreign Policy of John Hyrcanus I," *INJ* 12 (1992–1993): 1–12; Gerald Finkielsztejn, "More Evidence on John Hyrcanus I's Conquest: Lead Weights and Rhodian Amphora Stamps," *BAIAS* 16 (1998): 33–63; Yitzhak Magen, "The Dating of the First Phase of the Samaritan Temple on Mount Gerizim in Light of the Archaeological Evidence," in *Judah and the Judeans in the Fourth Century B.C.E.*, ed. Oded Lipschits, Gary N. Knoppers, and Rainer Albertz (Winona Lake, IN: Eisenbrauns, 2007), 193 n. 43.

Transjordan

Josephus provides no details regarding the fate of the inhabitants of Madaba, Samaga,[5] and their environs. Aryeh Kasher has proposed that both cities were ruled by the Arab tribe of the Jambrites/Ya'amri mentioned in 1 Macc 9:36–42, and Uriel Rappaport suggests that this area was taken from the Nabateans.[6] Because of the lack of archaeological data, the precise date of the campaign in Transjordan remains a moot point.[7] Some have even questioned the authenticity of the claim that Madaba was conquered by John Hyrcanus, on the grounds that, according to *Ant.* 14.18, it was his son Alexander Jannaeus (103–76 BCE) who took the city from the Arabs.[8] At any event, it may be useful to note here the results of the study by Jong-Keun Lee and Chang-Ho Ji of the settlement patterns in the zone surrounding Madaba in the late Hellenistic period. The area under discussion is delineated by Iraq al-Amir in the north and Machaerus in the south and includes Wadi Hesban in the east.[9] Lee and Ji note that, after a period of abrupt settlement decline in the mid-second century BCE, this area witnessed settlement intensification in the late second–early first century BCE. Interestingly enough, archaeological evidence has yielded no link between the Nabateans and this settlement growth; Lee and Ji have therefore ascribed it to John Hyrcanus and most probably to Alexander Jannaeus. This would mean that the area was reoccupied by Jews.

---

[5] The identity of this Samaga/Samoga is still debated. Michael Avi-Yonah identified it with the modern es-Samik (ca. 13 km northeast of Madaba) (*The Holy Land: A Historical Geography from the Persian to the Arab Conquest [536 B.C. to A.D. 640]* [Jerusalem: Carta, 2002], 64). This proposition was ruled out, however, by Robert D. Ibach Jr. (*Archaeological Survey of the Hesban Region: Catalogue of Sites and Characterization of Periods*, Hesban 5 [Berrien Springs, MI: Andrews University Press, 1987], 170). Gideon Foerster has proposed identifying this site with Mount Nebo ("The Conquests of John Hyrcanus I in Moab and the Identification of Samaga" [in Hebrew], *ErIsr* 15 [1981]: 353–55).

[6] Aryeh Kasher, *Jews, Idumaeans and Ancient Arabs: Relations of the Jews in Eretz-Israel with the Nations of the Frontier and the Desert during the Hellenistic and Roman Era (332 BCE–70 CE)*, TSAJ 18 (Tübingen: Mohr Siebeck, 1988), 44 n. 2; Uriel Rappaport, *The House of the Hasmoneans* [in Hebrew] (Jerusalem: Yad Ben Zvi, 2013), 257–58.

[7] Barag, "Foreign Policy of John Hyrcanus I," 11.

[8] See Joseph Sievers, *The Hasmoneans and Their Supporters from Mattathias to the Death of John Hyrcanus I*, SFSHJ 6 (Atlanta: Scholars Press, 1990), 142. In a personal communication, Professor Jonathan Fergusson (University of Toronto; Madaba Plains Project) informed me that it is hard to pinpoint definitive archaeological evidence for the conquest of Madaba by John Hyrcanus; however, nothing has yet been found to contradict Josephus's statement. I am grateful to him for sharing this information with me.

[9] Jong-Keun Lee and Chang-Ho Ji, "From the Tobiads to the Hasmoneans: The Hellenistic Pottery, Coins, and History in the Regions of 'Iraq al-Amir and the Wadi Hisban," *SHAJ* 8 (2004): 177–88. I thank Dr. Chang-Ho Ji (La Sierra University; Madaba Plains Project) for information on possible archaeological evidence for John Hyrcanus's campaign in Transjordan.

Idumea

Josephus provides more information about the treatment of the Idumeans. According to *Ant.* 13.257–258, Hyrcanus allowed the Idumeans to remain in their country on the condition that they submit to circumcision and adopt the laws of the Jews.[10] Like Josephus, Ptolemy (first century BCE, an otherwise unknown historian), depicts the conversion of the Idumeans as wholly coercive.[11] These accounts have been questioned by some[12] on the basis of Strabo (64/63 BCE–24 CE), who appears to describe this event as a voluntary association of the Idumeans with the Jews.[13] In support of this view, it has been argued that circumcision may have been a native custom of the Idumeans before the rise of the Hasmoneans.[14] Nevertheless, many scholars hold that the conversion of the Idumeans could not have been fully

---

[10] *Ant.* 13.257–258: "Hyrcanus also captured the Idumaean cities of Adora and Marisa, and after subduing all the Idumaeans, permitted them to remain in their country so long as they had themselves circumcised and were willing to observe the laws of the Jews [καὶ ἅπαντας τοὺς Ἰδουμαίους ὑπὸ χεῖρα ποιησάμενος ἐπέτρεψεν αὐτοῖς μένειν ἐν τῇ χώρᾳ, εἰ περιτέμνοιντο τὰ αἰδοῖα καὶ τοῖς Ἰουδαίων νόμοις χρήσασθαι θέλοιεν]. And so, out of attachment to the land of their fathers, they submitted to circumcision and to making their manner of life conform in all other respects to that of the Jews [οἱ δὲ πόθῳ τῆς πατρίου γῆς καὶ τὴν περιτομὴν καὶ τὴν ἄλλην τοῦ βίου δίαιταν ὑπέμειναν τὴν αὐτὴν Ἰουδαίοις ποιήσασθαι]. And from that time on they have continued to be Jews" (Marcus, LCL). The forced conversion of the Idumeans is not mentioned in *Jewish War*.

[11] See Menahem Stern, ed., *Greek and Latin Authors on Jews and Judaism*, 3 vols., FRJS (Jerusalem: Israel Academy of Sciences and Humanities, 1974–1984), vol. 1, no. 146.

[12] See, inter alios, Kasher, *Jews, Idumaeans and Ancient Arabs*, 45–85. According to Kasher, the assertion that the Idumeans were forcibly Judaized by John Hyrcanus derived from anti-Hasmonean propaganda. His proposition has been seriously challenged by several studies; see, e.g., *Jews in a Graeco-Roman World*, ed. Martin Goodman (Oxford: Clarendon, 1998), 94 n. 3; Richard A. Horsley, "The Expansion of the Hasmonean Rule in Idumea and Galilee: Toward a Historical Sociology," in *Studies in Politics, Class and Material Culture*, ed. Philip R. Davies and John M. Halligan, vol. 3 of *Second Temple Studies*, JSOTSup 340 (Sheffield: Sheffield Academic, 2002), 134–64, esp. 142–43. For an opinion in favor of Kasher, see Peter Richardson, *Herod: King of the Jews and Friend of the Romans*, Studies on Personalities of the New Testament (Columbia: University of South Carolina Press, 1996), 54–62.

[13] "The Idumaeans are Nabataeans, but owing to a sedition they were banished from there, joined the Judaeans, and shared in the same customs with them" (see Stern, *Greek and Latin Authors*, vol. 1, no. 115). According to Louis H. Feldman, however, Strabo's account "does not necessarily imply coercion, nor does it contradict it" (Feldman and Meyer Reinhold, eds., *Jewish Life and Thought among Greeks and Romans: Primary Readings* [Minneapolis: Fortress, 1996], 124).

[14] Jeremiah 9:24–25 is often quoted as evidence for the antiquity of the practice of circumcision among the Idumeans; see Uriel Rappaport, "The Hellenistic Cities and the Judaization of the Land of Israel in the Hasmonean Period," in *Doron: Eighteen Articles in Honor of the Sixtieth Birthday of Prof. Bentsiyon Kats* [in Hebrew], ed. Shmuel Perlman and Binyamin Shimron (Tel Aviv: University of Tel Aviv, 1967), 219–39, here 229; Kasher, *Jews, Idumaeans and the Ancient Arabs*, 56.

voluntary and that, at the very least, the more hellenized Idumeans residing in Adora and Marisa were compelled to be circumcised if they wished to remain in their homes.[15] Support for this, in their view, comes from Egyptian papyri that refer to the existence of several Idumean colonies in Egypt in the early part of the first century BCE, which may suggest that some Idumeans preferred exile to forced conversion and fled to Egypt in the wake of the Hasmonean conquest in the late second century BCE.[16]

Furthermore, the excavations in the lower part of Maresha appear to indicate that the buildings there were abandoned as a result of the conquest of John Hyrcanus.[17] There is also archaeological evidence to show that other parts of Idumea were severely affected by the warfare, as Josephus himself suggests when he writes, "He [John Hyrcanus] further took *numerous cities* in Idumaea, including Adora and Marisa" (*J.W.* 1.63). Thus, Hellenistic Beer-Sheva (Tel Beer-Sheva) was abandoned following the Hasmonean campaign (between ca. 112/111 and 104 BCE).[18] In addition, Abraham Faust and Adi Erlich have made a strong case that not only the Idumean urban centers but also numerous settlements in the rural sectors (Kh. er-Rasm, Tel Arad, Kh. Uza, Tel Ira, and Lachish) were destroyed or abandoned as a result of John Hyrcanus's conquest of Idumea.[19]

---

[15] See, e.g., Kasher, *Jews, Idumaeans and Ancient Arabs*, 74; Shaye J. D. Cohen, *The Beginnings of Jewishness: Boundaries, Varieties, Uncertainties*, HCS 31 (Berkeley: University of California Press, 1999), 110–19; Martha Himmefarb, *A Kingdom of Priests: Ancestry and Merit in Ancient Judaism*, Jewish Culture and Contexts (Philadelphia: University of Pennsylvania Press, 2006), 74–75. For an opposite view, see Benedikt Eckhardt, "An Idumean, That Is, a Half-Jew," in *Jewish Identity and Politics between the Maccabees and Bar Kokhba: Groups, Normativity, and Rituals*, ed. Benedikt Eckhardt, JSJSup 155 (Leiden: Brill, 2012), 91–115, esp. 103.

[16] Uriel Rappaport, "Les Iduméens en Égypte," *RevPhil* 43 (1969): 73–82, esp. 75–77.

[17] See Amos Kloner, "Maresha" [in Hebrew], *Qad* 95–96 (1991): 70–88, esp. 83; Israel Shatzman, "Jews and Gentiles from Judas Maccabaeus to John Hyrcanus according to Contemporary Sources," in *Studies in Josephus and the Varieties of Ancient Judaism: Louis H. Feldman Jubilee Volume*, ed. Shaye J. D. Cohen and Joshua J. Schwartz, AGJU 67 (Leiden: Brill, 2007), 237–70, esp. 267–68 n. 58.

[18] Barag, "Foreign Policy of John Hyrcanus I"; Alla Kushnir-Stein and Haim Gitler, "Numismatic Evidence from Tel Beer-Sheva and the Beginning of Nabatean Coinage," *INJ* 12 (1992–1993): 13–20, esp. 16–17; Finkielsztejn, "John Hyrcanus I's Conquest," 48, 55 n. 6. Finkielsztejn contends that the city of Lachish also was destroyed by John Hyrcanus during his conquest of Idumea, but this proposition has been seriously questioned by Alexander Fantalkin and Oren Tal ("Redating Lachish Level I: Identifying Achaemenid Imperial Policy at the Southern Frontier of the Fifth Satrapy," in *Judah and the Judeans in the Persian Period*, ed. Oded Lipschits and Manfred Oeming [Winona Lake, IN: Eisenbrauns, 2006], 167–98, esp. 177 n. 12).

[19] Abraham Faust and Adi Erlich, "The Hasmonean Policy toward the Gentile Population in Light of the Excavations at Kh. er-Rasm and Additional Rural Sites" [in Hebrew], *Jerusalem and Eretz Israel* 6 (2008): 5–32, esp. 10–18, 22. As mentioned in the preceding note, the destruction of Lachish by John Hyrcanus is questioned by certain scholars.

The theory of a wholly peaceful Judaization of Idumea can hardly be reconciled with the above data.[20] It is usually agreed that John Hyrcanus's policy was aimed at integrating the Idumeans into the Jewish state. Morton Smith, for instance, argued that this policy was designed to unify the country and consolidate Hasmonean rule, analogous to the Roman practice of extending citizenship to their allies and conquests.[21] According to Shaye J. D. Cohen, Hyrcanus's policy of integration of the Idumeans derived from his "conceiving Judaism as a *politeia*—a way of life and a citizenship."[22] Steven Weitzman has proposed a somewhat different solution; in his view, the compulsory circumcision of gentiles was a subterfuge of the Hasmonean rulers to overcome the lack of human resources without eroding their political legitimacy as the ones who continued "the Maccabean drive to retake the land for Judaism."[23]

Mount Gerizim and Shechem

Josephus relates that John Hyrcanus attacked Shechem and Gerizim, subduing "the nation of the Cutheans who dwelt round about that temple which was built in imitation of the temple at Jerusalem" (*J.W.* 1.62). As is well known, "Cuthean" is a derogatory term for the Samaritans, implying their alleged foreign origins.[24]

The account in *Ant.* (13.255) refers more explicitly to the destruction of the temple on Mount Gerizim:

> [Hyrcanus took] Shechem and Garizein and the Cuthaean nation, which lives near the temple built after the model of the sanctuary at Jerusalem, which Alexander permitted their governor Sanaballetes to build for the sake of his son-in-law Manasses, the brother of the high priest Jaddua as we have related before. Now it was two hundred years later that this temple was laid waste. (Marcus, LCL)[25]

---

[20] According to Josephus, John Hyrcanus's successors pursued a similar policy of forced conversions of non-Israelite populations; thus, Judah Aristobulus compelled Itureans to submit to circumcision (*Ant.* 13.257–258, 319), and Alexander Jannaeus devastated the city of Pella because its inhabitants "would not bear to change their religious rites for those peculiar to the Jews" (*Ant.* 13.397). Furthermore, Steven Weitzman has observed that Jewish sources of the second century BCE "seem to endorse forced circumcision as a legitimate practice" ("Forced Circumcision and the Shifting Role of Gentiles in Hasmonean Ideology," *HTR* 92 [1999]: 37–59, here 43, http://dx.doi.org/10.1017/S0017816000017843).

[21] Morton Smith, "Rome and the Maccabean Conversion: Notes on 1 Maccabees 8," in *Donum Gentilicium: New Testament Studies in Honour of David Daube*, ed. E. Bammel, C. K. Barrett, and W. D. Davies (Oxford: Clarendon, 1978), 1–7; see also Martin Goodman, *Mission and Conversion: Proselytizing in the Religious History of the Roman Empire* (Oxford: Clarendon, 1994), 61.

[22] Cohen, *Beginnings of Jewishness*, 125–29.

[23] Weitzman, "Forced Circumcision," 58.

[24] On this term, see n. 65 below.

[25] Josephus refers here to his account of the construction of the Samaritan sanctuary under

The gist of this account is confirmed by the archaeological record. Excavations at Tell Balâtah (ancient Shechem) indicate that the site ceased to be occupied in the late second century BCE. According to the stratification of G. Ernest Wright (repeated by Edward F. Campbell), the destruction of the city occurred in 107 BCE.[26] Dan Barag, however, favors the year 112–111 BCE.[27] Thus, the archaeological evidence for the devastation of Shechem by John Hyrcanus is very scanty and debated.[28]

Yitzhak Magen's excavations on the top of Mount Gerizim have revealed that John Hyrcanus not only demolished the Samaritan temple but also set fire to the surrounding city around 111–110 BCE.[29] On the basis of the discovery of a hoard of Hasmonean coins in the western part of the city (Building K-Ic), Magen has proposed that a Hasmonean garrison was subsequently stationed on the top of the mount in order to prevent the return of the Samaritans.[30] Interestingly enough, Megillat Ta'anit, which commemorates victories of the Hasmonaean period, celebrates "the day of Mount Gerizim" (יום הר גריזים) on 21 Kislev; this is generally

---

Alexander the Great (*Ant.* 11.302–325). According to this, renegade priests married to foreign women were expelled from Jerusalem and attached themselves to Sanballat, the governor of Samaria. As a reward, Sanballat established them as priests in the temple he had erected on Mount Gerizim (ca. 332 BCE). It has been proposed that this account is an elaboration of Neh 13:28, according to which Nehemiah expelled one of the grandsons of the high priest Eliashib because he was married to the daughter of "Sanballat the Horonite." See, e.g., Hans G. Kippenberg, *Garizim und Synagoge: Traditionsgeschichtliche Untersuchungen zur samaritanischen Religion der aramäischen Periode*, RVV 30 (Berlin: de Gruyter, 1971), 52. According to Yitzhak Magen, the construction of the Samaritan temple goes back to the mid-fifth century BCE; a city surrounding the sacred precinct was founded in the early second century BCE. On the Samaritan temple and its sacred precinct, and on the question of its dating, see Yitzhak Magen, *Mount Gerizim Excavations*, vol. 2, *A Temple City*, Judea and Samaria Publications 8 (Jerusalem: Staff Officer of Archaeology, Civil Administration of Judea and Samaria; Israel Antiquities Authority, 2008), 97–205; Magen, "Dating of the First Phase of the Samaritan Temple," 157–211. On the Hellenistic city surrounding the Samaritan temple on Mount Gerizim, see Magen, *Temple City*, 3–93.

[26] See, inter alios, G. Ernest Wright, "The Samaritans at Shechem," *HTR* 25 (1962): 357–66, esp. 358, http://dx.doi.org/10.1017/S0017816000007987; Wright, *Shechem: The Biography of a Biblical City*, Norton Lectures of the Southern Baptist Theological Seminary, 1963 (New York: McGraw-Hill, 1965), 47; Edward F. Campbell, *Shechem III: The Stratigraphy and Architecture of Shechem/Tell Balâtah*, 2 vols., ASORAR 6 (Boston: American Schools of Oriental Research, 2002), 1:1, 8.

[27] Barag, "Foreign Policy of John Hyrcanus I," 7–8.

[28] See Wright, *Shechem*, 183; Campbell, *Shechem III*, 1:316; Magnar Kartveit, *The Origin of the Samaritans*, VTSup 128 (Leiden: Brill, 2009), 205.

[29] Magen, "Dating of the First Phase of the Samaritan Temple," 193; Magen, *Temple City*, 98.

[30] Of the coins found in Building K-Ic, twenty-five are of John Hyrcanus and two of Alexander Jannaeus. See Yitzhak Magen, Haggai Misgav, and Levana Tsfania, *Mount Gerizim Excavations*, vol. 1, *The Aramaic, Hebrew and Samaritan Inscriptions*, Judea and Samaria Publications 2 (Jerusalem: Staff Officer of Archaeology, Civil Administration of Judea and Samaria; Israel Antiquities Authority, 2008), 12–13; Magen, *Temple City*, 81.

interpreted as a reference to the destruction of the Samaritan temple by John Hyrcanus.[31]

The Hellenistic Cities of Samaria and Beth Shean

According to Josephus, the conquest of the city of Samaria was particularly brutal. At the time, Samaria was a strong Hellenistic city inhabited primarily by the descendants of the original Macedonian settlers.[32] The capture of the city was undertaken by Aristobulus and Antigonus (John Hyrcanus's sons), who laid siege to the city for a year. Vain attempts to relieve Samaria were made by the Seleucid ruler of Coele-Syria, Antiochus IX Cyzicenus, and by Ptolemy Lathyrus, the coregent of Egypt. Eventually, John Hyrcanus had the city flooded by diverting a river and utterly destroyed it (*Ant.* 13.281). As if to present this as an extraordinary case, Josephus stresses John Hyrcanus's loathing of the inhabitants of the city of Samaria.[33] Although Josephus's report is certainly exaggerated, archaeological evidence does confirm the violent destruction of large parts of Samaria.[34] Similarly, the hinterland

---

[31] Megillat Taʿanit (Scroll of Fasting) is a treatise that originated in the late Second Temple period; it lists thirty-five festival days on which fasting was forbidden. See Megillat Taʿanit, line 24 (MS Parma de Rossi 117); Vered Noam, *Megillat Taʿanit: Version, Interpretations, History* [in Hebrew] (Jerusalem: Yad Izhak Ben-Zvi, 2003), 262–65; Noam, "*Megillat Taʿanit*: The Scroll of Fasting," in *The Literature of the Sages*, ed. Shmuel Safrai et al., 2 vols., CRINT, sect. 2, The Literature of the Jewish People in the Period of the Second Temple and the Talmud 3a (Assen: Van Gorcum, 2006), 339–62.

[32] See, e.g., Reinhard Pummer, *The Samaritans in Flavius Josephus*, TSAJ 129 (Tübingen: Mohr Siebeck, 2009), 204; Hanan Eshel, "The Growth of Belief in the Sanctity of Mount Gerizim," in *A Teacher for All Generations: Essays in Honor of James C. VanderKam*, ed. Eric F. Mason et al., 2 vols., JSJSup 153 (Leiden: Brill, 2012), 509–35, esp. 517; Gary N. Knoppers, *Jews and Samaritans: The Origins and History of Their Early Relations* (Oxford: Oxford University Press, 2013), 173.

[33] Josephus, *Ant.* 13.275: "… for he [Hyrcanus] hated the Samaritans [i.e., the inhabitants of the city of Samaria] as scoundrels because of the injuries which, in obedience to the kings of Syria, they had done to the people of Marisa, who were colonists and allies of the Jews" (Marcus, LCL). The identity of the "colonists and allies of the Jews" has proved controversial and has been widely debated; for different propositions on this issue, see inter alios, Ralph Marcus, *Josephus, Jewish Antiquities, Books XII–XIV*, LCL (Cambridge: Harvard University Press, 1943), 366; Aryeh Kasher, *Jews and Hellenistic Cities in Eretz-Israel: Relations of the Jews in Eretz-Israel with the Hellenistic Cities during the Second Temple Period (332 BCE–70 CE)*, TSAJ 21 (Tübingen: Mohr Siebeck, 1990), 30; Bezalel Bar-Kochva, "The Conquest of Samaria by John Hyrcanus: The Pretext for the Siege, Jewish Settlement in the ʿAkraba District, and the Destruction of the City of Samaria" [in Hebrew], *Cathedra* 106 (2000): 7–34.

[34] See George Andrew Reisner, Clarence Stanley Fisher, and David Gordon Lyon, *Harvard Excavations at Samaria 1908–1910* (Cambridge: Harvard University Press, 1924), 50, 252–73; William J. Fulco and Fawzi Zayadine, "Coins from Samaria Sebaste," *ADAJ* 25 (1981): 197–225; John B. Hennessy, "Excavations at Samaria-Sebaste, 1968," *Levant* 2 (1970): 1–21, http://dx.doi.org/10.1179/007589170790216981.

of the city appears to have suffered a great deal from John Hyrcanus's campaign: Adam Zertal's archaeological survey has revealed that a considerable decline in the number of settlements occurred in this area between the Hellenistic and the Roman periods (eleven registered Hellenistic sites compared to four Roman ones).[35] The conquest of (the wall of) Samaria is referred to in Megillat Taʿanit on the date of the 25th of Marheshvan.[36] Of prime interest for this study is the fate of the city's inhabitants, who, according to Josephus, were enslaved (J. W. 1.65).

Josephus relates that, during the siege of Samaria, "Scythopolis and other places near it" were also captured by the Jews.[37] Like Samaria, Scythopolis was a large Hellenistic city inhabited at that time primarily by gentiles (see 2 Macc 12:29–31).[38] The excavations of the site (Tel Istabah) exposed a Hellenistic layer (third-second centuries BCE) overlain by a destruction layer dated to ca. 108 BCE.[39] Megillat Taʿanit provides further information about the fate of its inhabitants: "On the fifteenth of it and on the sixteenth of it [the month of Sivan], the people of Beth Shean [Scythopolis] and the Valley went into exile" (גלו אנשי בית שאן ובקעתא) (line 10 [MS Parma de Rossi 117]).

There is general agreement that the reference here is to John Hyrcanus's conquest of Scythopolis[40] and its environs.[41] The results of the archaeological survey carried out by Nehemia Tsori in the Beth-Shean Valley and the eastern Jezreel Valley confirm the above passage from Megillat Taʿanit: only seven of the twenty-six Hellenistic sites recorded in this area continued into the Roman period.[42]

---

[35] Adam Zertal, *The Manasseh Hill Country Survey*, vol. 1, *The Shechem Syncline*, CHANE 21.1 (Leiden: Brill, 2004), 63.

[36] בעשרים וחמשה ביה אחידת שומרון שורא (Megillat Taʿanit, line 20 [MS Parma de Rossi 117]); see Noam, *Megillat Taʿanit*, 243–49.

[37] According to *Ant.* 13.280, Epicrates (one of Antiochus IX Cyzicenus's generals) treacherously surrendered Scythopolis to the Jews. A somewhat different account is found in *J. W.* 1.65, which intimates that, immediately after the fall of Samaria, the Hasmoneans marched against Scythopolis and "laid waste all the country that lay within Mount Carmel."

[38] See Emil Schürer, *The History of the Jewish People in the Age of Jesus Christ (175 B.C.–A.D. 135)*, rev. and ed. Geza Vermes, Fergus Millar, and Matthew Black, 3 vols. (Edinburgh: T&T Clark, 1973–1987), 2:15–16, 144.

[39] Rachel Bar-Nathan and Gaby Mazor, "Beth-Shean in the Hellenistic Period" [in Hebrew], *Qad* 107–8 (1994): 87–91; Finkielsztejn, "John Hyrcanus I's Conquest," 40–41.

[40] Noam, *Megillat Taʿanit*, 196–97.

[41] The "valley" (בקעתא) referred to in Megillat Taʿanit is usually understood as the Jezreel Valley; see Schürer, *History of the Jewish People*, 2:9 n. 19. Ido Hampel prefers to see here a reference to the Beth-Shean Valley (*Megillat Taʿanit* [in Hebrew] [PhD thesis, Tel Aviv University, 1976], 132–33).

[42] Nehemia Zori, "An Archaeological Survey of the Beth-Shean Valley," in *The Beth-Shean Valley: The 17th Archaeological Convention of the Israel Exploration Society* [in Hebrew] (Jerusalem: Israel Exploration Society, 1962), 135–98, esp. 197–98. This survey covered the area extending from Afula in the west, to the Jordan River in the east, to the Gilboa Mountains in the south, and to Ramat-Yavniel in the north.

Michael Avi-Yonah and Gideon Fuks proposed that, like the Idumeans, the inhabitants of Scythopolis were given the choice of conversion or forced exile from their city.[43] Although this proposition is not unlikely, a policy of forced conversion or expulsion toward Hellenistic cities is first recorded in the reign of Alexander Jannaeus.[44]

II. Interpretation of the Data

The difference in the ways in which the defeated peoples were treated calls for some comments. Menahem Mor and others have concluded that, while the Idumeans were regarded with some sympathy by Hyrcanus (on account of their supposedly practicing circumcision), the Samaritans were treated like "the Hellenistic cities in *Eretz Israel* which were burned to the ground and their population deported."[45] Zeev Safrai thinks that John Hyrcanus's treatment of the Samaritans was even more severe than his treatment of the Hellenistic cities, for while cities such as Samaria were later resettled by the Hasmoneans, Shechem remained abandoned.[46]

It is crucial to note, however, that the ancient sources report that the inhabitants of the city of Samaria were enslaved, while the people of Scythopolis and its environs and some of the Idumeans were driven out of their homes. Yet the Samaritans are nowhere said to have been sold into slavery or expelled by John Hyrcanus.

In this regard, the results of the modern Shechem Regional Survey headed by Edward F. Campbell are remarkable. The survey has examined a total of fifty-four sites in the vicinity of ancient Shechem (Tell Balâtha), within an area bounded by Kumeh to the north, Beit El-Kirbeh to the south, Kh. Kafrur to the west and Kh. Tana et-Tahta to the east.[47] Campbell has concluded from the results of the survey

---

[43] Michael Avi-Yonah, "Scythopolis," *IEJ* 12 (1962): 123–34, esp. 130; Gideon Fuks, *Scythopolis: A Greek City in Eretz-Israel* [in Hebrew] (Jerusalem: Yad Ben-Zvi, 1983), 63.

[44] As already seen (n. 20 above), Alexander Jannaeus demolished the city of Pella since its inhabitants "would not bear to change their religious rites for those peculiar to the Jews" (*Ant.* 13.397).

[45] Mor, "Persian, Hellenistic and Hasmonean Period," 16; Mor, *From Samaria to Shechem: The Samaritan Community in Antiquity* [in Hebrew] (Jerusalem: Zalman Shazar Center for Jewish History, 2003), 127. See also Samkutty, *Samaritan Mission in Acts*, 75; Terry Giles, "The Samaritans in the Time of Jesus," in *Encyclopedia of the Historical Jesus*, ed. Craig Evans (New York: Routledge, 2008), 539–42, esp. 540.

[46] Zeev Safrai, "The History of the Settlement in Samaria in the Roman and Byzantine Periods," in *Shomron Studies* [in Hebrew], ed. Zeev Safrai and Shimon Dar (Tel Aviv: Hakkibutz Hameuchad, 1986), 127–81, esp. 129.

[47] Edward F. Campbell Jr., *Shechem II: Portrait of a Hill Country Vale; The Shechem Regional Survey*, ed. Karen I. Summers, ASORAR 2 (Atlanta: Scholars Press, 1991).

that, in spite of the destruction of Shechem, life in the surrounding valley was not visibly affected at all by John Hyrcanus's military campaign.[48] Likewise, Israel Finkelstein's survey of southern Samaria indicates that the areas bordering Mount Gerizim in the east and in the south show no interruption of settlement following the Hasmonean conquests. Thus, in the surveyed zone delineated by Salim in the north, Beit Dajan in the east, Aqraba in the south, and Kh. Ed-Deir in the west, twenty-six of twenty-eight clearly identified Hellenistic sites appear to have continued to exist into the Roman period.[49] The same impression is given by the results of the archaeological survey conducted by Zertal in the Shechem syncline, from the Dothan Valley in the north to Nahal Shechem in the southwest and Mount Ebal in the southeast. It would seem that this area did not witness major changes in the number of sites in the Roman period in comparison with the Hellenistic period. As we have seen, the notable exception is the hinterland of the city of Samaria (the "Sebastiyeh section"), which shows a dramatic decrease in the number of settlements during the transition from the Hellenistic to the Roman period.[50] Furthermore, Zertal has observed that neither did the eastern valleys of the Manasseh hills (between the Jordan Valley and the Shechem syncline) suffer very much from the Hasmonean campaigns (although they do show some sign of a reduction).[51]

The general picture that emerges from the surveys of Samaria, and especially of the areas surrounding Mount Gerizim, is very different from the situations in the other territories conquered by John Hyrcanus. As we have seen, Faust and Erlich have shown that the rural settlements in Idumea suffered no less than the urban ones during John Hyrcanus's campaign, which resulted in their destruction or abandonment. The same impression arises from the archaeological evidence from the foothills of western Samaria. Finkelstein was the first to observe a large number of farmsteads there that had existed for hundreds of years.[52] According to him, their destruction or abandonment in the course of the second century BCE is to be ascribed to the Hasmonean conquests.[53] Further, farmhouses in which settlement ceased at the same time as the destruction or abandonment of the farms were

---

[48] Ibid., 97.

[49] Israel Finkelstein, Zvi Lederman, and Shlomo Bunimovitz, *Highlands of Many Cultures: The Southern Samaria Survey; The Sites*, 2 vols., Monograph Series 14 (Tel Aviv: Institute of Archaeology of Tel Aviv Publications Section, 1997), 2:907–19, 953–54.

[50] Zertal, *Shechem Syncline*, 63.

[51] Adam Zertal, *The Manasseh Hill Country Survey*, vol. 2, *The Eastern Valleys and the Fringes of the Desert*, CHANE 21.2 (Leiden: Brill, 2008), 93. Sixteen of the twenty-three clearly identified Hellenistic sites registered in this area continued into the early Roman period (ibid., 794).

[52] The areas in question are bounded on the south by Nahal Natuf, on the north by Nahal Qana, on the west by the Coastal Plain's alluvial valley, and on the east by the southern Samaria hill country.

[53] Israel Finkelstein, "Israelite and Hellenistic Farms in the Foothills and in the Yarkon Basin" [in Hebrew], *ErIsr* 15 (1981): 331–48, here 347.

identified at Tirat Yehudah (ca. 150 BCE)[54] and Mazor (in the days of John Hyrcanus).[55] The last of these farms seem to have disappeared in the late second century BCE (under John Hyrcanus).[56] Their original inhabitants, who were most likely of non-Jewish stock,[57] were subsequently replaced by Jewish settlers.[58] Similarly, Andrea Berlin has reported that, at the same time, a pagan shrine was destroyed at Ashdod and the area was immediately resettled, most likely by Jews. Likewise, the seaport of Yavne Yam was attacked, but it was not resettled.[59]

On the basis of these results, Faust and Erlich have concluded that the conquered gentile settlements as a whole, whether urban or rural, hellenized or not, suffered harshly from the Hasmonean expansion, which resulted in their abandonment or destruction. In contrast, the Jewish areas of settlement controlled by the Hasmoneans show no sign of disruption in the late second century BCE, as the archaeological evidence shows in sites such as Horvat Ethri, Khirbet Umm el 'Umdan, Har Adar, Kalandia, and others.[60]

Thus, John Hyrcanus's treatment of the Samaritans appears to be quite exceptional: on the one hand, his destruction of the temple on Mount Gerizim, together with its adjacent settlement and Shechem, recalls what happened in the conquered gentile territories; on the other hand, however, the Samaritans, in contrast to the gentiles, were apparently allowed to remain on their lands.

In the light of this evidence, it can hardly be maintained that John Hyrcanus's action was aimed against the Samaritans as a whole. Seth Schwartz has made an original and interesting proposition in this regard. He suggests that, following the persecution of Antiochus IV (167 BCE), the control of the temple on Mount Gerizim (henceforth dedicated to Zeus) passed to the reformist hellenized Samaritans (the so-called Sidonians who were in Shechem, mentioned in *Ant.* 12.257–264). This group then managed the sanctuary until John Hyrcanus's attack. According to

---

[54] Zeev Yeivin and Gershon Edelstein, "Excavation at Tirat Yehuda" [in Hebrew], *Atiqot* 6 (1970): 56–67, here 67.

[55] David Amit and Irina Zilberbod, "Mazor 1994–1995" [in Hebrew], *Hadashot Arkheologiyot* 106 (1996): 92–96, here 95. As it appears, Mazor was not resettled after it had been attacked; see Andrea M. Berlin, "The Hellenistic Period," in *Near Eastern Archaeology: A Reader*, ed. Suzanne Richard (Winona Lake, IN: Eisenbrauns, 2003), 418–35, esp. 425–26.

[56] Faust and Erlich, "Hasmonean Policy toward the Gentile Population," 20.

[57] Avraham Faust, "Farmsteads in the Foothills of Western Samaria: A Reexamination," in *"I Will Speak the Riddles of Ancient Times": Archaeological and Historical Studies in Honor of Amihai Mazar on the Occasion of His Sixtieth Birthday*, ed. Aren M. Maeir and Pierre de Miroschedji, 2 vols. (Winona Lake, IN: Eisenbrauns, 2006), 1:477–504, esp. 503 n. 121.

[58] See Shimon Applebaum, "The Hasmoneans: Logistics, Taxation and Constitution," in *Judaea in Hellenistic and Roman Times: Historical and Archaeological Essays*, SJLA 40 (Leiden: Brill, 1989), 9–29, esp. 13–14; Jack Pastor, *Land and Economy in Ancient Palestine* (London: Routledge, 1997), 62, http://dx.doi.org/10.4324/9780203410950.

[59] Berlin, "Hellenistic Period," 425–26.

[60] Faust and Erlich, "Hasmonean Policy toward the Gentile Population," 23–26.

Schwartz, the destruction of the sanctuary by Hyrcanus was supported by those "conservative" law-observant Samaritans who resented the reformist Samaritans.[61] Schwartz's theory, however, was questioned by Hanan Eshel, on the ground that, long before the time of John Hyrcanus, the religious decrees of persecution had been abolished by Antiochus V (2 Macc 11:22–25).[62]

I propose that John Hyrcanus's destruction of the Samaritan temple was intended not as an act of exclusion but as an act of integration of the Samaritans into the Hasmonean state. It was a radical but entirely logical attempt to rally them to his authority as high priest of the Jerusalem temple. In theory, no further step was necessary to fulfill this aim, in contrast to case of the Idumeans, who had to submit to circumcision and the laws of Moses to be incorporated with the Jews. In this respect, it is by no means unlikely that John Hyrcanus considered the Samaritans to be genuine Israelites. A roughly contemporaneous text, 2 Maccabees,[63] shows that, at this time, the Jews (or at least some of them) regarded the Samaritans as brethren. In two different accounts (2 Macc 5:22–23 and 6:1–28), the worshipers in the temple of Jerusalem and those in the Gerizim sanctuary fall into the category of Jews.[64] Josephus's mention that John Hyrcanus subdued the

---

[61] Seth Schwartz, "John Hyrcanus I's Destruction of the Gerizim Temple and Judaean-Samaritan Relations," *Jewish History* 7 (1993): 9–25, http://dx.doi.org/10.1007/BF01674492.

[62] Hanan Eshel, "The Development of the Attribution of Sanctity to Mount Gerizim," in *The Samaritans* [in Hebrew], ed. Ephraim Stern and Hanan Eshel (Jerusalem: Yad Ben Zvi, 2002), 192–209, esp. 208–9, published in English as "Growth of Belief in the Sanctity of Mount Gerizim," in Mason et al., *Teacher for All Generations*, 1:509–36, esp. 534.

[63] Second Maccabees claims to be an epitome of Jason of Cyrene's lost work that comprised five volumes. It treats of the Jews' revolt against Antiochus IV Epiphanes until the defeat of the Seleucid general Nicanor (161 BCE). While Jason's work is usually ascribed to the first Hasmonean generation, the date of its abridgment is still disputed; it has been variously dated between the reign of John Hyrcanus I and Pompey's conquest of Judea in 63 BCE. See, e.g., Jonathan A. Goldstein, *II Maccabees: A New Translation with Introduction and Commentary*, AB 41A (Garden City, NY: Doubleday, 1983), 3–188; Daniel R. Schwartz, *2 Maccabees*, CEJL (Berlin: de Gruyter, 2008), 3–126; Vasile Babota, *The Institution of the Hasmonean High Priesthood*, JSJSup 165 (Leiden: Brill, 2014), 15–20.

[64] Second Maccabees 5:22–23 depicts the situation in the land of Israel following the plundering of the temple of Jerusalem by Antiochus IV Epiphanes and his departure to Antioch (summer 168 BCE): "He [Antiochus] went so far as to leave officials in charge of maltreating our race [τὸ γένος]: at Jerusalem, Philip, a Phrygian by birth, but by character more barbaric than the man who appointed him; and at Mount Gerizim, Andronikos; and in addition, Menelaus, who was worse than the others inasmuch as he lorded it over his compatriots" (trans. Goldstein, *II Maccabees*, 245). It has been widely observed that the author explicitly recognizes the YHWH worshipers on Mount Gerizim and in Jerusalem as belonging to the same "race," that is, the Jewish people. See, e.g., Morton Smith, *Palestinian Parties and Politics That Shaped the Old Testament*, LHR NS 9 (New York: Columbia University Press, 1971), 189–90; Goldstein, *II Maccabees*, 261; Schwartz, *2 Maccabees*, 264; Robert Doran, *2 Maccabees: A Critical Commentary*, Hermeneia (Minneapolis: Fortress, 2012), 229.

Second Maccabees 6:1–28 reads, "Not long thereafter, the king sent Geron the Athenian to compel the Jews [τοὺς Ιουδαίους] to depart from their ancestral laws [τῶν πατρίων νόμων] and to

"Cuthean nation" (*J. W.* 1.62; *Ant.* 13.255), which implies the supposed foreign origins of the Samaritans, may be misleading and more likely reflects Josephus's own stance.[65]

---

cease living by the laws of God. He was also to defile both the temple in Jerusalem and the temple on Mount Gerizim and to proclaim the former to be the temple of Zeus Olympios and the latter (in accordance with the ... of the inhabitants of the place) to be the temple of Zeus Xenios [καὶ τὸν ἐν Γαριζιν, καθὼς ἐτύγχανον οἱ τὸν τόπον οἰκοῦντες, Διὸς Ξενίου]" (trans. Goldstein, *II Maccabees*, 268). Here again, the category of Jews encompasses both the YHWH worshipers in Jerusalem and those on Mount Gerizim. The author's stance toward the Samaritans, however, remains a matter of controversy. Much of the debate depends on the significance of the phrase καθὼς ἐτύγχανον οἱ τὸν τόπον οἰκοῦντες and the word Ξένιος in v. 2. Three main interpretations have been advanced: (1) Many have altered ἐτύγχανον to ἐνετύγχανον and have interpreted the passage as meaning that the temple on Mount Gerizim was renamed Zeus Xenios at the request of the inhabitants of the place; on this, see Robert Doran, "2 Maccabees 6:2 and the Samaritan Question," *HTR* 76 (1983): 481–85, here 481. This emendation makes 2 Macc 6:2 correspond to the letter preserved by Josephus from the group calling themselves the "Sidonians in Shechem" and demanding from Antiochus IV that their temple be renamed after Zeus Hellenios (*Ant.* 12.258–261). This translation, however, is by no means certain. As Reinhard Pummer has stressed, it finds no support in the manuscript evidence; according to Josephus, the Sidonians in Shechem requested that their sanctuary be dedicated to Zeus Hellenios, not Xenios (*Samaritans in Josephus*, 14–15). It can be further observed that the proposed emendation would create some inconsistency with the fact that Antiochus's emissary was sent to "compel" (ἀναγκάζειν) the Jews to rename both temples, in Jerusalem and in Gerizim. Furthermore, 2 Macc 6:3 states that these measures were grievous and vexing for the "whole [people]" (τοῖς ὅλοις), that is both in Jerusalem and in Gerizim. As in 2 Macc 5:22–23, Jews and Samaritans are depicted as covictims of Antiochus's measures. (2) It has also been advanced that 2 Macc 6:2 contains a polemical allusion to the supposed foreign origins of the Samaritans. This proposition rests on the premise that Διὸς Ξενίου here refers to "Zeus the protector of strangers"; this implies that the passage should be translated as "(the temple on Mount Gerizim was renamed after) Zeus the protector of strangers, as were they that dwelt in the place." On this basis, it has been suggested that 2 Macc 6:2 may be alluding to the interpretation of 2 Kgs 17 according to which the Samaritans were descended from foreign settlers. See, e.g., Robert Hanhart, "Zu den ältesten Traditionen über das samaritanische Schisma," *ErIsr* 16 (1982): 106*–15*, here 108*–10*; Ferdinand Dexinger, "Der Ursprung der Samaritaner im Spiegel der frühen Quellen," in *Die Samaritaner*, ed. Ferdinand Dexinger and Reinhard Pummer, WdF 604 (Darmstadt: Wissenschaftliche Buchgesellschaft, 1992), 67–140, esp. 129–30. This proposition, though, creates a discrepancy with the author's inclusion of the Gerizim worshipers in the Jewish category (both in 2 Macc 5:22–23 and in 6:1–2). Furthermore, it is conspicuous that the laws of God are here referred to as "the ancestral laws" of the YHWH worshipers both in Jerusalem and in Gerizim. This clearly shows that, from the author's point of view, the latter shared common ancestry. For the purpose of comparison, Josephus, in his repeated statements that the Samaritans were of pagan stock, felt it necessary to clarify that their seemingly Jewish practices did not derive from their own ancestral laws (*Ant.* 9.290; 12.258–259). (3) Others have interpreted Διὸς Ξενίου as designating Zeus Hospitable; if so, καθὼς ἐτύγχανον οἱ τὸν τόπον οἰκοῦντες, Διὸς Ξενίου would mean that the inhabitants of the place happened to be hospitable like Zeus. See, e.g., Doran, *2 Maccabees*, 124. Some support for this proposition may be found in a statement of Pseudo-Eupolemus that the inhabitants of the city at the Gerizim temple received Abraham hospitably (Eusebius, *Praep. ev.* 9.17.2–9 [GCS 43.1:502–4]).

[65] The term *Cuthean* (כותי) is derived from the name of the city of Cutha (כותה), whence, according to 2 Kgs 17:24, foreigners were brought into the former northern kingdom of Israel to

John Hyrcanus's action was aimed at divorcing the Samaritans not only from their temple on Mount Gerizim but also from the priesthood associated with it. Here it should be stressed that Hyrcanus derived his authority above all from the high priesthood in the Jewish temple. In this respect, his coins are very instructive, as they all bear the inscription "Yohanan the high priest" (יוחנן הכהן הגדול).[66] Nor is it accidental that, following the murder of Simon, his father, Hyrcanus's first official step was to assume the high priesthood and to carry out sacrifices in the Jerusalem temple (*J.W.* 1.56; *Ant.* 13.230). Furthermore, rabbinic sources present Hyrcanus as an active high priest who instituted a number of regulations in cultic and halakic matters (m. Maʿas. Š. 5:15).[67] According to many scholars, however, the Hasmoneans' right to the high priesthood was disputed, since they were not

---

replace the Israelites (who had been exiled from there after their defeat at the hands of the Assyrians in 722/721 BCE). Josephus explicitly identified the foreign colonists referred to in this biblical account as the Samaritans' forebears (*Ant.* 9.288–291); consequently, he very frequently (but not exclusively) calls them "Cutheans" (*J.W.* 1.63; *Ant.* 9.288, 290; 10.184; 11.19, 20, 88, 302; 13.255). This term is also used to designate the Samaritans in talmudic literature. Elsewhere in his writings, Josephus reports that the Samaritan community included also renegade priests and outcast Israelites who had left Jerusalem because of their marriage to foreigners and other impieties (*Ant.* 11.312, 346; see n. 25 above). The frequent allusions to the dubious origins of the Samaritans were clearly designed to challenge their claim to belong to the people of Israel. In this context, Josephus's repeated emphasis on the labile nature of the Samaritans is most edifying: when they see the Jews thriving they call them kinsmen, asserting (incorrectly in Josephus's opinion) that they derive from Joseph, but when the Jews are in difficulty, they deny that they have any kinship with them and claim to be of another race (*Ant.* 9.291; 11.341; 12.257). It is plain, then, that in Josephus's eyes, John Hyrcanus, by defeating the Samaritans, had subdued a foreign people. On the term *Cuthean*, see, e.g., Lawrence Schiffman, "Cuthaeans," in *A Companion to Samaritan Studies*, ed. Alan D. Crown, Reinhard Pummer, and Abraham Tal (Tübingen: Mohr Siebeck, 1993) 63–64. On Josephus's treatment of the Samaritans, see Richard J. Coggins, "The Samaritans in Josephus," in *Josephus, Judaism, and Christianity*, ed. Louis H. Feldman and Gohei Hata (Detroit: Wayne State University Press, 1987), 257–73; Louis H. Feldman, "Josephus' Attitude toward the Samaritans: A Study in Ambivalence," in *Jewish Sects, Religious Movements, and Political Parties: Proceedings of the Third Annual Symposium of the Philip M. and Ethel Klutznick Chair in Jewish Civilization, Held on Sunday–Monday, October 14–15, 1990*, ed. Menahem Mor, SJC 3 (Omaha, NE: Creighton University Press, 1992), 23–45. The anti-Samaritan bias of Josephus's writings has been seriously challenged by R. Egger ("Josephus Flavius and the Samaritans," in *Proceedings of the First International Congress of the Société d'étude samaritaines*, ed. Abraham Tal and Moshe Florentin [Tel Aviv: Tel Aviv University Press, 1991], 109–14), but her view remains a minority position among scholars.

[66] In addition to the dignity of high priest, Hyrcanus may have borne the title of ethnarch; see the note of Marcus on *Ant.* 14.148 in *Josephus: Jewish Antiquities, Books XII–XIV*, 526–27.

[67] See Saul Lieberman, "The Three Abrogations of Johanan the High Priest," in *Hellenism in Jewish Palestine: Studies in the Literary Transmission, Beliefs and Manners of Palestine in the I Century B.C.E.–IV Century C.E.*, TSJTSA 18 (New York: Jewish Theological Seminary of America, 1950), 139–43; Clemens Thoma, "John Hyrcnaus I as Seen by Josephus and Other Early Jewish Sources," in *Josephus and the History of the Greco-Roman Period: Essays in Memory of Morton Smith*, ed. Fausto Parente and Joseph Sievers, StPB 41 (Leiden: Brill, 1994), 127–40, esp. 133–35.

Zadokites but members of the lower priestly family of the Jehoiarib course (1 Macc 2:1).[68] In this context, the existence of another priesthood (even if based not in Jerusalem but on Mount Gerizim), which regarded itself and was regarded by many as the legitimate Aaronide priesthood, was certainly seen by John Hyrcanus as a potential threat to his authority and legitimacy as high priest, which had to be removed.[69] This may explain the fact that his troops almost completely destroyed the city adjacent to the Gerizim temple, whose population was, according to Magen, composed primarily of priests.[70]

It is also likely that John Hyrcanus expected substantial economic benefit from destroying the sanctuary on Mount Gerizim, in the anticipation that the offerings and tithes that had formerly been sent to Mount Gerizim would henceforth be redirected to the Jerusalem temple. We know that such contributions were brought not only from places in the vicinity of Mount Gerizim[71] but also from abroad.[72] Such hopes were not entirely baseless: we read in m. Menaḥ. 10:2 that it happened

---

[68] See, e.g., Jonathan A. Goldstein, *I Maccabees: A New Translation with Introduction and Commentary*, AB 41 (Garden City, NY: Doubleday, 1976), 71, 75; Daniel R. Schwartz, "Priesthood and Monarchy in the Hasmonean Period," in *Kehal Yisrael: Jewish Self-Rule through the Ages*, vol. 1, *The Ancient Period* [in Hebrew], ed. Isaiah Gafni (Jerusalem: Zalman Shazar Center, 2001), 13–25; Peter Schäfer, *The History of the Jews in the Greco-Roman World* (London: Routledge, 2003), 52. For a different opinion, see Eyal Regev, *The Hasmoneans: Ideology, Archaeology, Identity*, JAJSup 10 (Göttingen: Vandenhoeck & Ruprecht, 2013), 120–24.

[69] According to Josephus (*Ant.* 11.324), the first high priest to serve in the Gerizim temple, Manasseh, belonged to the Zadokite family of high priests from the temple of Jerusalem. As we have seen, though, the historicity of this account is questioned; see n. 25 above.

[70] Magen, *Temple City*, 89.

[71] The inscriptions discovered on the site of the Samaritan sacred precinct on Mount Gerizim have revealed some of the donors' places of residence, including Shechem (שכם), Kfar Ḥaggai (כפר חגי, probably modern Ḥajja, ca. 14 km west of Shechem), ʿAvarta or ʿAwarta (עברת[א], ca. 6 km south of Shechem). Interestingly enough, some of the donors apparently came from the city of Samaria (שמרין). See Magen, Misgav, and Tsfania, *Aramaic, Hebrew and Samaritan Inscriptions*, 28–30.

[72] In 1979–1980, the archaeologists of the École française d'Athènes discovered two Greek inscriptions engraved on marble stelae on the island of Delos. These are honorific dedications to some benefactors or patrons made by "the Israelites on Delos who make offerings to hallowed *Argarizein* [οἱ ἐν Δήλῳ Ἰσραελεῖται οἱ ἀπαρχόμενοι εἰς ἱερὸν Ἀργαριζείν]" and "the Israelites who make offerings to hallowed, consecrated *Argarizein* [Ἰσραηλῖται οἱ ἀπαρχόμενοι εἰς ἱερὸν ἅγιον Ἀργαριζείν]." On the basis of paleographic considerations, Philippe Bruneau has dated the first stela to between 150 and 50 BCE and the second to the period between 250 and 175 BCE ("Les Israélites de Délos et la juiverie délienne," *BCH* 106 [1982]: 465–504). This dating has been generally accepted. See, e.g., Alf T. Kraabel, "New Evidence of the Samaritan Diaspora Has Been Found on Delos," *BA* 47 (1984): 44–46. In an attempt to arrive at more precise dating than that proposed by Bruneau, L. Michael White has ascribed the first inscription to after 166 BCE and the second one to before this date ("The Delos Synagogue Revisited: Recent Fieldwork in the Graeco-Roman Diaspora," *HTR* 80 [1987] 133–60, here 144–45).

once that the two loaves for the celebration of Shavuot were brought to the temple in Jerusalem "from the plain of En-Soker" (מבקעת עין סוכר) since the crop in the vicinity of Jerusalem was not yet ripe. En-Soker has been identified by many as Sychar, which was located in the close vicinity of Shechem (the place where, according to John 4:4–42, Jesus met the Samaritan woman).[73] Shmuel Safrai points out that, according to t. Menaḥ. 64b, this occurred at the time of the civil strife between John Hyrcanus's grandsons, Hyrcanus II and Aristobolus II (ca. 65 BCE).[74]

A passage from Josephus may also be relevant here: in *Ant.* 18.29–30, we read that in the days of Coponius, the first Roman procurator of Judea (6–9 CE), some Samaritans (ἄνδρες Σαμαρεῖται) secretly entered the Jerusalem sanctuary on the eve of Passover and scattered human bones in "the porticoes and throughout the temple" in order to defile it. Josephus adds that "as a result, the priests, although they had previously observed no such custom, excluded everyone [i.e., of the Samaritans] from the temple, in addition to taking other measures for the greater protection of the temple" (Marcus, LCL).

The historicity of this account has been debated, inasmuch as it raises serious difficulties. In the first place, the identity of the ἄνδρες Σαμαρεῖται is not absolutely clear. Although the majority of scholars consider that they were Samaritans, some believe they were Samarians (i.e., gentile inhabitants of Samaria).[75] Besides, if it was Samaritans who committed this act, then, according to the law, they would have become unclean by touching human bones (Num 19:11–22). Furthermore, Morton Smith has considered it suspicious that nothing is said in this account about the fate of the offenders: if they were captured, we would expect to hear more about them. "If they were not caught, how was it known that they were Samaritans?"[76] We need to ask what the purpose of this account was. Clearly, it was designed to explain, if not to justify, the fact that the Samaritans had been forbidden to enter the temple since the days of Coponius. The interesting point is that the expulsion of the Samaritans from the temple here is set neither in the days of Nehemiah nor in those of

---

[73] Michael Avi-Yonah, *The World of the Bible: The New Testament* (Yonkers, NY: Education Heritage, 1964), 140; Jack Finegan, *The Archeology of the New Testament: The Life of Jesus and the Beginning of the Early Church* (Princeton: Princeton University Press, 1969), 70; Shmuel Safrai, *Pilgrimage at the Time of the Second Temple* [in Hebrew], 2nd ed. (Jerusalem: Akademon, 1985), 99–100.

[74] See also y. Šeqal. 48d; t. Soṭah 49b; b. B. Qam. 82b; Safrai, *Pilgrimage at the Time of the Second Temple*, 99.

[75] See, e.g., Refael Yankelevitch, "The Auxiliary Troops from Caesarea and Sebaste: A Decisive Factor in the Rebellion against Rome" [in Hebrew], *Tarbiz* 49 (1980): 33–42, esp. 40.

[76] Morton Smith, "The Gentiles in Judaism 125 BCE–AD 66," in Smith, *Studies in Historical Method, Ancient Israel, Ancient Judaism*, vol. 1 of *Studies in the Cult of Yahweh*, ed. Shaye J. D. Cohen, RGRW 130 (Leiden: Brill, 1996), 263–319, esp. 243, also published in *The Cambridge History of Judaism*, vol. 3, *The Early Roman Period*, ed. William Horbury, W. D. Davies, and John Sturdy (Cambridge: Cambridge University Press, 1999), 192–249, esp. 244.

Alexander the Great[77] but in the early first century CE. Furthermore, Josephus states that, prior to this incident, the priests did not prohibit Samaritan entry into the temple of Jerusalem, which implies that at least some of the Samaritans used to visit the temple. In fact, even if we consider the accusation against the Samaritans to be slanderous, it would be hard to explain why someone would have invented this story aimed at explaining why the Samaritans had been expelled from the temple in the days of Coponius, if before then no Samaritans had patronized the Jerusalem temple.[78]

III. Conclusion

John Hyrcanus's policy toward the Samaritans aimed at their forced integration into the Hasmonean state and was expected to lead to their exclusive dedication to the Jerusalem temple and its high priest. This effort constituted the radical continuation of the process begun under Jonathan the Hasmonean (161–142 BCE) when the three southern Samarian districts of Lydda (Lod), Aphairema (Ephraim), and Ramathaim (Rama) were officially annexed to Judea by Demetrius II Nicator (ca. 145 BCE; 1 Macc 11:34). It is interesting to note in this context that the grant of these districts was supplemented by the award of exemption from all royal taxes for "all those who offer sacrifices in Jerusalem" (πᾶσιν τοῖς θυσιάζουσιν εἰς Ἱεροσόλυμα). This clause, which certainly derived from a specific request of Jonathan, implies that those inhabitants of the three annexed districts who continued to bring sacrifices to the Samaritan temple on Mount Gerizim were denied the exemptions.[79]

Whereas Jonathan used persuasion, John Hyrcanus used coercion to force the Samaritans to recognize the Jerusalem temple as the only legitimate place of worship. His endeavors were not totally unsuccessful, since, as we have seen, Samaritans did patronize the Jerusalem temple at least up to the early first century CE. It is clear, however, that the majority of the Samaritans remained exclusively loyal to Mount Gerizim; furthermore, the destruction of their temple greatly enhanced the resentment and defiance of a certain segment of them toward the leadership in Jerusalem and its priesthood. The decision to exclude them from the Jerusalem temple, which attests to the worsening of the relations between Jews and Samaritans at the beginning of the Common Era, clearly meant the reversal of the policy used by John Hyrcanus.

---

[77] See n. 25 above.
[78] For a thorough discussion on this passage, see Pummer, *Samaritans in Josephus*, 222–30.
[79] See Goldstein, *I Maccabees*, 432–33; Joshua J. Schwartz, *Lod (Lydda), Israel: From Its Origins through the Byzantine Period, 560 B.C.E.–640 C.E.*, BARIS 571 (Oxford: Tempus Reparatum, 1991), 56; Knoppers, *Jews and Samaritans*, 172–73.

In any event, the study of John Hyrcanus's motivating factors for destroying the Samaritan temple offers a new perspective from which to examine the mechanism, significance, and implications of this event. If we are right to see this action as an attempt to integrate the Samaritans into the Hasmonean state by force, then it may be reductive, if not misleading, to consider it the ultimate expression of the Jewish–Samaritan schism in the sense of a mutual and definitive rupture between the two groups.

NEW FROM EERDMANS

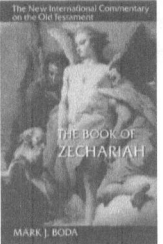

THE BOOK OF ZECHARIAH
THE NEW INTERNATIONAL COMMENTARY ON THE OLD TESTAMENT
Mark J. Boda

"Clear and profound, informative and illuminating. Everyone who studies Zechariah must read Boda's work, which makes an important contribution to scholarship and to the church." — Tremper Longman III

ISBN 978-0-8028-2375-5 • 935 pages • hardcover • $58.00

1 SAMUEL AS CHRISTIAN SCRIPTURE
A Theological Commentary
Stephen B. Chapman

"Rarely have I been so moved, informed, and delighted as I was in reading this book. Chapman's negotiation of matters historical and literary and theological, and his bibliography (is there anything he hasn't read?) are simply remarkable. And his christological reading of the tragedy of King Saul? Absolutely stunning."
— Brent A. Strawn

ISBN 978-0-8028-3745-5 • 357 pages • paperback • $36.00

A COVENANT WITH DEATH
Death in the Iron Age II and Its Rhetorical Uses in Proto-Isaiah
Christopher B. Hays
Foreword by **Matthew J. Suriano**

"A masterful and fascinating overview of death in Mesopotamia, Egypt, Ugarit, and Judah.... Christopher Hays offers a thorough discussion of ancient Near Eastern conceptions and imagery of the underworld and its deities, the afterlife, burials, and mourning." — Bernd U. Schipper

ISBN 978-0-8028-7311-8 • 465 pages • paperback • $50.00

WOMEN OF WAR, WOMEN OF WOE
Joshua and Judges through the Eyes of Nineteenth-Century Female Biblical Interpreters
Edited by **Marion Ann Taylor** and **Christiana de Groot**

"A spectacular corrective to stereotypes about 'women's writing' about the Bible.... Clearly, these writers unflinchingly took possession of the Bible — and the women of the Bible — for themselves and for their readers. The results are too impressive to be forgotten or ignored." — John L. Thompson

ISBN 978-0-8028-7302-6 • 288 pages • paperback • $35.00

WM. B. EERDMANS PUBLISHING CO.
2140 Oak Industrial Dr NE
Grand Rapids MI 49505

At your bookstore,
or call 800-253-7521
www.eerdmans.com

The Compositional Development of Qumran Pesharim in Light of Mesopotamian Commentaries

BRONSON BROWN-DEVOST
bronson.brown-devost@theologie.unigoettingen.de
Georg-August-Universität, Göttingen, DE 37073, Germany

The manuscript remains of Mesopotamian commentaries from the first millennium BCE provide ample evidence to construct a model for the creation of singular commentary texts out of widespread interpretive traditions. This model demonstrates how traditional interpretations of texts may be shared over a wide geographical area during a lengthy time span. What is more, the commentaries comprising these interpretations were neither static nor uniform; rather, they could represent interpretive traditions to varying extents, as well as grow and develop. A comparative application of the Mesopotamian model of commentary writing to the Qumran pesharim, which ostensibly lack manuscript evidence for their compositional history, provides solutions to a number of literary incongruities found in the pesharim as well as several scribal markings. This model also has important implications for the pesher genre and helps to highlight the similarity of several so-called thematic pesharim to the continuous ones, while at the same time further accounting for the variation attested in the continuous pesher category itself.

The textual development of the pesher commentaries from Qumran is not a common topic in studies of the genre,[1] but each of the pesharim represents the end

An earlier version of this article was presented at the Dead Sea Scrolls: Life in Ancient Times Graduate Symposium on 6 October 2013 at Brandeis University. I would like to thank Jonathan Klawans for his helpful comments on the paper. All transliterations, transcriptions, and translations (both Hebrew and Akkadian) are my own and have been carefully compared with photos.

[1] Important exceptions to this are Florentino García Martínez, "El pesher: Interpretación profética de la escritura," *Salm* 26 (1979): 137–38 (and esp. n. 45); Hanan Eshel, "The Two Historical Layers of Pesher Habakkuk," in *Northern Lights on the Dead Sea Scrolls: Proceedings of the Nordic Qumran Network 2003–2006*, ed. Anders Klostergaard Petersen et al., STDJ 80 (Leiden: Brill, 2009), 107–17, http://dx.doi.org/10.1163/ej.9789004171633.i-314.37; and Eshel, "Response to Bilhah Nitzan" [in Hebrew], *Zion* 72 (2007): 94–96.

product of a well-developed tradition of textual interpretation.² Yet no obvious witnesses to the earlier stages of the development of these texts have been preserved. Nor do any of these the Qumran pesharim exist in duplicate—each manuscript is the sole surviving representative of each literary work.³

Since no copies (or variant versions) of any single pesher remain to provide direct evidence for the compositional development of these works, other more intuitive methods must be employed to that end. In my own study of the pesher texts, I have found that form-critical analyses often reveal textual problems that find their solutions in the comparative study of similar textual remains. In the present study, a grouping of eight Mesopotamian commentaries on the Enuma Elish from the middle of the first millennium BCE will serve as the corpus to which the pesharim are compared.

Before beginning a comparative study of Mesopotamian commentaries and Qumran pesharim, a few remarks are in order with reference to the formal structure of these interpretive texts and the technical terminology used to describe them. The commentary texts are not all exactly the same, but the basic structure of their commentary units involves a citation of the base text (i.e., the text being commented on—this citation is labeled the *lemma*). In the Qumran pesharim, the lemma is usually followed by an introductory formula: a phrase with the word פשר ("interpretation") is customary (e.g., פשר הדבר, "the interpretation of the passage [is]" or פשרו על, "its interpretation concerns"). Introductory formulas are not customary in the Mesopotamian commentaries, but sometimes *ša* ("who/which") or *aššu*(MU) ("concerning") is used as a shorthand introduction to explanations. These expressions have the connotation "this word, phrase, or situation has to do with…." The

---

²Though the pesharim at Qumran are unique, some of the interpretive traditions in them have an origin in a wider Second Temple Jewish milieu. For traditional interpretations shared between 1QpHab and Targum Jonathan, see, e.g., N. Wieder, "The Habakkuk Scroll and the Targum," *JJS* 4 (1953): 14–18; and William H. Brownlee, "The Habakkuk Midrash and the Targum of Jonathan," *JJS* 7 (1956): 169–86. See also Géza Vermès, *Scripture and Tradition in Judaism: Haggadic Studies*, StPB 4 (Leiden: Brill, 1961), esp. 26–66.

³This does seem to be the prevailing opinion now, against Hartmut Stegemann's proposal of only two Isaiah commentaries, 4QpIsa[abd] and 4QpIsa[ce] (*The Library of Qumran: On the Essenes, Qumran, John the Baptist, and Jesus* [Grand Rapids: Eerdmans, 1998], 126, deemed possible by George Brooke ["Isaiah in the Pesharim and Other Qumran Texts," in *Writing and Reading the Scroll of Isaiah: Studies of an Interpretive Tradition*, ed. Craig C. Broyles and Craig A. Evans, 2 vols., VTSup 70 (Leiden: Brill, 1997), 618–19, http://dx.doi.org/10.1163/9789004275959_010]), and a single Psalms pesher, 1QpPs + 4QpPs[ab] (*Library of Qumran*, 127–29, largely accepted without further substantiation by Armin Lange and Zlatko Pleše, "The Qumran Pesharim and the Derveni Papyrus: Transpositional Hermeneutics in Ancient Jewish and Ancient Greek Commentaries," in *The Dead Sea Scrolls in Context: Integrating the Dead Sea Scrolls in the Study of Ancient Texts, Languages, and Cultures*, ed. Armin Lange, Emanuel Tov, and Matthias Weigold, 2 vols., VTSup 140 [Leiden: Brill, 2011], 910 n. 28). See the detailed arguments against both assertions in Bronson Brown-deVost, *Commentary and Authority in Mesopotamia and Qumran*, JAJSup (Göttingen: Vandenhoeck & Ruprecht, forthcoming), chapter 1.6.

interpretation of the lemma is called the *comment*; each lemma–comment pair constitutes a single commentary unit.[4] When presenting the commentary texts here, I use special formatting to make the individual elements of the commentary unit more easily identifiable: the lemma is indicated with a solid underline; the comment is presented in regular type; and citations of the lemma within the comment (i.e., internal citations) are indicated by a dotted underline.

I. Mesopotamian Commentaries

Mesopotamian commentary texts date between 800 and 100 BCE.[5] Scholars of ancient Mesopotamia divide these commentaries into two categories bearing Akkadian designations: the *ṣâtu* commentaries traditionally read like a glossary and list a single word or short phrase from the base text followed by a brief explanatory note;[6] the *mukallimtu* commentaries are more expansive and are characterized by the citation of a line from the base text, the lemma, followed by an interpretation, the comment.[7]

In order to demonstrate the structure and the transmission of Mesopotamian commentary texts, I have selected one particularly well-suited group of eight

---

[4] For the terminology "commentary unit" and a defense of its usefulness, see, e.g., Shani L. Berrin, *The Pesher Nahum Scroll from Qumran: An Exegetical Study of 4Q169*, STDJ 53 (Leiden: Brill, 2004), 19; and Gregory L. Doudna, *4Q Pesher Nahum: A Critical Edition*, JSPSup 35 (Sheffield: Sheffield Academic, 2001), 46.

[5] For an overview of Mesopotamian commentaries, see Eckart Frahm, *Babylonian and Assyrian Text Commentaries: Origins of Interpretation*, Guides to the Mesopotamian Textual Record 5 (Münster: Ugarit-Verlag, 2011), which supersedes his earlier "Royal Hermeneutics: Observations on the Commentaries from Ashurbanipal's Libraries at Nineveh," *Iraq* 66 (2004): 45–50. For a large-scale discussion of Mesopotamian interpretation in commentary texts compared to Jewish interpretation, especially in the pesharim, see Uri Gabbay, "Akkadian Commentaries from Ancient Mesopotamia and Their Relation to Early Hebrew Exegesis," *DSD* 19 (2012): 267–312, http://dx.doi.org/10.1163/15685179-12341235; and Gabbay, "Actual Sense and Scriptural Intention: Literal Meaning and Its Terminology in Akkadian and Hebrew Commentaries," in *Encounters by the Rivers of Babylon: Scholarly Conversations between Jews, Iranians, and Babylonians in Antiquity*, ed. Uri Gabbay and Shai Secunda, TSAJ 160 (Tübingen: Mohr Siebeck, 2014), 335–70.

[6] Frahm, *Babylonian and Assyrian Text Commentaries*, 34. In late Babylonian commentary texts, the term *ṣâtu* comes to be used for most commentary texts regardless of their formal characteristics.

[7] At an early stage of research, Gerhard Meier defined the *ṣâtu* commentaries as "linguistic explanation" (*sprachlichen Erklärung*) and *mukallimtu* commentaries as "factual interpretation" (*sachlichen Interpretation*) ("Kommentare aus dem Archiv der Tempelschule in Assur," *AfO* 12 [1937]: 239), but this definition is no longer tenable. For other terms sometimes associated with commentary texts (i.e., *malsûti*, "reading, lesson"; *maš²altu*, "questioning"; and *ša/šūt pî*, "oral lore [lit., those of the mouth]"), see, e.g., Gabbay, "Akkadian Commentaries from Ancient Mesopotamia," 281–84.

related commentary texts dealing with the Enuma Elish. The letter designations for these manuscripts follow Wilfred G. Lambert's recent edition of them.[8] As is often the case with cuneiform tablets, the fragmentary nature of the Enuma Elish commentaries obscures the full extent of each tablet's contents and makes it difficult to give a complete accounting of each manuscript. Nevertheless, none of them can demonstrably be a copy of any other, but they do overlap in a number of places. For this reason, it is best to think of these commentaries as a constellation of texts—that is, a group of very closely related works sharing much content with one another without being verbatim copies. To put it another way, they all appear to have access to more or less the same traditional interpretive content, but they differ in the extent to which they convey it. For instance, manuscript Z has more than thirty-eight commentary units, while manuscript y has little more than eleven.

The full contents of each manuscript can be charted as follows according to the lines of Enuma Elish that each commentary manuscript interprets (all breaks in the tablets are indicated by solid vertical lines):

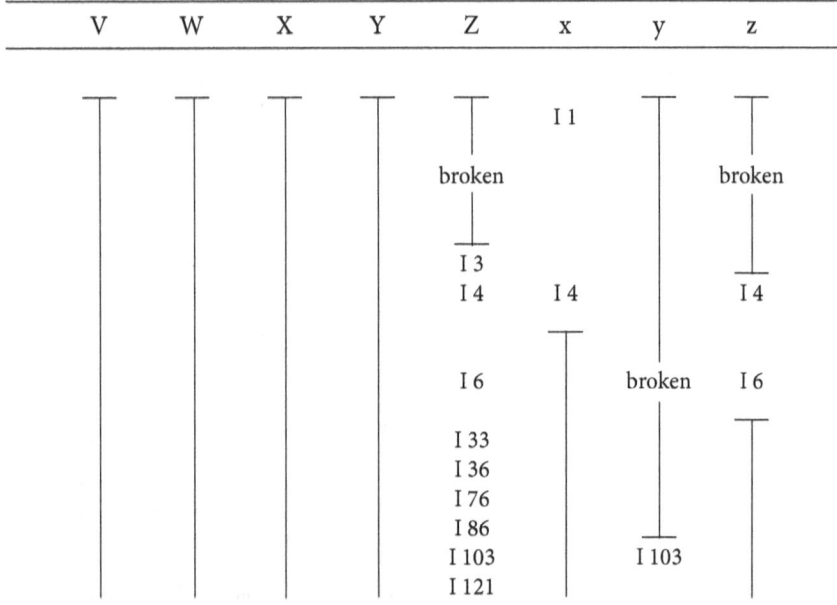

[8] Wilfred G. Lambert, *Babylonian Creation Myths*, MC 16 (Winona Lake, IN: Eisenbrauns, 2013). The manuscripts are as follows: Z = K 4657 + 7038 + 9427 + 9911 + 10008 + 12102 + 16818 + Sm 747; Y = Rm 395; X = K 8585; W = Rm II 538; V = VAT 10616(+)11616; z = BM 54228 (82-5-22, 379); y = BM 66606 + 72033 (82-9-18, 6599 + 12037); x = BM 69594 (82-9-18, 9591). While the present publication was in press, a full edition of these manuscripts was published by Eckart Frahm and Enrique Jiménez ("Myth, Ritual, and Interpretation: The Commentary on *Enūma eliš* I–VII and a Commentary on the Elamite Month Names," *HBAI* 4 [2015]: 293–343). They have identified yet another possible commentary manuscript (K 13866), which they designate Ω.

V	W	X	Y	Z	x	y	z
				I 122			
				I 139			
				I 159			
				II 1			
				II 53			
			broken	II 54			
				II 55			
				II 134			
				II 135			
	broken			IV 46–47[9]			
		broken		IV 62[10]			
				IV 113–114		IV 113	
				IV 124			
broken				IV 131–132		IV 131–132	
				IV 140			broken
				IV 145			
				V 21			
				V 22			
				V 24–25			
			V 33				
			V 55				
			V 59				
						V 64	
			V 70			V 70?	
						V 83	
						V 84	
			V 90				
			V 95				
			V 101/115				
			broken	broken			
		VI 94					
							V 157
						VI 89	VI 89
		VI 132	VI 132				

[9] These lemmas have no clear comment.
[10] These lemmas have no clear comment.

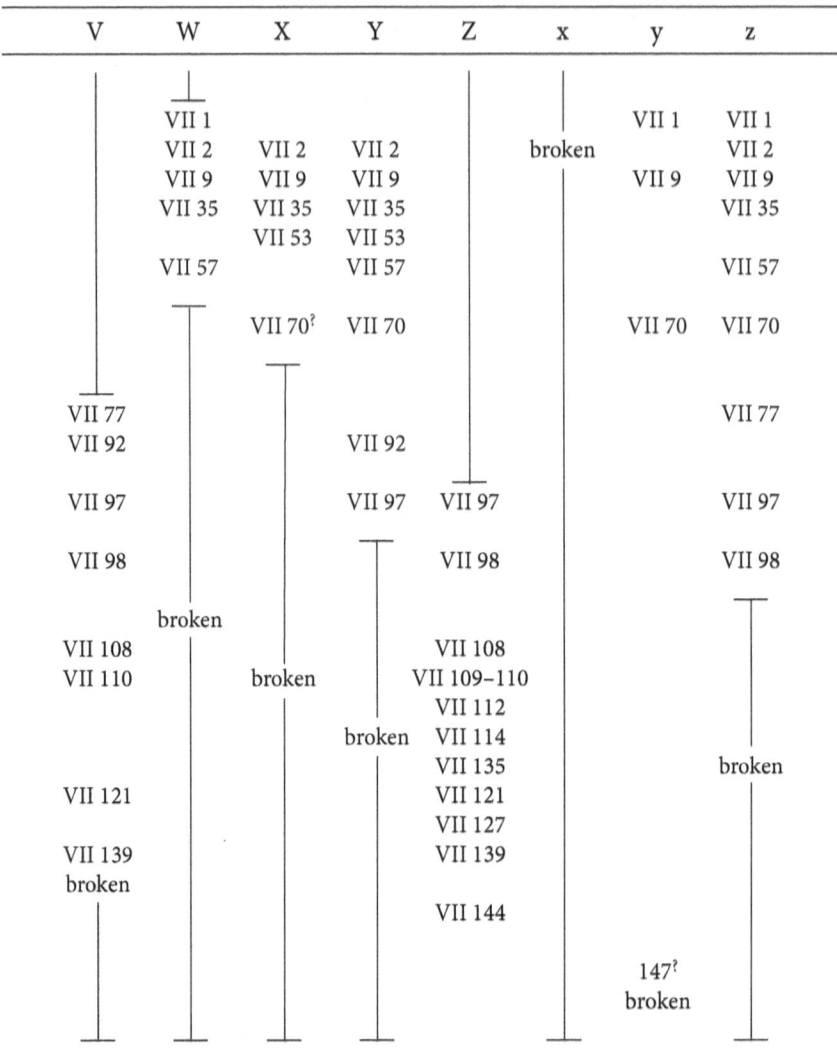

The constellatory nature of these manuscripts is evidenced by their large degree of overlap (when not broken). Five tablets contain a comment on Enuma Elish VII 9, and three of them are virtually identical (MSS Xyz; MS Y is broken): <u>ᵈTutu bān tēdištīšunu šū-ma</u> aššu(MU) ilānī(DINGIR.MEŠ) (ša) māḫāzi (...), "Tutu is he who accomplishes their renovation, (This has to do) with the gods of the cultic place (...)."[11] The manuscripts in synoptic (or scored) form are:

[11] Manuscript W appears to have a comment different from that of the other manuscripts, but it may be that this is a case of metathesis and that we should read for MS W ša ina Bābilim

Brown-deVost: The Compositional Development of Qumran Pesharim   531

W 5	ᵈ*tu-tu ba-an te-*[*diš-ti-šu-nu šu-ú-ma*]
X 5	[ᵈ*tu-tu ba-an te-diš-ti-šú-nu šu-ú-m*]*a* →
Y 4	[ᵈ*tu-tu b*]*a-ni te-diš-ti-šu-nu* [*šu-ú-ma*] →
y rev. 6	[ᵈ*tu-tu ba-an te-di-i*]*š-ti-šú-nu šu-ú* : →
z rev. 10	ᵈʳ*tu`-tu ba-an te-d*[*iš-ti-šu-nu šu-ú-ma*]
W 6	*šá ina* KÁ.DINGIR.RAᵏⁱ [...]
X cont.	MU DINGIR.MEŠ *šá ma-ḫ*[*a-zi* ...]
Y cont.	[MU? DINGIR?.MEŠ? (*šá?*) *ma?-ḫa?-zi?* ...]
y rev. 7	MU DINGIR.MEŠ *ma-ḫa-*[*zi* ...] (vacat) *it-ta-r*[*a* ...][12]
z rev. 11	MU DINGIR.MEŠ *šá ma-ḫa-zi* [...]

In fact, MSS W, X, Y, and z all have consecutive comments on Enuma Elish tablet VII lines 2, 9, and 35. In addition, the many other instances of overlap between commentary manuscripts, as noted in the chart above, further demonstrate that they all share access to a common interpretive tradition but record that tradition to different extents and sometimes with slight variation. These occasional variations in wording[13] and orthography[14] may be due to oral transmission. In addition to these minor differences between commentary manuscripts, a manuscript may also contain an expanded or updated version of a comment found in another.

The comment on Enuma Elish VII 109–110 in MS V 14 relates the base text to a cultic event: *qí-šá-a-ti šá* {*ina* ⁱᵗⁱBÁRA} *ul-tu* UD.6.KÁM E[N UD.12.KÁM SUM-*na* MU ᵈ*z*]*a-ba₄-ba₄* GIM DUG₄-*u*, "The gifts which [are given] {in the month of Nisan} from the 6th day t[o the 12th. This has to do with Z]ababa, as it is said." Manuscript Z rev. 7 contains this same comment but adds further information about the ritual, [...] x ᵈEN *šá ina a-ki-ti* UD.8.KÁM *uš-šá-bu*, "[...] ? Bēl who sits in the Akītu-house on the 8th," along with a lexical comment found in another source, <u>*kàt-ru-u*</u> *ṭa-ʾ-tu šá* ŠÀ *ṭup-pi šá-nim-ma*, "<u>katrû</u> (means) gift/bribe; (this explanation comes) from another tablet." Thus, the writer of MS Z had access to the same interpretive tradition as the writer of MS V but also knew of additional interpretive traditions and used those to create a conflated comment (i.e., a comment created by the combination of two or more originally discrete comments).

[*aššu ilānī māḫāzi*], "which is in Babylon, [(this has to do) with the gods of the cultic place]," and for MSS XYyz *aššu ilānī* (*ša*) *māḫāzi* [*ina Bābilim*], "(This has to do) with the gods of the cultic place [in Babylon]." Note that W again appears to have metathesis in its comment on VII 35 <u>*bārû libbi*</u> [*Šamaš*], "<u>the one who probes</u> hearts is [Šamaš]," where MSS XYz have *Šamaš* <u>*bārû libbi*</u>, "Šamaš is <u>the one who probes</u> hearts."

[12] The form *ittar*[*a-* ...] is unclear, but it probably belongs to a further interpretation of Enuma Elish VII 9 that is preserved only in MS y.

[13] The comment on Enuma Elish VII 9 in MSS X and z have a *ša*; MS Y does not. See also the possible instances of metathesis noted above in n. 11.

[14] Manuscript V 11 spells the divine name *Mār-bīti* with ᵈDUMU.É; MS Z rev. 5 spells it ᵈA.É (DUMU and A are variant logographic writings for Akkadian *māru*, "son").

Irrespective of the variation in the selection and presentation of comments, all of these Enuma Elish commentaries appear to have the same scope, with comments spanning the entire work: MS Z is the largest, with over sixty wide lines, and MS y was perhaps the briefest with only about twenty-six much shorter lines. The other commentaries, where there is enough tablet left to venture a guess, had lengths somewhere between these extremes. All the commentaries also share the same feature of devoting only about half their contents to Enuma Elish tablets I–VI and reserving most of the reverse side of the tablet for copious comments on tablet VII, Marduk's fifty names. What is more, the commentaries follow the order of lines in the base text, and in that sense they are somewhat continuous—to borrow a term from pesher scholarship—though MS Z does have one commentary unit on VII 135 placed out of order between the units covering VII 114 and VII 121.

Just as the tablets in this textual constellation each have a unique selection of commentary units, they also employ differing textual layouts, though they are all single-column tablets.[15] Manuscripts V, W, X, Y, y, and z use a format that situates the comment on the same line as the lemma; but in V, W, y, and z a single line was not always long enough to contain both the lemma and the comment, and in those particular cases the comment is placed directly underneath the lemma and indented—this is especially frequent in MS y. Manuscript Z, however, with its long lines, sometimes fits two commentary units on a single line and also uses *vacat*s as a dividing mark. Finally, MS x is a scrap of a tablet that presents only single words or short phrases from the lemma followed by very brief comments separated by cola. The differences in layout used by these manuscripts can be seen most readily in the commentary unit on Enuma Elish I 4 in MSS Z, z, and x:

Z obv. 2	[*mu-um-mu ti-amat mu-al-li*]-*da-at* ⸢*gim*⸣-*r*[*i-šú-un mu-um-mu*]
	(*vacat*) *nab-*⸢*ni*⸣-*t*[*um*]
Z obv. 2	[And demiurge Tiāmat, who ga]ve birth to them a[ll; … *mummu*]
	(*vacat*) (is related to) living cre[ation.]
z obv. 1	⸢*mu-um*⸣-[*mu ti-amat mu-al-li-da-at gim-ri-šú-un*]
z obv. 2	*mu-u*[*m-mu nab-ni-tu*]
z obv. 1	And demiu[rge Tiāmat, who gave birth to them all;]
z obv. 2	*mu*[*mmu* (is related to) living creation.]
x 3	⸢*mu-um-mu*⸣ *ti-*⸢*amat*⸣ [: …][16]
x 3	⸢*mummu*⸣ *ti*⸢*āmat*⸣ [: (means) …]

---

[15] For a discussion of Mesopotamian commentary text layouts, see, e.g., Frahm, *Babylonian and Assyrian Text Commentaries*, 33–37.

[16] Since the lemma of MS x, ⸢*mummu*⸣ *ti*⸢*āmat*⸣, does not match the lemma of MSS Z and z exactly, it is not certain that MS x should be restored ⸢*mummu*⸣ *ti*⸢*āmat*⸣ [: *nabnītu* …], "⸢*mummu*⸣ *ti*⸢*āmat*⸣ [: (is related to) living creation.…]."

This brief case study provides one model for the transmission of commentary traditions over a time span of about two hundred years[17] and over a wide geographical area encompassing Nineveh, Assur, and Sippar. These texts grew out of a scribal training curriculum that disseminated textual interpretations in both oral and written forms.[18] When a commentary text was copied down by a particular scribe, it was done in the length that was most useful and the format that was most familiar or apt. These commentaries were then used side by side with their base text as an aid for understanding that text and, perhaps more importantly, for relating it to the larger sphere of tradition.[19]

Even with the abundance of textual witnesses for commentary traditions surrounding the Enuma Elish, these fragmentary remains still do not admit of any confident conclusions about the dating of specific commentary units. Nevertheless, the variety of concerns treated in the comments—some dealing with lexical matters, others with cultic or astronomical events—as well as the differing styles of the individual comments argue against the assumption that every entry was the product of a single individual.[20] Rather, these comments were the product of an accretion of various ancient interpreters' research on the foundational creation epic Enuma Elish, and they bear witness to the great effort these commentators expended to understand the text and its place in their conception of the world.

The empirical evidence from this constellation of eight commentaries on the Enuma Elish provides a model for the creation of commentary texts out of interpretive traditions that can be applied to the continuous pesharim from Qumran and

---

[17] The Babylonian tablets are from Sippar and thus should not postdate the reign of Xerxes; see Caroline Waerzeggers, "The Babylonian Revolts against Xerxes and the 'End of Archives,'" *AfO* 50 (2003–2004): 150–73, noted in Frahm, *Babylonian and Assyrian Text Commentaries*, 287 n. 1362. The Nineveh tablets come from the seventh century BCE.

[18] For a discussion of the nature of oral traditions in Mesopotamian literature, see, e.g., Yaakov Elman, "Authoritative Oral Tradition in Neo-Assyrian Scribal Circles," *JANESCU* 7 (1975): 19–32. For Mesopotamian oral traditions in general, see the classic description in A. Leo Oppenheim, *Ancient Mesopotamia: Portrait of a Dead Civilization*, rev. ed. (Chicago: University of Chicago Press, 1977), 22–23.

[19] It is possible that, among the many Mesopotamian commentary texts, a few texts integrated comments into a running base text; see the texts described as "commented text" in Erica Reiner, "Celestial Omen Tablets and Fragments in the British Museum," in *Festschrift für Rykle Borger zu seinem 65. Geburtstag am 24. Mai 1994*, ed. Stefan M. Maul, CM 10 (Leiden: Brill, 1998), 215–302. One such manuscript that might be a running text with interspersed comments is VAT 10218 (see Erica Reiner and David Pingree, *Babylonian Planetary Omens*, 3 vols., CM 11 [Groningen: Styx, 1998], 3:29–36, 40–54). Though that text contains 127 omens concerning Venus (about 10 percent of the omens have variants or comments of some sort) it is uncertain whether this tablet is indeed tablet 61 of Enuma Anu Enlil or some other noncanonical collection of Venus omens (so Reiner and Pingree, *Babylonian Planetary Omens*, 3:1).

[20] *Pace* Frahm and Jiménez, "Myth, Ritual, and Interpretation," 332–33.

thereby can explain a number of difficulties in those texts.[21] This is an important heuristic since, as mentioned earlier, any statements about the literary development of the Qumran pesharim are difficult to justify because of the lack of manuscript evidence.

II. Qumran Pesharim

Against the idea that the pesharim are the product of the collection of various interpretative traditions surrounding their base texts, Bilhah Nitzan has argued for the literary unity of the pesher on Habakkuk—the most complete pesher text.[22] She attempts to substantiate this claim on the basis of a consistent interpretation of the terms רשע ("wicked"), בוגדים ("treacherous ones"), and צדיק ("righteous") throughout the text.[23] For all that, Hanan Eshel has argued for two literary strata in Pesher Habakkuk, one dealing with the Hellenistic period, where he situates the Teacher of Righteousness, and smaller additions made shortly after the Roman takeover of Judea.[24] He has defended this assertion against Nitzan's claims of textual unity by

---

[21] The category of continuous pesharim was first proposed by Jean Carmignac, "Le document de Qumrân sur Melkisédek," *RevQ* 7 (1969): 342–78; its coherence was first questioned by Moshe Bernstein, "Introductory Formulas for Citation and Re-Citation of Biblical Verses in the Qumran Pesharim: Observations on a Pesher Technique," *DSD* 1 (1994): 30–70, http://dx.doi.org/10.1163/156851794X00185. Some of the affinities of the thematic pesharim to the continuous type have been outlined by George Brooke, "Thematic Commentaries on Prophetic Scriptures," in *Biblical Interpretation at Qumran*, ed. Matthias Henze, SDSSRL (Grand Rapids: Eerdmans, 2005), 134–57. On the basis of Robert William Jr.'s recent application of cognitive theory to the genre of pesher ("Pesher: A Cognitive Model of the Genre," *DSD* 17 [2010]: 336–60, http://dx.doi.org/10.1163/156851710X513575), I have described a more comprehensive categorization of the Qumran pesher texts into four subtypes: (1) pesharim associated somewhat loosely with one or more base text(s) but still keyed to the sequential order of the base text(s) (e.g., 4QFlorilegium, 4QTanḥûmîm, and 4QCatena), frequently citing texts other than their base text; (2) pesharim that treat only excerpts from a single base text, employing simple or rather spare technical terminology and infrequently citing texts other than their base text (e.g., 4QpIsa[b], 4QpappIsa[c]); (3) pesharim on multiple complete psalms, which use short lemmas; and (4) pesharim on single self-standing literary units such as the Blessing of Jacob (Genesis 49) and the Enochic Apocalypse of Weeks, or on complete literary works such as Nahum and Habakkuk (chs. 1 + 2), which only rarely quote texts other than their base text (never with citation) (*Commentary and Authority*, chapter 1.8).

[22] See also Jutta Jokiranta, *Social Identity and Sectarianism in the Qumran Movement*, STDJ 105 (Leiden: Brill, 2013), 122, 163–65, though she refrains from asserting "that the pesher could not have been revised or even updated" (165). In a recent presentation at the Annual Meeting of the Society of Biblical Literature in Atlanta, Georgia, 23 November 2015, Jokiranta argued in favor of some revision in Pesher Habakkuk ("Paratextuality of *Pesher Habakkuk*: Case with the Prophet and the Teacher").

[23] Bilha Nitzan, "Are There Two Historical Layers in 1Q Pesher Habakkuk?" [in Hebrew], *Zion* 72 (2007): 91–93.

[24] Eshel, "Two Historical Layers of Pesher Habakkuk," 115. The later additions to the pesher are II, 10–IV, 13; V, 12–VI, 12; and the end of the comment in IX, 3–7.

noting that none of the passages in his proposed later strata uses the terms רשע, בוגדים, or צדיק.[25]

While historical concerns may be one way to discern literary strata in Pesher Habakkuk, form-critical discrepancies in the continuous pesharim strongly suggest multiple stages in their literary development. More specifically, these form-critical issues suggest there were stages in the development of these pesharim that were similar to the development of the Mesopotamian Enuma Elish commentaries. A basic example of this is the application of a new formatting system for the copy of the Habakkuk pesher in 1QpHab, where the first hand rather mechanically added a *vacat* before each instance of the introductory signal word פשר. The mechanical nature of the insertion of *vacat*s in this text is evidenced by the accidental misreading of פשו from the lemma of Hab 1:8 as פשר, which led the scribe to add a *vacat* before the word. The error was then ameliorated by thickening the vertical descender of the ר in order to make it look like a fat ו.[26]

A more hypothetical suggestion based on the Mesopotamian commentary model is that some of the Qumran pesharim would have had precursors with a structure similar to that found in the Mesopotamian commentaries. These earlier versions would have contained selected lemmas excerpted from the base text and the comments associated with them, but not a complete running presentation of the base text. In fact, several of the thematic pesharim (e.g., 4QFlorilegium, 4QTanḥûmîm, and 4QCatena) along with 4QpIsa[b] and 4QpappIsa[c] fit this model.[27] This understanding of the development of the Qumran commentaries can explain a number of difficulties encountered in 1QpHab and others of the continuous pesharim. I offer here four examples:

A. 1QpHab II, 15–III, 6 (comment on Hab 1:6b–7)

ההולך למרחבי ארץ לרשת II, 15	II, 15that roams the expanses of the land to take possession of
משכנות] [ול]וא לו איום ונורא16	habitations], 16even though (they) do n[ot belong to it. It is
הוא ממנו משפטו ושאתו יצא[	terrible and dreadful. Its justice and its majesty come forth
[... פשרו על הכתיאים אשר]17	from it itself.] 17[Its interpretation concerns the Kittim,
ובמישור ילכו לכות ולבוז את III, 1	who ...] III, 1and in the valley they will go to smite and
ערי הארץ 2כיא הוא אשר אמר	plunder the cities of the land, 2for it is the one concerning

---

[25] Eshel, "Response to Bilhah Nitzan," 94 n. 2.

[26] See, e.g., Maurya P. Horgan, *Pesharim: Qumran Interpretations of Biblical Books*, CBQMS 8 (Washington, DC: Catholic Biblical Association of America, 1979), 28.

[27] For several of the thematic pesharim as commentaries that are keyed sequentially to a base text without commenting on the entirety of that base text, see George Brooke, "Thematic Commentaries on Prophetic Scriptures." 4QpIsa[b] and 4QpappIsa[c], likewise follow the order of their base text (presumably) but do not comment on it in its entirety. 4QpIsa[b] moves directly from a commentary unit on Isa 5:11–14 to the next on 5:24β–25, and again the commentary jumps from a comment on Isa ?–5:30 to one on 6:9–?. 4QpappIsa[c] does not deal with Isa 10:14–18 and 14:9–25, and it is possible that 9:19 was left out of the commentary as well.

whom it says: to take possession of habitations not belonging to it. It is terrible ³and dreadful. Its justice and majesty come forth from it itself. [[ ]] ⁴Its interpretation concerns the Kittim, the dread and terror of whom are upon all ⁵ the nations, and with counsel their entire plan is to do evil, and in deceitfulness and trickery ⁶they walk with all the peoples.

³לרשת משכנות לוא לו איום ונורא הוא ממנו משפטו ושאתו יצא [[ ]] ⁴פשרו על הכתיאים אשר פחדם ואמתםᵒ על כול ⁵ הגואים ובעצה כול מחשבתם להרע ובגֹכל ומרמה ⁶ילכו עם כול העמים

The slightly variant internal citation of nearly the entire lemma (lines III, 2–3) in this commentary unit would seem unnecessary and is difficult to explain, especially since it seems to interrupt the comment more than anything else. What is more, the comment in lines III, 3–6 deals only with איום ונורא הוא ממנו משפטו ושאתו יצא ("It is terrible and dreadful. Its justice and majesty come forth from it itself") even though the internal citation also includes לרשת משכנות לוא לו ("to take possession of habitations not belonging to it"). If the comment were truly a single composition, the repetition of לרשת משכנות לוא לו ("to take possession of habitations not belonging to it") makes little sense, for that portion of the lemma had already been interpreted by לבוז ("to plunder") in III, 1. These difficulties can, however, be explained by positing that lines III, 2–6 originally constituted a separate commentary unit from another source, which was integrated, somewhat imperfectly, into the present text.

B. 4QcommGen A V, 1–7 (comment on Gen 49:10a)

ᵛ'¹[...לוֹ]אֹ יסור שליט משבט ² יהודה בהיות לישראל ממשל [ל²⁷ו]אֹ יֹ[כרת יושב כסֹא לדויד כי המחקק היא ברית המלכות ³[ואלו]פֹי ישראל המה הדגלים²⁸ [[ ]] עד בוא משיח הצדק צמח ⁴דויד כי לו ולזרעו נתנה ברית מלכות עמו עד דורות עולם אשר ⁵שמר [...]ᵒ התורה עם אנשי היחד כי ⁶[...]ᵒ היא כנסת אנשי⁷[...]ᵒ נתן

ᵛ'¹[...] a ruler shall [no]t depart from the tribe of Judah, while Israel has dominion ²[there shall not be] cut off one who sits upon the throne of David, for the scepter is the covenant of kingship,³[and the ch]iefs of Israel are the standards, [[ ]] until the coming of the righteous Messiah, the branch of ⁴David, for the covenant of the kingship of his people has been given to him and to his seed unto the eternal generations who ⁵have kept ? [...] the torah, with the men of the community, for ⁶[...] ? it is the congregation of the men of ⁷[...] ? he has given

A *vacat* in the middle of 4QcommGen A V, 3 separates two subcomments. The first subcomment links the promise of Judah's unending rulership to the Davidic dynasty and provides two keyword identifications from the base text

---

²⁸In PAM 41.816 there is a little speck of parchment with the top of a ל on it situated as though it is from this ל here. If that is correct, then we should read לוֹא.

²⁹This must be a variant reading for רגליו in the MT with ד/ר confusion (as also in the Samaritan Pentateuch); thus, it is an internal citation from the lemma.

(מְחֹקֵק, "scepter," and דְּגָלִים, "standards" [for MT רַגְלָיו]). The second subcomment begins rather abruptly with עד ("until"), which does not link well syntactically with the preceding remarks. The poor integration of these two subcomments with each other suggests that they originally existed as independent explanations, though both comments may indeed be trying to provide an apologetic defense for the current absence of a Davidic king.

C. 4QpNah 3–4 II, 7–10 (comment on Nah 3:4)

[ ] מֵרֹב זְנוּנֵי זוֹנָה טוֹבַת חֵן ^{II, 7} בַּעֲלַת כְּשָׁפִים הַמֹּכֶרֶת גּוֹיִם בִּזְנוּנֶיהָ וּמִשְׁפָּחוֹת בְּ[כְשָׁ]פֶיהָ ⁸פִּשְׁר[וֹ עַ]ל מַתְעֵי אֶפְרַיִם [[ ]] אֲשֶׁר בְּתַלְמוּד שְׁקָרָם וּלְשׁוֹן כְּזָבֵיהֶם וְשֶׂפֶת מִרְמָה יַתְעוּ רַבִּים ⁹מְלָכִים שָׂרִים כֹּהֲנִים וְעַם עִם גֵּר נִלְוֶה עָרִים וּמִשְׁפָּחוֹת יֹאבְדוּ בַּעֲצָתָם נִ[כְ]בָּדִים וּמוֹשְׁ[לִים] ¹⁰יִפֹּלוּ [מִזַּ]עַם לְשׁוֹנָם [[ ]]	^{II, 7}Because of the multitude of the harlotries of the whore, with good grace, [ ] lady of witchcraft, who deceives nations with her harlotry and families with her [witchc]rafts. ([[ ]]) ⁸[Its] interpretation [conc]erns those who lead Ephraim astray; [[ ]] those who with their teaching of a lie and their tongue of deceit and lip of treachery lead astray great ones, ⁹kings, princes, priests, and people along with resident alien. Cities and clans will perish with their counsel. Honored people and rul[ers] ¹⁰will fall [because of the insolence] their tongue. [[ ]]

4QpNah 2:8, like 4QcommGen A 5:3, has a *vacat* separating one subcomment in line 3–4 II, 8 from a second in lines 8–10. The first subcomment is very basic in its reference to people who lead Ephraim astray; the second is far more developed and describes the means of deception along with a detailed list of the people who were deceived.[30] In this instance, in contrast to 4QcommGen A, the two subcomments have been so well integrated that the *vacat* is the only overt clue that they form distinct units, though the difference in the level of detail they provide is also suggestive.

D. 1QpHab I, 16–II, 10 (comment on Hab 1:5)

¹⁶([[ ]]) רְאוּ בַגּוֹיִם וְהַבִּיטוּ] ¹⁷[וְהִתַּמְּהוּ תְּמָהוּ כִּיא פֹעַל פֹּעֵל בִּימֵיכֶם לוֹא תַאֲמִינוּ] כִּיא ^{II, 1}[יְסֻפָּר]] [[ ]] [פֵּשֶׁר הַדָּבָר עַל] הַבּוֹגְדִים עִם אִישׁ ²הַכָּזָב כִּי לוֹא[שָׁמְעוּ אֶל דִּבְרֵי] מוֹרֶה הַצְּדָקָה מִפִּי ³אֵל וְעַל הַבּוֹג[דִים	^{I, 16}[([[ ]]) Look among the nations and see,] ¹⁷[and be very amazed, for one is doing a deed in your days, you would not believe it even if] ^{II, 1}it were recounted. [[ ]] [The interpretation of the passage concerns] the treacherous ones along with the man ²of the lie, since [they did] not [listen to the words] of ^{the} teacher of what is right from the mouth ³of God. And (the interpretation of the passage)

---

[30] The list of deceived peoples here in 4QpNah bears a striking resemblance to the list of disrespected peoples in 1QpHab IV, 2–3, which also contains: רבים ("many"), מלכים ("kings"), שרים ("princes"), עם ("people"), and נכבדים ("honored people"). Perhaps both belong to a similar interpretative tradition.

בברית] החדשה כ֯יא לוא	concerns [those] who deal treacher[ously with the] new
⁴האמינו בברית אל [וכיא חללו]	[covenant], since they did not ⁴believe in God's covenant,
את ש֯[ם ק֯]וֿדשו ⁵וכן [[ ]] פשר	[and because they profaned] His holy na[me]. ⁵And
הדבר] על הבו[גדים לאחרית	thus, [[ ]] the interpretation of the passage [concerns the
א ⁶הימים המה עריצ֯[י הבר]יֿת	treach]erous ones at the end ⁶of days. They are the one[s]
אשר לוא יאמינו א ⁷בשומעם את	who violate the [coven]ant, who will not believe ⁷when
כול הבא֯]וֿת ע[ל] הֿדור האחרֿון	they hear all that is to co[me with resp]ect to the latter
מפי ⁸הכוהן אשר נתן אל ב]לבו	generation from the mouth of ⁸the priest in whose [heart]
בינ[ה ³⁰ ל֯פשור אֿת כול ⁹דברי	God has placed [understan]ding to interpret all ⁹the
עבדיו הנביאיםֿ] אשר [בֿידם	words of His servants, the prophets with [whose] hands
ספר אל את ¹⁰כול הבאות על	God recounted ¹⁰all that is to come with respect to His³¹
עמו וע֯]דתו […]	people and [His] cou[ncil …]

The ninth commentary unit in Pesher Habakkuk (I, 16–II, 10) includes a comment that deals with the בוגדים ("treacherous ones"), who are associated with the Man of the Lie. Florentino García Martínez understands this particular commentary unit as an example in which a newer comment is appended to another already existing one.³¹ Since there are three possible identifications of the בוגדים, García Martínez allows for as many as three subsequent comments in this commentary unit.³² Nevertheless, he ultimately argues that there are only two independent comments here (1QpHab II, 1–4 and 5–10) for the following reasons: (1) the traitors in lines 1–4 are contemporaries, but the ones in lines 5–10 are in the future, and this corresponds to the two types of traitors found in CD XIX and XX; (2) the usage of the terms וכן ("and thus"), המה ("they"), עמו ישראל ("his people Israel"), and כוהן ("priest," referring to the Teacher of Righteousness) in lines 5–10 is unique to this passage in the pesharim; and (3) because of the א at the end of line 5, which is certainly different from the X marks elsewhere, for example, 1QpHab III, 12, 14; IV, 11, 14 (unfortunately he provides no further explanation of the phenomenon).

The first four lines of this comment describe how the treacherous people did not believe the message of the Teacher of Righteousness, which came from the mouth of God. A second comment follows, in which each of the first two lines (II, 5 and 6) is marked by an א on the left margin. This second comment is set off with the phrase וכן followed by a *vacat*. It begins as a more condensed version of the first comment but introduces a new term עריצים ("violators"), a term found elsewhere in 1QpHab only at the end of the pesher in cols. IX and X. Lines II, 5 and 6 are followed by the well-known assertion that the Teacher of Righteousness received from God the understanding (בינה) to interpret (פשר) the words of the prophets.

---

³¹ García Martínez, "El pesher," 137–38, and esp. n. 45.

³² Horgan independently came to this same conclusion (*Pesharim: Qumran Interpretations of Biblical Books,* 24). She claimed that the first interpretation refers to the enemies in the time of the Teacher of Righteousness, the second refers to the enemies of the Qumran congregation, and the third is eschatological.

This second comment (II, 5–10) in commentary unit 9 (1) summarizes the first comment (II, 1–4), (2) refers to the Teacher of Righteousness's divinely apportioned understanding rather than his ability to relay the words of God, (3) calls him הכוהן ("the priest"), rather than מורה הצדקה ("teacher of what is right"),[33] (4) gives the interpretation a future time reference,[34] and (5) borrows the term עריצים ("violators") from the final columns of the Habakkuk pesher. These five points suggest that commentary unit 9 is a conflation of two commentary texts. The copyist first wrote a comment from one commentary source, then marked the insertion of a second, more developed comment by means of a *vacat* before its beginning and א's at the end of its first two lines.[35]

The common Mesopotamian practice of marking second comments with the terms *šanû* ("another [interpretation]") and *šanîš* ("secondly") might suggest that the א's at the beginning of the second comment stand for אַחֵר ("another

---

[33] The terms הכוהן and מורה הצדק appear to occur together in 4QpPs^a 1, 3–4 III, 15, פשרו על הכוהן מורה ה[צדק], "[Its interpretation concerns] the priest, the teacher of [righteousness]," where they must refer to a single person based on the usage of a singular pronoun in the following line. The two terms may also be used with the same referent in 4QpPs^b 1, 4 and 5. For possible connections between 1QpHab and 4QpPs^a, see George Brooke, "The Pesharim and the Origins of the Dead Sea Scrolls," in *Methods of Investigation of the Dead Sea Scrolls and the Khirbet Qumran Site: Present Realities and Future Prospects*, ed. Michael Wise et al., Annals of the New York Academy of Sciences 722 (New York: New York Academy of Sciences, 1994), 344; and the further analysis of Brown-deVost, *Commentary and Authority*, chapter 3.1.b.iii.

[34] See Karl Elliger, *Studien zum Habakuk-Kommentar vom Toten Meer*, BHT 15 (Tübingen: Mohr Siebeck, 1953), 126.

[35] Jokiranta's objections (*Social Identity and Sectarianism*, 164) to Hanan Eshel's proposition of textual strata in 1QpHab on the grounds that "scribal marks do not point to any redaction as such," while valid with regard to Eshel, cannot apply here, where a marginal scribal mark does indicate textual expansion (as does the dash at the beginning of 1QpHab 4:12). H. Gregory Snyder has similarly claimed that these alephs in 1QpHab II, 5 and 6 mark a second comment, though he does not discuss the issue of compositional history ("Naughts and Crosses: Pesher Manuscripts and Their Significance for Reading Practices at Qumran," *DSD* 7 [2000]: 40, http://dx.doi.org/10.1163/156851700509869). I do not follow the common opinion that these alephs were incorrectly copied X's from the *Vorlage* to 1QpHab (see, e.g., Emanuel Tov, "Scribal Markings in the Texts from the Judean Desert: Conference on the Texts from the Judean Desert, Jerusalem, 30 April, 1995," in *Current Research and Technological Developments on the Dead Sea Scrolls: Conference on the Texts from the Judean Desert, Jerusalem, 20 April 1995*, ed. Donald W. Parry and Stephen D. Ricks, STDJ 20 (Leiden: Brill, 1996], 43 n. 5).

This comment has previously been treated as an instance of "multiple interpretation" (Michael Fishbane, "The Qumran Pesher and Traits of Ancient Hermeneutics," in *Proceedings of the Sixth World Congress of Jewish Studies* [Jerusalem: World Union of Jewish Studies, 1977], 1:99). See also recently Matthias Weigold, "Ancient Jewish Commentaries in Light of the Dead Sea Scrolls: Multiple Interpretations as a Distinctive Feature?" in *The Hebrew Bible in Light of the Dead Sea Scrolls*, ed. Nóra Dávid et al., FRLANT 239 (Göttingen: Vandenhoeck & Ruprecht, 2012), 288; see his review of scholarship in n. 26. Such an assessment may still apply to the first comment in II, 1–5, which has two interpretations of בוגדים (one in lines 1–3 and another in lines 3–5).

[interpretation]"), a lexical equivalent to the Akkadian terms. The use of a lapidary *aleph* ✣ as a scribal marker (read אחר or אחרן) is known from the fifth-century BCE Aḥiqar manuscript found at Elephantine.³⁶ The rabbinic use of the abbreviation ד"א ("another interpretation" [דבר אחר]) to mark second interpretations or opinions in the Talmud may further substantiate this conjecture.³⁷

III. Conclusion

A number of other form-critical issues in the pesher corpus can be explained by positing a stage of pesher development that resembled the earlier Mesopotamian commentaries.³⁸ Like the Mesopotamian commentaries, the early pesher traditions would have consisted of a list of lemmas excerpted from the base text, mainly in order of occurrence, followed by interpretational comments. There may have even been multiple manuscripts of various lengths representing these interpretive traditions to different extents, just like the constellation of commentary texts on the Enuma Elish.³⁹ Yet sometime shortly before, or early in, the Herodian period,

---

³⁶ A. E. Cowley had first suggested that the lapidary *aleph* in the Aḥiqar text might be an abbreviation for אחר, an interpretation furthered by Ada Yardeni but with the reading אחרן ("another matter"). Yardeni further notes that the mark occurs in Eduard Sachau, *Aramäische Papyrus und Ostraka aus einer jüdischen Militärkolonie zu Elephantine: Altorientalische Sprachdenkmäler des 5. Jahrhunderts vor Chr.* (Leipzig: Hinrichs, 1911), Tafel 51. See Cowley, *Aramaic Papyri of the Fifth Century B.C.* (Oxford: Clarendon, 1923), 211; and Yardeni, "New Jewish Aramaic Ostraca," *IEJ* 40 (1990): 133–34. Emanuel Tov notes that a neo-paleo-Hebrew *aleph* is used similarly in several Qumran manuscripts as a section marker (*Scribal Practices and Approaches Reflected in the Texts Found in the Judean Desert*, STDJ 64 [Leiden: Brill, 2004], 185–87). The use of an Aramaic square script *aleph* here in 1QpHab would then constitute little more than an update in script form. George Brooke has independently come to the same conclusion, noting that the marginal א in II, 5 is similar in usage to the lapidary *aleph* "in some Aramaic texts of the 5th century B.C.E. by which scribes indicated new paragraphs or major subdivisions" ("Physicality, Paratextuality and Pesher Habakkuk," in *On the Fringe of Commentary: Metatextuality in Ancient Near Eastern and Ancient Mediterranean Cultures*, ed. Sydney Aufrère, Philip Alexander, and Zlatko Pleše, OLA 232 [Leuven: Peeters, 2014], 189). The anonymous *JBL* reviewer for this article has also independently made a similar suggestion.

No other known abbreviations are attested at Qumran, except the use of א as a numeral (4Q512 33–35, 3 and perhaps 51–55 II, 9). For the evidence of early abbreviations being the cause of some differences between the MT, LXX, and Samaritan Pentateuch, see Emanuel Tov, *Textual Criticism of the Hebrew Bible*, 3rd rev. and expanded ed. (Minneapolis: Fortress, 2012), 238–39, and the bibliography cited there.

³⁷ Gabbay has argued for a direct relationship between rabbinic דבר אחר and Akkadian *šaniš* ("Akkadian Commentaries from Ancient Mesopotamia," 308–9 and n. 128).

³⁸ See Brown-deVost, *Commentary and Authority*, chapter 3.3.

³⁹ This compositional model might seem to suggest that the pesharim as we now have them generally lack a sense of cohesion (as is largely the case with Mesopotamian commentaries), and they indeed do from time to time. But it should not be surprising that a more or less coherent

these early pesher interpretations would have been integrated into a running presentation of the base text, as was done with some Greek commentary traditions,[40] and the earlier, less-integrated materials largely passed out of the textual record.

---

message can be found within individual pesher texts (so, e.g., Bilhah Nitzan, *The Pesher Scroll of Habakkuk: A Scroll from the Wilderness of Judaea (1QpHab)* [in Hebrew] [Jerusalem: Bialik Institute, 1989]; and Jokiranta, *Social Identity and Sectarianism*), for the pesharim are the eschatological interpretations of a sect with a very particular ideology and idiolect, and the base texts of the pesharim lend their own internal coherence to the interpretive work. It must be noted, however, that in some cases a development in terminology can be detected in the sectarian works (see Annette Steudel, "Dating Exegetical Texts from Qumran," in *The Dynamics of Language and Exegesis at Qumran*, ed. Devorah Dimant and Reinhard G. Kratz, FAT 2/35 (Tübingen: Mohr Siebeck, 2009], 49–50).

[40] One such example would be the second-century CE commentary on Plato's *Theaetetus* (P.Berol. inv. 9782). For the relationship between Classical Greek commentary writing and the pesharim, see now Pieter Hartog, "Pesher and *Hypomnema*: A Comparison of Two Types of Commentary from the Hellenistic-Roman Period" (PhD diss., Catholic University of Leuven, 2015); and earlier Markus Bockmuehl, "Origins of Biblical Commentary," in *Text, Thought, and Practice in Qumran and Early Christianity: Proceedings of the Ninth International Symposium of the Orion Center for the Study of the Dead Sea Scrolls and Associated Literature, Jointly Sponsored by the Hebrew University Center for the Study of Christianity, 11–13 January, 2004*, ed. Ruth A. Clements and Daniel R. Schwartz, STDJ 84 (Leiden: Brill, 2009), 3–29; Reinhard G. Kratz, "Die Pescharim von Qumran: Im Rahmen der Schriftauslegung des antiken Judentums," in *Heilige Texte: Religion und Rationalität: 1. Geisteswissenschaftliches Colloquium 10.–13. Dezember 2009 auf Schloss Genshagen*, ed. Andreas Kablitz and Christoph Markschies (Berlin: de Gruyter, 2013), 101–2, http://dx.doi.org/10.1515/9783110296655.87; and Kratz, "Text and Commentary: The Pesharim of Qumran in the Context of Hellenistic Scholarship," in *The Bible and Hellenism: Greek Influence on Jewish and Early Christian Literature*, ed. Thomas L. Thompson and Philippe Wajdenbaum, Copenhagen International Seminar (London: Routledge, 2014), 212–29.

fortress press
scholarship that matters

biblical studies

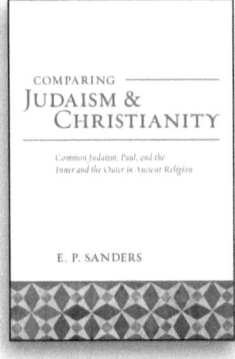

Comparing Judaism and Christianity
Common Judaism, Paul, and the Inner and the Outer in Ancient Religion
E.P. SANDERS

Gathered for the first time within one cover, here Sanders presents formative essays that show the structure of his approach and the insights it produces into Paul's relationship to Judaism and the Jewish law. These essays show a leading scholar at his most erudite as he carries forward and elaborates many of the insights that have become touchstones in New Testament interpretation.
9781506406077 526 pp pbk $39

The Structure of Romans
The Argument of Paul's Letter
PAUL B. FOWLER

The principles of Fowler's reading are that rhetorical questions in Romans 3–11 structure the argument, not as responses to criticism but as Paul's careful guiding of the reader, and that these chapters, like the paraenesis in Romans 12–15, address specific circumstances in Rome. Careful attention to the rhetorical structure of the letter points to tensions between Jew and Gentile that aggravate the already precarious situation of the Roman congregation. In the course of his argument, Fowler explodes the common conceptions that Paul employs diatribal technique to answer objections and that he is primarily engaged in a debate with Jews.
9781506416182 250 pp pbk $39

Available wherever books are sold or
800-328-4648
fortresspress.com

Baruch's Jerusalem: The Conception of Jerusalem in 1 Baruch 4:5–5:9

RUTH HENDERSON
rutihend@yahoo.com.au
Murdoch University, Western Australia, 6150

The final section of the book of 1 Baruch (4:5–5:9), which contains a song of exhortation and encouragement to Israel, is unified by a remarkably variegated emphasis on the city of Jerusalem. In this section, the city is dramatically personified as an aggrieved parent (4:5–9a), a lamenting, widowed mother (4:4:9b–16), an exhortatory prophet (4:17–29), and a glorious city of the future (4:30–5:9). While the personification of Jerusalem as a widowed, bereaved mother and glorious city of the last days is well known from scriptural texts such as Lam 1 and Isa 40–66, the conception of the city as an exhortatory prophet, not found in biblical sources, shows considerable development. Jerusalem is given a prophetic voice and role as one who intercedes for her exiled children, exhorts them to endurance and repentance and encourages them with the hope of restoration and return. The significance of this presentation of Jerusalem needs further investigation. The aim of this study is to explore this development in the conception of Jerusalem with particular emphasis on 1 Bar 4:17–29, against the background of its Second Temple provenance.

The final section of the book of 1 Baruch (4:5–5:9) is a poetic composition that shows considerable diversity, creativity, and originality in its development of some well-known prophetic themes—the destiny of Jerusalem and her relationship to her exiled children. Jerusalem, presented as a mother city, is viewed dramatically through the lens of a wide range of scriptural sources and from the perspective of two fixed points in her history and destiny—the Jerusalem of the past, destroyed by the Babylonians in 586 BCE, and the Jerusalem of the future, described in the yet-to-be-fulfilled prophecies of Isaiah and other prophets. In this composition, the author deals with the problem of how to bridge the gap between these two conceptions by relating his scriptural sources to the present situation of the city in the second century BCE.

For too long scholars have too readily attributed the entire final section of the book (4:4–5:9) to the influence of Isa 40–66. This misconception has been recently criticized by Sean A. Adams, who has questioned the extent of the formative and stylistic influence of these Isaianic chapters on 1 Bar 4:4–5:9.[1] Adams argues that, while it is obvious that the author of 1 Bar 4:5–5:9 knew and engaged with Isaiah and other Jewish writings, this pericope needs to be understood as a distinctive work in its own right, with a unique theological perspective, literary ingenuity, and creative purpose, rather than in terms of its literary borrowing of scriptural sources.[2] In this study I will reexamine the way in which Scripture has been creatively used in 1 Bar 4:5–5:9, with particular emphasis on the third section (4:17–29), in order to determine the ideological perspective of the author concerning the city of Jerusalem and his purpose in penning this creative poetic composition.

I. Jerusalem in the Introduction and Final Section of 1 Baruch

It is clear that a sense of unity in the composition of the book of 1 Baruch has been created by means of the juxtaposition of the focus on Jerusalem in the first (1:1–14) and final (4:5–5:9) sections of the work. The fourfold mention of Jerusalem in the introduction (1:2, 6, 8, 9) corresponds to the fourfold reference to her in the final section (4:30, 36; 5:1, 5). In these two sections the devastated, punished Jerusalem of the past has been intentionally contrasted with the glorious, vindicated Jerusalem of the future. In the introduction, the perspective is from the viewpoint of the exiles in Babylonia looking toward Jerusalem (1:7–14). In the final section, this perspective is reversed: Jerusalem looks toward her returning exiles (4:36–37, 5:5). In 1:5–7, 10–13, the exiles in Babylonia send gifts to the priests and all the people in Jerusalem with the request that they make intercession for them. In the final section, Jerusalem, personified as the mother city, promises to cry ceaselessly to God for her exiled children (4:20). Jerusalem appears in the introduction as a depopulated, devastated city burned with fire by the Babylonians as punishment for the sins of her people (1:2, 9). In the final section of the book, Jerusalem is depicted as a glorious city restored to God's favor (5:1–3). Her exiled children, whose loss she has lamented, are to be returned to her (4:36–37, 5:5–9), while the fate of Babylon, who appears as Israel's vanquisher and master in 2:2, 8–9, 11–12, is reversed at the end of the book. Babylon is herself to become depopulated, devastated by fire and a habitation of demons (4:31–35).[3]

---

[1] See Sean A. Adams, "Jerusalem's Lament and Consolation: Baruch 4:5–5:9 and Its Relationships with Jewish Scripture," in *Studies on Baruch: Composition, Literary Relations, and Reception*, ed. Sean A. Adams, DCLS 23 (Berlin: de Gruyter, 2016), 61–62, for a review of scholarly opinion.
[2] Ibid., 62–75
[3] Although Babylon is not named in the final section of the book, the primary reference appears to be to the destruction of Jerusalem by Babylon. The absence of specific mention of

II. Jerusalem in 1 Baruch 4:4-5:9

The fourth and final part of 1 Baruch (4:5-5:9) can be divided into four major poetic sections: an exhortation addressed by Baruch to exiled Israel, in which the people are arraigned for their sin of rebellion against God but, nevertheless, are encouraged with the hope of restoration (4:5-9a); a second section, in which Jerusalem utters a lament to her neighbors (4:9b-16); a third section, spoken by Jerusalem to her exiled children, in which she encourages them to endure exile, hoping and waiting for their restoration (4:17-29); and a fourth and final section, in which Jerusalem, addressed by the poet, is reassured with the hope of the overthrow of her enemies, her glorious destiny to come, and the return of her exiled children (4:30-5:9).

With the exception of the third section (4:17-29), the major scriptural source texts or models underlying each of these sections can be easily determined. In each case, however, 1 Baruch has imaginatively and creatively expanded on the source text/s.

The first section (4:5-9a) is modeled on the indictment speech of Moses in Deut 32, with particular reference to 32:15-18, to which the author alludes in 1 Bar 4:7-8.[4] The author has creatively expanded on this source by introducing Jerusalem (not mentioned explicitly in the book of Deuteronomy) as the mother city, which is to form the dominant image of the following sections. This has been achieved by the addition in 1 Bar 4:8 of the image of God as the angered father from Deut 32:18. By means of bold parallelism, Jerusalem, the aggrieved mother, has been juxtaposed with the Deuteronomic image of God as Israel's father and is thus presented as coparent with God.[5]

> And you forgot the one who nursed you, God everlasting (Deut 32:18)
>
> and you even grieved Ierousalem who reared you. (1 Bar 4:8 NETS)

In the second section (1 Bar 4:9b-16), Jerusalem appears as a widow bereaved of her sons and daughters, weeping, desolate, and alone (vv. 11-12). With no one to comfort her, she bewails her fate to her neighbors (vv. 9, 14). This motif of

---

Babylon in 4:31-35 may be deliberate, with the intention of making Babylon representative of all the of enemies of Jerusalem.

[4] See Odil Hannes Steck, *Das apokryphe Baruchbuch: Studien zu Rezeption und Konzentration "kanonischer" Überlieferung*, FRLANT 160 (Göttingen: Vandenhoeck & Ruprecht, 1993), 208-9; Ruth Henderson, *Second Temple Songs of Zion: A Literary and Generic Analysis of the Apostrophe to Zion (11QPs^a XXII 1-15); Tobit 13:9-18 and 1 Baruch 4:30-5:9*, DCLS 17 (Berlin: de Gruyter, 2014), 225-27; Géza G. Xeravits, *Take Courage, O Jerusalem: Studies in the Psalms of Baruch 4-5*, DCLS 25 (Berlin: de Gruyter, 2015), 57-60.

[5] Steck, *Das apokryphe Baruchbuch*, 190-93; Henderson, *Second Temple Songs*, 228-30. The extent of this influence has been disputed by Xeravits, *Take Courage, O Jerusalem*, 118-20.

Jerusalem as a widowed mother city, bereaved and weeping for her lost children, is well known from Isa 49:15–19, 51:17–22, 52:1–3, 54:1–11, and particularly Lam 1:12–16, 18b–22, in which Jerusalem is given an extended voice. Here again, however, the author of 1 Baruch has gone beyond his scriptural models. Whereas in the scriptural texts Jerusalem is identified with her children in having sinned against God,[6] in 1 Bar 4:9b–16, Jerusalem appears as innocent, suffering the consequences of her children's behavior.[7]

In the fourth and final section (1 Bar 4:30–5:9), the dominant motif is that of the transformation from Jerusalem's status as a widow grieving for her past destruction and depopulation to the future glorious mother city rejoicing in the return of her children. This motif is to be found in its most developed form in the Zion Songs of Isa 40–66.[8]

Two scholars have drawn particular attention to the development of the biblical motif of Jerusalem in the third section of this composition (1 Bar 4:17–29), where an underlying scriptural model is more difficult to determine. For Luis Alonso Schökel, this development can be seen in the representation of Jerusalem as one who intercedes for her children and advises and exhorts them. He first demonstrated how, in 1 Bar 4, the presentation of Jerusalem as the mother who, alongside the father, has the role of both educating and disciplining the children, in line, for example, with Prov 1:8 and Deut 21:18–24.[9] But, in the representation of Jerusalem as sending her children away in affirmation of their punishment by their father, God (1 Bar 4:11, 23), there is a development of biblical thought. Jerusalem, like the great prophetic intercessors such as Moses, Amos, and Jeremiah, intercedes for her children.[10] In this she also follows the line of biblical female intercessors such as Abigail, Bathsheba for Solomon, the wise woman from Tekoa, Judith, and Esther. In addition to interceding for her children, she exhorts them, again in a manner similar to the prophetic tradition, encouraging them to accept their punishment with patience, humility, and endurance (in line with Jer 27 and 29); to repent and turn back to God (in line with all the prophets, e.g., Zech 1:4); and to hope for restoration and repatriation (in line with Isa 40–66).[11] Thus, Jerusalem is presented not only as a weeping, bereft, widowed mother but also as a

---

[6] See Lam 1:8–9, 17–18, 20; see also Isa 1:21, Jer 32:31–32, Ezek 16; 23.

[7] See Luis Alonso Schökel, "Jerusalén inocente intercede: Baruc 4,9–19," in *Salvación en la Palabra Targum: Derash, Berith; En memoria del profesor Alejandro Díez Macho*, ed. Domingo Muñoz León (Madrid: Cristiandad, 1986), 44–48.

[8] Henderson, *Second Temple Songs*, 243–54; Xeravits, *Take Courage, O Jerusalem*, 79–87.

[9] Alonso Schökel, "Jerusalén inocente intercede," 39–51.

[10] Adams has objected to this view because no words of Jerusalem's intercession to God are given in the text ("Jerusalem's Lament and Consolation," 70). In 1 Bar 4:20, however, the motif of Jerusalem's putting on the sackcloth of petition and continually crying to God clearly indicate her role as intercessor.

[11] Alonso Schökel, "Jerusalén inocente intercede," 42–44.

prophet. According to Alonso Schökel, contrary to the biblical tradition in which Jerusalem is identified with her children in their rebellion against God (see, e.g., Isa 1:21–26; Jer 3:3, 10; 4:30; 13:25–27; 22:20–23; Ezek 16; 20; Lam 1:1, 8, 18; 2:14; 4:16), the author of 1 Bar 4 presents Jerusalem as one who suffers innocently for the sins of her children (4:12–13).[12] In contrast to the biblical depiction of personified Jerusalem, in which she is almost always silent, in 1 Bar 4:19–29 the city speaks at length. Alonso Schökel suggests that the representation of Jerusalem in a prophetic manner reflects a sentiment expressed in Second Temple literature such as Pss. Sol. 74:9 and 1 Macc 14:41, which mention the absence of a "faithful prophet." This role, he suggests, was given to Jerusalem to interpret and explain the exile to her children, advising them how to endure it and kindling their hope of restoration and return.[13]

Nuria Calduch-Benages, while concentrating on the social ramifications of the portrayal of Jerusalem as widow as one without protection or rights, also discusses the characteristics of Jerusalem's innocence and intercession.[14] She first explores the personification of Jerusalem in 1 Bar 4:3–5:9 against the background of the feminization of cities in antiquity and in Scripture. According to Calduch-Benages, the term *widow*, as used by the author of 1 Bar 4, pertains to social status. A widow is "a once married woman who has no means of financial support and who is thus in need of special legal protection."[15] Applied to Jerusalem, the term describes a once-independent city that has become the vassal of another state. Like Alonso Schökel, Calduch-Benages points to the twofold break with biblical tradition in 1 Bar 4, namely, the presentation of Jerusalem as completely innocent, suffering the punishment of the exile for the rebellion of her children (4:12–13), and her activity on behalf of her children in intercession and exhortation/encouragement.[16] Following Alonso Schökel, she concludes that, in this intercession and exhortation, Jerusalem takes on an undeniably prophetic character.

Although the development in the personification of Jerusalem from grieving widow to a prophetic figure who exhorts her children to repentance and encourages them with the hope of future restoration and return has been firmly established by Alonso Schökel and Calduch-Benages, the reasons underlying this development have not been fully investigated.[17]

---

[12] Ibid., 44–48.
[13] Ibid., 44.
[14] Nuria Calduch-Benages, "Jerusalem as Widow (Baruch 4:5–5:9)," in *Biblical Figures in Deuterocanonical and Cognate Literature*, ed. Hermann Lichtenberger, F. V. Reiterer, and Ulrike Mittmann-Richert, DCLY 2008 (Berlin: de Gruyter, 2009), 147–56.
[15] Ibid., 152.
[16] Ibid., 159–62.
[17] See ibid., 162. Calduch-Benages suggests that this aspect requires further investigation.

III. The Composition and Structure of 1 Baruch 4:17–29

The first and second sections of 1 Bar 4 (vv. 5–9a and vv. 9b–16) deal with the past, while the final section (vv. 17–29) is focused on the future. In the third section, however, the author uses the compositional technique of reversal, in which the past is constantly juxtaposed with and contrasted to the future. In this way, the author creates a picture of Jerusalem and her children suspended in the present, in a continuing pendulum of ongoing exile, which swings from remorse over the past to hope for the future.[18]

The section 4:17–29 is marked by a change of audience and tone, as Jerusalem turns from her neighbors, to whom she has been lamenting her distress (4:9–16), and addresses her exiled children with the rhetorical question, "But I, how am I able to help you?" (4:17). The *inclusio* in verses 18 and 29, which contains the words "For he who brought this evil upon you," coupled with a promise of salvation, marks the beginning and end of the section. Within this *inclusio* are two parallel subsections (vv. 19–24//vv. 25–28), each beginning with an imperative addressed by Jerusalem to her children, "Walk, children, walk" (v. 19) and "O children, bear patiently" (v. 25). Each subsection also contains the exhortation "take courage" (with the verb θαρσέω), a motif that characterizes the entire composition (see 4:5, 21, 27, 30), and ends with a comparison, "just as … so" (4:24, 28). This structure is set out in the table below with the English translation adapted from the NETS translation of Alexander A. Di Lella.

Transition	4:17 But I, how am I able to help you?
Inclusio	4:18 For he who brought these evil things upon you will deliver you from the hand of your enemies.
	Stanza 1
Imperative opening to Subsection 1	4:19 Walk, children, walk, for I have been left desolate.
	4:20 I have taken off the robe of peace and put on sackcloth for my petition; I will cry out to the Everlasting in all my days.
	4:21 Take courage, O children; call out to God, and he will deliver you from domination, from the hand of enemies.

---

[18] For the influence of ongoing exile on Second Temple thought, see M. A. Knibb, "The Exile in the Literature of the Intertestamental Period," *HeyJ* 17 (1976): 253–72, http://dx.doi.org/10.1111/j.1468-2265.1976.tb00590.x, and, more recently, Ehud Ben Zvi, "What Is New in Yehud? Some Considerations," in *Yahwism after the Exile: Perspectives on Israelite Religion in the Persian Era; Papers Read at the First Meeting of the European Association for Biblical Studies, Utrecht, 6–9 August 2000*, ed. Rainer Albertz and Bob Becking, STAR 5 (Assen: Van Gorcum, 2003), 34–46.

	4:22 For I have hoped in the Everlasting for your salvation, and joy has come to me from the Holy One because of the mercy that will soon come to you from your everlasting Savior.
	4:23 For I sent you out with mourning and weeping, but God will give you back to me with delight and joy forever.
Comparison—close of Subsection 1	**4:24** For **(just) as** the neighbors of Sion have seen your captivity **now, so** they will quickly see your salvation from God, which will come to you with the great glory and splendor of the Everlasting.
	Stanza 2
Imperative opening to Subsection 2	**4:25** O children, bear patiently the wrath that has come upon you from God. The enemy has pursued you, but you will quickly see their destruction and will tread upon their necks.
	4:26 My pampered children have traveled rough roads; they were taken away like a flock carried off by enemies.
	4:27 Take courage, O children, and call out to God, for there will be mention of you by the one who brought this.
Comparison—close of Subsection 2	**4:28** For **just as** your intention became to go astray from God, **(so)** multiply by ten when you return to seek him.
Inclusio	**4:29** For the one who brought these evil things upon you will bring you everlasting joy with your salvation.

IV. The Prophetic Elements in the Exhortation of Jerusalem in 1 Baruch 4:17–29

Although no clear biblical models can be singled out as underlying 1 Bar 4:17–29, the section is nevertheless infused with prophetic thought, as shown above by Alonso Schökel.[19] There are possible echoes of Zeph 3:15b–17 in 1 Bar 4:18, 19, and of Mic 1:16 in 1 Bar 4:26.[20] The language of the section is also overlaid with echoes of the prophets: the imperative to "have courage," which occurs quite frequently in the later Minor Prophets,[21] and the *inclusio* (4:18, 29), which attributes both the evils of exile and the good of future restoration to God. This motif may echo Jer 32:42 (39:42), although it is common throughout all the prophets. The idea of the glory of Jerusalem in the return of her children to her (1 Bar 4:24) being

---

[19] See pp. 546–47 above; see also Steck, *Das apokryphe Baruchbuch*, 190–93; and Xeravits, *Take Courage, O Jerusalem*, 106–9, 116–18.

[20] Henderson, *Second Temple Songs*, 208–11; Xeravits, *Take Courage, O Jerusalem*, 116–18.

[21] This imperative occurs twice in this section (1 Bar 4:21, 27) and also introduces the first (4:5) and final sections (4:30). It occurs also in the later Minor Prophets such as Joel 2:21–22; Zeph 3:16; Hag 2:5; and Zech 8:13, 15. See Xeravits, *Take Courage, O Jerusalem*, 116.

witnessed by the nations is reminiscent of Isa 60:1–2 and 62:11–12. The imminence of coming salvation for the exiles (1 Bar 4:22, 24) is found in Isa 51:5, 14; 56:8; and Ezek 36:8; the coming judgment on Israel's enemies (1 Bar 4:25) in Isa 13:22; Jer 48:16; Joel 1:15; Zeph 1:7, 14; and God's remembrance of the exiles (1 Bar 4:27) in Jer 31:20. These are not allusions to or echoes of particular prophecies but rather a compendium of prophetic thought on the theme of the restoration and return of Israel from exile, which bears witness to the prophetic corpus as a whole.

Ronald E. Clements demonstrates that 1 Baruch has imposed a unified understanding of the prophetic message on the canonical collection of the prophets, consisting of the three major prophets (Isaiah, Jeremiah, and Ezekiel) and the scroll of the Twelve (the Minor Prophets).[22] Older prophecies of restoration and return from the Babylonian exile have been extended and reinterpreted eschatologically in terms of ultimate salvation at the end of days. A structural sequencing, by which prophecies of hope and salvation have been placed after prophecies threatening doom and destruction, is evident throughout the entire collection. Both types of prophetic oracles are thus held together so that the prophetic corpus as a whole bears evidence of the purpose of God in bringing about both the disciplining and restoration of Israel.[23]

The interpretative patterning of prophecies of destruction followed by prophecies of salvation, which has been editorially imposed on the canonical prophetic corpus as a whole,[24] has been built into the very structure and fabric of 1 Bar 4:17–29. There are numerous references to prophecies of destruction that have found fulfillment in the past and present sufferings of the exile in relation to Israel's enemies and captivity as well as in the people's journey into exile (1 Bar 4:18, 21, 25, 26). These themes, however, are always juxtaposed with the promise of coming salvation.

This principle of duality in seeing both the evils of the past and the promise of coming salvation as part of the total plan of God is clearly laid down in the opening and closing *inclusio*:

> *For he who brought these evil things upon you will deliver you* from the hand of your enemies. (1 Bar 4:18)

> *For the one who brought these evil things upon you will bring you* everlasting joy with your *salvation*. (1 Bar 4:29)

It is also to be found in the comparison that concludes both stanzas:

---

[22] Ronald E. Clements, *Old Testament Prophecy: From Oracles to Canon* (Louisville: Westminster John Knox, 1996), 191–202.

[23] Ibid., 201–2.

[24] Ibid., 197. Clements notes, however, that this process should be seen as a development and extension of the original words of the prophets, who from the outset included words of hope in their prophecies of doom.

For *(just) as* the neighbors of Sion have seen your captivity now, *so* they will quickly see your salvation from God, which will come to you with the great glory and splendor of the Everlasting. (1 Bar 4:24)

For just as your intention became to go astray from God, *(so)* multiply by ten when you return to seek him. (1 Bar 4:28)

Duality forms the dominant element in the thought and fabric of the composition, with continual acknowledgment of the present exile as punishment for past rebellion juxtaposed with an affirmation of hope in an imminent salvation and restoration (1 Bar 4:21, 23, 25, 27).

The sequencing of prophecies of judgment followed by prophecies of hope has also been observed by Jakob Wöhrle in his study of a redaction of the twelve Minor Prophets that he calls the "Foreign Nations Corpus I," which he dates to the fifth–fourth centuries BCE.[25] This redaction, he claims, is further characterized by (1) a recognition of the present distress as the judgment of God on the exiles' own transgression; (2) a sharp distinction between Israel and the foreign nations, who are depicted as having exceeded their mandate as the instruments of God's punishment and who are treated homogeneously as one group; (3) the portrayal of Israel as a unity, whose people collectively bear the punishment of the past and present distress of exile with no differentiation among social groups or between the Jews of Yehud and those of the diaspora; and (4) the presentation of the Lord, who alone can change the present situation and bring salvation to his powerless people.

These features are all to be found in 1 Bar 4:17–29. Although the narrative setting of the book presupposes the Babylonian exile, the restoration and return of the exiles are here given an eschatological orientation. The historical return of the exiles from Babylon in the sixth century BCE has been passed over without mention, and the speaker, Jerusalem, perceives the exile of all Israel as a present and continuing event (1 Bar 4:20, 22, 24–25). She anticipates the hope of salvation as a future, soon-to-be-fulfilled event that will be brought about by God (4:20, 24). The enemy referred to in 4:17–28 is unspecified, represented with the vague designation "enemy" (4:18, 21, 25, 26). The enemy's excessive cruelty is referred to in 4:25 (cf. 4:15, 31–35). Israel is also referred to homogeneously with the term "(my) children" (4:19, 21, 25, 26, 29), with no hint of social distinction among them. Above all, God is continually represented as the One who alone can and will reverse Israel's present situation of distress (4:18, 21, 22, 23, 24, 25, 27, 29).

[25] Jakob Wöhrle, "Israel's Identity and the Threat of the Nations," in *Judah and the Judeans in the Achaemenid Period: Negotiating Identity in an International Context*, ed. Oded Lipschits, Gary N. Knoppers, and Manfred Oeming (Winona Lake, IN: Eisenbrauns, 2011), 153–72. See also Jill Middlemas, "The Shape of Things to Come: Redaction and the Early Second Temple Period Prophetic Tradition," in *Constructs of Prophecy in the Former and Latter Prophets and Other Texts*, ed. Lester L. Grabbe and Martti Nissinen, ANEM 4 (Atlanta: Society of Biblical Literature, 2011), 141–55, esp. 141–43, for a survey of current research on the editorial activity underlying the prophetic corpus.

It would appear, therefore, that Jerusalem's prophetic exhortation is modeled not on any particular prophet or prophecy but on the canonical prophetic corpus as a whole and that the shape and ideology of this corpus in written form were known to the writer of this composition.

V. The Later Development of Biblical Prophecy

In his historical survey of Hebrew prophecy, Joseph Blenkinsopp details a progression in the formation of the classical prophetic corpus from oral poetic utterances of individual prophets, to the writing down of these utterances, to the later collecting, editing, and interpretation of the words of the prophets and their compilation into a complete corpus. This is evident in the way postexilic prophets have reused and eschatologically reinterpreted the prophetic topoi of their eighth-century predecessors.[26] At a later stage, the process of scribal interpretation continued in parabiblical works and the prophetic pesharim from Qumran as well as in apocryphal writings.[27] In 1 Baruch, the author assumes the guise of the scribal prophet Baruch,[28] attributing the entire book to him. In 4:5–9a, the author addresses a "prophecy" to Israel in Baruch's name. What is intriguing is why Baruch, the "scribal prophet" who speaks prophetically to Israel in 1 Bar 4:5–9a and 4:30–5:9 places the prophetic message of 4:17–29 into the mouth of Jerusalem, the widowed mother city.

From a literary point of view, the leap from Jerusalem as widowed mother to Jerusalem as prophet is not so great as may first appear. The literary motif combining the widow with the prophetic word is to be found in the Bible itself and appears in many texts from the Second Temple period. By dint of her marginalized socio-economic position, the widow has the viewpoint of an onlooker who can see the implications of events more clearly than those directly involved in them. Elijah the fugitive prophet is sent to a Sidonian widow who sustains him during the famine. It is she, rather than Israel, who affirms his prophetic status in words that have a prophetic ring: "Now I know that you are a man of God and that the word of the Lord in your mouth is truth" (1 Kgs 17:24). The soon-to-be-widowed Abigail reaffirms the prophecy concerning the future dynastic reign of the house of David

---

[26] Joseph Blenkinsopp, *A History of Prophecy in Israel*, rev. and enl. ed. (Louisville: Westminster John Knox, 1996), 209, 227–39.

[27] See George J. Brooke, "Prophecy and Prophets in the Dead Sea Scrolls: Looking Backwards and Forwards," in *Prophets, Prophecy, and Prophetic Texts in Second Temple Judaism*, ed. Michael J. Floyd and Robert D. Haak, LHBOTS 427 (New York: T&T Clark, 2006), 151–65.

[28] On "scribal prophecy," see Blenkinsopp, *History of Prophecy*, 222–39; and Karel van der Toorn, *Scribal Culture and the Making of the Hebrew Bible* (Cambridge: Harvard University Press, 2007), 252–64.

(1 Sam 25:28–30). In the Apocrypha, the widowed Judith appears in a role similar to that of the prophet Deborah, speaking with prophetic authority of the Lord's deliverance of Israel (Jdt 8:33);[29] like Deborah, she sings a song of deliverance (Jdt 16:1–17).[30] In the pseudepigraphical 4 Ezra 9:38–10:27, the image of Jerusalem as widowed mother who speaks with the mourning Ezra is transformed into the image of the glorious future Jerusalem prophesied by Isaiah. In this transformation, she is presented as a self-fulfilling prophecy. In the New Testament, the pious, widowed Anna speaks in the temple of the child Jesus to those who await the redemption of Jerusalem (Luke 2:36–38).

From a sociohistorical point of view, the presentation of Jerusalem as prophet may reflect a final stage in the authorization of a corpus of sacred writings.[31] From the outset, prophecy was often closely linked to the Jerusalem temple.[32] During the Persian period, this connection strengthened with the reabsorption of prophecy into the cult, as can be seen in the predominance of liturgical forms in the later prophets such as Haggai, Zech 1–8, Isa 56–66, Malachi, and Joel and in the viewpoint of the Chronicler, for whom the composition and performance of liturgical music were a form of prophecy (1 Chr 25:1–8).[33] According to Blenkinsopp, the emergence and consolidation of an authoritative literary corpus of sacred Scripture were products of the historical/social situation of Jerusalem during the Second Temple period, under the dominant influence of a political, social, and religious organization based on the temple and promoted by the ruling Achaemenid power.[34]

Many studies subsequent to the work of Blenkinsopp, from both sociohistorical[35] and scribal perspectives, have focused on the centrality of Jerusalem in the

---

[29] According to Alonso Schökel, the prophetic accents are especially clear in Jdt 8:18 ("Jerusalén inocente intercede," 48 n. 12).

[30] Already in the book of Chronicles we see the conception of liturgy as prophecy (Blenkinsopp, *History of Prophecy*, 225–26).

[31] Although the word *canon* is an anachronism, there is a growing consensus that an authoritative collection of Law and Prophets existed by the second century BCE. See the survey in Stephen B. Chapman, *The Law and the Prophets: A Study in Old Testament Canon Formation*, FAT 27 (Tübingen: Mohr Siebeck, 2000), 170–88.

[32] Blenkinsopp, *History of Prophecy*, 222–23.

[33] Ibid.

[34] Joseph Blenkinsopp, "Temple and Society in Achaemenid Jerusalem," in *Second Temple Studies*, vol. 1, *Persian Period*, ed. Philip R. Davies, JSOTSup 117 (Sheffield: JSOT Press, 1991), 22–53; Blenkinsopp, *Sage, Priest, Prophet: Religious and Intellectual Leadership in Ancient Israel*, LAI (Louisville: Westminster John Knox, 1995), 166–68.

[35] See, e.g., Ehud Ben Zvi, "The Urban Centre of Jerusalem and the Development of the Literature of the Hebrew Bible," in *Urbanism in Antiquity: From Mesopotamia to Crete*, ed. Walter E. Aufrecht, Neil A. Mirau, and Steven W. Gauley, JSOTSup 244 (Sheffield: JSOT Press, 1997), 194–208.

process of collecting, editing, and annotating Scripture,[36] although a wide variety of opinion exists on the dating of the final editing of Scripture.[37]

Beyond this, attention has been drawn to the active role of the Hasmonean dynasty in promoting Jerusalem as the authoritative religious center of faith for the entire diaspora. In order to combat the pervasive influence of Greek langugage and culture, the Hasmoneans promoted the synagogue to establish the teaching of Scripture.[38]

It would appear, therefore, that the striking personification of Jerusalem as prophet in 1 Bar 4:17–29 is a reflection of the historical reality of the world of the author, in which the city and, more particularly, the temple, became the repository for the growing collection of sacred and authoritative Scriptures, which represented the voice of God to the people. Jerusalem, personified as a woman, is regarded by the author as the voice of God to the people. She speaks with the authority of the written scrolls of the Law and Prophets, which have been collected and stored within the city. From this corpus, Jerusalem addresses words of hope, exhortation, and encouragement to her children.

The sacred texts stored in the temple at Jerusalem represented "both symbolically and metaphorically a sense of the divine presence."[39] Just as the city of Jerusalem is presented as the authoritative locus of intercession offered either in her or toward her (1 Kgs 8:31–52, Dan 6:10, 9:17–19, 1 Bar 1:6–13), so also she embodies the entire authoritative prophetic witness to Israel both in Yehud and in the diaspora. In this sense, Jerusalem represents the prophetic voice to her children. At a time when an exilic mentality pervaded the consciousness of Israel,[40] Jerusalem stood as a concrete, living symbol of the veracity of the word of God and a real expectation that would be fulfilled in its time.

---

[36] In his study of the technical aspects of writing and copying scrolls, Emanuel Tov posited Jerusalem as the place in which scrolls were written, deposited, and rewritten ("The Writing of Early Scrolls as the Literary Analysis of the Hebrew Scripture," *DSD* 13 [2006]: 339–47, http://dx.doi.org/10.1163/156851706778884072). His ideas were confirmed and amplified on the basis of parallels in Mesopotamia and Egypt by van der Toorn, *Scribal Culture*, 75–141.

[37] Those who argue for an earlier date in the process of the formation of the Hebrew Scriptures include Chapman (*Law and the Prophets*, 276–92) and William M. Schniedewind (*How the Bible Became a Book: Textualization of Ancient Israel* [Cambridge: Cambridge University Press, 2007], 190–94). Among those who advocate a later view of the textualization of Scripture, Ben Zvi argues that the bulk of biblical literature as we know it is likely to be associated with the Persian II period ("Urban Centre of Jerusalem," 204–6). For a more extreme position, see K. L. Noll, "Did 'Scriptualization' Take Place in Second Temple Judaism?," *SJOT* 25 (2011): 201–16, esp. 208, and see also 203 n. 7 for bibliography, http://dx.doi.org/10.1080/09018328.2011.608541.

[38] Henderson, *Second Temple Songs*, 294–99.

[39] Ben Zvi refers to the prophetic texts and other written works that were composed, redacted, studied, stored, read, and reread in Yehud ("What Is New in Yehud?," 45).

[40] Ibid., 34–45.

VI. Conclusion

In 1 Baruch, the author has, as it were, updated the Zion Songs of Isaiah, viewing them from the perspective of Deuteronomy and the entire prophetic corpus in the light of the present reality of Second Temple Jerusalem. Like many of his contemporaries, the author of 1 Baruch wrestles with the problem of why the vision of Jerusalem's glorious destiny has not yet been fulfilled in the rebuilt Jerusalem of the Second Temple period and with how to understand the role of this present city in the total plan of God.

In response to this disjunction between the biblical ideal and the present reality, we see an imaginative development that goes beyond the biblical sources and reveals a disposition of growing love, veneration, and idealization of the city. Rather than being identified with the sins of her children, as in the biblical prophets, Jerusalem is depicted as pure and innocent, identified as the consort of God and aggrieved, as God is, over the iniquity that has caused her devastation and the exile of her children. She, like them, has suffered the wrath of God, but her suffering is innocent suffering.

In her dual relationship to both God and Israel, Jerusalem is invested with a new authority, on the basis of which she can pray and intercede for her children and exhort and encourage them to endure their punishment and turn back to God. In a concrete form, she represents the hidden face of a God who has withdrawn from Israel. Jerusalem witnesses to the love and compassion that God continues to hold for the people and will show them in response to their turning to God. At the same time, in her unceasing prayer to God for her children, Jerusalem becomes the embodiment of the totality of prayers and petitions of her children offered within or toward her (see 1 Kgs 8:22–53, Dan 6:10).

Thus, Baruch's Jerusalem of the Second Temple period provides a tangible, spatial affirmation that God had not deserted the people but will be faithful to the promises of the divne word. Jerusalem embodies the hope of God's return in response to the continuing prayer and supplication offered in the city and the assurance that to this place all Israel will one day return as a result of an act of divine intervention in their history. Jerusalem has become both a concrete symbol and a voice affirming the validity of her hope as promised in the words of the sacred Scriptures. This conception of Jerusalem, which spans the past in the destroyed Jerusalem of the First Temple, the present in the reality of the Jerusalem of the Second Temple, and the future in the vision of the glorious Jerusalem yet to come, perhaps represents the most multifaceted, comprehensive, and original description of its kind to be found in biblical and postbiblical literature.

It is remarkable that this conception of Jerusalem became so fixed and enduring in the memory of the Jewish people that it outlived the destruction of the city and the Second Temple to become a cornerstone of Jewish faith and practice. In

4 Ezra and 2 Baruch, the vision of a restored Jerusalem provides the basis for the consolation and hope of Israel after the destruction of the city.[41] Prayers for the restoration of Zion and the regathering of the people of Israel to their land form a central motif in the prayers of the Jewish prayer book (Siddur) and in the piyyutim. The way in which the significance of Zion/Jerusalem was developed and continued to function in Judaism after the destruction of the Second Temple in 70 CE would be worthy of further investigation.

---

[41] See George W. E. Nickelsburg, *Jewish Literature between the Bible and the Mishnah: A Historical and Literary Introduction,* 2nd ed. (Minneapolis: Fortress, 2005), 270–83.

Semitic Poetic Techniques in the Magnificat: Luke 1:46–47, 55

HUGO MÉNDEZ
hmendez@email.unc.edu
University of North Carolina at Chapel Hill, Chapel Hill, NC 27599

Two peculiar alternations of grammatical form appear in the Magnificat: a tense shift in verses 46b–47 and an alternation of object constructions in verse 55. Though most studies treat these phenomena as outlying examples of Greek usage, a better explanation is found in the marked language character of the canticle itself. A previous study by Randall Buth (1984) has argued that the tense shift in verses 46b–47 reflects a common Semitic poetic device. I defend that analysis and extend it to verse 55, identifying the preposition/case shift there as a second stylistic grammatical alternation in the canticle, specifically: an instance of reversed ballast prepositions. The presence of these devices in the Magnificat demonstrates that its poet possessed an interior grasp of the conventions of Semitic poetry and could execute a hymn in that tradition with skill. Furthermore, with the goal of supplementing inventories of the Magnificat's poetic features, I undertake a literary and linguistic analysis of both devices, giving particular attention to the negotiation of likeness and unlikeness in parallelisms, ambiguity as a vehicle of poetic expression, and the impact of these devices in a Greek presentation.

The Magnificat (Luke 1:46b–55) imitates the form and content of various biblical psalms and odes, including the Song of Hannah (1 Sam 2:1–10). But to what extent does it show flashes of its own poetic sophistication? How convincing is the pastiche? In this article, I will address these questions through the lens of two grammatical peculiarities in the hymn that are generally dismissed as nonstandard Greek usage. The first aligns two verbs in a synonymous parallelism but sets them in diffferent tenses (vv. 46b–47). The second references the same object through two different object constructions (v. 55).

An earlier study has already argued that the first alternation finds a background in Hebrew poetry.[1] In this article I will elaborate on this thesis and discuss

---

[1] Randall Buth, "Hebrew Poetic Tenses and the Magnificat," *JSNT* 21 (1984): 67–83, http://dx.doi.org/10.1177/0142064X8400602104.

the literary merits of this technique in the broader hymn. In turn, I will apply a poetic analysis to the second construction as well. I believe the two anomalies are comparable and can be classed together as stylistic or nonsemantic grammatical alternations. This category of poetic devices is amply attested in the Hebrew Bible and evidently plays a vital role in the marked language of this hymn as well. When one adds these techniques to the inventories of the hymn's poetic features, the skill of its poet stands out in stronger relief.[2]

I. Tense Alternation (Luke 1:46b–47)

A. Analysis of the Greek

In the opening couplet of the Magnificat, a present-tense verb (μεγαλύνει, "magnifies," v. 46b) stands opposite an aorist (ἠγαλλίασεν, "rejoiced," v. 47) in a synonymous parallelism:

Luke 1:46b–47
Μεγαλύνει ἡ ψυχή μου τὸν κύριον,   (pres. act. indic. 3rd sg.)
καὶ ἠγαλλίασεν τὸ πνεῦμά μου   (aor. act.[3] indic. 3rd sg.)
ἐπὶ τῷ θεῷ τῷ σωτῆρί μου

My soul magnifies the Lord,
 and my spirit rejoiced in God my savior.

The juxtaposition of these tenses has attracted considerable attention in secondary literature. Since for most interpreters, the immediate occasion of Mary's song justifies the present tense of μεγαλύνει, those treatments focus almost exclusively on the choice of an aorist form in verse 47.

Interpretations of the Aorist in Verse 47

One set of approaches identifies ἠγαλλίασεν with one of several non-past uses of the aorist. BDF, for instance, identifies ἠγαλλίασεν as a gnomic aorist.[4] This type,

---

[2] A partial catalog of the Magnificat's poetic features, neglecting the devices considered in this article, appears in Robert C. Tannehill, "The Magnificat as Poem," *JBL* 93 (1974): 263–75, http://dx.doi.org/10.2307/3263096.

[3] Notably, ἠγαλλίασεν appears in the active voice, rather than in its more common middle form. It is possible that this choice allows ἠγαλλίασεν more readily to parallel μεγαλύνει (Stephen Farris, *The Hymns of Luke's Infancy Narratives: Their Origin, Meaning and Significance*, JSNTSup 9 [Sheffield: JSOT Press, 1985], 186). The verb ἀγαλλιάω is used only one other time in Luke's Gospel, there in the middle voice with reference to Jesus's rejoicing in the Spirit (Luke 10:21). First Peter 1:8 and Rev 19:7 represent the only other active instances of the verb in the New Testament.

[4] BDF §333.2; see also Joseph A. Fitzmyer, *The Gospel according to Luke I–IX: Introduction, Translation, and Notes*, AB 28A (Garden City, NY: Doubleday, 1981), 366; John T. Carroll, *Luke: A Commentary*, NTL (Louisville: Westminster John Knox, 2012), 48.

rare in Hellenistic Greek, is associated with aphorisms and statements of general fact. Since the motive clauses following this couplet identify Mary's rejoicing as a reaction to particular events of her recent experience (vv. 48–49), however, a gnomic sense is unlikely in this instance. It is still less likely when one compares ἠγαλλίασεν to the true gnomics in verses 51–53.[5] The aorist in verse 47 differs considerably from these verbs, which include "features of proverbial statement, such as nouns with generic articles, indefinite noun or pronoun reference," and an eye toward "universal occurrences of the event."[6]

An alternative explanation would identify ἠγαλλίασεν as one of the few New Testament examples of a dramatic aorist, or an "aorist of present state."[7] A dramatic aorist here would represent a Hebraism, capturing qualities of the stative perfect (a type emphasizing a present condition resulting from a past, completed action).[8] The LXX translates some 47 percent of Hebrew perfects with a present or future value as aorists.[9] Four such verbs appear in the first line of the Song of Hannah, an obvious template for the phrasing of Luke 1:46b–47:[10]

1 Sam [LXX 1 Kgdms] 2:1
Ἐστερεώθη ἡ καρδία μου ἐν κυρίῳ   (aor. pass. indic. 3rd sg.)
ὑψώθη κέρας μου ἐν θεῷ μου   (aor. pass. indic. 3rd sg.)
ἐπλατύνθη ἐπὶ ἐχθροὺς τὸ στόμα μου   (aor. pass. indic. 3rd sg.)
εὐφράνθην ἐν σωτηρίᾳ σου   (aor. pass. indic. 1st sg.)

---

[5] On the gnomic character of the aorists in vv. 51–53, see Max Zerwick, *Biblical Greek: Illustrated by Examples*, SPIB 114 (Rome: Pontificio Istituto Biblico, 1963), §256.

[6] Buist M. Fanning, *Verbal Aspect in New Testament Greek*, OTM (Oxford: Clarendon, 1990), 266, 279–80.

[7] Ibid., 278–80; Daniel B. Wallace, *Greek Grammar beyond the Basics: An Exegetical Syntax of the New Testament* (Grand Rapids: Zondervan, 1996), 565.

[8] Fanning, *Verbal Aspect*, 276–79; see also Matthew Black, *An Aramaic Approach to the Gospels and Acts*, 2nd ed. (Oxford: Clarendon, 1967), 129.

[9] Steven Thompson, *The Apocalypse and Semitic Syntax*, SNTSMS 52 (Cambridge: Cambridge University Press, 2005), 37–40. Insofar as the original language of the Magnificat is still an open question, it is best to avoid models that absolutely require a Hebrew original for the hymn. On this ground, Fitzmyer discounts the related proposal that the aorist in v. 47 renders an original Hebrew perfect + *vav*-consecutive (*Luke I–IX*, 366; against Zerwick, *Biblical Greek*, §260; Heinz Schürmann, *Das Lukasevangelium*, 2 vols., HThKNT 3 [Freiburg: Herder, 1982], 1:73 n. 216; Paul Joüon and T. Muraoka, *A Grammar of Biblical Hebrew*, rev. ed., SubBi 27 [Rome: Pontificio Istituto Biblico, 2006], §118r; I. Howard Marshall, *The Gospel of Luke*, NIGTC [Grand Rapids: Eerdmans, 1978], 82), and related explanations (fem. jussive: Hans Klein, *Das Lukasevangelium*, KEK 1.3 [Göttingen: Vandenhoeck & Ruprecht, 2006], 105, 114–15; fem. part.: Ulrike Mittmann-Richert, *Magnifikat und Benediktus: Die ältesten Zeugnisse der judenchristlichen Tradition von der Geburt des Messias*, WUNT 2/90 [Tübingen: Mohr Siebeck, 1996], 107–8).

[10] Three other possible models for Luke 1:46–47 employ Hebrew imperfects. The LXX translates these as futures: LXX Ps 68:31: μεγαλυνῶ αὐτόν; LXX Ps 35:9: ἡ δὲ ψυχή μου ἀγαλλιάσεται ἐπὶ τῷ κυρίῳ; LXX Hab 3:18: ἐγὼ δὲ ἐν τῷ κυρίῳ ἀγαλλιάσομαι χαρήσομαι ἐπὶ τῷ θεῷ τῷ σωτῆρί μου.

> My heart has been made to exult in the Lord.
> My horn has been exalted in my God.
> My mouth has been enlarged against my enemies,
> Because I have been gladdened in your salvation.

Although this comparison provides a compelling explanation for the aorist form in verse 47, it ignores the fundamental difficulty of verses 46b–47, namely, the shift in tense. Why does the poet[11] of the Magnificat use a different tense in each line? Why not render both verbs as dramatic aorists, especially with 1 Sam 2:1 as a model? In effect, this explanation exchanges one problem for another, illuminating the aorist at the expense of understanding the straightforward use of a present in verse 46b. By taking too narrow an interest in one verb, the explanation loses sight of the organic unity of verses 46b and 47.

Another set of inteptretations avoids this error, arguing that the shift in tense is a means of contrasting the two verbs. Certainly, the aorist does not indicate a strictly past experience of rejoicing vis-à-vis the present act of praise; the entire hymn carries a joyful tone.[12] On the one hand, the aorist may denote "a past so recent as to be directly contiguous with the present";[13] that is, it may carry an anterior sense. Alternatively, the aorist may carry a distinctly ingressive value vis-à-vis the present verb, highlighting Mary's past entrance into her current state of rejoicing.[14] In both readings, the choice of the aorist introduces a past event as the basis of Mary's rejoicing: the annunciation. Mary engages in an act of praise in the present but continues to "rejoice" in, and after, the recent message of the angel (vv. 26–38).[15]

This approach certainly has its merits. Like the Hebrew stative perfects in 1 Sam 2:1 (and, by extension, the Greek aorists that translate them), the aorist in verse 47 has some view toward a past event. This is apparent not only from the narrative context of the canticle but also from the formal similarity of the aorist in verse 47 with the aorists in verses 48a, 49a, both of which share a definite past reference: Mary's election and miraculous conception (cf. the aorist in v. 45). But is past reference really a point of contrast between ἠγαλλίασεν and μεγαλύνει? Is

---

[11] I refer to the author of this text merely as "the poet," taking no stance on whether a particular community, individual, or editor (e.g., Luke himself) stands behind the final form of the hymn. An excellent survey of continuing debate surrounding the authorship and original language of the Lukan infancy hymns can be found in Farris, *Hymns of Luke's Infancy Narratives*, 31–66.

[12] François Bovon, *Luke 1: A Commentary on the Gospel of Luke 1:1–9:50*, trans. Christine M. Thomas, Hermeneia (Minneapolis: Fortress, 2002), 60.

[13] Jared S. Klein, "On the Independence of Gothic Syntax I: Interrogativity, Complex Sentence Types, Tense, Mood, and Diathesis," *JIES* 20 (1992): 368.

[14] Raymond E. Brown, *The Birth of the Messiah: A Commentary on the Infancy Narratives in the Gospels of Matthew and Luke*, ABRL (New York: Doubleday, 1993), 336; John Nolland, *Luke 1–9:20*, WBC 35A (Dallas: Word, 1990), 69.

[15] Kindalee Pfremmer De Long, *Surprised by God: Praise Responses in the Narrative of Luke-Acts*, BZNW 166 (Berlin: de Gruyter, 2009), 146.

Mary's attitude of praise not also rooted in the same past event as her rejoicing?[16] Given the synonymous force of the parallelism, Joseph Fitzmyer concludes that the verbs function in precisely the same manner.[17] I agree.

A Nonsemantic Tense Shift

Nonsemantic aspect/tense shifting within synonymous parallelisms is a well-documented feature of Hebrew, Ugaritic, and Akkadian poetry, still attested through the end of the Second Temple period.[18] The Psalms, for instance, contain dozens of examples of this device:

Ps 38:12

אהבי ורעי מנגד נגעי יעמדו   (*qal* impf. 3rd pl.)
וקרובי מרחק עמדו: (*qal* pf. 3rd pl.)

My loved ones and friends stand far from my plague,
 And my kinsmen stand far off.

Ps 46:10

קשת ישבר   (*piel* impf. 3rd sg.)
וקצץ חנית   (*piel* pf. 3rd sg.)
עגלות ישרף באש   (*qal* impf. 3rd sg.)

---

[16] This problem cuts both ways. Brown, Bovon, and Hans Klein focus on the peculiarity of the aorist (see nn. 11-13 above). But if the LXX of 1 Sam 2:1 (with its string of dramatic aorists) shapes Luke 1:46b-47, which seems likely, the most peculiar feature of the latter may be its present-tense verb. This form certainly stands out in a canticle relying almost exclusively on dramatic and gnomic aorists. Again, it makes little sense to dissociate Mary's attitude of praise from God's recent intervention in her life.

[17] Fitzmyer, *Luke I-IX*, 366; also Farris, *Hymns of Luke's Infancy Narratives*, 117-18.

[18] Adele Berlin, *The Dynamics of Biblical Parallelism* (Bloomington: Indiana University Press, 1985), 35-36; James L. Kugel, *The Idea of Biblical Poetry: Parallelism and Its History* (New Haven: Yale University Press, 1981), 17-19; Mitchell Dahood, *Psalms: Introduction, Translation, and Notes*, 3 vols., AB 16-17A (Garden City, NY: Doubleday, 1966-1970), 3:420-23; see also Moshe Held, "The YQTL-QTL (QTL-YQTL) Sequence of Identical Verbs in Biblical Hebrew and in Ugaritic," in *Studies and Essays in Honor of Abraham A. Neuman, President, Dropsie College for Hebrew and Cognate Learning*, ed. Meir Ben-Horin, Bernard D. Weinryb, and Solomon Zeitlin (Leiden: Brill, 1962), 281-90; Umberto Cassuto, *Biblical and Canaanite Literatures* [in Hebrew], 2 vols. (Jerusalem: Magnes, 1972-1979), 2:57-58. For instances of the device in Qumranic hymns, see Buth, "Hebrew Poetic Tenses," 71-73.

Throughout this study, I use "aspect/tense" for Semitic languages, and "tense" for New Testament Greek, where aspect has largely disappeared. For an introduction to Hebrew forms and aspect, see discussion and sources cited in Joüon and Muraoka, *Grammar of Biblical Hebrew*, §§111-13; IBHS, 346-47; Bill T. Arnold and John H. Choi, *A Guide to Biblical Hebrew Syntax* (Cambridge: Cambridge University Press, 2003), 36-37, 53-60. An introduction to the problem of aspect in New Testament Greek appears in D. A. Carson, "An Introduction to the Porter/Fanning Debate," in *Biblical Greek Language and Linguistics: Open Questions in Current Research*, ed. Stanley E. Porter and D. A. Carson, JSNTSup 80 (Sheffield: JSOT Press, 1993) 18-25.

The bow he has broken,
  And he has snapped the spear,
  And the shield he burns up in fire.

In these texts, the juxtaposition of Hebrew perfect (*qtl*) and imperfect (*yqtl*) verbs represents a form of grammatical parallelism that "occurs not for semantic reasons (it does not indicate a real temporal sequence) but for what have been considered stylistic reasons,"[19] that is, a desire for "poetic beauty and embellishment."[20] The translators of the LXX were sensitive to the nonsemantic character of these shifts, at times freely leveling these forms.[21] In Isa 60:16, for instance, recognizing the nonsemantic character of the shift, the Greek does not capture the aspect/tense distinction of the Hebrew text:

Isa 60:16

וְיָנַקְתְּ חֲלֵב גּוֹיִם   (*qal* pf. 3rd sg.)
וְשֹׁד מְלָכִים תִּינָקִי   (*qal* impf. 3rd sg.)

You have sucked the milk of nations,
  And the breasts of royalty you will suck.

LXX Isa 60:16
καὶ θηλάσεις γάλα ἐθνῶν   (fut. act. indic. = *qal* pf.)
καὶ πλοῦτον βασιλέων φάγεσαι   (fut. act. indic. = *qal* impf.)

Notably, verses 46b–47 juxtapose those tenses that characteristically translate the Hebrew *qtl* and *yqtl* in the LXX: the aorist and present, respectively. On this basis, Randall Buth suggests that the tense shift in Luke 1:46b–47 is a stylistic grammatical alternation in the Semitic tradition—an assessment with which I concur.[22] Of all the interpretations canvassed above, only this one finds a precedent for the tense shift in an identical context: Semitic-style poetic parallelisms. It is, in fact, precisely the character of verses 46b–47 as a synonymous parallelism that marks the tense shift as peculiar. For this reason, Stanley Porter is too optimistic when he seeks parallels for the phenomenon in Hellenistic Greek poetry, cautioning that Luke's use of the device may not necessarily represent a Semitic influence, "although

---

[19] Berlin, *Dynamics of Biblical Parallelism*, 35–36.

[20] Buth, "Hebrew Poetic Tenses," 67, 69.

[21] Ibid., 68–70. Wrongly assuming that all tense alternations in the Hebrew Bible are leveled in the LXX, Buth concludes that vv. 46b–47 must represent the translation of an underlying Hebrew source. Richard J. Dillon, however, catalogs numerous examples of such alternations appearing on the surface of the LXX Greek text (*The Hymns of Saint Luke: Lyricism and Narrative Strategy in Luke 1–2*, CBQMS 50 [Washington, DC: Catholic Biblical Association of America, 2013], 22 n. 21).

[22] Buth, "Hebrew Poetic Tenses," 67–83.

Semitic enhancement on the basis of a Semitic source may remain a possibility."[23] Porter finds unusual tense shifts in Hellenistic Greek poetry, but none arranged across synonymous parallelisms as in Luke 1:46b–47. The Lukan hymn is pervasively shaped by the known inventory of Hebrew forms, expressions, and devices. It stands to reason that this particular peculiarity of that hymn would also find its origin in that inventory.

B. Purpose

Of course, to conclude that the tense shift in verses 46b–47 is "stylistic," as Buth has done, still leaves a great deal unsaid. What motivates this form of "style"? Why does it occur precisely here in the hymn? In what ways does it support the poetic character of the entire canticle? These questions must be addressed if we will construct a descriptive inventory of the Magnificat's poetic features and understand any related phenomena (i.e, other stylistic alternations) in the hymn.

On the one hand, this task is made easier by the sheer number of aspect/tense alternations in Hebrew and Ugaritic poetry. The Psalms alone contain dozens of parallels against which we can compare the function of the device. Because the Lukan hymn is a Greek text, however, we must approach these parallels with a certain degree of caution. One cannot expect that a device developed within a Semitic framework will function identically within the parameters of the Indo-European verb. If this disclaimer warns us against drawing quick equivalences, however, it also invites us to deep and extended reflection. It is, after all, precisely the distance between the verbal systems of Hebrew and Greek that make a study of the μεγαλύνει–ἠγαλλίασεν pair so attractive. In Luke 1:46b–47, we are given a rare glimpse of how a Semitic language poetic device might operate within the parameters of Greek tense and, in turn, of the impression that device might have made on a Greek-speaking audience.

Variety

Perhaps the most apparent consequence of tense alternation is the introduction of variety in the couplet. Whereas a version of the text with no tense alternation is characterized by uniformity, a version of the text with tense alternation has an additional layer of diversity:

---

[23] Stanley E. Porter, *Verbal Aspect in the Greek of the New Testament, with Reference to Tense and Mood*, Studies in Biblical Greek 1 (New York: Lang, 1989), 131–32. Porter's endorsement of these Greek parallels but openness to "Semitic enhancement on the basis of a Semitic source" leaves a weak impression. It strikes me as an admission that the features of vv. 46b–47 cannot be fully understood on the basis of Hellenistic poetry.

Without tense alternation (possible):
My soul <u>magnifies</u> the Lord / (pres.)
and my spirit <u>rejoices</u> in God my savior. (pres.)

With tense alternation:
My soul <u>magnifies</u> the Lord / (pres.)
and my spirit <u>rejoiced</u> in God my savior. (aor.)

According to Wilfred G. E. Watson, instances of minor variety supplement the phenomenon of parallelism in significant ways. The genius of parallelism is its forging of a middle way between pure repetition and total dissimilarity, constantly resisting the extremes of one or another approach.[24] By means of tense alternations, the poet peels away at repetition, introducing elements of unlikeness into the text. If two verbs are too similar or interrelated semantically, they can be distanced in grammatical form. The biblical poet negotiates between the uninteresting (repetition) and the prosaic (dissimilarity), finding a balanced and interesting mean of expression.

In this light, it should come as no surprise that the Magnificat's only tense alternation appears in its most complex but congruent parallelism. Each line of the couplet observes a verb–subject–object word order, aligning the positions of the two verbs. Following these verbs is a pair of complementary synecdochic expressions replacing a first person singular subject (ἡ ψυχή μου || τὸ πνεῦμά μου).[25] These noun phrases are even constructed identically, with a nominative article, a nominative noun, and a first person singular possessive pronoun. Finally, each line concludes with an object phrase referencing God (τὸν κύριον || ἐπὶ τῷ θεῷ τῷ σωτῆρί μου). It is precisely in this parallelism that the poet fears an excess of identical elements.[26] He or she embeds what amounts to an antithetical grammatical parallelism within the synonymous parallelism. The impression is made all the more striking by the introduction of this discord to the clause-initial verbs in particular.

This analysis is not without its critics, however. In his treatment of the device in the Hebrew, James L. Kugel denies that the tense alternations are designed to supply variety. He observes that alternating verbs are often "very distinct and not even conventional pairs."[27] Since such verbs already manifest variety on the lexical level, he claims, "something closer to completion" seems to be supplied by tense

---

[24] Wilfred G. E. Watson, *Traditional Techniques in Classical Hebrew Verse*, JSOTSup 170 (Sheffield: JSOT Press, 1994), 45.

[25] Marshall, *Gospel of Luke*, 82.

[26] Artful repetition is not mere duplication but something more like reverberation. Readers encounter the content of v. 46b only once but are meant to recall it, feel it, throughout the second line. The poet must put distance between the two lines to achieve the desired effect. In this light, we can conceptualize the second colon as an interaction of (1) the text itself, which is always a novel statement, and (2) the reader's recollection of the preceding line. The poet gently draws out what now exists in the readers' memories—a craft of subtlety and suggestion.

[27] Kugel, *Idea of Biblical Poetry*, 19.

alternation, namely, "the integration of A and B into a single whole."[28] No doubt, certain instances of the device reinforce a semantic impression of "completion" in couplets (i.e., not only A but B as well). Still, completion presupposes complementarity and, by extension, variety. An insistence on completion in all cases also overlooks occasions in which the device occurs within tricola or at the beginning or middle of series of parallel couplets (see Ps 110:5–7 for both situations). These instances cannot be reduced to a mere relation of A and B elements. Finally, Kugel seems to overstate the unlikeness of lexically distinct verbs in parallelisms. His claim that variation "should operate … on the level of *lexis*"[29] fails to appreciate the possibility that, in parallelisms, lexical variation may not be enough. Parallelisms exist precisely to highlight a semantic relationship between two actions. Although the actions "to magnify" and "to rejoice" may not be synonymous, or even conventional complementary pairs, they are logically interrelated. One can express joy through praise (Luke 10:21), which is precisely why these verbs are aligned in the parallelism before us. The poet reacts against semantic relation of any kind when introducing grammatical discord—not only repetition.

Variety as Complementarity

One dimension of the Semitic device as a source of variety does not transfer well into Greek. Hebrew and Ugaritic recognize only a binary opposition of aspect/tense in finite verbs. Accordingly, an alternation of *qtl* and *yqtl* exhausts all possible forms in this category. A definite impression of grammatical wholeness can emerge in couplets containing the device. Greek, however, boasts eight tenses, three of which are represented in the canticle (aorist, present, future). Among so many options, a distinction between aorist and present cannot register as a simple $X:X^1$ opposition. In Luke 1:46b–47, the alternation introduces variety but not grammatical complementarity. There has been loss in the Greek transmission or imitation of the device.

Ambiguity

From the perspective of the reader, the tense alternation is no mere instance of variety. It is a difficulty, a peculiarity. Consider for a moment the reader's real-time encounter with the phenomenon. As I noted earlier, the present tense of verse 46b appears to be straightforward at first glance, suiting the immediate occasion of Mary's song. Only the second verb, the unexpected aorist, raises a red flag. The reader's first inclination is to read the verb as a straightforward past. Unlike Hebrew, Greek boasts an unambiguous "tense" category that situates events precisely in time. The logical interrelatedness of praise and rejoicing and the impression of the parallelism as a unity, however, cause the reader to second-guess that

[28] Ibid., 17.
[29] Ibid., 23.

first instinct. The tense alternation creates tension and ambiguity in the reading. The reader can either proceed to the next line or linger on these lines to clarify the temporal sphere of each verb. That lingering, that pause, is key.

Ambiguity is a well-documented facet of poetry, famously explored by William Empson. According to Empson, ambiguity fosters "indecision" in the reader with respect to meaning, forcing the reader "to consider ... relations for himself," and "invent" them as necessary.[30] Apparently, tense alternation fosters this very response. This analysis is widely overlooked in studies of the Hebrew device because alternation occurs so frequently in that literature as to seem routine or familiar. After encountering so many dozen examples in the Psalms, any impression of difficulty or confusion is reduced to a minimum, if not eliminated altogether. One learns to suspend judgments of aspect/tense in the poetic texts.[31] A Greek audience, on the other hand, cannot but be struck by the device. Studied in this isolated instance, the raw potential for tense alternation to create ambiguity shines through.

Unspecific Temporal Reference

Poetic ambiguity does not always exist for its own sake. As Empson observes, one of its uses is to imbue a statement with several meanings at once.[32] The confusion and indecision of the reader call attention to more than one deliberate sense of the text. It is in this light that we might understand the alternation of tenses in particular. At least two studies have suggested that aspect/tense alternations can signal "temporally inclusive" values in Hebrew; that is, the juxtaposition of two forms may indicate a "both/and" time reference relative to the characteristic values of these forms, rather than a "neither/nor" or "either/or."[33] Mitchell Dahood catalogs nineteen *qtl*//*yqtl* and *yqtl*//*qtl* alternations in the Psalms with ostensibly present or future reference. By my count, at least twelve of his examples (63 percent) have a more generalized scope than a simple present or future, whether gnomic, customary, iterative, or other (Pss 4:3; 46:4, 9; 50:19; 56:1; 63:6; 83:2; 102:14; 138:4; 139:5; 140:2; 146:4). Added to this number are a few that Dahood identifies as past, including Ps 26:4, which aptly illustrates this type:[34]

---

[30] William Empson, *Seven Types of Ambiguity*, 2nd rev. ed. (New York: New Directions, 1947), 5, 25.

[31] "Prose and poetry should be treated separately as O.T. scholars usually do, despite the difficulty of always making sharp distinction in practice between prose and poetry.... Poetry might have an atemporal nature, and it could be suspected that the time aspect ("tense") fully depends on context" (Yoshinobu Endō, *The Verbal System of Classical Hebrew in the Joseph Story: An Approach from Discourse Analysis*, SSN 32 [Assen: Van Gorcum, 1996], 30).

[32] Empson, *Seven Types of Ambiguity*, 5–6. This point is elaborated in subsequent chapters.

[33] John A. Cook, "The Biblical Hebrew Verbal System" (PhD diss., University of Wisconsin–Madison, 2002), 221–22; Randall J. Buth, "The Taxonomy and Function of Hebrew Tense-Shifting in the Psalms (qatal-yiqtal-yiqtal-qatal, Antithetical Grammatical Parallelism)," *Selected Technical Articles Related to Translation* 15 (1986): 31.

[34] See also Pss 20:6, 111:5, 131:1. For an example outside the Psalms, see Prov 11:7.

Ps 26:4

לֹא־יָשַׁ֥בְתִּי עִם־מְתֵי־שָׁ֑וְא   (*qal* pf. 1st sg.)
וְעִם נַעֲלָמִ֗ים לֹ֣א אָבֽוֹא   (*qal* impf. 1st sg.)

I have not sat with scoundrels,
And I do not go in with hypocrites.

An alternation in the above text works especially well since that text contains a general or customary statement—one as interested in past affairs as in continuing affairs. In both lines, the psalmist means to affirm that he has not done X in the past (a sense consistent with the *qtl*), nor does he currently (a sense ordinarily captured by the *yqtl*). Although tense alternations do appear in statements with a definite temporal reference,[35] there is something natural about utilizing this device in contexts where neither of two grammatical forms is inappropriate, that is, in a "primary area of semantic or functional overlap" between inflectional categories.[36] In those instances, one can arbitrarily apply grammatical forms without significant violence to the sense of the text.

In this light, consider again three of the interpretations of the aorist discussed in the last section: gnomic, anterior, and ingressive. All three interpretations agree that ἠγαλλίασεν is past, though not exclusively past. Phrased a different way, all seem to share an underlying suspicion that the verb ἠγαλλίασεν participates in more than one temporal sphere. This suspicion may not be inaccurate. The nonsemantic character of the tense shift does not demand that both verbs exist in only one time. That is, there is no need to suggest that both are present and that ἠγαλλίασεν is only a present verb under a different guise in verse 47. As I noted above, both Mary's praise and her rejoicing are rooted in the annunciation, and both are certainly present realities. In fact, one loses little of the force of this couplet if one interchanges the tenses of the two verbs: "My soul has magnified (aorist) the Lord, / and my spirit rejoices (present) in God my savior." These tense choices are at least as justifiable as the ones in our text. Indeed, an aorist verb in the first line would match the aorist used in the opening line of the LXX Song of Hannah: ἐστερεώθη ἡ καρδία μου ἐν κυρίῳ ("my heart has been made to exult in the Lord"; 1 Sam 2:1). In this light, it seems only too appropriate that the couplet juxtaposes past and present tense forms and only arbitrarily or casually assigns these tenses to one or another verb. The two verbs transcend a particular time category (i.e., they are inclusive, generalized, or unspecific to some extent) and overlap in time reference.

To a certain extent, one appreciates the inclusive or unspecific character of these verbs through the tense alternation. Consider renderings of verses 46b–47 that use a consistent tense throughout:

---

[35] Numerous examples are included in Dahood's inventory of verb form alternations (Dahood, *Psalms*, 3:420–23).

[36] This is Cook's characterization of the gnomic sense ("Biblical Hebrew Verbal System," 220). He suggests that "in the majority of instances [of Hebrew aspect/tense alternation] both the *qatal* and *yiqtol* forms have a present gnomic sense" (pp. 220–21).

	past
[+ past]	
My soul <u>magnified</u> the Lord,	(+)
And my spirit <u>rejoiced</u> in God my savior.	(+)
[- past]	
My soul <u>magnifies</u> the Lord,	(-)
And my spirit <u>rejoices</u> in God my savior.	(-)

Using a consistent tense obscures the participation of the verbs in more than one time category. As pasts, the verbs seem exclusively past; as presents, they appear to be exclusively present. There is little room for nuance or breadth in these verbs. If not for the stylistic tense alternation, we might not be attuned to the inclusive semantics of the verbs.

II. Alternation of Object Constructions (Luke 1:55)

A. Analysis of the Greek

The second syntactic peculiarity in the canticle appears in its final bicolon (v. 55). This peculiarity represents a device analogous to the tense shift in verses 46b–47—one designed to produce similar effects, including variety and ambiguity:

Luke 1:54–55
ἀντελάβετο Ἰσραὴλ παιδὸς αὐτοῦ,
  μνησθῆναι ἐλέους,
καθὼς ἐλάλησεν <u>πρὸς τοὺς πατέρας ἡμῶν</u>,
  <u>τῷ Ἀβραὰμ καὶ τῷ σπέρματι</u> αὐτοῦ εἰς τὸν αἰῶνα.

He has helped his servant Israel,
  in remembrance of his mercy,
according to the promise he made to our ancestors,
  to Abraham and to his descendants forever.

A complex dative noun phrase introduces the final line of these verses (v. 55b). Unfortunately, it is unclear which preceding verb—μνησθῆναι ("to remember," v. 54b) or ἐλάλησεν ("to speak," v. 55a)—governs the phrase. If μνησθῆναι governs it, verses 54b, 55b represent a single complete thought ("to remember [his] mercy … to Abraham and to his seed"), and verse 54a ("as he spoke to our fathers"), a parenthetical statement.[37] This reading finds a parallel in Mic 7:20b, an apparent model for the text, which treats the promise to the fathers as a distinct notion from the extension of covenant "mercy" to Abraham:[38]

---

[37] Nolland, *Luke 1–9:20*, 73; Marshall, *Gospel of Luke*, 85; Mittmann-Richert, *Magnifikat und Benediktus*, 16; Carroll, *Luke*, 48; Klein, *Das Lukasevangelium*, 105, 114–15; see also RV, NEB, NIV.

[38] For "mercy" as a metonym for "covenant," see LXX Ps 104:8 (MT Ps 105:8); LXX Ps 110:5

LXX Mic 7:20
δώσεις ἀλήθειαν τῷ Ιακωβ
ἔλεον τῷ Αβρααμ
καθότι ὤμοσας τοῖς πατράσιν ἡμῶν
κατὰ τὰς ἡμέρας τὰς ἔμπροσθεν

You will give truth to Jacob,
   mercy to Abraham,
As you promised our fathers,
   from former days.

Given the significant semantic overlap between the phrases τοὺς πατέρας (v. 55a) and τῷ Ἀβραὰμ καὶ τῷ σπέρματι αὐτοῦ (v. 55b), however, it seems more likely that the same verb that governs the first phrase also governs the second.[39] In this reading, the two phrases stand in apposition to each other, and the concluding formula εἰς τὸν αἰῶνα refers, in turn, to "the length of time for which the spoken promise is valid."[40] The resulting reading, though unusual, is perfectly grammatical. The verb λαλέω, like λέγω, takes objects of address either in the dative case or, less commonly, within a πρός + accusative construction.[41] Luke-Acts freely moves between

---

(MT 111:5). On the similarity of Luke 1:54–55 to Mic 7:20b, see Marshall, *Gospel of Luke*, 85; Mittmann-Richert, *Magnifikat und Benediktus*, 16. Even studies that disagree on this point see the influence of Mic 7:20 on Luke 1:54–55 (e.g., Fitzmyer, *Luke I–IX*, 368). Luke 1:54–55 is also compared to Ps 98:3 (LXX 97:3), see Bovon, *Luke 1*, 63.

[39] Brown, *Birth of the Messiah*, 338. This synonymity makes it unlikely that the datives of v. 55b have a different thematic relation to ἐλάλησεν than the accusatives of v. 55a. They are neither datives of interest (Zerwick, *Biblical Greek*, §55) nor of advantage (Paul Joüon, "Notes de philologie évangélique: Luc 1.54–55; Une difficulté grammaticale du Magnificat," *RSR* 15 [1925]: 440–41).

[40] Tannehill, "Magnificat as Poem," 271 n. 19. This adequately refutes the claim that the prepositional phrase εἰς τὸν αἰῶνα is in an awkward position if v. 55b continues the thought of v. 55a (so Marshall, *Gospel of Luke*, 85). Appeals to texts linking the prepositional phrase εἰς τὸν αἰῶνα with ἐλέους (e.g., LXX Pss 135:1–26, 95:5) also fall short, as none of them seems to inspire Luke 1:54–55. The second analysis of Luke 1:54–55 outlined above is endorsed in E. Klostermann, *Das Lukasevangelium*, HNT 5 (Tübingen: Mohr Siebeck, 1929), 21; John Martin Creed, *The Gospel according to St. Luke: The Greek Text with Introduction, Notes, and Indices* (London: Macmillan, 1930), 24; Fitzmyer, *Luke I–IX*, 116; J. Reiling and J. L. Swellengrebel, *A Translator's Handbook on the Gospel of Luke*, HeTr 10 (Leiden: Brill, 1971), 79; Brown, *Birth of the Messiah*, 338; also KJV, NASB, ESV. Schürmann agrees with this reading but believes that all of v. 55 except the final εἰς τὸν αἰῶνα is parenthetical to vv. 54–55 (Schürmann, *Das Lukasevangelium*, 1:72, 77, nn. 252–53; see also Wilfried Eckey, *Das Lukasevangelium: Unter Berücksichtigung seiner Parallelen*, 2 vols. [Neukirchen-Vluyn: Neukirchener Verlag, 2004], 1:98). As Hans Klein notes, this argument does nothing to resolve the syntactic difficulty of the case juxtaposition (Klein, *Das Lukasevangelium*, 114 n. 81).

[41] In general, the use of simple case constructions has decreased relative to prepositional phrases in Hellenistic and New Testament Greek (Zerwick, *Biblical Greek*, §80a). Fitzmyer links the more frequent use of πρός + accusative in Luke-Acts to its frequent use in the LXX, where it translates Hebrew ל- or אל before a noun (Fitzmyer, *Luke I–IX*, 116).

these alternatives, not least in the infancy narrative (e.g., Luke 2:15, 17, 18, 20).[42] Unfortunately, this is the only instance in the entire work in which a single verb governs both constructions.

In defense of this reading, two other verses of Luke-Acts identify the establishment of the "covenant" with the "fathers" precisely with a spoken promise to "Abraham," leaving no distance between the two concepts:

> To perform the mercy promised to our fathers,
>   and to remember his holy covenant,
>   the oath which he swore to our father Abraham. (Luke 1:72–73)

> You are the sons of the prophets and of the covenant, which God gave to your fathers, saying to Abraham, "And in your posterity shall all the families of the earth be blessed." (Acts 3:25)

As in the first example, taken from the Benedictus (Luke 1:68–79), the synonymity of the phrases τοὺς πατέρας (v. 55a) and τῷ Ἀβραὰμ καὶ τῷ σπέρματι αὐτοῦ (v. 55b) in the Magnificat seems to support the synonymous parallelism in which they are embedded.[43]

In light of these observations, the highly peculiar syntax of Luke 1:54–55 would appear to be no mere syntactic difficulty but another deliberate poetic device of the canticle. Specifically, the alternation of πρός + accusative and the two datives in verse 55a, b seems to represent a second instance of stylistic alternation or grammatical parallelism in the Magnificat. A particular technique of Hebrew poetry, the use of "reversed ballast prepositions," provides an analogy to the phenomenon observed in Luke 1:55a, b. In this device, the first colon of a parallelism employs a "heavier" alternative to or variant of a preposition found in the second colon. In turn, the second colon takes additional elements to compensate for the brevity of its own preposition.[44] In the following examples, a single verb in the first line governs two prepositions, one free, the other a prefix:

Ps 78:69

ויבן כמו־רמים מקדשו
כארץ יסדה לעולם

---

[42] Tannehill observes that Luke "tends to shift from one construction to the other in the same context for purposes of variation" ("Magnificat as Poem," 271 n. 19, with further examples cited), but he fails to see the poetic character of that variation as it appears in v. 55.

[43] Brown, *Birth of the Messiah*, 338.

[44] See discussion and examples in Wilfred G. E. Watson, *Classical Hebrew Poetry: A Guide to Its Techniques*, JSOTSup 26 (Sheffield: JSOT Press, 1984), 345; Kugel, *Idea of Biblical Poetry*, 45–48. The reversed type is rarer among ballast prepositions (Watson, *Classical Hebrew Poetry*, 344–45). Compare this phenomenon to more general forms of prepositional or prepositional prefix alternation in Hebrew poetry (Kugel, *Idea of Biblical Poetry*, 22), or to more general forms of ballast variation (Watson, *Classical Hebrew Poetry*, 344–45). One should consider ballast prepositions a subtype of both categories.

And he builds his sanctuary <u>like</u> high palaces
<u>Like</u> the earth, which he established forever

Job 40:21

תַּחַת־צֶאֱלִים יִשְׁכָּב
בְּסֵתֶר קָנֶה וּבִצָּה

<u>Under</u> shady trees he lies,
<u>Under</u> the cover of reed and marsh.

In each case, the second coda compensates for the shorter prepositional construction in the first. Psalm 78:69b adds a relative clause, while Job 40:12 expands the object of the preposition.

The Lukan canticle appears to use a similar device in verse 55, with ἐλάλησεν governing two synonymous (object) constructions available in the syntax of Luke-Acts:

Luke 1:55
καθὼς ἐλάλησεν <u>πρὸς τοὺς πατέρας</u> ἡμῶν,   (πρός + acc.)
<u>τῷ Ἀβραὰμ καὶ τῷ σπέρματι</u> αὐτοῦ εἰς τὸν αἰῶνα.   (dat.)

In verse 55, the second colon compensates for the brevity of its simple datives by creating a more complex object phrase (τῷ Ἀβραὰμ καὶ τῷ σπέρματι αὐτοῦ) and/or by adding a final adverbial phrase (εἰς τὸν αἰῶνα).[45] Notably, the LXX utilizes both πρός + accusative and simple datives as equivalents of both bound and free prepositions with Hebrew verbs of speaking (table 1). An attempt to imitate or translate a reverse ballast construction could surely utilize both constructions, though, admittedly, neither the Hebrew prepositions nor their Greek equivalents are ever juxtaposed in this manner.

TABLE 1. LXX TRANSLATIONS OF HEBREW VERB + PREPOSITION

	Heb. verb + אל	Heb. verb + (prep. prefix) ל־
Gk. verb + πρός + acc.	Ezek 37:11 Heb. ויאמר אלי Gk. καὶ ἐλάλησεν ... πρός με	1 Sam [LXX 1 Kgdms] 31:4 Heb. ויאמר ... לנשא Gk. καὶ εἶπεν ... πρὸς τὸν αἴροντα
Gk. verb + simple dat.	Gen 12:4 Heb. דבר אליו Gk. ἐλάλησεν αὐτῷ	Isa 49:3 Heb. ויאמר לי Gk. καὶ εἶπέν μοι

---

[45] The presence of both may address a need to compensate further for the adverb + predicate (καθὼς ἐλάλησεν) introducing v. 55a.

Intriguingly, Franz Delitzsch's Hebrew translation of the New Testament alternates precisely between these prepositions in its rendering of verse 55:[46]

Luke 1:55, Delitzsch

כאשר דבר אֶל־אבותינו
לְאברהם ולזרעו עד־עולם

The resulting translation is easily recognizable as a ballast variation in Hebrew. This analysis should hold for its Greek source as well. Once again, only Semitic poetry provides a precedent for a syntactic peculiarity in the Magnificat within an identical genre (i.e., poetry) and structural context (i.e., parallelism).

B. Purpose

If the alternation in verse 55 is a poetic device, why has the poet chosen to utilize it? How does it contribute to the literary quality of the hymn? The formal similarities between this device and the tense shift in verses 46b–47 reflect their similar functions in the hymn, especially their support of variety and ambiguity.

Variety

Like the tense shift in verses 46b–47, the alternation in verse 55 introduces a measure of grammatical discord into the hymn, undermining related elements in a parallelism. As synonymous and appositional phrases, τῷ Ἀβραὰμ καὶ τῷ σπέρματι αὐτοῦ and πρὸς τοὺς πατέρας should take identical grammatical forms. Both phrases, after all, share a syntactic relation to the other elements in the sentence. The poet, however, has chosen to limit the likeness of these elements, resisting repetition on the morphosyntactic plane while permitting it on the semantic plane.

As I noted above, this change affords the poet the flexibility to introduce an extra element to the end of the second colon, consistent with the convention of ballast variants. That additional element, the prepositional phrase εἰς τὸν αἰῶνα, only increases the dissimilarity of the two lines and the instances of variety in the couplet. On a related note, this element also reinforces the poetic character of the hymn. The expression εἰς τὸν αἰῶνα is a well-known concluding element of hymns and prayers (Rom 11:36, 16:27, 1 Pet 5:11, LXX Pss 40:14, 88:53). In the Magnificat, εἰς τὸν αἰῶνα provides a formulaic conclusion typical of the genre. A variant of the expression appears in LXX Ps 17:51b, c, a unit strikingly similar to verse 55:

LXX Ps 17:51
καὶ ποιῶν ἔλεος τῷ χριστῷ αὐτοῦ
τῷ Δαυιδ καὶ τῷ σπέρματι αὐτοῦ ἕως αἰῶνος

And showing mercy to his anointed one,
to David and to his seed <u>unto ages</u>.

---

[46] Franz Delitzsch, *Delitzsch's Hebrew New Testament* (Leipzig: Ackermann, 1877), 98.

Ambiguity

The alternation of object constructions in verse 55 also confirms that the verse constitutes a single bicolon, contradicting studies that treat the verse as a single line.[47] In Hebrew poetry, ballast variants occur across line breaks. Consistent with this pattern, one should recognize a line break between πρὸς τοὺς πατέρας ἡμῶν and τῷ Ἀβραὰμ καὶ τῷ σπέρματι αὐτοῦ. In this way, the device reinforces the couplet structure of the entire composition, allowing the canticle to conclude on a single, metrically balanced (5:5) bicolon.

Naturally, a line break in verse 55 disrupts the syntactic unity of ἐλάλησεν and εἰς τὸν αἰῶνα and creates an impression of compactness, or terseness, in the couplet. Here again, the device reinforces the poetic character of the composition. As Adele Berlin notes, terseness is a fundamental aspect of biblical poetry.[48] Lines of Hebrew poetry are brief, and paratactically conjoined, if at all. This brevity and loose syntax allow ambiguity to flourish:

> Two statements are made as if they are connected, and the reader is forced to consider their relations for himself. The reasons why these facts should have been selected for a poem is left for him to invent; he will invent a variety of reasons and order them in his own mind.[49]

The added peculiarity of the case alternation only increases the disjointed and confusing impression of verse 55a, b. The device upsets the reader's expectation that nouns in apposition should agree in case with their referents—a principle observed elsewhere in the canticle (e.g., Ἰσραήλ and παιδός in v. 54; in the Benedictus: κέρας σωτηρίας [v. 69a] and σωτηρίαν [v. 71]). Consequently, the reader is left to "invent a variety of reasons" to explain the syntax of verse 55, as illustrated in our survey of previous analyses of the Greek text.[50] The interpretive challenge of this couplet is, at its heart, a poetic one and owes itself precisely to this stylistic device.

Enveloping

I cannot conclude this discussion without addressing the intriguing fact that these two grammatical alternations occur in the first and last couplets of the canticle, respectively. Although the position of each device suits

---

[47] Tannehill, "Magnificat as Poem," 271, 265; Tannehill, *The Narrative Unity of Luke-Acts: A Literary Interpretation*, 2 vols., FF (Minneapolis: Fortress, 1986–1990), 1:27–28.

[48] Berlin, *Dynamics of Biblical Parallelism*, 6.

[49] Empson, *Seven Types of Ambiguity*, 25.

[50] In this instance, it is difficult to imagine that the author intended to affirm more than one deliberate sense of the text (like the unspecific temporal reference of the tense alternation in vv. 46b–47). The preposition/case alternation in v. 55 depends on only one of the possible interpretations described above (in which τῷ Ἀβραὰμ καὶ τῷ σπέρματι αὐτοῦ [v. 55b] stands in apposition to πρὸς τοὺς πατέρας [v. 55a]). At best, the datives could double as datives of interest or advantage (see n. 41). Recognizing, however, that ambiguity can exist for its own sake in biblical poetry, I prefer to characterize this alternation as a purely nonsemantic device.

couplet-internal factors, the manner in which these devices "envelop" the poem is striking and deepens the suspicion that these alternations are elements of the author's deliberate style. Previous studies have noted an occasional, though nonpredictable, tendency for both devices to open or conclude poems or their individual strophes.[51] In the Psalms, I have recorded instances of hymn-initial tense alternation in at least Pss 56:1, 116:1–2, and 131:1, and hymn-final ballasting of a preposition in Pss 114:8, 116:19a, b. Perhaps the poet considered these phenomena "boundary devices" (as has been proposed for Hebrew examples[52]), choosing to utilize them only at transitional points. At the very least, it is worth noting the consistency of these examples with Semitic patterns of use. That the function, positions, and semantics of these constructions align with Hebrew and Ugaritic precedents validates the findings of this study.

III. Conclusion

Notably, none of the texts that influence the content of Luke 1:46b–47 (i.e., 1 Sam 2:1) or Luke 1:55 (i.e., Mic 7:20, LXX Ps 17:51) contains stylistic alternations, though the features they export to Luke 1 seem to justify the use of the devices there (e.g., the striking likeness of vv. 46b and 47, the additional elements in v. 55b, and so on). Though previous studies have characterized the canticle as "a mere pastiche of OT fragments,"[53] my study suggests that the poet was capable of reshaping and improving upon the style of these apparent sources. The author of the Magnificat possessed an interior grasp of the theory and conventions of Semitic poetry. He or she knew when and how to raise mere allusions to the realm of literary artistry. That the poet's genius is evident in a Greek text—whether by his or her own hand or by that of a later translator—is still more remarkable.

Unfortunately, it is precisely the Greek language of the composition that has obscured the poet's genius. In Hebrew, these devices would be unmistakably stylistic. In Greek, they have been cast aside as syntactic peculiarities or difficulties—obstacles to understanding the canticle—despite their prominent positions within it. Descriptions of the poetry of the Magnificat cannot afford to neglect these constructions any longer. In a genre characterized by marked syntax, peculiar constructions such as these deserve to be explored in a subgenre-specific manner, with due attention to possible literary and linguistic backgrounds. The brief lingering of our eyes on any grammatical difficulty in biblical poetry may occur by deliberate design. It is especially worth lingering a little longer on these examples.

---

[51] Buth, "Taxonomy and Function," 31; Watson, *Classical Hebrew Poetry*, 346–47. Watson also cites examples of hymn-final ballasting in Ugaritic.

[52] Buth, "Taxonomy and Function," 31.

[53] See Farris, *Hymns of Luke's Infancy Narratives*, 113.

One of the Days of the Son of Man: A Reconsideration of Luke 17:22

RYAN P. JUZA
ryan.juza@asburyseminary.edu
Asbury Theological Seminary, Wilmore, KY 40390

This article challenges two interpretive decisions related to "one of the days of the Son of Man" in Luke 17:22. (1) Instead of interpreting the "days" as a temporal period, I suggest that the "days" be understood as a collection of similar yet distinct days. If Luke employs this tactic, it frees the interpreter from having to synchronize the "days of the Son of Man" temporally in 17:22 with the same phrase in 17:26 and brings "one of the days of the Son of Man" into harmony with the "day of the Son of Man" (17:24, 30, 31). (2) Instead of interpreting Luke 17:22–37 as referring to the parousia, I suggest that this passage be interpreted in relation to the destruction of Jerusalem. This interpretation is encouraged by a close reading of 17:22–37 in order to identify Luke's primary points of comparison between the "days" and "day" of Noah and Lot, and those of the Son of Man. I conclude that the disciples' desire to see "one of the days of the Son of Man" is their desire to witness Jesus's glorious coming as the suffering-yet-vindicated king of Israel, but they will not see it because Jesus commands them to escape Jerusalem's ruin.

And he said to the disciples, "The days will come when you will long to see one of the days of the Son of Man, and you will not see it." (Luke 17:22)

Luke 17:22 is a puzzle that has confounded interpreters for generations. There are several pieces to the puzzle but no clear way of fitting them together without apparently leaving out a piece or two. The main difficulty revolves around what the disciples will desire to see but will not see, "one of the days of the Son of Man" (μίαν τῶν ἡμερῶν τοῦ υἱοῦ τοῦ ἀνθρώπου). Scholars describe this phrase as "unusual,"[1] "enigmatic,"[2] "highly problematic,"[3] and a "*crux interpretum*."[4] A. R. C. Leaney's

---

[1] John Nolland, *Luke*, 3 vols., WBC 35A–C (Dallas: Word, 1989–1993), 2:858.
[2] Joseph A. Fitzmyer, *The Gospel according to Luke: Introduction, Translation, and Notes*, 2 vols., AB 28, 28A (Garden City, NY: Doubleday, 1981–1985), 2:1164.
[3] I. Howard Marshall, *The Gospel of Luke: A Commentary on the Greek Text*, NIGTC (Grand Rapids: Eerdmans, 1978), 658.
[4] T. J. Lang, "'You Will Desire to See and You Will Not See [It]': Reading Luke 17.22 as Antanaclasis," *JSNT* 33 (2011): 281, http://dx.doi.org/10.1177/0142064X10382073.

assessment still holds true today: Luke 17:22 "is a verse for which no satisfactory explanation has been given."[5] Any interpretation of this phrase must account for two significant problems associated with it.

First, it is not readily apparent how the phrase is to be synchronized with the other temporal designations in 17:22–37. We can list them here:

- Days will come (v. 22)
- One of the days of the Son of Man (v. 22)
- The Son of Man [in his day][6] (v. 24)
- But first it is necessary (v. 25)
- In the days of Noah (v. 26)
- In the days of the Son of Man (v. 26)
- Until the day Noah entered the ark (v. 27)
- In the days of Lot (v. 28)
- But on the day Lot left Sodom (v. 29)
- On the day that the Son of Man is revealed (v. 30)
- On that day (v. 31)
- On this night (v. 34)

The basic problem is that "one of the days of the Son of Man" seems to align itself temporally with the "days of the Son of Man" (v. 26), which, according to the analogies of Noah and Lot (vv. 26–29) should occur *before* the "day" of the Son of Man (vv. 24, 30). This creates the scenario where "one of the days of the Son of Man" cannot refer to the "day" of the Son of Man (i.e., the parousia) because it is part of a period that should precede the "day." This requires a significant interpretive decision. How does one interpret the phrase in relation to Luke's other temporal designations?

Second, the phrase presents the idea of multiple "days" of the Son of Man, but this is unprecedented in the rest of the New Testament, which speaks of the parousia only as a singular "day."[7] It is not as though Luke is unfamiliar with this idea of the parousia, since he uses "day" elsewhere in Luke-Acts to refer to it (e.g., Acts 2:20). Furthermore, he uses "day" in the immediate context (17:24, 30, 31). Why, then, does Luke break consistency in 17:22? Why does he write "days" if he supposedly means "day"? In view of the unanimous agreement among the New Testament writers concerning the parousia, Luke's uncommon expression suggests that he is *not* referring to the parousia.

---

[5] A. R. C. Leaney, *The Gospel according to St. Luke*, HNTC (1958; repr., Peabody, MA: Hendrickson, 1988), 68.

[6] "In his day" may not be original. Its absence may be explained as a result of homoeoteleuton (skipping ahead from ἀνθρώπου to αὐτοῦ). Its presence or absence does little to alter the meaning of 17:24.

[7] See Matt 24:36, Mark 13:32, 1 Cor 1:8, 5:5, 2 Cor 1:14, Phil 1:10, 2:16, 1 Thess 5:2, 1 Pet 2:12, 2 Pet 3:10.

In this study, I challenge two interpretive decisions that I believe led to the problems discussed above: (1) that the "days" in "one of the days of the Son of Man" are a temporal period, and (2) that Luke 17:22–37 is about the parousia. These interpretive decisions are difficult to sustain when the evidence is examined. I argue here for two alternative interpretations: (1) The "days" in "one of the days of the Son of Man" are a collection of similar yet distinct days.[8] In other words, the "days" refer to a set of individual days that can all be classified as a "day of the Son of Man." The "one," then, distinguishes a specific "day of the Son of Man" from another "day of the Son of Man." (2) Luke 17:22–37 is best understood as describing the events surrounding the destruction of Jerusalem (ca. 70 CE).[9] Consequently, I argue that the "days of the Son of Man" (17:26) was a period prior to the destruction of Jerusalem when Jesus and his witnesses suffered and were rejected by "this generation," Jesus's wicked and unperceptive Jewish contemporaries (17:25). The "day of the Son of Man," then, entailed a revelatory theophany of Jesus as the glorious and suffering-yet-vindicated Messiah in order to condemn "this generation" (17:24, 30). The disciples will "long to see" this "day" (17:22) because it will answer their prayers for justice against their oppressors (18:1–8). They "will not see" it, however, because Jesus commanded them to escape from Jerusalem as the "day" drew near (17:31–32). Thus, "one of the days of the Son of Man" is not the parousia but the "day" when Jesus was gloriously revealed as the suffering-yet-vindicated Messiah to those who rejected him.

My argument begins with a survey of previous proposals for interpreting "one of the days of the Son of Man." Following this I will discuss the advantages and challenges of interpreting the "days of the Son of Man" in 17:22 as a collection of similar yet distinct days. Finally, I will offer an interpretation of Luke 17:22–37 that demonstrates how the evidence suggests a portrayal of Jerusalem's divine judgment.

I. INTERPRETATIONS OF LUKE 17:22

There are six major proposals for the meaning of the phrase "one of the days of the Son of Man."[10] The first five proposals understand the "days of the Son of

---

[8] As far as I am aware, this was first proposed by A. R. C. Leaney, "The Days of the Son of Man (Luke xvii. 22)," *ExpTim* 67 (1955): 28–29, http://dx.doi.org/10.1177/001452465506700108; see also Leaney, *Gospel according to St. Luke*, 68–72.

[9] This is not a new proposal, but it has not received detailed exegetical support or much recent attention. See André Feuillet, "La venue du Règne de Dieu et du Fils de l'homme (d'après Luc 17,20 à 18,8)," *RSR* 35 (1948): 544–65; Leaney, *Gospel according to St. Luke*, 68–72, 230–32; G. B. Caird, *Saint Luke*, Westminster Pelican Commentaries (Philadelphia: Westminster, 1963), 196–200; Bernard De Souza, "The Coming of the Lord," *SBFLA* 20 (1970): 166–208; N. T. Wright, *Jesus and the Victory of God*, vol. 2 of *Christian Origins and the Question of God* (Minneapolis: Fortress, 1996), 365–67.

[10] With a text as difficult as 17:22, there are naturally more views than can be expressed here.

Man" *temporally* as a unified period of time consisting of several consecutive days. The "one," then, singles out a specific day within that period of time. The sixth proposal understands the "days of the Son of Man" *collectively* as a group of similar yet distinct "days." The "one," then, distinguishes a specific "day" from other like days.

1. The expression "days of the Son of Man" corresponds to "the days of the Messiah," which is found in rabbinic literature to describe the period of the Messiah's reign (see m. Ber. 1:5).[11] Thus, the "days of the Son of Man" refers to the period after the parousia when the Son of Man will exercise his reign. Some interpret μίαν as "one," suggesting that the disciples will long to see any day during the period. But others interpret μίαν as "first," suggesting that the disciples will long to see the initial day of the Son of Man's reign, the parousia. One of the problems with this view is the probable late date of rabbinic literature. More critically, this view conflicts with the analogies of Noah and Lot (17:26–29), which imply that the "days" should come *before* the "day." Finally, if the phrase refers to the parousia (μίαν = "first"), which is an improbable translation of μίαν in this context, why did Luke not just use the singular expression "day," similar to 17:24, 30, 31?[12]

2. The "days of the Son of Man" refers to a general period of time before the parousia.[13] This view relies on the analogies of Noah and Lot (17:26–29). Thus, the

---

See the similar surveys in Fitzmyer, *Gospel according to Luke*, 2:1168–69; Marshall, *Gospel of Luke*, 658–59; Darrell L. Bock, *Luke*, 2 vols., BECNT 3 (Grand Rapids: Baker, 1994–1996), 2:1426–28; Steven L. Bridge, *Where the Eagles Are Gathered: The Deliverance of the Elect in Lukan Eschatology*, JSNTSup 240 (London: Sheffield Academic, 2003), 33–35; Lang, "'You Will Desire to See,'" 284–87.

[11] This is the current majority view. See Bock, *Luke*, 2:1427–28; E. Earle Ellis, *The Gospel of Luke*, NCBC (Grand Rapids: Eerdmans, 1981), 211; Leon Morris, *Luke: An Introduction and Commentary*, rev. ed., TNTC 3 (Grand Rapids: Eerdmans, 1988), 284; Walter Grundmann, *Das Evangelium nach Lukas*, THKNT 3 (Berlin: Evangelische Verlagsanstalt, 1961), 343; Wolfgang Wiefel, *Das Evangelium nach Lukas*, THKNT 3 (Berlin: Evangelische Verlagsanstalt, 1987), 311. Calling it the "least unsatisfactory" option is Marshall, *Gospel of Luke*, 659. Holding this view but not advocating for a connection to the "days of the Messiah" is Frederick W. Danker, *Jesus and the New Age: A Commentary on St. Luke's Gospel*, 2nd rev. ed. (Philadelphia: Fortress, 1988), 292; see also Luke Timothy Johnson, *The Gospel of Luke*, SP 3 (Collegeville, MN: Liturgical Press, 1991), 263–64; Robert H. Stein, *Luke*, NAC 24 (Nashville: Broadman, 1992), 438; Michael D. Goulder, *Luke: A New Paradigm*, 2 vols., JSNTSup 20 (Sheffield: JSOT Press, 1989), 2:651; W. Powell, "The Days of the Son of Man," *ExpTim* 67 (1956): 219.

[12] It is probable that the plural genitive "of the days" is a partitive genitive that "denotes *the whole of which* the head noun is a part" and is consistently employed when the head noun is "one" (εἷς). This is how Luke employs the same phrase in the rest of his Gospel (see 5:17, 8:22, 20:1). See Daniel B. Wallace, *Greek Grammar beyond the Basics: An Exegetical Syntax of the New Testament* (Grand Rapids: Zondervan, 1996), 84–85; BDAG, s.v. εἷς.

[13] See E. Ashby, "The Days of the Son of Man," *ExpTim* 67 (1956): 124–25; T. Francis Glasson, *The Second Advent: The Origin of the New Testament Doctrine*, 3rd rev. ed. (London: Epworth, 1963), 78–83.

disciples will desire to see but will not see "one" of the days in the period leading up to the parousia. The main difficulty here, as regularly noted, is understanding why the disciples would "desire to see" a day *prior* to the parousia, especially if this period is going to be characterized by suffering and other eschatological birth pangs.[14]

3. The "days of the Son of Man" refers to the period extending from Jesus's resurrection to his parousia, the period of his exaltation.[15] Thus, the disciples will desire to see the exalted Jesus but will not because he must remain in heaven until the parousia (cf. Acts 3:21). Instead of seeing him, they must believe. This view also aligns itself with the analogies of Noah and Lot by placing the "days" before the "day." The problem with this view, however, again as noted by many, is that the disciples *did* "see" this period, at least at the beginning.[16]

4. The "days of the Son of Man" refers to the period of Jesus's earthly life.[17] The disciples will long for the time when Jesus was present with them in bodily form. This sort of nostalgia for Jesus's ministry, however, is unprecedented in the New Testament. The hope of the early church is always future-oriented. In addition, for Jesus to say that the disciples "will not see" the past is superfluous (unless it is for purely rhetorical reasons). Furthermore, this interpretation also breaks with the analogies of Noah and Lot by positing a gap between the "days" (Jesus's earthly ministry) and the "day" (his parousia).

5. The "days of the Son of Man" refers to the entire period extending from Jesus's earthly ministry into the eschaton.[18] The "one day" the disciples will desire to see because of future suffering is the parousia. This proposal, however, also violates the analogies to Noah and Lot by suggesting that the "day" can be inserted into the "days" instead of following them. This also brings us back to the issue of why Luke used such an awkward phrase if he simply meant the "day of the Son of Man."

6. The "days of the Son of Man" refers to a collection of glorious appearances by Jesus that can each be identified as a "day of the Son of Man."[19] These

---

[14] E.g., Bock, *Luke*, 2:1428; Bridge, *Where the Eagles Are Gathered*, 34.

[15] Josef Zmijewski, *Die Eschatologiereden des Lukas-Evangeliums: Eine traditions- und redaktionsgeschichtliche Untersuchung zu Lk 21,5–36 und Lk 17,20–37*, BBB 40 (Bonn: Hanstein, 1972), 399–403; Helmut Flender, *St. Luke: Theologian of Redemptive History*, trans. Reginald H. Fuller and Ilse Fuller (Philadelphia: Fortress, 1967), 94–95.

[16] E.g., Bock, *Luke*, 2:1427; Lang, "'You Will Desire to See,'" 285.

[17] Nolland, *Luke*, 2:858; John T. Carroll, *Luke: A Commentary*, NTL (Louisville: Westminster John Knox, 2012), 349; C. F. Evans, *Saint Luke*, 2nd ed. (London: SCM, 2008), 631. Seeing the disciples' longing as a desire for Jesus's presence, which includes the past (proposal 4) and the future (proposal 1) is Bridge, *Where the Eagles Are Gathered*, 34–35; François Bovon, *Das Evangelium nach Lukas*, 4 vols., EKKNT 3 (Zurich: Benziger; Neukirchen-Vluyn: Neukirchener Verlag, 1989–2009), 3:169.

[18] Joel B. Green, *The Gospel of Luke*, NICNT (Grand Rapids: Eerdmans, 1997), 631–33.

[19] Leaney, *Gospel according to St. Luke*, 68–72, 230–32; Leaney, "Days of the Son of Man,"

appearances include the transfiguration, the resurrection and ascension, the appearances to Stephen and Paul, the restoration of Jerusalem and Israel (by which Leaney means the salvific aspects of the destruction of Jerusalem seen in the redemption of the disciples and the establishment of the kingdom), and the parousia. The characteristic that binds this set of "days" together is a revelation of Jesus's glorious presence. The one "day" under consideration in 17:22–37 is Jerusalem's destruction. This proposal is also unparalleled in the New Testament. More problematic, however, is that Luke does not indicate in his accounts of the transfiguration, resurrection and ascension, and so on, that he considers each of them to be a "day" of the Son of Man.

In conclusion, we can visually represent each proposal below in comparison to the "days" and "day" of Noah and Lot (17:26–29).

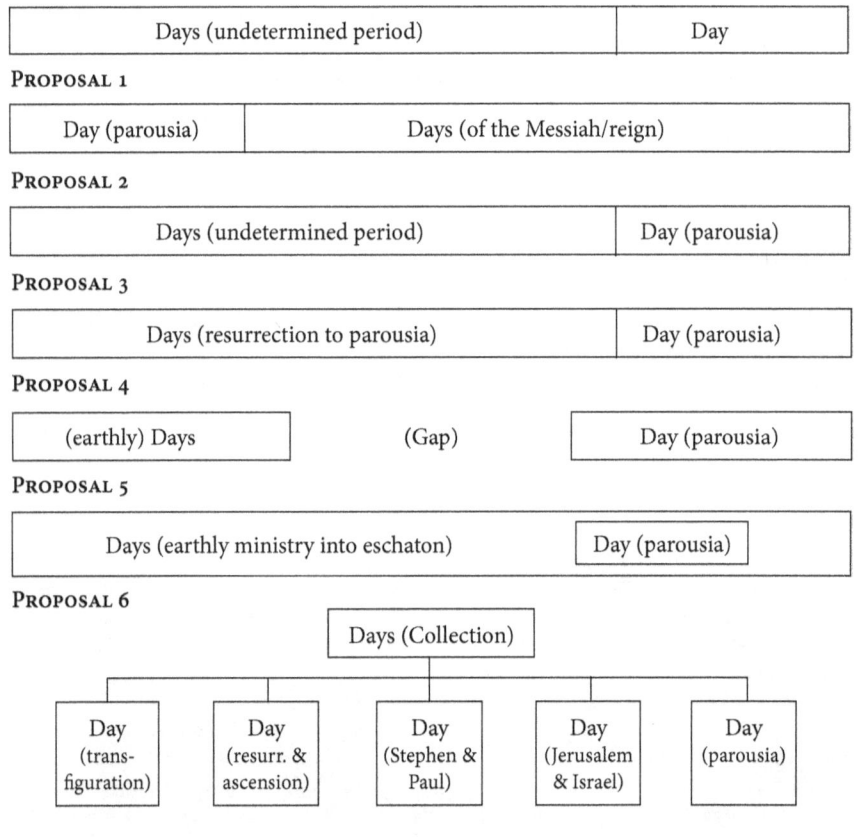

28–29; Carroll Stuhlmueller, *The Gospel of Saint Luke,* 2nd ed., NTRG 3 (Collegeville, MN: Liturgical Press, 1964), 117–18.

Every proposal encounters problems. Those attempting to interpret the "days of the Son of Man" as a temporal period (proposals 1–5) cannot escape the conflicting data between the "days" and "day" while at the same time trying to coordinate these time periods with the disciples' "desire to see" something that they "will not see." Proposals 1, 4, and 5 break with the temporal sequence in the Noah and Lot analogies. In addition, while proposals 2 and 3 temporally synchronize their scheme with the analogies, proposal 2 fails to explain why the disciples would "desire to see" this period, and proposal 3 fails to explain why they "will not see" this period. Overall, Luke 17:22 appears to be a temporal puzzle that cannot be solved. As T. J. Lang aptly observes, "All of the temporal possibilities for understanding the 'one of the days of the Son of Man' expression have been exhausted."[20] The temporal approach seems to have nowhere left to go. This leaves us with proposal 6, a view that also has significant problems (as it is currently advocated). The basic claim of this proposal, however, that the "days of the Son of Man" could refer to a *collection* of similar yet distinct "days," holds potential for further investigation. It appears to be the only route left for exploring this *crux interpretum*.

II. Exploring the Idea of a Collection of Days

Interpreting the "days of the Son of Man" in 17:22 as a collection of similar yet distinct days has two notable advantages over a temporal interpretation. First, it frees the interpreter from the impenetrable problem of having to synchronize temporally "one of the days of the Son of Man" (v. 22) with the "days of the Son of Man" (v. 26), which, in light of the survey above, cannot be done without causing other major interpretive problems. But if the "days" in verse 22 denote a collection of events, the interpreter is not required to synchronize the phrase with the temporal period in verse 26.[21] While it may seem problematic to treat the two occurrences of the "days of the Son of Man" in verses 22 and 26 differently, Luke does not connect these two phrases as much as is commonly assumed. In fact, because Luke parallels 17:20–21 and 17:22–23, "one of the days of the Son of Man" (v. 22) is more closely aligned with an event, "the coming of the kingdom of God" (v. 20), than it is with the temporal period "in the days of the Son of Man" (v. 26).[22] Furthermore, because of Luke's two analogies in 17:26–29, "in the days of the Son of Man" (v. 26) is more closely aligned with "in the days of Noah/Lot" (vv. 26, 28) than it is with verse 22.

---

[20] Lang, "'You Will Desire to See,'" 287.

[21] Both Ashby ("Days of the Son of Man," 124) and Lang ("'You Will Desire to See,'" 286) are incorrect to suggest that proposal 6 disregards the analogies of Noah and Lot.

[22] On the relation of 17:20–21 and 17:22–23, see Lang, "'You Will Desire to See,'" 291; Green, *Gospel of Luke*, 632.

Second, interpreting "one of the days of the Son of Man" as a collection of similar yet distinct "days" harmonizes the phrase with the "day" of the Son of Man (17:24, 30, 31). Under the assumption that "one of the days of the Son of Man" is temporal in orientation, the phrase *cannot* refer to the "day of the Son of Man" (vv. 24, 30, 31) because the logic of the Noah/Lot analogies requires that the "one day" (which is part of the "days") must occur *prior* to the "day."[23] Thus, a temporal reading forces the interpreter to speak of two "days." This is why several scholars have postulated an alternative sense of εἷς (i.e., "first") in an attempt to merge the period of the "days" with the "day." But even if this improbable translation were granted, it still disregards Luke's analogies to Noah and Lot, since it would require the "days" to follow the "day." Therefore, if one assumes a temporal reading, Luke's logic does not allow "one of the days of the Son of Man" to be equated with the "day of the Son of Man." If we understand the phrase as a collection, however, the "one" selects a specific "day" from the collection to address in 17:22–37. Thus, the collection view equates "one of the days of the Son of Man" with the "day of the Son of Man" (17:24, 30, 31).[24] The result is a unified presentation concerning "one day of the Son of Man."

There are, of course, challenges to the concept of a collection. First, the idea of more than one "day of the Son of Man" is unprecedented in the rest of the New Testament, which raises the question, Where did Luke come up with such an idea? While the notion of multiple "days" is foreign to the New Testament, it is not unprecedented in the Old Testament with regard to the day of YHWH/the Lord (to which the day of the Son of Man clearly alludes).[25] In the Old Testament, it was common practice among the prophets to associate multiple events with the day of YHWH. While the prophets were united in speaking of only one genuine "Day" envisioned in the eschatological future (which the New Testament takes up as the parousia), they routinely applied the concept to a number of historical situations, specific "days" when God acted in history to judge and to save.[26] For example, Babylon (Isa 13:1–14:32), Edom (Isa 34:1–17), Egypt (Ezek 30:1–19), Moab (Jer 48:1–47), the Philistines (Jer 47:1–7), Tyre (Isa 23:1–18), and others, even Israel (Isa 2:5–22, Jer 18:13–17, Amos 5:18–27) and Jerusalem (Isa 3:1–4:6, Joel 2:1–17), were all characterized by the prophets as experiencing a "day" of YHWH. Yet none

---

[23] Zmijewski, *Die Eschatologiereden des Lukas-Evangeliums*, 400–401.

[24] De Souza, "Coming of the Lord," 187.

[25] On the New Testament's use of the day of YHWH/the Lord, see De Souza, "Coming of the Lord," 166–208; T. Francis Glasson, "Theophany and Parousia," *NTS* 34 (1988): 259–70, http://dx.doi.org/10.1017/S0028688500020051; Mark D. Vander Hart, "The Transition of the Old Testament Day of the Lord into the New Testament Day of the Lord Jesus Christ," *MAJT* 9 (1993): 3–25.

[26] See Richard H. Hiers, "The Day of the Lord," *ABD* 2:82–83; J. D. Barker, "Day of the Lord," in *Dictionary of the Old Testament: Prophets*, ed. Mark J. Boda and J. Gordon McConville (Downers Grove, IL: IVP Academic, 2012), 132–43.

of these "days" was *the* "day." In other words, the prophets took the liberty of calling other manifestations of God's judgment and salvation in history a "day" of YHWH, even though they knew it was not the final "Day." The prophets did this whenever they saw or foresaw a historical manifestation of God's judgment and salvation that foreshadowed the great "Day" to come.[27] In other words, the historical manifestation of YHWH's "day" of judgment against a particular locality embodied and anticipated his "Day" to come. I suggest that Luke is doing the same thing in 17:22–37. He knows that the ultimate "day of the Son of Man" (the parousia) is coming (see Acts 2:20), but Luke saw or foresaw another "day" that embodied and anticipated the parousia, and so he called it "one of the days of the Son of Man" so as to distinguish it from the parousia while at the same time communicating its typological relationship. The event that I think Luke saw or foresaw as embodying and anticipating the parousia was a revelatory theophany of the Son of Man, enacted in the destruction of Jerusalem and its temple.

Even if it is granted that the Old Testament concept of the day of YHWH allows for multiple "days," what events (apart from the parousia) would Luke consider a "day of the Son of Man"? If Luke is following the Old Testament pattern of naming "days" that prefigure the "Day," then it would seem reasonable for him to describe these events in terms reminiscent of the day of YHWH. This is where the current collection view falters. The only criterion in proposal 6 for grouping events together is that each "day" must be a glorious appearance of Jesus. This opens the door for all kinds of events that do not resemble a day of YHWH. Therefore, the criterion is not stringent enough. If Luke follows the Old Testament pattern, then he should describe each "day" in ways that allude to the day of Yahweh. He does this with one other event besides the parousia in Luke-Acts, the divine judgment of Jerusalem (see Luke 13:33–35, 19:42–44, 20:16, 21:20–36, 23:28–31).

Even if it is granted that Luke describes the destruction of Jerusalem in terms reminiscent of the day of YHWH, it still does not demonstrate that he addresses this subject in Luke 17:22–37. This can be established only by a careful examination of 17:22–37. If my proposal is correct, then we should be able to observe several points of contact between 17:22–37 and Luke's portrayal of Jerusalem's divine judgment. At the same time, we should also be able to observe several points of disconnect between 17:22–37 and the parousia.

III. Interpreting Luke 17:22–37

I begin by examining the analogies of Noah and Lot. Luke writes that these two stories function to explain what the "days" and "day" of the Son of Man will be

---

[27] G. B. Caird, *The Language and Imagery of the Bible* (Philadelphia: Westminster, 1980), 256–60; George R. Beasley-Murray, *Jesus and the Kingdom of God* (Grand Rapids: Eerdmans, 1986), 11–16.

like. Thus, the analogies should provide us with some parameters to help guide our interpretation of the "days" and "day" of the Son of Man.

The Analogies of Noah and Lot (Luke 17:26–29)

The stories of Noah and Lot have a considerable tradition of development in literature beyond Genesis, both in the Hebrew Bible and in extrabiblical writings.[28] It is common to find these stories being used together as prototypes of divine judgment on the ungodly.[29] The Noah analogy is paralleled in Matt 24:37–39 but with significant differences.[30] The Lot analogy is Lukan alone.

We can compare the analogies of Noah (17:26–27) and Lot (17:28–29). Luke has paralleled them following a five-part sequence:[31]

1. Just as it was in the *days* of Noah/Lot
2. They were eating, drinking, and so on
3. Until/But on the *day* Noah entered the ark/Lot left Sodom
4. The flood came/It rained fire and sulfur from heaven
5. And destroyed all

The first two parts of the sequence describe the "days," while the last three parts describe the "day." Below I will discuss each part of the sequence with the intention of observing how 17:26–29 connects to the remainder of 17:22–37. This is of vital importance to help identify the most significant points of comparison that Luke wants to emphasize. The key, then, will be accurately to assess the similarities between the analogies of Noah and Lot, and the "days" and "day" of the Son of Man. I will also intersperse comments about the implications for my interpretation of the "days" and "day" of the Son of Man.

1. The "days" of Noah and Lot are nonspecific periods of time. They gain their definition only in relation to the "day." Chronologically speaking, then, the "days"

---

[28] See Jack P. Lewis, *A Study of the Interpretation of Noah and the Flood in Jewish and Christian Literature* (Leiden: Brill, 1968); J. A. Loader, *A Tale of Two Cities: Sodom and Gomorrah in the Old Testament, Early Jewish and Early Christian Traditions*, CBET 1 (Kampen: Kok, 1990).

[29] See 2 Pet 2:5–8, Wis 10:4–7, 3 Macc 2:4–5, T. Naph. 3:4–5, LAE 49:3.

[30] First, Luke uses the analogy to illustrate the "day(s) of the Son of Man," while Matthew illustrates the "coming." Second, the Noah analogy functions differently in Luke by explaining a course of events, while Matthew substantiates the claim that no one "knows" the timing of the parousia (24:36). Third, the analogy provides the basis for a different exhortation in Luke to "escape" (17:31–32), while in Matthew everyone must "keep awake" (24:42). The point is that we cannot uncritically assume that Luke's Noah analogy refers to the parousia (as it does in Matthew).

[31] Zmijewski contends that the two analogies are not parallel to each other (*Die Eschatologiereden des Lukas-Evangeliums*, 442–44). Luke, however, has carefully crafted them using the same pattern and indicates by writing "in the same way" (17:28) that the Lot analogy serves the same purpose as the Noah analogy.

of Noah and Lot occur prior to the "day" and end when the "day" arrives. *Therefore, the analogies imply that the days of the Son of Man will be a general period of time that precedes, and is terminated by, the day of the Son of Man.* Similarly, in 17:25 Luke describes another general period of time that precedes the "day of the Son of Man": "but first … this generation" (distinguished as a period of time). Luke uses the expression "this generation" to describe simultaneously a period of time and a class of people.[32] We are concerned here with its temporal connotation, which describes a general period contemporary to Jesus. By apparently making "this generation" analogous to the "days" of Noah and Lot, Luke seems to equate "this generation" with the "days of the Son of Man."

2. While Luke surely assumes, along with the biblical tradition, that Noah's generation and the people of Sodom were wicked, he describes activities that appear to be normal everyday behaviors (eating, drinking, etc.). Luke may suggest, however, that these activities reveal an orientation directed away from God and God's kingdom.[33] By interrupting the direct succession of Greek verbs with the arrival of the "day," Luke appears to emphasize that the people went about their daily lives without any recognition that divine judgment was coming. They were unaware. *Therefore, the analogies imply that, during the days of the Son of Man, the general population of people are presumed to be wicked, and their actions demonstrate a lack of awareness of God's plan.* According to this inference, we can identify another group of people in 17:25 who are considered by Luke to be wicked and whose actions demonstrate a lack of awareness of God's plan: "this generation" (distinguished as a class of people). As a class of people, "this generation" in Luke refers to Jesus's Jewish contemporaries, who are wicked and unperceptive.[34] Furthermore, their repetitive actions, which Luke describes in 17:25 as causing the suffering and rejection of the Son of Man, demonstrate a keen lack of awareness of God's plan. Thus, Luke appears to make "this generation" (of people) analogous to Noah's generation and the people of Sodom.[35]

I can now shift the discussion to the "day," which is described in the final three parts of the Noah and Lot analogies.[36]

3. In contrast to those who would be destroyed, Luke probably assumes, along with the biblical tradition, that Noah and Lot were faithful to God, although he does not single out anything particularly righteous about them. The actions of

---

[32] See Luke 7:31; 11:29, 30, 31, 32, 50, 51; 17:25; 21:32; Acts 2:40; Friedrich Büchsel, "γενεά," *TDNT* 1:662–63.

[33] See Luke 8:14; 12:18–19, 29, 31, 45; 14:18–20; 19:45; Green, *Gospel of Luke*, 634–35; Carroll, *Luke*, 350–51.

[34] See Luke 7:31–35; 11:29–32, 39–52.

[35] So Fitzmyer, *Gospel according to Luke*, 2:1170.

[36] Lang misconstrues the nature of the "day" by focusing exclusively on the departure of Noah and Lot ("'You Will Desire to See,'" 294–95).

Noah and Lot on the "day" involve escape prior to judgment. Luke does not frame their departure as salvation by God. Instead, Noah and Lot take action to save themselves, presumably based on the warning they received ahead of time (Gen 6:13–14; 19:12–13, 17).[37] Thus, what appears to separate them from those who perished was their ability to recognize that divine judgment was coming and to act on their awareness of God's plan. *Therefore, the analogies imply that the day of the Son of Man will involve an escape prior to judgment by the ones who are presumed to be faithful and are able to perceive God's plan.* According to this inference, we can observe another group of people in the immediate context whose faithfulness will be challenged as they are called upon to perceive God's plan and escape judgment: "the disciples" (17:22, 23, 31–37). Thus, Luke appears to make Jesus's disciples analogous to Noah and Lot.[38]

4. Next, the "day" is when the "flood came" and "fire and sulfur rained down from heaven." These (multiple!) "days" were unquestionably viewed as divine judgments executed by YHWH.[39] The flood and rain of fire are portrayed by Luke as instruments of YHWH's condemnation, not salvation. Luke also frames his other reference to "Sodom" in terms of condemnation (cf. 10:12). *Therefore, the analogies imply that the day of the Son of Man will involve a divine judgment executed for the purpose of condemnation.* In this context, Luke makes the Son of Man analogous to YHWH. His divine appearance from heaven is readily apparent in 17:24, 30. Whether the lightninglike revelation of the Son of Man is condemnatory in nature remains to be seen.

5. Finally, Luke characterizes the judgment of the "day" with the same phrase in both analogies, "and [it/he] destroyed all [of them]" (καὶ ἀπώλεσεν πάντας). Luke's repetition of this phrase suggests its prominence as a description of the "day" (which would also substantiate the previous point about the condemnatory nature of the "day"). The stories of both Noah and Lot report the destruction of "all things" as a result of YHWH's judgment (Gen 7:21–23, 19:25). Luke seems more focused, however, on the death of those who did not recognize that judgment was coming.[40] *Therefore, the analogies imply that the day of the Son of Man will involve utter destruction, resulting in the death of all those who are wicked and unperceptive of God's plan.* Luke appears to be saying that the death of Noah's generation and the people of Sodom will be analogous to the death of "this generation." They are the ones who try to secure their lives but "will perish" (ἀπολέσει, 17:33–35).

---

[37] Note Luke's use of the active voice: Noah "entered" and Lot "left."

[38] Lang considers the Son of Man to be analogous to Noah and Lot ("'You Will Desire to See,'" 294), but this is certainly an incorrect point of comparison based on Luke's language of escape.

[39] See Gen 6:7, 13; 7:4, 23; 19:13, 24–25, 29.

[40] Most translations add "of them" in v. 29, under the assumption that what is "destroyed" are people. This is probably correct in terms of balancing those who escape versus those who perish (cf. Luke 13:1–5).

In summary, we can chart the most significant points of comparison between the analogies of Noah and Lot, and Luke's description of the "days" and "day" of the Son of Man.

Days of Noah/Lot	Days of the Son of Man
1. Days of Noah/Lot	1. This generation (as period of time)
2. Activities of Noah's generation/people of Sodom lack perception	2. Activities of this generation (as class of people) lack perception

Day of Noah/Lot	Day of the Son of Man
3. Escape of Noah/Lot	3. Escape of Jesus's disciples
4. Condemnatory judgment by YHWH	4. Condemnatory judgment by Jesus, the Son of Man
5. Death of Noah's generation/people of Sodom	5. Death of this generation (as class of people)

Having established some of Luke's points of comparison between 17:26–29 and the rest of 17:22–37, we can use them as interpretive parameters that will help guide our interpretation. The next step will be to look at Luke's presentation of the "days" of the Son of Man (v. 25), followed by the "day" of the Son of Man (vv. 24, 30). Then I will focus on Luke's exhortations and elaboration on the "day" (vv. 31–37). Finally, I will return to the central text under consideration, "one of the days of the Son of Man" (vv. 22–23).

The Days of the Son of Man (Luke 17:25)

Luke 17:25 is an abbreviated passion prediction, formulated on the basis of an earlier prediction in 9:22. We can set the two verses side by side for comparison purposes.

Luke 9:22	Luke 17:25

δεῖ τὸν υἱὸν τοῦ ἀνθρώπου
πολλὰ παθεῖν
καὶ ἀποδοκιμασθῆναι ἀπὸ
   τῶν πρεσβυτέρων καὶ ἀρχιερέων
   καὶ γραμματέων
καὶ ἀποκτανθῆναι
καὶ τῇ τρίτῃ ἡμέρᾳ ἐγερθῆναι
	πρῶτον δὲ δεῖ αὐτὸν
	πολλὰ παθεῖν
	καὶ ἀποδοκιμασθῆναι ἀπὸ
	   τῆς γενεᾶς ταύτης

It is necessary for the Son of Man
  to suffer many things,
  and to be rejected by
    the elders and chief priests
    and scribes,
  and to be killed,
  and to be raised on the third day.
	But first it is necessary for him
	  to suffer many things,
	  and to be rejected by
	    this generation.

In these two sayings, Luke has basically repeated 9:22 in 17:25 with the exception of three important features.

First, in 17:25 Luke omits the references to Jesus's crucifixion and resurrection, the two elements most commonly associated with Jesus's passion. This omission dramatically alters the saying by disconnecting it from the events that temporally situate it. In other words, Jesus's crucifixion and resurrection can be pinpointed to specific days, but his suffering and rejection, when standing alone, cannot. Furthermore, with the addition of "this generation" (as a designation of time) Luke resituates Jesus's suffering and rejection in relation to a new period of time. *Thus, Luke's alteration creates a generalized saying that no longer functions as a definitive passion prediction.* "This generation," then, indicates a general period of time, contemporary to Jesus, which extends both before *and after* Jesus's crucifixion and resurrection (cf. Acts 2:40). One may object to the idea of Jesus's suffering and rejection after his death. But Luke insists that the exalted Jesus continues to experience these things through his witnesses, the disciples. For example, the exalted Jesus questions Saul, "Why are you persecuting *me*?" (see Acts 9:4–5, 22:7–8, 24:14–15, Luke 10:16). This is significant because it characterizes the "days" as a period that includes *also* the disciples' suffering and rejection (cf. Luke 18:1–8, 21:12–19, Acts 14:22). Therefore, Luke's alterations create a general period of time (about thirty to forty years) that overlaps with the ministry of Jesus (ca. 30 CE) and extends beyond his crucifixion and resurrection. If this chronology is roughly accurate, then the "day" that both follows and terminates "this generation" appears to be not the parousia but the destruction of Jerusalem (ca. 70 CE).

Second, Luke expands the scope of "the elders and chief priests and scribes" (9:22) to "this generation" of people (17:25).[41] Thus, Luke generalizes the population to include a wider group of Jewish contemporaries of Jesus. This would suggest that the people who perish during the "day" are not wicked people in general (as in a parousia reading) but a certain class of Jews who participated in the suffering and rejection of Jesus and his witnesses during the period before Jerusalem's destruction.

Third and finally, Luke adds "but first" to organize 17:24 and 17:25 temporally. As a result, "it is necessary" for Jesus's suffering and rejection to occur before the "day." When Luke addresses what follows Jesus's suffering and rejection in the rest of Luke-Acts, he does not speak of the parousia.[42] Instead, *what follows is the destruction of Jerusalem* (see Luke 9:26–27, 13:33–35, 19:39–44, 20:9–19, 23:28–31). For example, Luke's only other use of the word *reject* (ἀποδοκιμάζω) in Luke-Acts is in the parable of the wicked tenants, where Jesus condemns the temple authorities for rejecting him (Luke 20:17). The consequence of their rejection is

---

[41] Fitzmyer, *Gospel according to Luke*, 2:1170.

[42] Most interpreters note the unique (or even odd) inclusion of 17:25 in a discourse supposedly about the parousia.

that YHWH "will come [ἐλεύσεται] and destroy [ἀπολέσει] these tenants and give the vineyard to others" (20:16).

To sum up, Luke temporally situates the "days of the Son of Man" as the period between the beginning of Jesus's ministry and the destruction of Jerusalem. These "days" were characterized as a period of suffering and rejection experienced by Jesus directly during his ministry and indirectly through the suffering and rejection of his disciples. "This generation" is the group who carried out these wicked and unperceptive behaviors, actions that necessarily led to their condemnation.

The Day of the Son of Man (Luke 17:24, 30)

On the "day" when the Son of Man "is revealed" (17:30), Luke writes that he will "shine" like "flashing lightning" when it lights up the entire sky (17:24). Matthew has parallels to both of these verses in 24:27 and 24:39, using παρουσία in each. The majority of scholars take this as a clear indication that Luke is also speaking about the parousia. I agree that Matthew refers to the parousia, but I think Luke does not. As noted above, Matthew and Luke employ the Noah analogy differently, and the same is true for their use of lightning imagery. Luke uses the imagery to describe the Son of Man himself (17:24), whereas Matthew describes the Son of Man's παρουσία (24:27). The point of comparison is different, especially since Luke connects the "day" in 17:24 to the suffering and rejection of the Son of Man (17:25). Thus, it cannot be assumed that Luke is talking about the parousia in 17:24 and 17:30.

The revelation of the Son of Man like flashing lightning implies that the "day" will be a *revelatory theophany*. While the ideas of a theophany and revelation are certainly interconnected, I will separate them for discussion purposes below.

First, the lightning imagery implies that the "day" will involve a *theophany*. In Old Testament theophany accounts, YHWH is often described as coming in a thunderstorm when he acted in history for purposes of judgment and salvation.[43] "Lightning" (ἀστραπή) is an essential component in many of these accounts, the majority of times functioning as YHWH's implement of war to execute judgment on his enemies (see Deut 32:41, 2 Sam 22:14–15, Ps 18:13–14 [17:14–15 LXX], Hab 3:11, Zech 9:14).[44] Thus, lightning is not normally a positive image, but one that evokes the terrifying presence of YHWH and judgment.[45] Luke's image of "flashing lightning" (ἀστραπὴ ἀστράπτουσα) may allude to Ps 144:6 (143:6 LXX), which is the only verse in the LXX to link the two words, "Flash lightning [ἄστραψον

---

[43] See Exod 19:16, Ps 77:18 [76:19 LXX], 97:4 [96:4 LXX]; Beasley-Murray, *Jesus and the Kingdom*, 3–10; Jörg Jeremias, *Theophanie: Die Geschichte einer Alttestamentlichen Gattung*, WMANT 10 (Neukirchen-Vluyn: Neukirchener Verlag, 1965), 97–100.

[44] Feuillet, "La venue du Règne de Dieu," 550.

[45] "Lightning," in *Dictionary of Biblical Imagery*, ed. Leland Ryken, James C. Wilhoit, and Tremper Longman III (Downers Grove, IL: InterVarsity, 1998), 512–13.

ἀστραπήν] and you will scatter them; send forth your arrows and you will confuse them." This appears to cohere with our finding from the analogies of Noah and Lot that the Son of Man's actions on the "day" will be condemnatory in nature. Luke may even employ lightning imagery to draw comparisons to the firestorm that "rained" on Sodom (17:29; cf. Gen 19:24). Other contemporary writers described Sodom's destruction as YHWH hurling "thunderbolts" (κεραυνός) upon the city.[46]

Closely related to the concept of a theophany is that the "day" will be a *revelation* of the Son of Man. In Luke's Gospel, being "revealed" (ἀποκαλύπτω) involves the disclosure of something that was previously hidden (see 2:35; 10:21, 22; 12:2).[47] When the entire sky is lit up by a flash of lightning, everything becomes visible.[48] Things once hidden in darkness are able to be seen. Hidden before the "day," the Son of Man will then be *seen*. But seen by whom? It will not be the disciples (17:22). Furthermore, the context does not suggest a revelation to all people (as is commonly assumed in a parousia reading). Instead, "this generation" will *see* him. They demonstrated an inability to perceive the Son of Man by their actions (17:25). Luke repeatedly emphasizes that "this generation" failed to perceive God's plans (see Luke 7:30–35, 8:10, 10:21, 11:29–32, 12:54–56, Acts 28:25–27) and did not recognize Jesus as God's chosen Messiah who must suffer, die, and be raised (see Luke 13:33–35; 19:41–44; 23:34; Acts 2:36, 40; 3:17–18; 4:27–28; 13:27). Their inability to recognize Jesus as the Messiah will lead to their destruction. Luke shows this by contrasting God's plan with this generation's response. At the beginning of Luke's Gospel, Zechariah speaks of Jesus coming to Israel as the sunrise-like revealer of God's salvation.

> Because of the tender mercy of our God, the sunrise [i.e., Jesus] from on high will visit [ἐπισκέψεται] us, to shine [ἐπιφᾶναι] upon the ones sitting in darkness and in the shadow of death, to guide our feet in the way of peace [εἰρήνης]. (Luke 1:78–79)

But as Jesus approaches Jerusalem, Luke makes painfully clear that this generation was unable to perceive (i.e., see the light of) God's salvation in Jesus.[49] Jesus weeps over Jerusalem's rejection and prophesies its judgment (alluding to 1:78–79).

> If you, even you, had only recognized [ἔγνως] on this day the things that make for peace [εἰρήνην]! But now they are hidden [ἐκρύβη] from your eyes. For the days will come upon you when your enemies will set up a barricade against you, and surround you and hem you in on every side, and they will level you to the

---

[46] Josephus, *J.W.* 4.484; 5.566; *Ant.* 1.203; Philo, *Mos.* 2.56.

[47] BDAG, s.v. ἀποκαλύπτω; De Souza, "Coming of the Lord," 181–83; Lang, "'You Will Desire to See,'" 295.

[48] Some argue that the lightning imagery communicates "suddenness," but in consideration of Luke's emphasis on "seeing" (17:22, 23, 24, 30), "visibility" is more likely. See Zmijewski, *Die Eschatologiereden des Lukas-Evangeliums*, 415; Stein, *Luke*, 439; Bock, *Luke*, 2:1429.

[49] When Luke speaks of "Jerusalem," he often identifies it as wicked and unperceptive, like "this generation" (13:33–35, 19:42–44, 23:28–31).

ground and your children within you, and they will not leave in you one stone upon another, because you did not recognize [ἔγνως] the time of your visitation [ἐπισκοπῆς]. (Luke 19:42-44)

Commenting on this passage, David Tiede writes, "God's visitation was intended to be the redemption and salvation of God's people. But now it has turned tragically into a visitation of judgment."[50] When Jerusalem was destroyed, this generation finally saw what it had been unable to perceive, Jesus coming as Israel's Messiah/king. Luke seems to imply a contrast between Jesus coming as a "sunrise" for the purpose of salvation (1:78-79) and Jesus coming as "lightning" for the purpose of condemnation (17:24). "This generation" finally saw its king, an event that Luke describes in a variety of ways (see 9:27, 13:35, 21:27, 23:30).[51] For example, Jesus describes the response of a general group of people ("they") to Jerusalem's destruction, "Then they will begin to say to the mountains, 'Fall on us,' and to the hills, 'Cover [καλύψατε] us'" (Luke 23:30). This verse is similar to Rev 6:16, which also employs Hos 10:8 (cf. Isa 2:10, 21) in a context of divine wrath where God comes to judge the wayward people who persecute his witnesses. The apparent contrast between ἀποκαλύπτω (17:30) and καλύπτω (23:30) should not be missed. Confronted with the glorious revelation of the Son of Man as the suffering-yet-vindicated Messiah, this generation will call upon the mountains and hills to conceal them from his presence.

In summary, the evidence seems to imply that the "day of the Son of Man" will be a revelatory theophany of the Son of Man as the glorious and suffering-yet-vindicated messianic king of Israel to pass judgment on this generation, the wicked and unperceptive Jews who persistently rejected and caused the suffering of Jesus and his witnesses. This condemnatory judgment will be enacted in the utter destruction of Jerusalem and its temple.

Exhortations and Explanations concerning the Day (Luke 17:31-37)

Luke turns attention toward the disciples and this generation in 17:31-37. Jesus commands his disciples concerning the "day" (vv. 31-33) and explains about how it will divide the disciples from this generation (vv. 34-35).[52] Jesus then responds to a follow-up question about "where" these events will occur (v. 37).

Luke develops the theme of escape in 17:31-33. Verse 31 is parallel to Matt 24:17-18 and Mark 13:15-16, both of which describe escaping from Jerusalem before it is destroyed (also see Luke 21:21). Luke does little to dispel the idea that he is talking about the same event. Here Jesus addresses his historical disciples (not future Christians). Luke 17:31-32 raises major problems for a parousia reading of

---

[50] David L. Tiede, *Luke*, ACNT (Minneapolis: Augsburg, 1988), 333.

[51] Note the impersonal subjects in each passage, which probably refer to "this generation."

[52] Luke 17:36 is most likely a harmonization with Matt 24:40 and thus not original to Luke's text. I will not discuss it here.

17:22–37. For example, how can one flee from the parousia?[53] If we read these verses in light of the analogies of Noah and Lot (especially on account of Luke's reference to "Lot's wife"), however, then we see that Jesus's followers are to pattern their lives after Noah and Lot. They need to perceive when the "day" of judgment is at hand and escape (21:20–21). These exhortations to flee evoke images of an approaching army in the Old Testament (see Jer 6:1; 48:6; 49:8, 30; 51:6).[54] There will be no time to gather one's possessions, only time to run. The command to "remember" Lot's wife underscores the severity of turning back and is a negative example of the saying in 17:33.[55] Luke 17:33 probes the heart-level commitment necessary to remain faithful and preserve one's "life" (ψυχή) from certain destruction. The disciples will have to adopt a daily lifestyle of cross-bearing discipleship that is not controlled by the wants of worldly living (9:23–25). "This generation" does not live with this commitment, seeking to live their lives like the inhabitants of Sodom (eating, drinking, buying, selling, etc.). As a result, they will perish. At its core, what divides those who live from those who die is an inner commitment that exalts Jesus as God's chosen Messiah.

Closely linked to 17:33 are verses 34–35, in which Luke develops the theme of division (cf. 2:34–35). Some interpreters question why Luke appears to change settings from "on that day" (v. 31) to "on this night" (ταύτῃ τῇ νυκτί) in verse 34, but this seems to confuse categories. The "day" of the Son of Man is not something that happens during the daytime since it is an *event*, like the day of YHWH. Furthermore, in 17:24 Luke has already used nighttime imagery to describe the "day," when lightning flashes and illuminates (presumably) the entire night sky. "Night," then, serves as part of Luke's imagery to describe the "day" (cf. Amos 5:18–20).[56] "On this night" appears to allude to the parable of the rich fool, who (like those who will perish in 17:33) attempts to secure his life through an abundance of possessions (12:13–21). Jesus declares, "You fool! On this night [ταύτῃ τῇ νυκτί] your life [ψυχήν] is demanded [ἀπαιτοῦσιν] from you" (12:20). If Luke follows the same line of thought in 17:33–35 (which appears likely), then those who are "taken" have their lives "demanded" from them by God.[57] Put another way, "this generation," who rejected God's salvation in Jesus and chose to secure their lives through possessions, had their lives taken from them amid Jerusalem's ruin. Those "left," then,

---

[53] The majority of commentators acknowledge this difficulty but then tend to "spiritualize" 17:31–35 in order to apply it to the parousia.

[54] Stein, *Luke*, 440.

[55] Cf. Luke 9:62, 18:8, Gen 19:26; Beasley-Murray, *Jesus and the Kingdom*, 319.

[56] Lang ("'You Will Desire to See,'" 296–97) attempts to link the "night" to the Passover, following August Strobel ("In dieser Nacht [Luk 17,34]: Zu einer älteren Form der Erwartung in Luk 17,20–37," *ZTK* 58 [1961]: 16–29), but this is unwarranted.

[57] Several commentators argue that those "taken" are the disciples (e.g., Bock, *Luke*, 2:1437; Marshall, *Luke*, 668; Fitzmyer, *Gospel according to Luke*, 2:1172). They suggest (rightly) that Luke associates the disciples with Noah and Lot, but they assume (wrongly) that Noah and Lot are "taken" by God for salvation. According to Luke 17:27, 29, however, Noah and Lot act to save themselves.

were Jesus's disciples, who were willing to leave everything (including their possessions in Jerusalem) in order to follow Jesus. The main point is that the "day" will involve a division of persons based on an inner commitment to Jesus that manifests itself in how one secures one's life.

In 17:37, the disciples ask a follow-up question ("Where, Lord?"), to which Jesus offers an obscure response, "Where the body is, there also the eagles will be gathered together" (ὅπου τὸ σῶμα, ἐκεῖ καὶ οἱ ἀετοὶ ἐπισυναχθήσονται).[58] Here again, a parousia reading encounters great difficulty. Why are the disciples asking about "where" the parousia will occur? Is not this question misplaced?[59] "Where," however, is a legitimate question if the "day of the Son of Man" is understood as a divine judgment against a particular historical locality. The "body" probably refers to Jesus's corpse (cf. Luke 22:19; 23:52, 55; 24:3, 23).[60] The "eagles" are probably Roman armies, who had eagles depicted on their standards, and whom Luke later describes as "surrounding" (κυκλουμένην) Jerusalem (21:20; cf. 19:43).[61] Jesus's answer, then, is something like, "The location where I die is also the place where the Roman armies will be gathered." This cryptic answer contrasts Jerusalem's fate with what might have been. Earlier Jesus lamented, "Jerusalem, Jerusalem, the city that kills the prophets and stones those who are sent to it! How often I desired to gather [ἐπισυνάξαι] your children together as a hen gathers her brood under her wings, and you were not willing!" (13:34). Jerusalem initially had the opportunity to be gathered under the nurturing wings of a mother hen, depicting God's salvation in Jesus. Yet, because of its unwillingness, Jerusalem was handed over to another bird, a bird of prey, which swooped down to destroy them.

One of the Days of the Son of Man (Luke 17:22–23)

Jesus begins by referring to a future time in the lives of his disciples by saying, "the days will come" (ἐλεύσονται ἡμέραι). Luke uses this exact phrase in 5:35 and 21:6 and a minor variation in 19:43 (ἥξουσιν ἡμέραι) and 23:29 (ἔρχονται ἡμέραι). Strikingly, in three of these four occurrences (17:22, 19:43, 21:6, 23:29), Luke's subject is Jerusalem's destruction. The other occurrence (5:35) refers to a future period when Jesus will no longer be present with his disciples. Thus, Jesus is probably referring to the segment of the "days of the Son of Man" after he has ascended,

---

[58] Again, the context of the parallel in Matt 24:28 is different.

[59] E.g., Johnson, *Luke*, 267; Evans, *Saint Luke*, 634; Marshall, *Gospel of Luke*, 669.

[60] Lang argues that σῶμα refers to Jesus's *living* body when he is surrounded by the Jewish authorities ("'Where the Body Is, There Also the Eagles Will Be Gathered': Luke 17:37 and the Arrest of Jesus," *BibInt* 21 [2013]: 326–27). His conclusion builds on the argument of Bridge (*Where the Eagles Are Gathered*, 51–52), but when Luke refers to Jesus's "body," it is always to his *dead* body.

[61] On Roman "eagles," see Josephus, *J. W.* 3.123; Lang, "'Where the Body Is,'" 324–27; Warren Carter, "Are There Imperial Texts in the Class? Intertextual Eagles and Matthean Eschatology as 'Lights Out' Time for Imperial Rome," *JBL* 122 (2003): 473–76, http://dx.doi.org/10.2307/3268387.

when the disciples will experience suffering and rejection in his name prior to Jerusalem's ruin (17:25, 21:12–19).

It is during this period of suffering that the disciples will desire to see "one of the days of the Son of Man." They long to see *the "day" when Jesus will be publicly revealed as the glorious and suffering-yet-vindicated Messiah* (cf. 17:24, 30). In other words, they long to see Jesus's coming as the exalted king of Israel. There are hints at the beginning of this longing (i.e., before the disciples comprehended the necessity of Jesus's, and their own, suffering and rejection) in the following narrative. First, in Luke 19:11 the disciples supposed (wrongly) that the kingdom of God was to "appear immediately" because Jesus was drawing close to Jerusalem. Jesus challenges their thinking, however, by telling a parable about how his own countrymen (i.e., this generation) will reject him as "king" (19:12–27). Second, two disciples lament the crucified Jesus, "But we had hoped that he was the one to redeem Israel" (24:21). But the resurrected Jesus corrects them by explaining that it was necessary for the Messiah to "suffer" before entering "glory" (24:26). Finally, the disciples inquire of Jesus, "Is it at this time when you will restore the kingdom to Israel?" (Acts 1:6). While the disciples now know that Jesus had to suffer, their question reveals a failure to understand the necessity of their own suffering and rejection as Jesus's witnesses (Acts 1:7–8). It was not yet time for them to "stand looking up into the sky" (Acts 1:11) because the time of their "liberation" from their oppressors had not yet come (Luke 21:28).

Why, then, do the disciples "long to see" Jesus gloriously revealed as the suffering-yet-vindicated Messiah? Their longing appears to be grounded in a desire for justice and relief from the suffering they will experience at the hands of "this generation" during the "days of the Son of Man" (17:25).[62] Jesus addresses the disciples' future longing in the parable of the widow and the unjust judge (18:1–8). There will come a time when the disciples will be in danger of "losing heart" amid their suffering (18:1). The lure of other messianic claimants, wherever they might show themselves, will be enticing (17:23; cf. 21:8), especially when it seems that God will not grant their requests for justice (18:3–4). But instead of turning away, Jesus exhorts the disciples to "cry out" to God continually day and night for "justice/vindication" (ἐκδίκησις) against their oppressors (18:7). Jesus declares that God will act quickly on their behalf, but they must remain faithful (18:8; cf. 17:31–33, 21:19). Later we find that the longing expressed in the disciples' prayers is answered during the "days of justice/vindication" (ἡμέραι ἐκδικήσεως) against Jerusalem (21:22), which will grant the disciples' "liberation" from their oppressors, "this generation" (21:28).

Despite the disciples' desire to see Jesus's glorious coming as the suffering-yet-vindicated Messiah, Jesus says they "will not see" (i.e., witness) it.[63] Many

---

[62] So De Souza, "Coming of the Lord," 176–77; Green, *Gospel of Luke*, 633; Danker, *Jesus and the New Age*, 292.

[63] Lang argues that Luke uses two different senses of "seeing" in the two occurrences of ὁράω

interpreters take this assertion to mean that the disciples will no longer be alive when the parousia occurs. Yet, if the disciples are analogous to Noah and Lot, then they should be alive when the "day" arrives and should perceive the need to depart. This is precisely what Jesus instructs the disciples to do: "escape" (17:31–32) and "flee" (21:21) when they perceive that the "day" is at hand. When they see the eagles surrounding Jerusalem, the city where Jesus was crucified, they need to run (17:37, 21:20). As with Noah and Lot, their very lives depend on their getting out and not turning back. Consequently, they will not "see" Jesus's glorious revelation as the suffering-yet-vindicated Messiah. The ones who will "see" his coming will be "this generation," those who persist in their wicked and unperceptive ways. Instead of experiencing Jesus's messianic reign as salvation, they will experience it as condemnation.

IV. Conclusion

I have attempted to challenge two interpretive decisions related to "one of the days of the Son of Man." (1) Instead of interpreting the "days" as a temporal period, I suggest that we understand the "days" as a collection of similar yet distinct days. This interpretive decision is made possible when one recognizes that the Old Testament prophets spoke of multiple "days" of divine judgment on historical localities in association with the day of YHWH. These "days" typologically prefigured the great "Day" of YHWH. If Luke employs the same tactic, it frees the interpreter from having to synchronize temporally the "days of the Son of Man" in 17:22 with the same phrase in 17:26 and brings "one of the days of the Son of Man" (17:22) into harmony with the "day of the Son of Man" (17:24, 30, 31). These interpretive moves appear to solve the puzzle presented by Luke's variation of temporal language in 17:22–37. (2) Instead of interpreting Luke 17:22–37 as referring to the parousia, I suggest that we interpret it in relation to the destruction of Jerusalem. This interpretation is encouraged by Luke's description of Jerusalem's demise as a "day" of YHWH that embodies and anticipates the great "Day" (i.e., the parousia) to come. As a result, the "day of the Son of Man" refers to a revelatory theophany of the Son of Man as the Messiah/king of Israel in order to condemn "this generation," Jesus's wicked and unperceptive Jewish contemporaries who persist in rejecting God's revelation of salvation through Jesus and his witnesses. This condemnatory judgment was witnessed by "this generation" amid Jerusalem's destruction. The disciples' desire to see "one of the days of the Son of Man," then, was their desire to witness Jesus's glorious coming as the suffering-yet-vindicated king of Israel, but they will not see it because Jesus commanded them to escape Jerusalem's ruin.

---

in 17:22 ("'You Will Desire to See,'" 281–302). He takes the first experientially (i.e., witness) and the second cognitively (i.e., understand), but this is unnecessary.

NEW FROM IVP ACADEMIC

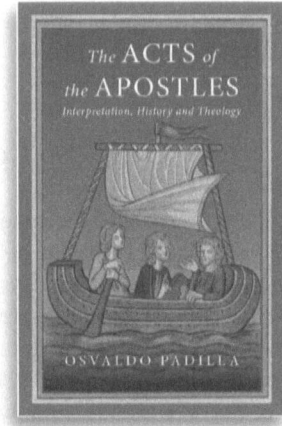

DELIVERED FROM THE ELEMENTS OF THE WORLD
Atonement, Justification, Mission

Peter J. Leithart

In this wide-ranging study bursting with insights, Peter Leithart explores how and why Jesus' death and resurrection address the deepest realities of this world. This biblical and theological examination of atonement and justification challenges conventional perceptions and probes the depths of the death that changes everything.

368 pages, paperback,
978-0-8308-5126-3, $30.00

THE ACTS OF THE APOSTLES
Interpretation, History and Theology

Osvaldo Padilla

Osvaldo Padilla explores fresh avenues of understanding the book of Acts by examining the text in light of the most recent research on the book itself, philosophical hermeneutics, genre theory, and historiography. This advanced introduction to the study of Acts covers important questions about authorship, genre, history, theology, and interpretation.

264 pages, paperback,
978-0-8308-5130-0, $26.00

Visit **ivpacademic.com/examcopy** to request an exam copy.

 800.843.9487 | ivpacademic.com

On Paul's Second Visit to Corinth: Πάλιν, Parsing, and Presupposition in 2 Corinthians 2:1

STEPHEN C. CARLSON
stephen.carlson@acu.edu.au
Australian Catholic University, Fitzroy, VIC 3065, Australia

The supposition that Paul's second visit to Corinth was a painful visit between the writing of 1 and 2 Corinthians is a staple of modern reconstructions of Paul's biography, but its basis is surprisingly thin. It rests in large part on a presupposition generated by a particular parsing of the adverb πάλιν in 2 Cor 2:1 τὸ μὴ πάλιν ἐν λύπῃ πρὸς ὑμᾶς ἐλθεῖν. This article revisits the semantics and pragmatics of πάλιν from a contemporary linguistic perspective and concludes that πάλιν, in this particular context, cannot bear the exegetical weight placed upon it. Reconstructions of Paul's travels need to look elsewhere for evidence.

I. The Pivotal πάλιν of 2 Corinthians 2:1

The occasional nature of Paul's letters to various Christian congregations in the first century presents at least two difficulties for his interpreters in the twenty-first century. First, statements that were clear to Paul and his recipients can be obscure to us because we lack much of the necessary background to interpret them. Second, the issues discussed in detail in Paul's letters are those that were important back then, but some issues of interest to us—such as the finer points of his theology or his biography—may be only briefly or incidentally treated, if at all. These two difficulties come to a head when we consider one of the thorniest questions of Paul's career: Did he make a painful visit to Corinth after the writing of 1 Corinthians? Although the existence and nature of this visit seem crystal clear in some contemporary English translations of the last half of 2 Cor 2:1, τὸ μὴ πάλιν ἐν λύπῃ πρὸς ὑμᾶς ἐλθεῖν as "not to make another painful visit" (NRSV),[1] this dynamic

[1] Scholars who hold this view today include Ivar Vegge, *2 Corinthians—A Letter about Reconciliation: A Psychogogical, Epistolographical and Rhetorical Analysis*, WUNT 2/239 (Tübingen: Mohr

translation irons a critical ambiguity out of Paul's Greek. What πάλιν actually presupposes about a prior visit to Corinth depends on how it is parsed, and the Greek clause in isolation is actually ambiguous as to whether the previous visit had been painful.[2] This article is about the meanings of πάλιν, how they can be disambiguated, and whether the syntax and semantics of this word can bear the interpretive weight placed upon it. I conclude that such exegetical reliance on the meaning of πάλιν is misplaced, for its meaning in this context is too underdetermined to warrant an otherwise unattested, painful interim visit to Corinth.

The debate over the meaning of πάλιν in 2 Cor 2:1 is no modern controversy. The fifth-century exegete Theodoret of Cyrus, in his commentary on the letters of Paul, interprets this verse by explaining that Paul decided not to come back to Corinth and cause the Corinthians grief:

> 1. Ἔκρινα δὲ ἐμαυτῷ τοῦτο, τὸ μὴ πάλιν ἐν λύπῃ πρὸς ὑμᾶς ἐλθεῖν. According to the construction, μέν is left out, so that it should be τῇ μὲν γὰρ πίστει ἑστήκατε ("for, on the one hand you are standing in faith…"). He says this: While I am by no means blaming you on account of your faith (for you are endowed with its soundness), there are some other things from you that are in error, which are resisting some correction. I decided not to grieve those who sinned when I come to you. The πάλιν goes with the arrival, not with the grief [Τὸ δὲ πάλιν, τῇ παρουσίᾳ, οὐ τῇ λύπῃ συνέζευκται].[3]

The first part of Theodoret's remarks pertains to the construal of the connective marker δέ, which is no longer read in the Nestle-Aland critical text.[4] Theodoret

---

Siebeck, 2008), 88–89; Murray J. Harris, *The Second Epistle to the Corinthians: A Commentary on the Greek Text*, NIGTC (Grand Rapids: Eerdmans, 2005), 54–59; Margaret E. Thrall, *A Critical and Exegetical Commentary on the Second Epistle to the Corinthians*, 2 vols., ICC (Edinburgh: T&T Clark, 1994–2000), 50–55; Ralph P. Martin, *2 Corinthians*, WBC 40 (Waco, TX: Word, 1986), 35; and C. K. Barrett, *A Commentary on the Second Epistle to the Corinthians*, BNTC (London: Black, 1973), 5–8, 85–86.

[2] This is routinely pointed out by those challenging the existence of such a painful, interim visit. See, e.g., Douglas A. Campbell, *Framing Paul: An Epistolary Biography* (Grand Rapids: Eerdmans, 2014), 83–84, esp. n. 41; Troels Engberg-Pedersen, "2. Korintherbrevs indledningsspørgsmål," in *Tro og historie: Festskrift til Niels Hyldahl, I anledning af 65 års fødselsdagen den 30. december 1995*, ed. L. Fatum and M. Müller, FBE 7 (Copenhagen: Museum Tusculanums, 1996), 69–88, esp. 75–76; Bärbel Bosenius, *Die Abwesenheit des Apostels als theologisches Programm: Der zweite Korintherbrief als Beispiel für die Brieflichkeit der paulinischen Theologie*, TANZ 11 (Tübingen: Franke, 1994), 10; Niels Hyldahl, *Die paulinische Chronologie*, ATDan 19 (Leiden: Brill, 1986), 36–37; Richard Batey, "Paul's Interaction with the Corinthians," *JBL* 84 (1965): 139–46 esp. 144–45; and C. F. Georg Heinrici, *Der zweite Brief an die Korinther*, 8th ed., KEK 6 (Göttingen: Vandenhoeck & Ruprecht, 1900), 86–87.

[3] My translation from *Interpretatio in xiv epistulas sancti Pauli* (PG 82:385). Another English translation of Theodoret's commentary is that of Robert C. Hill, *Theodoret of Cyrus: Commentary on the Letters of St. Paul* (Brookline, MA: Holy Cross Orthodox Press, 2001).

[4] In a change from the 25th edition, the more recent Nestle-Aland editions read γάρ instead, on the strength of 𝔓46 B 0223 0243 33 1739. This change ought to be reconsidered. The external

goes on to explain that the Corinthians were in need of correction and that they would be grieved by that correction if Paul were to come. In other words, his explanation is that Paul wanted to spare the Corinthians (φειδόμενος ὑμῶν, 2 Cor 1:23) from punishment for their sinning, despite his praise of their faith in verse 24. Finally, Theodoret concludes his interpretation with an explicit parsing of the adverb πάλιν (usually glossed as "back" or "again"): it is to be construed with the infinitive ἐλθεῖν, not with the immediately following preposition phrase ἐν λύπῃ ("with grief").[5] Thus, Theodoret's parsing supports a translation of the infinitival phrase along the lines of "not to come back to you with grief." With this understanding, the text says nothing about the painfulness of any prior visit to Corinth, only that Paul put off an upcoming visit that could prove painful to the Corinthians. The very fact that Theodoret was so explicit about his preferred parsing, however, suggests that another parsing is not just possible but that it may have even been made. In fact, this is the parsing of John Chrysostom a generation earlier.

One of the foremost expositors of Scripture in late antiquity, John Chrysostom handled this verse in a series of homilies on 2 Corinthians. In the fourth of these homilies he has this to say about 2:1:

> Ἔκρινα δὲ ἐμαυτῷ τοῦτο, τὸ μὴ πάλιν ἐν λύπῃ ἐλθεῖν πρὸς ὑμᾶς. The πάλιν also shows that he had already been grieved from there (Τὸ, Πάλιν, δείκνυσι καὶ ἤδη λυπηθέντα ἐκεῖθεν).[6] And while he seems to defend himself, he furtively upbraids them. If they had already grieved [him], and they are about to grieve [him] again, consider how much displeasure it will be. But he does not say this: "you grieved [me]." He crafts the message in a different way to hint at the same thing as saying "For this reason I did not come, so that I would not grieve you." His statement has the same force as what I said, but it is rather more tactful.[7]

---

evidence for the competing variant reading δέ is just as strong: ℵ A C (D) F G Byz lat, and so the variation unit ought to be decided on internal grounds. Both discourse markers fit the context, but the transcriptional probabilities suggest that the reading γάρ is a local scribal harmonization to the instances of γάρ in 1:24 and 2:1. Nothing in this article, however, turns on this variation unit.

[5] Though commonly glossed as "pain," λύπη does not refer to pain in the physical sense but in the mental, spiritual, or emotional sense; see BDAG, s.v. λύπη: "pain of mind or spirit, grief, sorrow, affliction." Likewise, the cognate verb λυπεῖν signifies "to grieve."

[6] The expression is somewhat obscure, and later catenists quote this comment with varying wording. For example, Pseudo-Oecumenius has Τὸ "πάλιν" εἰπών, δείκνυσι καὶ ἤδη λυπηθέντα αὐτὸν ἐπ' αὐτοῖς ("By saying the πάλιν he shows that he was already grieved at them") (*Catenae graecorum patrum in Novum Testamentum*, ed. J. A. Cramer, 8 vols. [Oxford: Oxford University Press, 1841], 5:358, 450). As another example, Hans Windisch (*Der zweite Korintherbrief*, 9th ed., KEK 6 [Göttingen: Vandenhoeck & Ruprecht, 1924], 78 n. 1) cites Theophylact of Ohrid for τὸ "πάλιν" δείκνυσιν αὐτὸν καὶ ἄλλοτε λυπηθέντα ("the πάλιν shows that he was also grieved at another time").

[7] My translation of Chrysostom, *Homiliae in epistulam ii ad Corinthios* (PG 61:419).

Unlike Theodoret, Chrysostom takes πάλιν with ἐν λύπῃ and suggests that Paul had been grieved once before by the Corinthians.[8] The particular grief Chrysostom has in mind is the grief that a father feels when correcting his son, likening this grief later in the homily to what a father feels when forced to amputate his son's leg due to gangrene.[9] As for the prior bout of grief Paul had, Chrysostom identifies it with Paul's "great affliction and anguish of heart" when he wrote the tearful letter of 2:4 (which Chrysostom equates with 1 Corinthians).[10] In other words, Chrysostom took πάλιν in conjunction with ἐν λύπῃ to refer to an earlier time of grief, but that earlier time was the writing of 1 Corinthians, not an earlier visit. Though Chrysostom chooses another path through the parsing—that is, associating πάλιν with ἐν λύπῃ instead of with ἐλθεῖν—his conclusion is much the same as Theodoret's: Paul canceled his visit to Corinth to spare the Corinthians from his having to punish them in person. Like Theodoret, Chrysostom infers no prior painful visit with πάλιν.

By contrast, many modern commentators interpret τὸ μὴ πάλιν ἐν λύπῃ πρὸς ὑμᾶς ἐλθεῖν in 2 Cor 2:1 differently from either of these great Greek exegetes. Rather than taking πάλιν either with just the verb ἐλθεῖν or with just the prepositional phrase ἐν λύπῃ, their preference is to construe the adverb with the infinitival phrase as a whole and draw the inference that Paul's statement presupposes a prior, painful visit to Corinth.[11] Whereas Theodoret inferred a prior visit not associated with pain and Chrysostom inferred a prior bout of grief not associated with a visit, this modern interpretation draws both inferences as evidence for a prior, painful visit. Despite the various interpretative ambiguities for 2 Cor 2:1, it is this understanding that is unambiguously reflected in dynamic English translations of the infinitival

---

[8] A potential explanation for the different parsing is the slight difference in word order, in that Chrysostom's text reads ἐλθεῖν πρὸς ὑμᾶς instead of πρὸς ὑμᾶς ἐλθεῖν. The placement of πρὸς ὑμᾶς after the infinitive ἐλθεῖν disrupts the elegant hyperbaton of Theodoret's (and the Nestle-Aland edition's) word order, and it could suggest a closer grouping of πρὸς ὑμᾶς with ἐλθεῖν, allowing πάλιν to be likewise grouped with ἐν λύπῃ. But, as will be seen with 2 Cor 1:16, this word order is not dispositive to the logical grouping.

[9] Chrysostom (PG 61:421): ὥσπερ ἂν ἔχων τις παῖδα γνήσιον σηπεδόνα ἔχοντα, ἀναγκαζόμενος τέμνειν καὶ καίειν, δι' ἀμφότερα πάσχοι, καὶ ὅτι νοσεῖ, καὶ ὅτι ἀναγκάζεται αὐτὸν τέμνειν.

[10] Chrysostom (PG 61:420–421).

[11] So Vegge, *2 Corinthians*, 87: "The alternative in 2:1, however, is not whether πάλιν only modifies ἐν λύπῃ or ἐλθεῖν, but whether πάλιν modifies the *whole* expression, including ἐν λύπῃ, or only qualifies the aorist infinitive ἐλθεῖν." So also Thrall, *Second Epistle to the Corinthians*, 54–55. The earliest commentator I could find for this interpretation is Friedrich Bleek, "Erörterungen in Beziehung auf die Briefe Pauli an die Korinther," *TSK* 3 (1830): 614–32, here 620: "Deutlich liegt hierin daß der Apostel schon ein Mal zu ihnen ἐν λύπῃ gekommen war." Less careful commentators, however, tend to speak only of the two options as laid out by Theodoret (πάλιν construed with either ἐλθεῖν or ἐν λύπῃ), as if the second option amounts to the modern interpretation rather than to Chrysostom's.

phrase at issue.¹² Under the modern view, then, Paul already had a painful visit to Corinth once and canceled his planned trip to avoid another one.

Getting this interpretation right is no idle exercise in Greek exegetical trivia. It shapes our understanding of Paul's activities at this point in his career. C. K. Barrett, in discussing the ambiguity of 2 Cor 2:1, notes that construing πάλιν with the verb ἐλθεῖν but without the adjunct ἐν λύπῃ "unfortunately leads to no possibility of reconstructing the events behind 2 Corinthians."¹³ Although Barrett's strong statement is probably too pessimistic about the implications of this reading,¹⁴ it correctly senses the importance of πάλιν's scope. If 2 Cor 2:1 does indeed refer to a prior, painful visit to Corinth, then the silence of 1 Corinthians about it readily leads to the inference that it took place after the writing of 1 Corinthians.¹⁵ This interim visit, rather than the issues of 1 Corinthians, then becomes the key for understanding Paul's interaction with the Corinthians in the rest of 2 Corinthians, and scholars are especially keen to connect this painful interim visit with the offender of 2 Cor 7:12.¹⁶ On the other hand, if there was no prior painful visit or if there was a prior visit but it was not painful, then the silence of 1 Corinthians about it is insufficient to suppose an otherwise unattested visit to Corinth after 1 Corinthians, let alone to connect this visit with the offender.

At the time of Margaret Thrall's commentary on 2 Corinthians, she could cite no one after 1962 for the position that Paul's second visit to Corinth happened before the writing of 1 Corinthians.¹⁷ Since the publication of her commentary, however, three scholars have come forward in favor of placing the second visit before 1 Corinthians, the most recent being Douglas A. Campbell in his comprehensive reframing of Paul's biography.¹⁸ Given the importance of πάλιν in 2 Cor 2:1

---

¹²For instance, the RSV and NRSV render it as "not to make you another painful visit," and the NIV translates it as "that I would not make another painful visit to you."

¹³Barrett, *Second Epistle to the Corinthians*, 85.

¹⁴Without the painful interim visit implied by Barrett's preferred reading, 1 Corinthians can be closer in time to the writing of (the partitions of) 2 Corinthians, and so it can be more reasonable to coordinate the travel plans of 1 Cor 16 with those canceled in 2 Cor 1 in order to reconstruct the events between 1 Corinthians and Romans.

¹⁵Barrett, *Second Epistle to the Corinthians*, 85: "1 Corinthians gives no hint to this effect." So also Thrall, *Second Epistle to the Corinthians*, 53: "And why, lastly, should Paul have said nothing in the first letter about his sorrowful recollection of this visit, only to revive the memory of it in 2 Corinthians? If there was a second visit, it must have followed 1 Corinthians."

¹⁶E.g., Thrall, *Second Epistle to the Corinthians*, 165 n. 256: "In relation to the actual interim visit it refers to the state of grief in which Paul found himself once he had arrived in Corinth and the unhappy incident of the offender had taken place."

¹⁷Ibid., 51, esp. n. 325, naming Friedrich Bleek, Albert Klöpper, Heinrich August Wilhelm Meyer, Theodor Zahn, Paul Wilhelm Schmiedel, and Philip Edgcumbe Hughes. It should be pointed out that some interpreters, such as Niels Hyldahl and Troels Engberg-Pedersen, deny the existence of a second visit altogether.

¹⁸Campbell, *Framing Paul*, 83–84; Richard G. Fellows, "Was Titus Timothy?" *JSNT* 81

for Pauline biography, then, there is a need for a fresh analysis of πάλιν in this passage. As the following discussion aims to show, the semantics, syntax, and context of πάλιν constitute an inadequate basis to suppose a painful interim visit on the part of Paul to Corinth.

II. The Senses of πάλιν and Their Disambiguation

The meanings of πάλιν have been studied in recent years from a number of linguistic perspectives. In 1994, Juan Mateos offered a detailed treatment of this word as used in the New Testament based on his Method for Semantic Analysis.[19] More recently, Antonio R. Revuelta Puigdollers published a summary of his analysis of πάλιν in classical Greek based in part on Simon Dik's Functional (Discourse) Grammar.[20] In addition, analogous iterative adverbs in English (*again*) and German (*wieder*) have been extensively studied in contemporary linguistics literature.[21] What this research shows is that—aside from an obsolescing spatial sense of counter-directionality[22] and a more productive use as a discourse marker[23]—the iterative adverb πάλιν presupposes that some state of affairs within its scope in the clause

---

(2001): 33–58, esp. 52–53; and David R. Hall, *The Unity of the Corinthians Correspondence*, JSNTSup 251 (London: T&T Clark, 2003), 243–46.

[19] Juan Mateos, "Contribuciones al DGENT (Diccionario Griego-Español del Nuevo Testamento): πάλιν en el Nuevo Testamento," *Filología Neotestamentaria* 7 (1994): 65–80.

[20] Antonio R. Revuelta Puigdollers, "Word Classes, Functions and Syntactic Level: The Case of πάλιν," in *Word Classes and Related Topics in Ancient Greek: Proceedings of the Conference on 'Greek Syntax and Word Classes' Held in Madrid on 18–21 June 2003*, ed. E. Crespo, J. de la Villa, and A. R. Revuelta, BCILL 117 (Louvain-la-Neuve: Peeters, 2006), 455–70.

[21] See esp. Arnim von Stechow, "The Different Readings of *Wieder* 'Again': A Structural Account," *Journal of Semantics* 13 (1996): 87–138, http://dx.doi.org/10.1093/jos/13.2.87; Cathrine Fabricius-Hansen, "Wi(e)der and again(st)," in *Audiatur Vox Sapientiae: A Festschrift for Arnim von Stechow*, ed. C. Féry and W. Sternefeld (Berlin: Akademie, 2001), 101–30, http://dx.doi.org/10.1515/9783050080116.101; and, in the same volume, Wolfgang Klein, "Time and Again," 267–86.

[22] The best candidate for this meaning in the New Testament is perhaps Gal 4:9a πῶς ἐπιστρέφετε πάλιν ἐπὶ τὰ ἀσθενῆ καὶ πτωχὰ στοιχεῖα ("How is it that you are turning back to the weak and poor elements?"). See further BDAG, s.v. πάλιν, 1a: "turn back"; Walter Bauer, *Griechisch-deutsches Wörterbuch zu den Schriften des Neuen Testaments und der frühchristlichen Literatur*, 6th ed., ed. Kurt Aland, Barbara Aland, and Viktor Reichmann (Berlin: de Gruyter, 1988 [hereinafter BAAR]), s.v. πάλιν, 1a, 1227: "sich zurückwenden"; Mateos, "πάλιν en el Nuevo Testamento," 77: "volvéis de nuevo / atrás."

[23] This use of πάλιν is particularly common in the New Testament to introduce another scriptural text in an argument. For example, Paul uses the introductive expression καὶ πάλιν to punctuate a series of scriptural proofs in Rom 15:10–12. See further BDAG, s.v. πάλιν, 3; BAAR, πάλιν 3, 1227; Mateos, "πάλιν en el Nuevo Testamento," 77–78. Other examples include 1 Cor 3:20 and Heb 1:5, 2:13a, b, and 10:30.

has occurred before. The repeated state of affairs presupposed by πάλιν may include a prior position or state (as with Theodoret[24] and Chrysostom[25]), or it may comprise the whole event (as with the modern interpretation).[26] Though there is a vague sense of some kind of repetition beneath these competing interpretations, they all feature an ambiguity of scope as to what precisely is presupposed as repeated.

The problems of ambiguity and vagueness can be lessened in communication when the speaker and the listener share a common context that makes it clear what is meant. In the case of 2 Cor 2:1, the scopal ambiguity of πάλιν would not have been an issue for Paul's recipients because the Corinthians already knew whether Paul had made a prior painful visit to them. This ambiguity is a problem for us, not them. Because we lack this information today, those of us interested in Paul's biography must discern this missing background information by careful exegesis, if at all.

Despite this ambiguity, there are cases in which the context can disfavor—if not exclude altogether—some of the potential senses. A good example is 2 Cor 1:16, which occurs in the midst of Paul's description of his canceled travel plans (vv. 15-16). This example is especially important because it is one of the few places in the New Testament with the same word order, πάλιν + adjunct(s) + verb, and it has the additional linguistic benefit of having been written by the same author at the same time. No other example of πάλιν is as precisely on point to the interpretation of 2 Cor 2:1 as 1:16.[27] In 2 Cor 1:16, then, Paul mentions his previous intention to go first to Corinth (v. 15, ἐβουλόμην πρότερον πρὸς ὑμᾶς ἐλθεῖν), then

---

[24] So BDAG, s.v. πάλιν, 1: "pert[aining] to [a] return to a position or state, *back*"; Revuelta Puigdollers, "Word Classes, Functions," 458: "The second value [of πάλιν] introduces a presupposition that refers only to the final state." Specifically, Theodoret identifies the final state of the movement verb ἐλθεῖν for the scope of πάλιν, a common use of this adverb in Greek (ibid., 459) and in Paul, e.g., 2 Cor 1:16, καὶ πάλιν ἀπὸ Μακεδονίας ἐλθεῖν πρὸς ὑμᾶς; 12:21, πάλιν ἐλθόντος μου; Gal 1:17, καὶ πάλιν ὑπέστρεψα εἰς Δαμασκόν.

[25] Chrysostom identifies Paul's state of being ἐν λύπῃ for the scope of πάλιν. In the analysis of Revuelta Puigdollers, this would be a use of πάλιν as a contrastive focusing device, in which πάλιν does not describe a spatial or temporal iteration but "contrasts the information provided in it with some previous piece of information or common background" (Revuelta Puigdollers, "Word Classes, Functions," 461-63; quotation from 463).

[26] So BDAG, s.v. πάλιν, 1: "pert[aining] to repetition in the same (or similar) manner, *again, once more, anew* of someth[ing] a pers[on] has already done"; Revuelta Puigdollers, "Word Classes, Functions," 457: "In the first case the adverb [πάλιν] presupposes that the whole SoA [state of affairs] has taken place at least once before."

[27] Other examples include Matt 26:42, πάλιν ἐκ δευτέρου ἀπελθὼν προσηύξατο ("Again he went away for the second time and prayed"); John 4:54, τοῦτο δὲ πάλιν δεύτερον σημεῖον ἐποίησεν ὁ Ἰησοῦς ("this was the second sign that Jesus did"); and Gal 4:9b, οἷς πάλιν ἄνωθεν δουλεύειν θέλετε ("How can you want to be enslaved to them again?"). Though these are pleonastic uses of πάλιν, they demonstrate that the following adverbial is not within the scope of πάλιν. Both 1 Cor 7:5, καὶ πάλιν ἐπὶ τὸ αὐτὸ ἦτε ("and then be together again"), and Gal 5:1, καὶ μὴ πάλιν ζυγῷ δουλείας

to go from Corinth to Macedonia (v. 16, καὶ δι' ὑμῶν διελθεῖν εἰς Μακεδονίαν), and "to go back from Macedonia to you" (v. 16, καὶ πάλιν ἀπὸ Μακεδονίας ἐλθεῖν πρὸς ὑμᾶς). Paul's intention here is not to *go from Macedonia again*, because the first trip to Corinth on his plan was not from Macedonia at all but from Asia (2 Cor 2:13–14). The adjunct ἀπο Μακεδονίας does not fall within the scope of πάλιν, since Paul is not referring to repeating the action of coming to them from Macedonia. Rather, only ἐλθεῖν πρὸς ὑμᾶς can be within its scope, and so πάλιν here refers to Paul's repeating his state of being with Corinthians according to his original travel plans, that is, to Paul's coming *back* to them from Macedonia.[28]

Although context is certainly vital for interpreting such ambiguous adverbs as πάλιν, some languages, notably Germanic languages like English and German, offer syntactic and prosodic means for resolving the scope ambiguity of their corresponding iterative adverbs.[29] For example, in German the iterative adverb *wieder* scopes to the right, such that adjuncts to the right of *wieder* are repeated while those to the left of *wieder* are not necessarily repeated.[30] In English, the syntax is somewhat more complicated, but restitutive meanings (that is, repetition of a result state) can generally be licensed only if the adverb *again* immediately follows the verb and necessary arguments.[31] In both languages, phonological emphasis on the adverb forces the broader event scope to the exclusion of the narrower state scope.[32] In the

---

ἐνέχεσθε ("and do not be subject again to a yoke of slavery"), involve repetitions of state, as indicated by their stative verbs, but there is no action to repeat.

[28] So also BDAG, s.v. πάλιν, 1a, 752; BAAR, "πάλιν 1a," 1227; Campbell, *Framing Paul*, 84 n. 41; Engberg-Pedersen, "2. Korintherbrevs," 75. Many commentators construe or translate this sense of *coming back* for πάλιν ... ἐλθεῖν in 2 Cor 1:16 without raising any concern about its ambiguity. See, e.g., Thomas Schmeller, *Der zweite Brief an die Korinther (2Kor 1,1–7,4)*, EKK 8.1 (Neukirchen-Vluyn: Neukirchener Theologie, 2010), 96; Jan Lambrecht, *Second Corinthians*, SP 8 (Collegeville, MN: Liturgical Press, 1999), 27–28; Thrall, *Second Epistle to the Corinthians*, 1:139; Victor Paul Furnish, *II Corinthians: Translated with Introduction, Notes, and Commentary*, AB 32A (Garden City, NY: Doubleday, 1984), 132; Barrett, *Second Epistle to the Corinthians*, 75; and Alfred Plummer, *A Critical and Exegetical Commentary on the Second Epistle of St Paul to the Corinthians*, ICC (Edinburgh: T&T Clark, 1915), 30.

[29] The availability of these internally disambiguating devices for German *wieder* and English *again* has been of intensive interest to linguists because these devices may imply the existence of syntactic structure buried inside the morphological verb. See, e.g., von Stechow, "Different Readings," 88.

[30] Klein gives the examples of *Frau Rubi hatte das Lädchen wieder für drei Tage geöffnet* (presupposing that she also had the shop open for three days a previous time) and *Frau Rabi hatte das Lädchen für drei Tage wieder geöffnet* (presupposing that she had opened the shop a previous time but without committing to a particular duration) ("Time and Again," 271).

[31] See Karin Pittner, "Process, Eventuality, and *Wieder/Again*," in *Modifying Adjuncts*, ed. Ewald Lang, Claudia Maienborn, and Cathrine Fabricius-Hansen, Interface Explorations 4 (Berlin: de Gruyter, 2003), 365–91, here 368–69.

[32] See generally Sigrid Beck, "Focus on 'Again,'" *Linguistics and Philosophy* 29 (2006): 277–314, http://dx.doi.org/10.1007/s10988-005-5794-z.

copious literature on 2 Cor 2:1, each of these disambiguating devices in English and German has been proposed and applied to the Greek wording to argue that the entirety of ἐν λύπῃ πρὸς ὑμᾶς ἐλθεῖν falls within the scope of the πάλιν and to infer from this that Paul had a prior painful visit to Corinth. As the following discussion makes clear, however, none of these proposals is actually reliable in other contexts of πάλιν, especially 2 Cor 1:16.[33]

For example, in a recent commentary on 2 Corinthians, Thomas Schmeller argues emphatically that the exegetical alternative "not to come back to you in pain" is "practically excluded by the word order."[34] Schmeller's understanding of the syntax is consistent with his rendering of the Greek τὸ μὴ πάλιν ἐν λύπῃ πρὸς ὑμᾶς ἐλθεῖν into the same German word order as *nicht wieder im Schmerz zu euch zu kommen*. Since *wieder* scopes to the right in German, it is true that the German word order of his translation effectively excludes any but the broadly scoped repetitive meaning of πάλιν. Yet, when Schmeller translates 2 Cor 1:16, καὶ πάλιν ἀπὸ Μακεδονίας ἐλθεῖν πρὸς ὑμᾶς, which cannot include "from Macedonia" within its scope for the reasons given above, he changes the word order and moves *wieder* to the right, so as not to encompass "from Macedonia" in its scope: *und von Makedonien wieder zu euch kommen*.[35] His accurate translation of 2 Cor 1:16 demonstrates that the proper German word order and its inferences as to the scope of the iterative adverb do not necessarily follow from the Greek word order. These are different languages with different rules, and 2 Cor 1:16 shows that Paul's Greek does not follow the German word order rule.[36]

Similarly, the infinitive phrase in 2 Cor 1:16 also belies the appeals to juxtaposition for disambiguating the scope of πάλιν. Several exegetes of 2 Cor 2:1 have

---

[33] In an attempt to marginalize the significance of 2 Cor 1:16 for the interpretation of 2:1, E.-B. Allo (*Saint Paul Seconde épître aux Corinthiens*, EBib [Paris: Gabalda, 1956], 33) and Windisch (*Der zweite Korintherbrief*, 78) contend that this word order rule applies only in ambiguous cases. Yet both 1:16 and 2:1 are equally ambiguous at the clause level. It is only because of 2:13–14, where we learn that Paul's itinerary began from Asia, that we can disambiguate 1:16 at all.

[34] Schmeller, *Der zweite Brief an die Korinther*, 122: "Die Alternative, πάλιν ausschließlich auf ἐλθεῖν zu beziehen (also: 'nicht wiederzukommen, [diesmal] im Schmerz') ist von der Wortstellung her praktisch ausgeschlossen" (footnote omitted to proponents of the alternative, including the fluent Greek speaker Theodoret). Schmeller is not alone on this point; he is part of an exegetical tradition that includes Rudolf Bultmann, *Der zweite Brief an die Korinther*, 10th ed., KEK 6 (Göttingen: Vandenhoeck & Ruprecht, 1976), 49; and Windisch, *Der zweite Korintherbrief*, 78.

[35] Schmeller, *Der zweite Brief an die Korinther*, 92. In his detailed treatment of this verse (p. 96), Schmeller does not discuss the word order issue of πάλιν, which he had to move to the right after the prepositional phrase.

[36] As another example, John 4:54, τοῦτο δὲ πάλιν δεύτερον σημεῖον ἐποίησεν ὁ Ἰησοῦς, does not mean that Jesus did this second sign again (as if δεύτερον were in the scope of πάλιν), but simply that he repeated the making of a sign and that this is the second instance of it (with δεύτερον outside of scope of πάλιν). Similarly with Matt 26:42, πάλιν ἐκ δευτέρου ἀπελθὼν προσηύξατο.

argued that the fact that πάλιν is closer to the adverbial adjunct ἐν λύπῃ than to the infinitive ἐλθεῖν means that the adverbial adjunct is under the scope of πάλιν.[37] While this rule generally fits the syntax of the English *again*, this rule too fails to construe 2 Cor 1:16 correctly, for the adverbial adjunct ἀπὸ Μακεδονίας immediately follows πάλιν and separates πάλιν from the infinitive ἐλθεῖν.[38] This rule also fails to distinguish Chrysostom's alternative of reading only ἐν λύπῃ within the scope of πάλιν.

Some exegetes have argued that the prominent position of πάλιν at the beginning of the infinitival clause favors the broadest scope of the iterative adverb.[39] Since the initial position in a Greek clause is the favored position of emphasis,[40] this argument corresponds to the English and German behavior that emphasizing *again* or *wieder* forces a broadly scoped repetitive reading. Again, this rule fails to account for the word order of 2 Cor 1:16, with πάλιν in the initial and prominent position in its infinitive clause there.[41] Furthermore, there is the additional complication that πάλιν may not even be the most prominent word in its clause in 2:1, since it is preceded by the negative μή. This negative is a variable prosody particle,[42] and so there is an ambiguity of intonation on top of the ambiguity of scope, which cannot be resolved by looking at the word order.

By contrast, other interpreters claim that the emphasis does not fall on πάλιν but on ἐν λύπῃ, thereby favoring the broadly scoped repetitive reading of πάλιν.[43] It is hard to know what to make of this argument. Factually, the argument seems

---

[37] See, e.g., Paul A. Toseland, "The Corinthian Crisis: A Reconstruction of the Events Leading Up to the Composition of the Letter of Tears, and of 2 Corinthians" (PhD diss., Trinity College, Bristol, 1999), 27; N. H. Taylor, "The Composition and Chronology of Second Corinthians," *JSNT* 44 (1991): 67–81, esp. 80 ("proximity"); Martin, *2 Corinthians*, 31 ("immediately follows"); Barrett, *Second Epistle to the Corinthians*, 85 ("immediately follows"); and Windisch, *Der zweite Korintherbrief*, 78 ("die Stellung des πάλιν [vor ἐν λ. und getrennt von ἐλθ.]").

[38] This proposed rule also fails to handle John 4:54 and Matt 26:42.

[39] E.g., Thrall, *Second Epistle to the Corinthians*, 55; and Philipp Bachmann, *Der zweite Brief des Paulus an die Korinther*, 2nd ed., KNT 8 (Leipzig: Deichert, 1909), 88 ("Hier steht πάλιν an entscheidend betonter Stelle").

[40] E.g., BDF, 248, §472: "Any emphasis on an element in the sentence causes that element in the sentence to be moved forward." See also Stephen H. Levinsohn, *Discourse Features of New Testament Greek: A Coursebook on the Information Structure of New Testament Greek*, 2nd ed. (Dallas: SIL International, 2000), 39.

[41] As another example, the proposed rule fails to explain the preverbal prominent position of πάλιν with the *back* meaning in Gal 1:17, ἀλλὰ ἀπῆλθεν εἰς Ἀραβίαν καὶ πάλιν ὑπέστρεψα εἰς Δαμασκόν ("but I went away at once into Arabia, and afterwards I returned to Damascus" [NRSV]), for Paul did not repeat an act of returning to Damascus from Arabia. He repeated the state of being in Damascus.

[42] See, e.g., David Michael Goldstein, "Wackernagel's Law in Fifth-Century Greek" (PhD diss., University of California, Berkeley, 2010), 58–60, published as *Classical Greek Syntax: Wackernagel's Law in Herodotus*, Brill's Studies in Indo-European Languages and Linguistics 16 (Leiden: Brill, 2016).

[43] E.g., Vegge, *2 Corinthians*, 87; Furnish, *II Corinthians*, 140; Windisch, *Der zweite*

wrong since ἐν λύπῃ would normally be fronted if it had the emphasis. Logically, the argument seems wrong since emphasis on ἐν λύπῃ should suggest that only it is within the scope of πάλιν, which would lead instead to Chrysostom's focused reading of πάλιν.[44] This argument has the additional problem of having no parallel cited in support, so it ought to be retired for its lack of foundation.

Still another syntactic argument comes from the observation that πάλιν lies within an articular infinitive clause, τὸ μὴ πάλιν ἐν λύπῃ πρὸς ὑμᾶς ἐλθεῖν. Thrall, for instance, argues, "The inclusion of this phrase [ἐν λύπῃ] in its [πάλιν's] scope is also demanded by the introductory τό, which serves to integrate the whole clause as a unified concept. Paul wishes to avoid a second *sorrowful* visit."[45] While it is true that the whole clause is unified as a single syntactic constituent, this fact does not, by itself, establish the interrelationship of its parts, especially as to whether πάλιν refers to the whole or to the main constituent. Indeed, Georg Heinrici draws the opposite conclusion from the same syntactic observation, arguing that in such a construction each constituent is subordinated to the construction's head, ἐλθεῖν.[46] Neither exegete, however, supplies any example supporting her and his diametrically opposed arguments. Lacking such evidence, both arguments are difficult to evaluate, and thus the safest route would be to conclude that the syntax of the

---

Korintherbrief, 78: "Offenkundig liegt der Ton auf ἐν λ., dann wird ein vorangehendes πάλιν dazu dienen, dies betonte Wort näher zu bestimmen."

[44] The actual inference from the focused reading, however, is sensitive to some salient open proposition with which to contrast, but there is no such explicit proposition available in the context and the interpreter would have to supply a plausible one. One possibility is that this reading could indicate that Paul's next coming to Corinth would be "with grief" (ἐν λύπῃ), in contrast to an earlier time that did not involve grief (i.e., a rendering, "to not come to you again, this time with grief"). This reading has much in common with Theodoret's reading, in that only the upcoming, canceled visit involves grief. Another possibility, here mooted by Chrysostom, is to contrast a personal visit to Corinth with a letter to Corinth. In view of the lack of contextual support for either possibility, it is unclear which one is better for 2 Cor 2:1; but it is clear enough that neither requires a prior, painful visit on the part of Paul to Corinth.

[45] Thrall, *Second Epistle to the Corinthians*, 55 (emphasis original). Though not entirely clear due to its brevity, Thrall's argument seems to depend on an analogy between articular infinitive phrases and definite noun phrases, in that modifiers between the article and the head noun are attributive, while modifiers that follow the noun without an article of their own are predicative. Attributive modifiers are integral parts of the nominal's unified concept, while predicative attributes are not. There is no such thing, however, as attributive and predicate positions for articular infinitives, and the modern trend in research on the articular infinitive is to abandon the analogy with definite noun phrases in favor of the view that the article is a syntactic structuring device. See Denny Burk, *Articular Infinitives in the Greek of the New Testament: On the Exegetical Benefit of Grammatical Precision*, New Testament Monographs 14 (Sheffield: Sheffield Phoenix, 2006), 141.

[46] Heinrici, *Der zweite Brief an die Korinther*, 87: "Der Artikel τό vor dem Inf. fordert die Unterordnung der übrigen Theile der Aussage unter ἐλθεῖν." Heinrici goes on to conclude: "Sinn: Meine Entschlüsse gingen darauf, meine Wiederkehr nicht ἐν λύπῃ zu vollziehen."

articular infinitive is of no help here in disambiguating the scope of πάλιν's presupposition.

What this discussion shows is that the attempts of commentators to disambiguate the sense of πάλιν in 2 Cor 2:1 in isolation from the context have been misguided. Notwithstanding their usefulness in English and German, the disambiguation rules proposed for πάλιν, whether by word order or by prosody, do not seem to work for Greek generally, and they do not work specifically for the Greek of 2 Cor 1:16 by the same author in the same part of the letter.[47] In retrospect, the failure of Greek to disambiguate πάλιν by word order should not be surprising, since Greek generally does not use word order to express syntactic relations that are necessary in many modern European languages. Consequently, with word order out of the picture, context must be our guide to the meaning of πάλιν in 2 Cor 2:1.[48]

III. Πάλιν in the Broad and Narrow Contexts of 2 Corinthians 2:1

To evaluate whether πάλιν in 2 Cor 2:1 could presuppose an earlier painful visit, it is important to ascertain whether there is indeed independent evidence of a second visit to Corinth that could be part of the contextual background known to both Paul and his recipients in Corinth. As it turns out, there is inferential evidence of such a second visit in two statements in 2 Cor 12:14 and 13:1–2.[49] The first of these passages reads as follows:

> 12:14 Look, this is the third time I am ready to come to you ['Ἰδοὺ τρίτον τοῦτο ἑτοίμως ἔχω ἐλθεῖν πρὸς ὑμᾶς], and I will not be a burden to you. For I am not seeking your things, but you. For children should not save up for their parents but parents for their children.

Here, Paul's explicit mention of a third time presupposes that there were two other times, but there is some initial ambiguity concerning the point of reference of those two times. Should we take τρίτον τοῦτο with the immediately following ἑτοίμως ἔχω

---

[47] Engberg-Pedersen makes the opposite claim, that πάλιν in Paul generally applies only to the verb and not to any adverbial adjuncts, even those that follow right afterward: "Pointen er, at hvis der i en sætning med *palin* optræder en vedføjet *løsere* bestemmelse af verbet, fx af adverbial karakter, så vil *palin* lægge sig *til verbet* og *ikke* til den løsere bestemmelse, selv om det står tættere på den løsere bestemmelse" ("2. Korintherbrevs," 75). Unfortunately, the restriction of his corpus to Paul seems too narrow a basis to justify the conclusion as a reliable rule, but the Pauline data examined by Engberg-Pedersen ought to caution against jumping to the opposite conclusion.

[48] So Plummer, *Second Epistle of St Paul to the Corinthians*, 47.

[49] This is in distinction to those who support excluding ἐν λύπῃ from the scope of πάλιν in 2 Cor 2:1, including Engberg-Pedersen ("2. Korintherbrevs," 76) and Hyldahl ("Die Frage nach der literarischen Einheit des Zweiten Korintherbriefes," *ZNW* 64 [1973]: 289–306).

and hold that Paul meant that it was the third time he was prepared to come to Corinth?⁵⁰ Or should we take τρίτον τοῦτο with the infinitive ἐλθεῖν so that Paul meant that he had been there twice before and was ready to come for a third time? Notwithstanding the closeness in word order of these two phrases, modern commentators overwhelmingly choose the latter alternative and construe τρίτον τοῦτο with ἐλθεῖν.⁵¹ This conclusion makes the best sense of the context, for the number of visits is more relevant to Paul's being a burden to the Corinthians than the number of his preparations for visits, which would instead burden the sending congregation.⁵²

The inference of two earlier visits to Corinth in 2 Cor 12:14 is confirmed a little later in 13:1-3, as follows:

> 13:1 This is the third time I am coming to you [Τρίτον τοῦτο ἔρχομαι πρὸς ὑμᾶς]: *every matter will stand on the mouth of two and three witnesses.* 2 I have declared before and I declare now, as present the second time and absent now [ὡς παρὼν τὸ δεύτερον καὶ ἀπὼν νῦν], to the ones who have sinned before and to all the others, that if I come again I will not spare [ὅτι ἐὰν ἔλθω εἰς τὸ πάλιν οὐ φείσομαι], 3 since you seek proof of Christ speaking in me, who is not weak to you but strong among you.

In 13:1, Paul explicitly mentions the "third time" in connection with his coming to the Corinthians, and this mention presupposes two earlier times. As with 12:14, the statement in 13:1 has some ambiguity if taken on its own, since the present tense ἔρχομαι can denote a present plan (as if "I am going to come to you") as well as a future result.⁵³ Here, too, context helps to resolve the ambiguity. The Deuteronomistic citation seems to refer to two speaking opportunities and thus implies something more than a mere plan to communicate (as with a visit), but the occasion itself to communicate.⁵⁴ Thus, the presupposition behind the τρίτον τοῦτο of 2 Cor 13:1 suggests that Paul had visited Corinth twice before. The conclusion here

---

⁵⁰ So Engberg-Pedersen, "2. Korintherbrevs," 76; and Hyldahl, "Die Frage nach der literarischen Einheit," 303, as if this is the clearly obvious conclusion, presumably due to the word order.

⁵¹ E.g., Thrall, *Second Epistle to the Corinthians*, 843; Lambrecht, *Second Corinthians*, 212-13; Rudolf Bultmann, *The Second Letter to the Corinthians*, trans. Roy A. Harrisville (Minneapolis: Augsburg, 1985), 233; Furnish, *II Corinthians*, 557-58; Barrett, *Second Epistle to the Corinthians*, 323; and Plummer, *Second Epistle of St Paul to the Corinthians*, 360-61, usually on the basis of 2 Cor 13:1.

⁵² Thrall, *Second Epistle to the Corinthians*, 843, also pointing out that Paul would be averse to calling attention to the times that he prepared to come in light of the Corinthians' exasperation with his changes in travel plans.

⁵³ E.g., Thrall, *Second Epistle to the Corinthians*, 872.

⁵⁴ Laurence L. Welborn understands the Deuteronomic statute literally and suggests that there was only one such visit and that Paul was demanding a second or third witness against a (false) charge of embezzlement (inferred from 2 Cor 12:14-18) ("'By the Mouth of Two or Three Witnesses': Paul's Invocation of a Deuteronomic Statute," *NovT* 52 [2010]: 207-20, http://dx.doi.org/10.1163/004810010x12471172125751). Even so, there was a prior visit.

reinforces the conclusion there in 12:14 that Paul is talking about his third visit, not his third plan or preparation to visit.

In 2 Cor 13:2, Paul says more about what happened at the second visit. He says that he declared to the "ones who have sinned before [τοῖς προημαρτηκόσιν] and all the rest" that when he comes again he will not spare. The object of the verb φείσομαι is implicit, but the implication is that it is the Corinthian sinners. Corroborating this implication is Paul's hope that he not be severe with his authority when he comes (2 Cor 13:10, ἵνα παρὼν μὴ ἀποτόμως χρήσωμαι κατὰ τὴν ἐξουσίαν; cf. also 1 Cor 4:19–21). In other words, Paul promises at the second visit not to spare those Corinthians from punishment on the third visit.[55] Such a promise, reaffirmed by letter in his absence (v. 2, προλέγω, ὡς ... ἀπὼν νῦν), suggests that the problem requiring discipline for the Corinthians' sinning had not been dealt with decisively at the second visit, if at all. Coupled with the charge of Paul's opponents that he is weak in person but strong in his letters (2 Cor 10:1), it is reasonable to postulate that Paul did not punish the Corinthian sinners at the second visit but rather deferred discipline for the next visit, perhaps in the hope that they would come to repent of their uncleanness, fornication, and licentiousness (12:21, τῶν προημαρτηκότων καὶ μὴ μετανοησάντων ἐπὶ τῇ ἀκαθαρσίᾳ καὶ πορνείᾳ καὶ ἀσελγείᾳ ᾗ ἔπραξαν; cf. also 2 Cor 7:9). As he says a bit later, Paul would rather use his authority for building up not tearing down (13:10, εἰς οἰκοδομὴν καὶ οὐκ εἰς καθαίρεσιν).

Although 2 Cor 12:14 and 13:1–2 are not entirely free of ambiguity, the best reading of these passages is that Paul had made at least two visits to Corinth prior to the writing of 2 Cor 10–13.[56] This last proviso is unfortunately necessary on account of complications in the literary history of 2 Corinthians, as it cannot be assumed that 2 Cor 13:1–2 was written at the same time as 2 Cor 2:1. Indeed, partition theories of 2 Corinthians routinely hold that 2 Cor 10–13 originally belonged to a letter separate from the one that contained 2 Cor 2:1 and written at another time.[57] If 2 Cor 10–13 was written after 2 Cor 2:1, then it is conceivable that the second visit had not yet happened then. Few scholars have endorsed this scenario, but it would decisively settle the scope of πάλιν as not including ἐν λύπῃ, since only the founding visit could be that prior visit, which is hardly characterizable as painful.[58] Nevertheless, in order to explore the meaning of πάλιν more fully, I will put

---

[55] So Thrall, *Second Epistle to the Corinthians*, 877–78, canvassing various suggestions for the nature of the punishment.

[56] It should be pointed out that this assumption is at odds with some proponents of the reading of πάλιν in 2 Cor 2:1 as "back" (e.g., Engberg-Pedersen, "2. Korintherbrevs," 76), but the denial of a second visit to Corinth is merely a sufficient condition for that reading. The following discussion addresses whether it is a necessary condition.

[57] On partition theories of 2 Corinthians, see generally Thrall, *Second Epistle to the Corinthians*, 3–49.

[58] E.g., Batey, "Paul's Interaction," 139–46, who identifies the second visit with the one mentioned in Acts 20:1–6.

this scenario aside and continue to examine the issue on the premise that this second visit also took place before the writing of 2 Cor 2:1.

With a prior second visit in the background, it is now time to take a closer look at the local context of 2 Cor 2:1. This statement occurs in a section relating to Paul's defense of his changed travel plans. As he admits in 1:15-17, he originally planned a double visit to Corinth, with Macedonia in the middle, before taking his collection for the saints to Jerusalem. When Paul canceled those plans after visiting Macedonia first so that he would visit Corinth only once, the Corinthians were not pleased at his vacillation, which forced Paul to defend his sincerity at the beginning of this letter (1:12-22). Then, Paul twice tells the Corinthians why he canceled the earlier visit:

> 1:23 Ἐγὼ δὲ μάρτυρα τὸν θεὸν ἐπικαλοῦμαι ἐπὶ τὴν ἐμὴν ψυχήν, ὅτι φειδόμενος ὑμῶν οὐκέτι ἦλθον εἰς Κόρινθον. 24 οὐχ ὅτι κυριεύομεν ὑμῶν τῆς πίστεως ἀλλὰ συνεργοί ἐσμεν τῆς χαρᾶς ὑμῶν· τῇ γὰρ πίστει ἑστήκατε. 2:1 Ἔκρινα δὲ ἐμαυτῷ τοῦτο τὸ μὴ πάλιν ἐν λύπῃ πρὸς ὑμᾶς ἐλθεῖν. 2 εἰ γὰρ ἐγὼ λυπῶ ὑμᾶς, καὶ τίς ὁ εὐφραίνων με εἰ μὴ ὁ λυπούμενος ἐξ ἐμοῦ;

> 1:23 Now, I call upon God as a witness against my life that in sparing you I no longer came to Corinth. 24 Not that we lord over your faith but we are coworkers of your joy: for you stand in faith. 2:1 Now, I decided for myself this: to not come to you again with grief.[59] 2 For if I grieve you, then who would make me glad except the one being grieved from me?

The first reason in 1:23 is emphatic. Paul swears a strong oath, upon his own life, that the reason he did not come to Corinth was to spare the Corinthians (φειδόμενος ὑμῶν). Here, he is less vague about the object of his sparing compared to 2 Cor 13:1-2, and the upshot is the same: he had threatened that his next visit would involve his punishment of the Corinthian sinners. What Paul's avowal means is that, rather than coming and punishing them as he promised, he instead canceled the visit to spare them. Paul explains, in the following verse 24, that he does not want to see his relationship with Corinth as involving a position of dominance over them; rather, he views himself as being a fellow coworker for their joy in the faith in which they all stand.

Shortly thereafter, in 2 Cor 2:1, Paul tells the Corinthians again why he canceled the visit: τὸ μὴ πάλιν ἐν λύπῃ πρὸς ὑμᾶς ἐλθεῖν. The question of the painful interim visit thus hangs on the understanding of the scope of πάλιν in this context. Since the syntactic arguments for ascertaining its scope lack a sufficient basis, especially in the light of 2 Cor 1:16 as explained above, the crucial issue remaining is how well each reading fits the context.

---

[59] The rendering here is an attempt to translate the clause as ambiguously as possible into English, relying on the scope ambiguity of *again* in this particular word order with default prosody (i.e., main accent on the final constituent *with grief*).

The sense of πάλιν ... πρὸς ὑμᾶς ἐλθεῖν in 2 Cor 2:1 fits this context well. Paul decided not to come back to Corinth, this time with grief. Though Paul is again somewhat vague in verse 2 as to whose grief is meant, the following sentence expressly shows Paul's concern for the Corinthians' grief: "For if I grieve you, then who would make me glad except the one being grieved from me?" (v. 2). Paul is worried about the Corinthians' grief, and this continues his desire to spare them from being punished in his solemn oath of 1:23. To be sure, verse 3 goes on to suggest that Paul could be grieved as well from the upcoming visit (ἵνα μὴ ἐλθὼν λύπην σχῶ ἀφ' ὧν ἔδει με χαίρειν, "so that when I come I would not get grief from the ones who should make me rejoice"), but, as verse 2 indicates, those who should make Paul rejoice are the ones Paul needs to punish. In other words, Paul is talking about the grief he expects to get from having to exact punishment on those he loves.[60] He prefers joy to pain and does not want the Corinthians to receive grief from his visit. Under this interpretation of πάλιν, then, Paul reinforces the reason he had just avowed, but with a shift in perspective from himself to the Corinthians. First he says he did not want to punish the Corinthians (1:23), and then he says he did not want the Corinthians to experience the punishment (2:1).

By contrast, including ἐν λύπῃ within a broadly scoped construal of πάλιν in 2 Cor 2:1 is contextually awkward. If this πάλιν presupposes a repetition of grief, it is unclear whose grief it was, and resolving this vagueness creates an exegetical dilemma with no good answer that fits the context as well as the alternative discussed above.[61] On the one hand, if the grief is the Corinthians' grief,[62] it would certainly fit both Paul's avowal to spare them in 1:23 and the Paul's concern for grieving anyone in 2:2. But if this grief falls under the scope of πάλιν, it goes against the characterization of the second visit in 2 Cor 13:1–2 as involving Paul's forbearance in punishing the Corinthians, a restraint he extended in 2 Cor 1:23. On this

---

[60] An early textual variant in 2 Cor 2:3 supporting this interpretation reads λύπην ἐπὶ λύπην ("grief upon grief"), that is, so that Paul would not get the grief added to their grief (cf. Phil 2:27, ἵνα μὴ λύπην ἐπὶ λύπην σχῶ, for the same expression and thought but in a different context). This variant reading could well be what Paul wrote, since it is attested in some early witnesses (especially the well-regarded 1739 plus the Western D F G), it fits the context and his style, and the shorter reading could easily have arisen from a scribal mistake, by skipping from one λύπην to the next. See Furnish, *II Corinthians*, 154, arguing that this scribal scenario "cannot be ruled out entirely."

[61] To be sure, Andreas Lindemann considers the question irrelevant, ("'... an die Kirche in Korinth samt allen Heiligen in ganz Achaja': Zu Entstehung und Redaktion des '2. Korintherbriefs,'" in *Der zweite Korintherbrief: Literarische Gestalt - historische Situation - theologische Argumentation: Festschrift zum 70. Geburtstag von Dietrich-Alex Koch*, ed. Dieter Sänger, FRLANT 250 [Göttingen: Vandenhoek & Ruprecht, 2012], 131–59, here 138 n. 28, http://dx.doi.org/10.13109/9783666535338), but he does not really offer a way out of the dilemma.

[62] So, e.g., L. L. Welborn, "Paul and Pain: Paul's Emotional Therapy in 2 Corinthians 1.1–2.13; 7.5–16 in the Context of Ancient Psychagogic Literature," *NTS* 57 (2011): 547–70, here 555, http://dx.doi.org/10.1017/S0028688511000142: "Paul then explains to the Corinthians that he had no intention of causing them sorrow," in conformity with attested contemporary practices.

interpretation, then, if 2 Cor 2:1 refers to a prior visit at all, it is not the visit mentioned in 2 Cor 12:14 and 13:1-2.

On the other hand, if it is Paul's grief that was to be repeated by the πάλιν in 2:1, then, as an explanation for Paul's decision (ἔκρινα γὰρ ἐμαυτῷ τοῦτο), it would be to avoid a repetition of the grief.[63] Paul's prior grief is not the grief that results from punishing the Corinthians (e.g., v. 3 ἵνα ... λύπην σχῶ ἀφ' ὧν ἔδει με χαίρειν), since Paul did not in fact punish them on the earlier visit (2 Cor 13:1-2).[64] As a result, commentators propose that Paul referred to the grief he got during a quick, interim trip, unmentioned in the travel plans of either 1 Cor 16 or 2 Cor 1, where Paul was personally attacked by the offender of 2 Cor 7:12.[65] Yet this understanding of Paul's grief is unsupported by the characterization of the second visit in 2 Cor 13:1-2, which concerns his warning the whole group of Corinthians about their sexual sins (12:21).[66] Furthermore, even if Paul did in fact get grief from the offender despite how he characterized the visit in 13:1-2, his alluding to it in 2:1 with πάλιν would offer a different reason for canceling the trip—to avoid another encounter with the offender. The reason is an excuse from a position of weakness, and it vitiates the reason he just gave from a position of strength and underscored with a solemn oath in 1:23 to spare the Corinthians. Granted, Paul does not always make the most cogent argument, but when evaluating two exegetical alternatives, it seems to best to avoid the route that gratuitously leads to an ineffective whipsaw.

Thrall, who supports the broad scope of πάλιν in 2 Cor 2:1, points out this

---

[63] So, e.g., Furnish, *II Corinthians*, 149: "He wanted to avoid the kind of unpleasantness which had marred a previous visit to Corinth"; Taylor, "Composition and Chronology," 80: "Paul had already experienced one unpleasant visit to Corinth, and had avoided a second."

[64] If it is merely the grief from realizing the need to punish his flock, this pain is so attenuated that the argument *ex silentio* from 1 Corinthians cannot be used to locate the second visit relative to the writing of 1 Corinthians.

[65] So, e.g., Jerome Murphy-O'Connor, *Paul: A Critical Life* (Oxford: Oxford University Press, 1996), 293: "a single Christian (2:6; 7:12) made a serious attack (2:1, 3, 4) on Paul personally (2:5, 10)." The appeal to the section beginning with 2:5 is explained in more detail by Thrall, *Second Epistle to the Corinthians*, 171–73, who claims support from 2:5, Εἰ δὲ τις λελύπηκεν, οὐκ ἐμὲ λελύπηκεν ("Now, if anyone has grieved, he has not grieved me"), but this statement actually denies the point. Even if the denial can be mirror-read to conclude that Paul had indeed been grieved despite his protestation against it, it hardly makes sense that Paul would admit such grief in v. 1 with πάλιν only to deny shortly thereafter in v. 5. In a context much closer to v. 5 than to v. 1, Paul does admit grief but at a different occasion: in writing the letter "with many tears" (v. 4).

[66] In fact, J. M. Gilchrist argues that 2 Cor 13 and 2 Cor 2 refer to two different visits after 1 Corinthians because "the troubles are different: the visit of 2 Cor. 2.1 concerned a personal insult to Paul by one man (2 Cor. 2.6), whereas the second visit of 2 Cor. 13.1 concerned immorality by many (2 Cor. 12.21). Once again we find two distinct visits, neither of which is the original evangelistic visit" ("Paul and the Corinthians—The Sequence of Letters and Visits," *JSNT* 34 [1988]: 47–69, here 53, http://dx.doi.org/10.1177/0142064x8801103403). A much simpler solution to these incompatibilities is to recognize that the meaning and syntax of πάλιν in 2 Cor 2:1 do not refer to a painful visit at all.

tension in the understandings of ἐν λύπῃ between the proposed visit and the presupposed visit:

> The two occasions (the actual past visit and the present hypothetical one) would not have been exactly identical, since on the actual earlier occasion it seems likely that it was primarily Paul himself who experienced the sorrow, whilst on the visit he refrained from making he would have been the cause of sorrow to the Corinthians (2.2), although this would not have excluded sorrow on his own part.[67]

In a footnote, Thrall attempts to account for the difference by arguing that "the phrase ἐν λύπῃ has an implicit dual reference," the first being to Paul's past grief and the second to the Corinthians' prospective grief.[68] Though Thrall is perceptive to spot the tension, her proposal that Paul actually intended this equivocation follows from her prior decision to infer the painful visit on, as it turns out, inadequate syntactic grounds.[69] Indeed, her exegetical expedience would be unnecessary on Theodoret's narrow reading of πάλιν's scope. The surface appeal of the broadly scoped reading of πάλιν ἐν λύπῃ πρὸς ὑμᾶς ἐλθεῖν is that it enables the juxtaposed ἐν λύπῃ to be repeated as part of the presupposition, while the more narrow scoping skips over it. Yet, with Thrall's acknowledgment of an "implicit dual reference," the attractiveness of the broadly scoped reading proves to be illusory: the kinds of grief associated with the visits are not in fact repeated.

IV. Conclusion

Paul's letters are contemporary, eyewitness evidence of his career. Though all evidence must be critically evaluated, contemporary, eyewitness evidence is the gold standard for historians of antiquity. It is understandable, therefore, that scholars of Paul are particularly keen to find any nugget of information in his letters about his activities. Yet not all that glitters is gold. In the case of 2 Cor 2:1, scholars should resist the temptation to unearth an otherwise unattested painful visit to Corinth after 1 Corinthians in the possible presuppositions of πάλιν. Entities should not be multiplied without necessity, and for lexical, syntactic, and contextual reasons, πάλιν generates no need to suppose that there was such a painful, interim visit. It is true that πάλιν presupposes the repetition of some state of affairs, but what it presupposes has to be inferred from the context. Indeed, the reading of πάλιν that makes the best sense of the context is the one that Theodoret noted long

---

[67] Thrall, *Second Epistle to the Corinthians*, 165.

[68] Ibid., 165 n. 256: "In relation to the actual interim visit it refers to the state of grief in which Paul found himself once he had arrived in Corinth and the unhappy incident of the offender had taken place. In relation to the projected but abandoned visit the ἐν λύπῃ ... ἐλθεῖν would refer to the grief he would, as it were, bring with him and inflict on the Corinthians."

[69] Ibid., 54–55.

ago: πάλιν only has ἐλθεῖν in its scope and so Paul decided not to come back to Corinth with grief for them to experience. Although there probably was a second visit to Corinth (2 Cor 12:14 and 13:1–2), πάλιν in 2 Cor 2:1 thus does not actually say enough to characterize further its nature or to place it relative to the writing of 1 Corinthians. In fact, it probably does not refer to it at all. As a result, πάλιν should not be used to justify the existence of a painful, interim visit by Paul to Corinth.

JBL 135, no. 3 (2016): 617–637
doi: http://dx.doi.org/10.15699/jbl.1353.2016.3094

Paulus als Yischmaelit? The Personification of Scripture as Interpretive Authority in Paul and the School of Rabbi Ishmael

MICHAEL BENJAMIN COVER
michael.cover@marquette.edu
Marquette University, Milwaukee, WI 53201

While a growing body of scholarship suggests that Paul's scriptural hermeneutics may fruitfully be illuminated "backwards" in the light of his early Christian reception and interpretation, the enigma of the precise Jewish character of his exegetical method remains tantalizingly unsolved. Any attempt to illuminate this obscurity by way of Paul's Jewish matrix must wrestle with one intractable fact and its correlative question: Paul was a Pharisee (Phil 3:5), but what kind of Pharisee? Past answers to this question in terms of various first-century rabbis—as exemplified by the studies of Joachim Jeremias, Hans Hübner, and, more recently, N. T. Wright—stumble upon the methodological *skandalon* of the late dating of Tannaitic sources. The present article proposes a new way through this impasse, in the form of a twofold contribution. First, a comparison of the scriptural hermeneutics of the Pauline letters—particularly Galatians—and the midrash attributed to the school of Rabbi Ishmael reveals an important and overlooked similarity: their common personification of "Scripture" as a self-interpreting authority. Triangulating between this common complex of hermeneutical features and Essene and Alexandrian exegetical methods, one can then recover with reasonable probability some contours of Paul's first-century Pharisaism that have ramifications for understanding Paul's Jewish education, his relationship to Torah, and his apocalypticism and mysticism.

While a growing body of scholarship suggests that Paul's scriptural hermeneutics may fruitfully be illuminated "backwards" in the light of his early Christian

This paper was presented in the "Paul" section of the Midwest Regional SBL Meeting, Bourbonnais, Illinois, 8 February 2014; the "Paul and Judaism" section of the SBL Annual Meeting, San Diego, California, 24 November 2014; and the Valparaiso University theology faculty research symposium. Thanks especially to Tzvi Novick, Magnus Zetterholm, Richard Choi, Andrei Orlov, Ron Rittgers, Tyler Stewart, and the two anonymous *JBL* reviewers for their valuable suggestions. All mistakes remain my own.

617

reception and interpretation,[1] the enigma of the precise Jewish matrix of his exegetical method remains tantalizingly unsolved. Some have emphasized Paul's debt to Hellenistic rhetorical and philosophical methods drawn from Alexandrian and Antiochene diaspora communities and their allegorical "yearning for the One."[2] Other studies have highlighted the distinctly Palestinian, Semitic, apocalyptic, or otherwise "midrashic" character of his biblical interpretation.[3] Still others construe Paul's relationship to Israel's Scriptures in primarily canonical terms.[4] Any attempt to root Paul's hermeneutics in his Jewish education and identity, however, must wrestle with one intractable fact and its correlative question: Paul was a Pharisee (Phil 3:5), but what kind of Pharisee?[5] Despite the difficulties of answering this

---

[1] See, e.g., Margaret M. Mitchell, *Paul, the Corinthians, and the Birth of Christian Hermeneutics* (Cambridge: Cambridge University Press, 2010); Matthew W. Bates, *The Hermeneutics of the Apostolic Proclamation: The Center of Paul's Method of Scriptural Interpretation* (Waco, TX: Baylor University Press, 2012).

[2] See, e.g., Udo Schnelle, "Das frühe Christentum und die Bildung," *NTS* 61 (2015): 113–43, esp. 136, http://dx.doi.org/10.1017/S0028688514000344: "Denkfiguren antiker Philosophie finden sich vielfach in den Paulusbriefen"; Gudrun Holtz, "Von Alexandrien nach Jerusalem: Überlegungen zur Vermittlung philonisch-alexandrischer Tradition an Paulus," *ZNW* 105 (2014): 228–63, http://dx.doi.org/10.1515/znw-2014-0013; Volker Rabens, "Pneuma and the Beholding of God: Reading Paul in the Context of Philonic Mystical Traditions," in *The Holy Spirit, Inspiration, and the Cultures of Antiquity: Multidisciplinary Perspectives*, ed. Jörg Frey and John R. Levison, Ekstasis 5 (Berlin: de Gruyter, 2014), 293–329, http://dx.doi.org/10.1515/9783110310252.293; Gregory E. Sterling, "'Wisdom among the Perfect': Creation Traditions in Alexandrian Judaism and Corinthian Christianity," *NovT* 37 (1995): 355–84, http://dx.doi.org/10.1163/1568536952663096; Daniel Boyarin, *A Radical Jew: Paul and the Politics of Identity*, Contraversions 1 (Berkeley: University of California Press, 1994); and Hans Dieter Betz, "The Literary Composition and Function of Paul's Letter to the Galatians," *NTS* 21 (1975): 353–79, http://dx.doi.org/10.1017/S0028688500009619.

[3] See, e.g., Mark D. Nanos and Magnus Zetterholm, eds., *Paul within Judaism: Restoring the First-Century Context to the Apostle* (Minneapolis: Fortress, 2015); Thomas G. Casey and Justin Taylor, eds., *Paul's Jewish Matrix*, Bible in Dialogue 2 (Mahwah, NJ: Paulist, 2011); Menahem Kister, "Romans 5:12–21 against the Background of Torah-Theology and Hebrew Usage," *HTR* 100 (2007): 391–424, http://dx.doi.org/10.1017/S0017816007001642; Francis Watson, *Paul and the Hermeneutics of Faith* (London: T&T Clark, 2004); Timothy H. Lim, *Holy Scripture in the Qumran Commentaries and Pauline Letters* (Oxford: Clarendon, 1997), http://dx.doi.org/10.1093/acprof:oso/9780198262060.001.0001; Joseph A. Fitzmyer, "Glory Reflected on the Face of Christ (II Cor. 3.7–4.6) and a Palestinian Jewish Motif," *TS* 42 (1981): 630–44, http://dx.doi.org/10.1177/004056398104200405; W. D. Davies, *Paul and Rabbinic Judaism: Some Rabbinic Elements in Pauline Theology*, rev. ed. (New York: Harper & Row, 1967).

[4] Christopher R. Seitz, *Colossians*, Brazos Theological Commentary on the Bible (Grand Rapids: Brazos, 2014), esp. 19–56; Brevard S. Childs, *The Church's Guide for Reading Paul: The Canonical Shaping of the Pauline Corpus* (Grand Rapids: Eerdmans, 2008).

[5] The literature on the Pharisees is vast. For a recent *Forschungsbericht*, see John P. Meier, *A Marginal Jew: Rethinking the Historical Jesus*, 5 vols., ABRL (vols. 1–3, New York: Doubleday, 1991–2001), AYBRL (vols. 4–5, New Haven: Yale University Press, 2001–2016), 3:342–46, n. 4.

question, the quest remains legitimate,[6] and outlining two classic answers will help contextualize the contribution of this study—to identify mutually illuminating similarities between Paul's exegesis and the later exegesis of the school of Rabbi Ishmael—while also indicating a road not taken.

The first position is that of Joachim Jeremias, the renowned Göttingen Semitist, who, in a 1969 Festschrift for Matthew Black, made his own position on the subject crystal clear:

> Wir können nun aber die theologische Heimat des Apostels im Raum der zeitgenössischen Theologie noch genauer fixieren. Zahlreiche Einzelbeobachtungen lassen erkennen, *dass Paulus Hillelit war.*[7]

Paul was a Hillelite. In defense of this position, Jeremias rallies a host of arguments, including their shared Stoicized Jewish doctrine that the entirety of Torah could be reduced to a single summary *Kerngesetz*; belief in the resurrection of the dead; an openness to the inclusion of the gentiles; and preference for proselyte baptism rather than circumcision as the primary rite of initiation.[8]

Many of Jeremias's methods and presuppositions have been challenged by subsequent scholarship.[9] Most glaring is his dependence on the *beraitot* of the Talmud Bavli for his reconstruction of Tannaitic tradition. The echoes he hears of 1 Cor 10:12 in m. Avot 2:4 and of Rom 12:15 (χαίρειν μετὰ χαιρόντων, κλαίειν μετὰ κλαιόντων, "Rejoice with those who rejoice, weep with those who weep" [NRSV]) in t. Ber. 2:21, on the other hand, remain intriguing.[10] Nonetheless, the contemporaneous critiques of Klaus Haacker and Hans Hübner significantly problematized Jeremias's conclusions, and, following the more trenchant skepticism of Jacob Neusner, almost everything that had been said about first-century Pharisees has now been called into question.[11]

For a short introduction to Paul's Pharisaism, see Martin Hengel, *The Pre-Christian Paul*, trans. John Bowden (London: SCM, 1991), 40–53.

[6] Meier, *Marginal Jew*, 3:300: "This is a delicate business at best, but better than nothing. By reading between the lines in Paul's epistles, one can try to intuit the *sort of* Pharisaism—and Pharisaism was no monolith in the 1st century—that Paul had known and embraced."

[7] Joachim Jeremias, "Paulus als Hillelit," in *Neotestamentica et Semitica: Studies in Honour of Matthew Black*, ed. E. Earle Ellis and Max Wilcox (Edinburgh: T&T Clark, 1969), 88–94, here 89.

[8] Ibid., 88–91.

[9] For a debate on the relative merits of Jeremias's work and construction of Judaism, see the *sic et non* posed by Ben F. Meyer ("A Caricature of Joachim Jeremias and His Scholarly Work," *JBL* 110 [1991]: 451–62, http://dx.doi.org/10.2307/3267782) and E. P. Sanders ("Defending the Indefensible," *JBL* 110 [1991]: 463–77, http://dx.doi.org/10.2307/3267783).

[10] For a similar critical appreciation of Jeremias's work on Pharisees, see Roland Deines, *Die Pharisäer: Ihr Verständnis im Spiegel der christlichen und jüdischen Forschung seit Wellhausen und Graetz*, WUNT 1/101 (Tübingen: Mohr Siebeck, 1997), 461–67.

[11] See Klaus Haacker, "War Paulus Hillelit?" *Institutum Judaicum Tübingen* (1971–1972): 106–20; Haacker, "Die Berufung des Verfolgers und die Rechtfertigung des Gottlosen," *TBei* 6

All the more interesting, then, that a second, more recent scholar, N. T. Wright, using much the same evidence as Jeremias, has revived just the opposite conclusion: Paul was a Shammaite Pharisee. Wright claimed this confidently in his 1992 work *The New Testament and the People of God*, following the earlier thesis of Hübner, and has reiterated it in his most recent study, *Paul and the Faithfulness of God*.[12] For Wright, it is precisely Paul's later opposition to the Shammaite zeal for circumcision and their exclusion of the gentiles that suggest this as the tradition in which he was schooled. Paul's later apparent affinities with Hillel are simply a natural result of his shedding the scales of his Shammaite past.[13]

The ability of Jeremias and Wright to place Paul in conflicting schools on the basis of his position vis-à-vis gentiles and circumcision suggests that further evidence is needed to make headway on the question of Paul's Pharisaism. It furthermore confirms that, given the current state of the evidence, attempting to plot Paul's Pharisaism along the Hillel–Shammai grid is probably quixotic.[14] Jeremias himself, however, offers an alternative way forward in the second half of his essay in the Black Festschrift: the comparison of hermeneutical method. For Jeremias, Paul's implicit use of all seven of Hillel's *middôt* represents the single most impressive argument in favor of his belonging to this school.[15] These *middôt* were not the sole property of the school of Hillel and probably constitute a shared early Jewish (and indeed Greek/Latin rhetorical) inheritance.[16] Nonetheless, Jeremias's instinct to turn to scriptural hermeneutics in the comparative study of Paul and early Judaism remains a critical part of mapping Paul's religious identity and praxis.[17]

(1975): 1–19; Hans Hübner, "Gal 3, 10 und die Herkunft des Paulus," *KD* 19 (1973): 215–31 (Hübner argues that Paul was a Shammaite—or, better, that Paul was not a Hillelite); and Jacob Neusner, *The Rabbinic Traditions about the Pharisees before 70* (Leiden: Brill, 1971). So also Meier, *Marginal Jew*, 3:311: "The dirty little secret of NT studies is that no one really knows who the Pharisees were."

[12] N. T. Wright, *The New Testament and the People of God*, Christian Origins and the Question of God 1 (Minneapolis: Fortress, 1992), 202; Wright, *Paul and the Faithfulness of God*, 2 vols., Christian Origins and the Question of God 4 (Minneapolis: Fortress, 2013) 2:1415–16.

[13] Wright, *Paul and the Faithfulness of God*, 1:86: "We should not be surprised if his Christian rethinking made some opinions come out looking like cousins of Hillel rather than Shammai."

[14] So Hengel, *Pre-Christian Paul*, 28: "Gamaliel I was possibly a man of compromise, who attempted to stand above the schools. So the argument as to whether Paul was a Hillelite or Shammaite is also an idle one."

[15] Jeremias, "Paulus als Hillelit," 92: "Noch eindrucksvoller als durch diese theologischen Berührungen erweist sich die hillelitische Schulung des Apostels an seiner glänzenden *Beherrschung der exegetischen Methodik Hillels*" (emphasis original).

[16] See Hengel, *Pre-Christian Paul*, 28; Saul Lieberman, *Hellenism in Jewish Palestine: Studies in the Literary Transmission, Beliefs and Manners of Palestine in the I Century B.C.E.–IV Century C.E.*, TSJTSA 18 (New York: Jewish Theological Seminary of America, 1950). For a list of six Latin legal controversy subtypes, with apparent kinship to Pauline and rabbinic *middôt* (including *scriptum et sententia, contrariae leges,* and *ratiocinatio*), see Rhet. Her. 1.19.

[17] Meier, *Marginal Jew*, 3:325: "It seems likely that Paul's way of reading the Jewish Scriptures

Taking a cue from the exegetical portion of Jeremias's study, albeit an indirect one, I tentatively suggest a thesis to be tested: *dass Paulus Yischmaelit war*. Such a claim, construed literally, would be anachronistic. Thus, in suggesting the seemingly tendentious thesis that Paul was an "Ishmaelite," I intentionally bypass the thorny crux of determining the particular stripe of Paul's Pharisaism and begin with a comparative hermeneutical observation: that Paul's interpretation of Scripture and position vis-à-vis Torah mirror, in certain ways, the later scriptural hermeneutics of the school of Rabbi Ishmael.

In looking to the next generation(s) of Tannaim as a means of illuminating Paul's Judaism, I take a cue not only from Jeremias but also from Wright, who draws some striking analogies between Paul and Rabbi Akiva.[18] Akiva's messianism and his martyrdom at the hands of Rome are particularly important for Wright. On the exegetical plane, Menahem Kister has recently argued that an "intimate relationship" exists between Rom 5:12–21 and an Adamic tradition that surfaces in two Akivan collections—and that Paul used a similar passage "as a source" in Romans.[19] While such comparisons are primarily typological and hermeneutical, they nonetheless help plot Paul's thought within the landscape of early Judaism and can, as I argue below, be used carefully to draw out historical conclusions.

Following Jeremias's exegetical instinct, I ask the question reciprocal to Wright's and Kister's: whether the school of Akiva's rival Rabbi Ishmael—with its universalist view of Torah and its eponymous hero's later connection with *merkabah* mysticism—might equally shed some light on Paul's pattern of religion and his particular stripe of Judaism.[20] I answer with a qualified affirmative. The structure of this study is twofold. First, I compare the scriptural hermeneutics of Paul (and, in the case of 1 Timothy, the Pauline "school") and the school of Rabbi Ishmael and discover some previously overlooked similarities in their personifications of Scripture as a self-interpreting authority. These proto-Ishmaelian tendencies are especially prominent in Paul's letter to the Galatians. This discovery, in its own right, makes a contribution to the study of comparative exegesis and can be appreciated independently of the historical conclusions that follow. Second, I use the comparative evidence to triangulate between the hermeneutical features shared by Paul and the Rabbi Ishmael school, on the one hand, and Essene and Alexandrian

---

from an eschatological and messianic perspective did not begin simply after he became a Christian. If the Pharisees engaged in the exact, precise interpretation of *all* the Scriptures, and not just some legal texts, it is hardly surprising that their exegesis should have had an eschatological and messianic as well as legal (halakhic) dimension."

[18] Wright, *Paul and the Faithfulness of God*, 2:1409, 1415–16.

[19] Kister, "Torah-Theology and Hebrew Usage," 400, 422.

[20] For Rabbi Ishmael and the *merkabah* tradition, see Andrei A. Orlov, *The Enoch-Metatron Tradition*, TSAJ 107 (Tübingen: Mohr Siebeck, 2005), 116–17; cf. 2 Cor 12:1–10. My concern in this study is not with the historical Rabbi Ishmael but, first, with the hermeneutics affiliated with his Tannaitic "school" and, second (at a later stage), with the mystical pattern of religion attributed to him in legend.

exegetical methods, on the other. By highlighting the elements unique to Paul and Rabbi Ishmael, one can recover with reasonable probability some contours of Paul's first-century Pharisaism. These features help illuminate Paul's Jewish education, his hermeneutics and relationship to Torah, and his apocalyptic and mystical worldview.

I. Paul, Rabbi Ishmael, and the Construction of Scriptural Authority

In his study of the exegetical method of the school of Rabbi Ishmael, Azzan Yadin-Israel pinpoints a previously underappreciated characteristic of this school of Tannaitic midrash: the personified Scripture (הכתוב)—in contradistinction to the personified Torah (תורה)—interprets itself. In short, "Scripture speaks."[21] This exegetical phenomenon, which distinguishes Ishmaelian hermeneutics from Akivan hermeneutics, finds important counterparts, according to Yadin-Israel, in the scriptural exegesis of 4QMMT and Clement of Alexandria.[22] Yadin-Israel leaves largely unexplored, however, a more intuitive lexical and exegetical parallel: the personification of ἡ γραφή as an interpretive authority in the New Testament, particularly in the letters of Paul.[23]

There are at least five features of Ishmaelian midrash identified by Yadin-Israel that distinguish it from Akivan midrash and simultaneously link it to Paul's exegesis. These are (1) the personification of Scripture and Torah as distinct "speaking" characters; (2) the particular interpretive tasks performed by both הכתוב and ἡ γραφή;[24] (3) the rhetorical construction of an implied reader whose role is to "hear Scripture"; (4) the relative eclipse of halakah and other nonscriptural authorities;[25] and (5) an assertion of the universal audience of Scripture's message, or what Marc

---

[21] Azzan Yadin, *Scripture as Logos: Rabbi Ishmael and the Origins of Midrash*, Divinations (Philadelphia: University of Pennsylvania Press, 2004). See now Azzan Yadin-Israel, *Scripture and Tradition: Rabbi Akiva and the Triumph of Midrash*, Divinations (Philadelphia: University of Pennsylvania Press, 2015).

[22] Yadin, *Scripture as Logos*, 155–75.

[23] Yadin-Israel brings Paul briefly into dialogue with Akivan and Ishmaelian tradition as a "foil" (*Scripture and Tradition*, 166–67, 186). I respond to his suggestions in subsection I, D and section II below.

[24] Yadin-Israel suggests that the personified *hakkātûb* is a shared figure in the Ishmaelian and Akivan schools (*Scripture and Tradition*, 130)—and similarly, that the named Akivan *dərāšôt* in Sifra are "closely aligned with the Rabbi Ishmael midrashim" (ibid., 100). This does not obliterate the distinction between the schools or their hermeneutics but cautions against overdrawing their differences. Shared *formulae*, however, sometimes "camouflage" distinct school hermeneutics (ibid., 53).

[25] For the Akivan school's coordination of oral tradition and midrash as distinguishing it from Ishmaelian scripturalism, see Yadin-Israel, *Scripture and Tradition*, 103 and esp. 138.

Hirshman has called, in the Ishmaelian case, "Torah for all who come into the world."²⁶ In what follows, I treat each of these subjects in turn, and then draw a more comprehensive conclusion regarding the degree of continuity between Pauline and Ishmaelian hermeneutics.

A. The Personification of Scripture and Torah as Distinct "Speaking" Characters

One of the most prominent features of Ishmaelian midrash illustrated by Yadin-Israel's study is the personification of *hakkātûb* and *tôrâ* as distinct personifications of Scripture.²⁷ The primary personification is carried out by four speaking formulae: הכתוב מדבר ("Scripture speaks"), מגיד הכתוב ("Scripture states"), אמרה תורה ("Torah said"), דיברה תורה ("Torah spoke"). Paul similarly personifies both ἡ γραφή ("the writing," "Scripture") and ὁ νόμος ("the law") in his letters, using the phrases (or their near equivalents) λέγει ἡ γραφή ("the Scripture says") and ὁ νόμος λέγει ("the law says").²⁸

In the Ishmaelian midrashim, *hakkātûb* and *tôrâ* differ in the way that each personified speaker relates to the biblical text. The first question, then, is whether Paul makes any similar hermeneutically important distinctions between ἡ γραφή and ὁ νόμος. To answer this question, I turn to the four primary distinctions between *hakkātûb* and *tôrâ* identified by Yadin-Israel,²⁹ and ask whether the same distinctions are present in Paul's letters.

First, "TORAH is figured almost exclusively as a speaker of scriptural passages, while HA-KATUV never cites Scripture."³⁰ This distinction clearly does not hold for Paul's personifications. Despite the fact that ἡ γραφή may in fact simply *be* the verse elsewhere in the New Testament, in all five instances of λέγει ἡ γραφή in Paul's undisputed letters, Scripture cites itself in a manner primarily reserved for Torah in the Rabbi Ishmael midrashim.

Second, "TORAH is an authoritative voice, deciding halakhic questions, while HA-KATUV is part of the midrashic give-and-take."³¹ This distinction provides a closer parallel to the Pauline usage. The speech of ὁ νόμος, as in Rom 3:19, has a "mouth-stopping" quality within its own sphere; ἡ γραφή, to the contrary, enters in the present into the halakic debate of Gal 4:30, arguing alongside Paul and making its own case.

---

²⁶ Marc Hirshman, "Rabbinic Universalism in the Second and Third Centuries," *HTR* 93 (2000): 101–15, here 104.

²⁷ Yadin, *Scripture as Logos*, 12.

²⁸ For λέγει ἡ γραφή, see Gal 4:30, Rom 4:3, 9:17, 10:11, 11:2, and 1 Tim 5:18 (see also Rom 10:8, and the reading in D). For ὁ νόμος λέγει, see Rom 3:19, 7:7 (imperfect), 1 Cor 9:8, 14:34.

²⁹ Yadin, *Scripture as Logos*, 32.

³⁰ Ibid.

³¹ Ibid.

Third, in the Rabbi Ishmael midrashim, "TORAH's non-speech actions are very limited, almost non-existent, while HA-KATUV is presented as an active teacher that employs a wide range of interpretive techniques."³² Here again, Paul's letters evince a similar distinction in the nonspeech actions of ἡ γραφή and ὁ νόμος. These can be witnessed in Gal 3. As in the Ishmaelian midrashim, ἡ γραφή emerges by far as the more imaginative personification, both "seeing beforehand" (προϊδοῦσα) and "pre-evangelizing Abraham" (προευηγγελίσατο) in Gal 3:8 and then "locking all things up under sin" (συνέκλεισεν) in Gal 3:22. Ὁ νόμος, by contrast, is also vividly personified as παιδαγωγός, but its actions per se are not specifically detailed, as in the case of ἡ γραφή.³³

Finally, in the Rabbi Ishmael midrashim, "TORAH belongs decisively to the past: its statements already made, its actions (few as they are) already performed, while HA-KATUV is very much part of the present."³⁴ Again, one finds a near but not perfect point of correspondence in Paul. Whereas ἡ γραφή always "speaks" in the present, ὁ νόμος, at least on one occasion (Rom 7:7) "was speaking" (ἔλεγεν) in the imperfect. Of course, one may object that ἡ γραφή did "pre-evangelize" in Gal 3:8, but that is not technically a breach of the present formula "Scripture speaks."

Despite some salient differences, then, Law and Scripture do emerge as distinct personifications in Paul's letters. These two personifications are not coextensive (Gal 3:22–25),³⁵ despite the fact that they may at times partially overlap. Even in one potentially critical counterexample, Gal 4:21, where Paul's initial question, "do you not hear the law?," is resumed in Gal 4:30 with the question, "but what does Scripture say?," there is reason to suspect that Paul maintains a degree of distinction between his two personifications. For although τὸν νόμον is the expressed object of the interlocutor's "hearing" in Gal 4:21, the accusative case of "the law" suggests that τὸν νόμον is not "the one speaking" (which ought to be in the genitive), but "the thing heard" (properly rendered in the accusative).³⁶ This construction leaves

---

³²Ibid.

³³Cf. Rom 5:20, where νόμος is said to "enter in" (παρεισῆλθεν) in order to increase the trespass.

³⁴Yadin, *Scripture as Logos*, 32.

³⁵See, e.g., David J. Lull, "'The Law Was Our Pedagogue': A Study in Galatians 3:19–25," *JBL* 105 (1986): 481–98, http://dx.doi.org/10.2307/3260514.

³⁶Herbert Weir Smyth, *Greek Grammar*, rev. Gordon M. Messing (Cambridge: Harvard University Press, 1956 [1920]), §1361: "The person or thing, whose words, sounds, etc. are perceived by the senses, stands in the genitive; the words, sound, etc. generally stand in the accusative." See BDF §173, which notes the New Testament's partial adherence to this pattern. Hans Dieter Betz observes that "Paul ... intentionally uses the term νόμος ambiguously: the first time, it refers to Jewish Torah, the second time to 'Scripture' or, more precisely, to Scriptural tradition, interpreted allegorically" (*Galatians: A Commentary on Paul's Letter to the Churches in Galatia*, Hermeneia [Philadelphia: Fortress, 1979], 241).While I agree with Betz in spirit (and with regard to Paul's slippage or "ambiguous vacillation" in his meaning of νόμος), my reading differs from Betz's in that τὸν νόμον in the second instance does in fact refer to Jewish Torah (or, in this instance, a verse

the personified speaker of "the law" unidentified in Gal 4:21, only to be revealed by Paul as ἡ γραφή in Gal 4:30.[37]

B. The Interpretive Tasks Performed by הכתוב and ἡ γραφή

The distinct personifications of Law and Scripture constitute an initial similarity between Pauline exegesis and Ishmaelian midrash. A second connection between their respective hermeneutics can be established by comparing the particular interpretive activities of the personified Scripture in each corpus. I focus on two hermeneutical similarities: the way the personified Scripture (1) introduces nonscriptural categories and (2) distinguishes between legal cases. Both of these features can be seen in a passage from Mekilta, interpreting the law concerning injuries to slaves in Exod 21:20:

"כי יכה איש את עבדו" (שמות כא כ): רבי ישמעאל אומר, בכנעני הכתוב מדבר.
את אומר בכנעני הכתוב מדבר או אינו מדבר אלא בעברי. תלמוד לומר "לא יוקם כי
כספו הוא." מה כספו שקנינו קנין עולם וירושתו גמורה לו...

"When a man strikes his slave" (Exod 21:20): ... Rabbi Ishmael says: *ha-katuv* here speaks of a Canaanite slave. You say *ha-katuv* speaks of a Canaanite slave, but perhaps it speaks of a Hebrew slave? [Scripture] teaches, saying: "He is not to be avenged since he is the other's property" (Exod 21:21), just as his property can be acquired by him as a lasting possession, and when acquitted by inheritance is completely his... (Mek. Nez. 7, p. 272; Lauterbach 3:57–58)[38]

In this *dərāšâ*, the personified Scripture clarifies that Exod 21:20 is speaking not about just any slave but about a Canaanite slave. The *stam* (סתם) objects, saying that a Hebrew slave may also be intended. But Scripture offers a rebuttal: a Hebrew slave could not be considered property (כסף), which is a lasting possession (קינין עולם), since he must be released every Jubilee. Here Yadin-Israel sees several of

---

or pericope of Torah). The anarthrous ὑπὸ νόμον is distinct from the arthrous τὸν νόμον in that the former refers to "law" as a signifier of a cosmic, apocalyptic domain or power, whereas the latter points to a scriptural verse and a personified "scriptural" speaker. Thus, Law is personified as a mythic power in Gal 4:21a but not personified in Gal 4:21b.

[37] God's command to Abraham in Gen 21:12 LXX provides a useful, if imperfect, comparison in this case: πάντα, ὅσα ἐὰν εἴπῃ σοι Σάρρα, ἄκουε τῆς φωνῆς αὐτῆς ("whatever Sarah says to you, do as she tells you"). The foregrounded accusative (cf. Gal 4:21) signifies the content of the proclamation, while the genitive points to the speaker and her "voice." Sarah's "voice" here is hypostatized as the authoritative speaker of the foregoing (accusative) commands, even as it depends for its genitive case on the prepositional construction of the Hebrew *Vorlage* (שמע בקל). For a narratological account of how Sarah's role as authoritative speaker to Abraham in Genesis mirrors Scripture's role as authoritative "speaker" to the Galatians (construed as an Abrahamic people) in Paul's letter, see Michael Cover, *Lifting the Veil: 2 Corinthians 3:7–18 in Light of Jewish Homiletic and Commentary Traditions*, BZNW 210 (Berlin: de Gruyter, 2015), 45–48.

[38] Cited in Yadin, *Scripture as Logos*, 23.

hakkātûb's characteristic interpretive moves present at once. "The phrase 'Hakatuv speaks' provides information omitted by Scripture, concerning the status or the identity of the legal category under discussion, and usually appears at the beginning of the derashah."[39]

Even this cursory description of Mek. Nez. 7 reveals thematic parallels with Gal 4:21–31. Both texts treat issues of slavery and ethnicity, and both make distinctions about inheritance. There are, moreover, several important similarities between Scripture's exegetical moves here and its interpretive actions in Paul's "*midraschartige Stücke*."[40] Several excerpts from this passage warrant closer attention, the first of which is Gal 4:22–23:

> For it has been written [γέγραπται] that Abraham had two sons, one from the slave woman and one from the free. But the son of the slave woman was born according to the flesh, while the son from the free woman was born through the spirit.

Just as in Mekilta, so here in Galatians, Scripture's self-interpreting activity comes at the beginning of the *dərāšâ*. In Gal 4:22, Scripture does two self-interpreting things: first, it paraphrases itself; second, it adds nonscriptural information.

It is immaterial, in this case, whether Scripture is paraphrasing Gen 16:15 and Gen 21:2–3 or simply Gen 21:9–10. In none of these passages is Sarah identified as a free-woman (ἐλευθέρα), as she is in Gal 4:22. Neither is it a given that "free" would be the natural opposite of slave. A more logical, etymological, and culturally appropriate antithesis would have been "lady" or "mistress," δέσποινα or ἀρχή μου, as Philo designates Sarah in several places,[41] presumably playing on the Hebrew etymology of Sarah's name. Thus, Paul's personified Scripture, like Rabbi Ishmael's *hakkātûb* in Mekilta, introduces a foreign category, which will have halakic consequences as the exegesis ensues.

The point is made in the following verse (Gal 4:23), where Paul uses Scripture's previous introduction of the nonbiblical language of "free-woman" to distinguish between two halakic categories—another interpretive activity carried out by Rabbi Ishmael's *hakkātûb*. In the case of Galatians, these are the son of the slave-woman

---

[39] Ibid., 24.

[40] For a description of this passage as "*midraschartig*," see Hans Windisch, *Der zweite Korintherbrief*, KEK 6 (Göttingen: Vandenhoeck & Ruprecht, 1924), 112; and Jeremias, "Paulus als Hillelit," 89. Jürgen Becker considers the allegory to stem from a prophetic tradition of Antiochene provenance ("Der Brief an die Galater," in *Die Briefe an die Galater, Epheser und Kolosser*, ed. Jürgen Becker and U. Luz, NTD 8.1 [Göttingen: Vandenhoeck & Ruprecht, 1998], 70–74). Gerhard Sellin thinks it belongs to the world of Hellenistic Judaism ("Hagar und Sara: Religionsgeschichtliche Hintergründe der Schriftallegorese Gal 4,21–31," in *Das Urchristentum in seiner literarischen Geschichte: Festschrift für Jürgen Becker zum 65. Geburtstag*, ed. Gerhard Sellin, BZNW 100 [Berlin: de Gruyter, 1999], 59–84, http://dx.doi.org/10.1515/9783110821017-005).

[41] See Philo, *Congr.* 14, 23 (δέσποινα); *Congr.* 1 (ἀρχή μου).

and the son of the free(d)-woman, who represent two different ethical and eschatological paradigms for gentile Christians. Paul's aim, however, is not to argue this on his own authority but to let ἡ γραφή make the point for him. Thus, when Scripture finally speaks at the end of the allegory in Gal 4:30, it says, again modifying and interpreting its own words: "the son of the slave woman will not inherit with the son of the *free woman.*"

C. An Emphasis on "Hearing Scripture"

The foregoing two sections have focused on the construction of Scripture as a self-interpreting hypostasis in Paul and the school of Rabbi Ishmael. I turn now to the related question of how allowing Scripture to speak in this fashion shapes the rhetorical characterization of the implied audience in each corpus.

In his analysis of the Rabbi Ishmael midrashim, Yadin-Israel argues that an integral component of the personification of Scripture as a self-interpreting figure is the restriction of the role of the reader to that of "inaction and attention." Scripture speaks, the reader hears. This focus on the implied audience's hearing in Ishmaelian midrash is typified, in Yadin-Israel's analysis, by three hearing formulas: כשמועו ("as it is heard"), שומע אני ("I hear"), and, perhaps most important for Paul's usage, the phrases שמענו ("we have heard") and לא שמענו ("we have not heard").[42]

Paul similarly constructs his readers as hearers of the personified Scripture in several ways. Remaining with the Galatians passage for the moment, one may point to the question with which Paul begins the allegory of Sarah and Hagar: "Tell me, you who wish to be under law, do you not hear (Scripture speaking) the law?" (Gal 4:21).

Paul is one of the only two New Testament authors to use the idiom "hear the law" (Gal 4:21).[43] The other, the author of the Fourth Gospel, also employs the phrase in an Ishmaelian sense in John 12:34. There, however, it is the crowd that says, "We have heard *from the law* [ἐκ τοῦ νόμου] that the Messiah is staying forever; so how do you say that it is necessary for the Son of Man to be exalted?" Strictly speaking, the law is not personified here, and John's verb, ἠκούσαμεν, which echoes the Ishmaelian שמענו (*šāmaʿnû*), introduces the exegetical view that stands in need of correction. The Fourth Gospel, however, does help to corroborate the theory that

---

[42] Yadin, *Scripture as Logos*, 34–47.

[43] Betz links this formula explicitly to the diatribal style of Epictetus (*Galatians*, 241). Although I think this is plausible, Richard B. Hays has convincingly argued that this formula may well be derived from Pharisaic custom ("'Have We Found Abraham to Be Our Forefather according to the Flesh?' A Reconsideration of Rom 4:1," *NovT* 27 [1985]: 76–98, http://dx.doi.org/10.1163/156853685x00175). The two are not mutually exclusive, however, and many rabbinic *middôt* are now recognized, following the seminal work of Lieberman (see n. 16 above), as having their origin in Greco-Roman rhetoric.

this formula was in use in Jewish circles of the first century and was not exclusively rooted in the Hellenistic diatribe.

In contrast to the usage attested in John, in Gal 4:21 the law is not merely a textual authority, as John's prepositional phrase ἐκ τοῦ νόμου suggests, but the active speech of a personified *speaker*, Scripture, who appears in Gal 4:30. Paul, moreover, appropriates the Ishmaelian emphasis on hearing Scripture into his *own* voice. By translating the negative form of the Ishmaelian formula, "we have not heard" (לא שמענו), into the second person plural, Paul even more aggressively constructs his readers as hearers of Scripture's law.[44]

D. The Relative Eclipse of Halakah and Other Nonscriptural Authorities

One final point of continuity between Paul's and Rabbi Ishmael's hermeneutical stances, which goes hand in hand with the foregoing features, is the relative eclipse of halakah attributed to specific teachers. For both Paul and Rabbi Ishmael, Scripture, as its own exegete, must become greater and human tradition must become less. This hermeneutical decision, according to Yadin-Israel, was of extreme consequence for the school of Rabbi Ishmael: there is no Ishmaelian Mishnah and Tosefta, "because the group that produced the Rabbi Ishmael midrashim does not (except for rare exceptions) recognize legal argument divorced from the authority of scripture."[45]

As a parallel, one might point to Paul's famous disregard for the "traditions of the fathers" in Gal 1:12, 14. Of course, as Yadin-Israel notes, Paul does on occasion make room for views attributed to human tradents, primarily his own views, those of Jesus, and anonymous apostolic tradition (1 Cor 7:25, 15:3).[46] But to suggest that in Paul "we find a generally positive view of received tradition and regular recourse to the terminology of oral transmission" is to ignore the evidence of Galatians in favor of the Corinthian correspondence. The tension between the positive and negative valuations of tradition in Pauline and Deutero-Pauline writings remains unresolved.[47] At the risk of oversimplification, one might say that Paul's Ishmaelian

---

[44] See Gal 4:21; cf. 4QMMT^c (4Q396) 1–2, IV, 9, etc., for the related formula אתם יודעים ("you know"). For a comparative study of the rhetorical construction of boundaries in 4QMMT and Galatians, see Adele Reinhartz, "We, You, They: Boundary Language in 4QMMT and the New Testament Epistles," in *Text, Thought, and Practice in Qumran and Early Christianity: Proceedings of the Ninth International Symposium of the Orion Center for the Study of the Dead Sea Scrolls and Associated Literature*, ed. Ruth A. Clements and Daniel R. Schwartz, STDJ 84 (Leiden: Brill, 2009), 89–105, esp. 97–98, http://dx.doi.org/10.1163/ej.9789004175242.i-326.27.

[45] Yadin, *Scripture as Logos*, 146.

[46] Yadin-Israel, *Scripture and Tradition*, 186.

[47] The positive valuation of tradition in 1 Corinthians is reiterated, albeit in a metaphorical way, by Paul himself in Rom 6:17 and again, in the Pauline school, in 2 Thess 2:15. Galatians' negative valuation is reiterated by Paul in Phil 3:5, and again, among the disputed epistles, in Col

Cover: Paul and the School of Rabbi Ishmael 629

scripturalism in Galatians is offset by his more Akivan balance of Scripture and tradition in 1 Corinthians. In this, Paul proves himself once again a hermeneutical Proteus.[48] It is striking that the Pauline letter in which proto-Ishmaelian formulae and features sound most strongly is also the letter in which Pharisaic (Gal 1:14; cf. Phil 3:5) and apostolic "flesh and blood" traditions (Gal 1:1, 11–12, 15–23) are most clearly rendered suspect.

In defense of this point, it is noteworthy that 1 Tim 5:18 stands in continuity with Paul's hermeneutics in Galatians. The former epistle's disputed authenticity need not detain us, for, as in the case of Rabbi Ishmael, so with Paul we are concerned with the hermeneutics not only of a historical individual but also (and perhaps primarily) of a school.[49]

In 1 Tim 5:17, Paul informs Timothy that elders in the churches who are of upstanding reputation are worthy of a "double honor/compensation" (διπλῆ τιμή), insofar as they labor in both "word and teaching." In light of the various doublets in this opening verse, it is unsurprising that Paul then sets in the mouth of the personified γραφή a *double proof* supporting this opinion: "For Scripture says: 'you shall not muzzle a threshing ox' and 'the worker is worthy of his payment.'" The first saying, about the threshing ox (Deut 25:4) is an established Pauline prooftext, which occurs in 1 Cor 9:9; the second text cited by ἡ γραφή here, however, is of disputed provenance. The author of 1 Timothy may be paraphrasing *Paul's* second prooftext of 1 Cor 9:10, whose origins are similarly murky.[50] If this is the case, the double proof of 1 Cor 9:9–10 has apparently attained a "scriptural" status for the author of 1 Timothy. For the Pauline school, this double proof rests on the words of both Moses and Paul. In this creative rewriting, however, both Pauline and Mosaic authority are eclipsed by the authority of the personified Scripture, who speaks for them, paraphrasing their content and interpreting them to a new generation of Pauline churches.

This is one option. The closest verbal parallel to Scripture's second prooftext in 1 Tim 5:18, however, is not 1 Cor 9:10 but the saying of Jesus in Luke 10:7 (cf.

2:8. As in Paul's letters, there remains diversity in hermeneutics and rhetorical strategy within the Pauline school. For further consideration, see the discussion of 1 Tim 5:18 below.

[48] See Wayne A. Meeks, "The Christian Proteus," in *The Writings of St. Paul*, ed. Wayne A. Meeks (New York: Norton, 1972), 435–44; Mark D. Nanos, "Paul's Relationship to Torah in Light of His Strategy 'to Become Everything to Everyone' (1 Corinthians 9.19–23)," in *Paul and Judaism: Crosscurrents in Pauline Exegesis and the Study of Jewish–Christian Relations*, ed. Reimund Bieringer and Didier Pollefeyt, LNTS 463 (London: T&T Clark, 2012), 106–40.

[49] For the Pauline school hypothesis (and its discontents), see David Lincicum, "Learning Scripture in the School of Paul: From Ephesians to Justin," in *The Early Reception of Paul*, ed. Kenneth Liljeström, Publications of the Finnish Exegetical Society 99 (Helsinki: Finnish Exegetical Society, 2011), 148–70.

[50] Johannes Weiss is surely right that 1 Cor 9:10 includes "[ein] Zitat eines ... unbekannten Schriftwortes," perhaps drawn from Sir 6:19 or 2 Chr 15:7 (*Der erste Korintherbrief*, KEK 5 [Göttingen: Vandenhoeck & Ruprecht, 1910], 237).

Matt 10:10), "the worker is worthy of his wages." The syntactic similarities between these verses and the fact that each verse serves as a source of scribal corruption for the other make hearing an *echo* of Luke's saying in 1 Tim 5:18 unavoidable. The direction of influence is, of course, difficult to determine. It is worth asking, however, as an alternative to the theory posed above, whether the author of 1 Timothy may have intentionally echoed a dominical saying here.[51] If that is the case, then the author of 1 Timothy has rewritten 1 Cor 9:10 and attributed the halakic positions of Moses *and* Jesus to Scripture. As in the case of the school of Rabbi Ishmael, so here in the school of Paul, the authority of human halakic tradition—even the authority of Jesus himself—is eclipsed in light of the authoritative self-interpretation of Scripture.

E. Corroborating Features: Torah for the Entire World and Mystical Ascent

Two typological similarities between the Pauline tradition and that of Rabbi Ishmael will serve to strengthen and broaden the present comparison between the Pauline corpus, especially Galatians, and the school of Rabbi Ishmael.

The first of these is the "universalism" of both Pauline and Ishmaelian thought.[52] Paul's ethnic expansion of the boundaries of God's covenant family are well documented, even as the precise soteriological mechanisms of this expansion remain vigorously debated.[53] Hirshman has intriguingly claimed that the Ishmaelian tradition evinces traces of a different kind of *nomistic* universalism, most particularly in its notion that Torah was presented on Mount Sinai "publically, openly ... so that everyone wishing to accept it could come and accept it."[54] Torah, in other words, was given "for all who come into the entire world." The (nomistic)

---

[51] According to Martin Dibelius and Hans Conzelmann, Luke 10:7 gives the impression that Jesus himself may be "appealing" to another "saying" (*The Pastoral Epistles: A Commentary on the Pastoral Epistles*, trans. Philip Buttolph and Adela Yarbro, Hermeneia [Philadelphia: Fortress, 1972], 79). They suggest a scriptural source, but there is no reason why Jesus could not be drawing on oral halakah or wisdom here.

[52] Jeremias attributes this to Paul's Hillelite affiliation: "Im Untershied zu den Schammaiten waren [die Hilleliten], wie schon Hillel selbst, offen für den Anschluß der Heiden an das Gottesvolk" ("Paulus als Hillelit," 90).

[53] Udo Schnelle states Paul's dilemma eloquently: "[Paul] had to think through disparate issues and bring into some kind of conceptual consistency what could not really be harmonized: God's first covenant remains valid, but only the new covenant saves" (*Theology of the New Testament*, trans M. Eugene Boring [Grand Rapids: Baker Academic, 2009], 203). For a list of scholars espousing the "two-ways" or "one way" versions of the New Perspective, see Pamela Eisenbaum, "A Remedy for Having Been Born of Woman: Jesus, Gentiles, and Genealogy in Romans," *JBL* 123 (2004): 671–702, esp. 672 n. 3, http://dx.doi.org/10.2307/3268465.

[54] Hirshman, "Rabbinic Universalism," 103; cf. Mek. Bahodesh 1.

differences with Paul, of course, are striking,[55] but so are the (scriptural) proximities.[56] Scripture, in both traditions, speaks to all the nations.

A second point of continuity derives from the fact that both Paul and Rabbi Ishmael become religious heroes or typological exemplars in early Christian and Jewish mystical theology. Paul's reputation as a visionary likely has historical roots. His rapture into the third heaven, recounted in 2 Corinthians and various other passages, has lent credibility to his later portrayal in Acts and to the mystical interpretation of his theology in Valentinus, Gregory of Nyssa, and Ps.-Dionysius.[57] Paul's narrative of ascent finds a parallel in the traditional attribution of "many mystical statements and literary works, Ma'aseh Bereshit and Ma'aseh Merkevah" to Rabbi Ishmael.[58] The connections between these two exegetes and their schools thus extend beyond their hermeneutics and are corroborated by deeper similarities between their patterns of religion.

Here, I have extended Ishmaelian tradition beyond reconstructions of the rabbinic school to include other clusters of tradition associated with Rabbi Ishmael in 3 Enoch and the Hekhalot Rabbati. Such traditions are by no means of a kind with the Tannaitic school and, in fact, may have been composed in a polemical relationship with it.[59] Nonetheless, it is worth asking whether the mystical legacies and scripturalist hermeneutics attributed to both Paul and Rabbi Ishmael bear some relationship to one another. The experience of apocalyptic ascent, resulting in an apophatic response to divine revelation, has a certain phenomenological similarity to the quest to hear the "unveiled" teaching of Scripture, not mediated through human tradition but immediately in the voice of the hypostatized word. Any discussion of Paul's relationship to Torah "within Judaism," then, cannot speak

---

[55] See, e.g., Magnus Zetterholm, who suggests that those Jews who "welcomed non-Jewish participation in Jewish affairs such as Torah" may well be the variety that caused Paul so much consternation ("Paul within Judaism: The State of the Question," in Nanos and Zetterholm, *Paul within Judaism*, 31–51, esp. 48–49).

[56] For the notion that Paul's ethical "rule" for the gentiles, while not requiring circumcision, was nonetheless not "law-free," see Paula Fredriksen, "Judaizing the Nations: The Ritual Demands of Paul's Gospel," in Casey and Taylor, *Paul's Jewish Matrix*, 327–54.

[57] On Paul's mysticism generally, see Rabens, "Pneuma and the Beholding of God"; Daniel Marguerat, "Paul le Mystique," *RTL* 43 (2012): 473–93. For Paul's ascent in 2 Cor 12:1–12, see Christopher Morray-Jones, "Paradise Revisited (2 Cor 12:1–12): The Jewish Mystical Background of Paul's Apostolate; Part 2, Paul's Heavenly Ascent and Its Significance," *HTR* 86 (1993): 265–92; Alan F. Segal, *Paul the Convert: The Apostolate and Apostasy of Saul the Pharisee* (New Haven: Yale University Press, 1990); Peter Schäfer, "New Testament and Hekhalot Literature: The Journey to Heaven in Paul and in Merkavah Mysticism," *JJS* 35 (1984): 19–35.

[58] Shmuel Safrai, "Ishmael ben Elisha," *JE* 9:83–86. Both Rabbi Akiva and Rabbi Ishmael appear together as descenders in Hekhalot Rabbati §106, and Rabbi Akiva is the legendary hero of the earlier collection, Hekhalot Zutarti.

[59] So, e.g., Rachel Elior, *Temple and Chariot, Priests and Angels, Sanctuary and Heavenly Sanctuary in Early Jewish Mysticism* [in Hebrew] (Jerusalem: Magnes, 2002), 170, cited in Yadin-Israel, *Scripture and Tradition*, 171.

simply of his engagement with particular laws and traditions but must wrestle with the way those traditions are authorized, nullified, artificialized,[60] or otherwise reinterpreted through the personification of Law and Scripture as actors on the apocalyptic stage.

F. An "Akivan" Counterexample: Galatians 3:16 and m. Sanh. 4:5

This recognition of some proto-Ishmaelian elements in Paul's exegesis throughout Galatians should not be overextended to support the stronger conclusion that Paul *always* leans in a proto-Ishmaelian rather than in a proto-Akivan direction. As already noted, Kister has made a strong case for a parallel between Rom 5 and Sifra, and Paul's correlation of Scripture and oral tradition in 1 Corinthians fits more readily into an Akivan mold. As a relevant counterexample in Galatians, one may consider m. Sanh. 4:5, a text that, on Yadin-Israel's reading, belonged to the cluster of writings associated with Rabbi Akiva.[61] In this passage, which contains an important parallel to Gal 3:16,[62] the *stam* exhorts witnesses in capital cases to use only well-attested evidence against the defendant, given the gravity of unjust shedding of human blood. To buttress this exhortation, the *stam* introduces a biblical proof, Gen 4:10.

ודני נפשות — דמו ודם זרעיותיו תלויים בו עד סוף כל העולם. שכן מצינו בקין [בשהרג את חבל] שנאמר: "קול דמי אחיך צועקים אלי מן־האדמה" (בראשית ד י); אינו אומר 'דם אחיד', אלא "דמי אחיד" — דמו ודם זרעיותיו.

> And [in] capital cases—his blood and the blood of his offspring [lit. "his seeds"] is "hung" on him [*viz.* the murderer] until the end of all the world.[63] And thus we find was the case with Cain [who killed Abel] as it is said:[64] "the voice of your brother's bloods are crying out to me from the earth" (Gen 4:10); it does not say, "your brother's blood," but your brother's "bloods"—[i.e.] his blood and the blood of his offspring ["seeds"]. (m. Sanh. 4:5)[65]

This text demonstrates midrashic and conceptual similarities to Gal 3:16 and complicates the notion that Paul's exegesis stands cleanly within an Ishmaelian genealogy. In particular, the *stam*'s meditation on the construct plural דמי (Gen 4:10) is reminiscent of Paul's exegetical ruminations on the σπέρμα(τα) of Gen 13:15 LXX. That "bloods" (דמי) are interpreted as "seeds" (זרעיותיו) in m. Sanh. 4:5 in the context of a discussion of genealogy and offspring strengthens this connection.[66]

---

[60] For the term *artificialization*, see n. 85 below.

[61] For the Akivan character of the Mishnah, see Yadin, *Scripture as Logos*, 146; Yadin-Israel, *Scripture and Tradition*, 190.

[62] Str-B recognizes this parallel (1:267; 3:553).

[63] MS Parma: כל הדורות.

[64] MS Parma: כשהרג את חבל נאמר בו.

[65] Text from MS Kaufmann (A 50), checked against MS Parma (De Rossi 138). Translation is my own, in consultation with Herbert Danby, *The Mishnah* (Oxford: Clarendon, 1933).

[66] According to one dominant position, such biblical prooftexts are likely additions to the

Paul's creative misreading of the plural in Gen 3:16 demonstrates an affinity with a tendency of later Akivan hermeneutics to ascribe midrashic significance to morphological or syntactic markers that might easily be otherwise explained by grammatical analysis. The Ishmaelian school, by comparison, was more reluctant to see halakic significance in every one of Biblical Hebrew's idiosyncrasies. Perhaps the most famous example of this division occurs in Sifre Num. 112, where, in response to Rabbi Akiva's attachment of halakic significance to the Hebrew infinitive absolute (*hikkārēt tikkārēt*), Rabbi Ishmael retorts: דיברה תורה לשון בני אדם; "Torah spoke human language."

Of course, attention to the hermeneutic markedness of particular biblical lexemes is both a "bone of contention" between and a shared feature of the Ishmaelian and Akivan schools, and attention to plural forms does not appear to be one of the distinctive markers of Akivan hermeneutics.[67] One typical Akivan marker, the independent preposition *min*—if it formed an original part of the biblical lemma from Genesis—goes undiscussed by the *stam*. Nonetheless, the *dərāšâ* does not strike one as explicitly Ishmaelian either, and its attention to "extra features" in the biblical text (in this case, a *yod*) does comport with Rabbi Akiva's apparent interests. In addition to its appearance in a text broadly associated with the Akivan school, one finds a similar attention to the singular and plural of זרע in m. Šabb. 9:2.[68] There, in an interpretation of Isa 60:11, the argument [זרעה] לא נאמר כן אלא זרועיה ("it does not say here 'its seed' but 'its seeds'")[69] occurs in a string of *minayin* questions attributable to Rabbi Akiva, who is explicitly named in m. Šabb. 9:1.[70]

The upshot of this "Akivan" counterexample is to reassert the difficulty of tracing the midrashic and hermeneutical particularities of later schools even within the

---

halakic collections that were later redacted into the Mishnah and do not reflect the origin of rabbinic law. See Paul Mandel, who suggests a post-70 origin for the prooftexting phenomenon ("Legal Midrash between Hillel and Rabbi Akiva: Did 70 C.E. Make a Difference?" in *Was 70 CE a Watershed in Jewish History? On Jews and Judaism before and after the Destruction of the Second Temple*, ed. Daniel R. Schwartz, Zeev Weiss, and Ruth A. Clements, AGJU 78 [Leiden: Brill, 2012], 343–70). This position comports well with the Akivan portrait of this collection. For a counterpoint, see James L. Kugel, *Traditions of the Bible: A Guide to the Bible as It Was at the Start of the Common Era* (Cambridge: Harvard University Press, 1998), 2–3. The evidence presented here, which demonstrates a strong exegetical similarity between Gal 3:16 and m. Sanh. 4:5, as well as the shared central importance of the personified Scripture in both Paul and the school of Rabbi Ishmael, suggests that halakah and scriptural exegesis were indeed intertwined in Paul's brand of Pharisaic Judaism in the first century.

[67] For attention to textual "markedness" in both schools, and a list of typical Akivan markers, see Yadin-Israel, *Scripture and Tradition*, 10–11; for the (usually) marked character of plurals and unmarked character of singulars in most languages, see Yadin, *Scripture as Logos*, 49.

[68] Str-B recognizes this parallel (3:553).

[69] MS Kaufmann and MS Parma omit זרעה printed in Hanoch Albeck, *Shisha Sidrei Mishnah* (1952; repr., Jerusalem: Dvir, 2008).

[70] For the unique function of *minayin* statements in Akivan midrash, see Yadin-Israel, *Scripture and Tradition*, 55–57.

Mishnah, let alone across the narrow Pharisaic bridge into Paul's Greek corpus. Certain midrashic features, such as the personification of *hakkātûb* and even the use of particular verbal formulae, are shared by both schools.[71] At the same time, these schools were not identical, and attention to the hermeneutical differences between them provides a sharper analytical heuristic by which to assess the unique contours of Paul's Judaism within the more diverse literary landscape of Judaism before 70 CE.

II. Paul and Pre-70 Pharisaic Exegesis

How might these conclusions help us redescribe Paul's relationship to Pharisaic and rabbinic Judaism? At minimum, the evidence suggests that Paul anticipates some exegetical and theological features that distinguish the later school of Rabbi Ishmael, and he also shares some of the hermeneutical methods and religious patterns associated with the cluster of traditions surrounding both Rabbi Ishmael and Rabbi Akiva. In terms of Paul's Judaism, this study helps confirm in part a tenet of Jeremias's earlier study: despite Paul's evident growing awareness and use of Hellenistic, Platonizing allegory, "seine geistige Heimat ist jedoch die palästinische Exegese."[72]

This point gains significance in light of the fact that Paul's Jewish contemporary, Philo, despite the significantly larger size of his corpus, never once uses the formula λέγει ἡ γραφή and only twice uses the formula λέγει ὁ νόμος.[73] Josephus, who purportedly joined the Pharisees at the age of nineteen,[74] never uses either formula. Whatever the reasons for the absence of λέγει ἡ γραφή in Philo's corpus, it demonstrates Paul's affinity with the rabbinic Judaism of a later era.

But there is more we can say. As mentioned earlier, Yadin-Israel has claimed that the hermeneutics of the school of Rabbi Ishmael have a salient first-century analogue in the Essene document 4QMMT. The document is well known to Pauline scholars through its use of the critical phrase "works of the law," as well as its similar recourse to the covenantal narrative of Deut 28–30.[75] To this body of evidence

---

[71] Yadin-Israel, *Scripture and Tradition*, 130.

[72] Jeremias, "Paulus als Hillelit," 89.

[73] Philo, *Det.* 159; *Deus* 99. These data were gleaned from a TLG advanced string search of Philo's works.

[74] Josephus, *Vit.* 12; Steve Mason, *Flavius Josephus on the Pharisees: A Composition-Critical Study*, StPB 39 (Leiden: Brill, 1991), 18–39; Meier, *Marginal Jew*, 3.301–5.

[75] 4QMMT[e] (4Q398) 14–17 II, 3: מקצת מעשי התורה. For the significance of the phrase "works of the law," see James D. G. Dunn, "4QMMT and Galatians," *NTS* 43 (1997): 147–53, http://dx.doi.org/10.1017/S0028688500022554. For 4QMMT's "Deuteronomistic view of history," see N. T. Wright, "4QMMT and Paul: Justification, 'Works,' and Eschatology," in *History and Exegesis:*

linking 4QMMT and the Pauline corpus, we can now add a scripturalist hermeneutic. The connection with 4QMMT gives this study an even more concrete historical reference point in the apocalyptic Judaism of the Essene settlements. Might Paul's personification of Scripture derive, in part, from this thought world as well? While personification and *prosopopoeia* are well-known Hellenistic rhetorical devices, Paul's personification of Scripture in Galatians also owes a debt to early Jewish traditions that identify Torah and personified Wisdom. The difference for Paul is that, while ὁ νόμος remains distinctly propaedeutic (Gal 3:24), ἡ γραφή speaks with comparatively more immediate pedagogical and halakic authority (Gal 4:30).

The similarities between 4QMMT and the school of Rabbi Ishmael, however, are not as exact as one might wish: first, while the form כתוב does occur in 4QMMT in halakic contexts, it is anarthrous and has a participial rather than a substantival usage.[76] Hence, one cannot speak about Scripture's personification here to the same degree as in Paul and the Rabbi Ishmael tradition. Second, while we do encounter a similar construction of "reader as hearer" in both Paul and 4QMMT, the latter text also uses the first person plural to construct a community of inspired halakic speakers through such formulae as אנחנו חושבים ("we think") and אנחנו אמרים ("we say") in a positive sense—precisely in those places where כתוב also appears.[77] Here, 4QMMT combines inspired interpretation and "sober midrash" in a way Yadin-Israel describes as antithetical to the Ishmaelian resistance to esoteric understandings of Torah.[78]

Paul stands as a kind of middle term between these traditions.[79] At times he shares with the author of 4QMMT a certain oracular understanding of the prophetic texts and an authoritative sense of the communal "we." Like Philo, therefore, he finds a place for charismatic exegesis and esoteric meaning.[80] But at other times—and especially in Galatians—Paul recognizes the essential fallibility of "we"

New Testament Essays in Honor of Dr. E. Earle Ellis for His 80th Birthday, ed. Sang-Won [Aaron] Son (London: T&T Clark, 2006), 104–32.

[76] For כתוב in 4QMMT, see 4Q394 3–7 II, 14; 8 III, 8 (הדבר כתוב); IV, 16 (restored); 4Q395 5 (restored); 4Q396 1–2 I, 4; III, 10; IV, 5, 6; 4Q397 frags. 6–13, lines 7, 9 (restored), 12, 13; frags. 14–21, lines 6, 10 (the finite form, כתבנו), 11, 12 *bis*, 15 (restored); 4Q398 frags. 11–13, line 4; 14–17 I, 2 (כתבנום), 3, 5 *bis*; 14–17 II, 2 (אנחנו כתבנו); 4Q399 I, 10 (כתבנ[ו אנחנו]).

[77] For hearing statements, see 4Q394 8 IV, 2–3 (לוא שמעו, ולוא שמע); for the construction of the halakically authoritative "we," see, e.g., 4Q394 3–7 II, 16 (אנחנו חושבים); 8 IV, 5 (אנחנו אמרים); 4Q398 frags. 11–13, line 3 (אנחנו מכירים, "we are aware"); 14–17 II, 2 (אנחנו כתבנו, "we have written").

[78] Yadin-Israel, *Scripture and Tradition*, 164–65, 168–70.

[79] Similarly, Kister sees Paul drawing elements from contrasting systems attested at Qumran and in Sifra and "combin[ing] [them] into a novel system of his own" ("Torah-Theology and Hebrew Usage," 405–6).

[80] See Rom 3:2; 1 Cor 1:23; 2:6, 7; Yadin-Israel, *Scripture and Tradition*, 166–67.

and subjects it to the authority of ἡ γραφή.[81] In this letter, Paul's exegesis takes a turn away from the apocalyptic toward the rhetorical, allegorical, and agonistic,[82] in a way that finds special affinity with the Tannaim, particularly Rabbi Ishmael.

It seems, then, that the personification of Scripture as self-interpreting authority in the school of Rabbi Ishmael, conceived as both a set of formulae and a complex of motifs, finds a closer parallel in Galatians than in either 4QMMT or Philo's corpus. In these respects, Mekilta and Sifre Numbers reflect first-century Pharisaic tradition, certain vestiges of which we find in the writings of Paul.[83] To insist on too rigid a distinction between Essene, Pharisaic, and Alexandrian hermeneutics in the first century would be problematic.[84] Nonetheless, one expects to be able to detect certain hallmark features of Paul's various stages of education, and the contours of this Pharisaism anticipate not only the midrashic playfulness of Rabbi Akiva but also the "scripturalist warrant" of Rabbi Ishmael. Both of these traditions have a firm foothold in the Pharisaism of the first century, as Paul's letters attest.

This conclusion represents an important gain for the study of first-century Pharisaism. Whereas attempts to triangulate between later Tannaitic and Amoraic

---

[81] See Gal 1:8; 2:16, 17. On Paul as a partially noncharismatic exegete, see Yadin-Israel, *Scripture and Tradition*, 167.

[82] For the "agonistic paradigm" as a lens for understanding Paul's rhetorical hermeneutics more generally, see Mitchell, *Paul, the Corinthians*, 21.

[83] In light of this conclusion, it is worth considering whether the terminology "works of the law" in 4QMMT might stem, at least in part, from its Pharisaic audience. The Pharisaic "addressee" of 4QMMT has been suggested, more broadly, on the basis of the phrase "seekers after smooth things" (דורשי החלקות) in CD 1:18 and 4QpNah 3–4 II, 2, 4; III, 3 (see, e.g., James C. VanderKam, "Those Who Look for Smooth Things, Pharisees, and Oral Law," in *Emanuel: Studies in the Hebrew Bible, Septuagint, and Dead Sea Scrolls in Honor of Emanuel Tov*, ed. Shalom M. Paul et al., VTSup 94 [Leiden: Brill, 2003], 465–77, http://dx.doi.org/10.1163/9789004276215_031) and in terms of the particular halakic issues being discussed (see, e.g., Eyal Regev, "The Sectarian Controversies about the Cereal Offerings," *DSD* 5 [1998]: 33–56, esp. 37, http://dx.doi.org/10.1163/156851798X00226, who makes the case that a dispute between the more lenient Pharisaic laws of the cereal offering and the more stringent Essene position can be identified in 4QMMT[b]). The claim, moreover, that "we separated from the mass of people" (פרשנו מרוב הע[ם]) in 4QMMT[d] (4Q397), frags. 14–21, line 7, is similarly suggestive that the author is trying to forge a bond with a Pharisaic or proto-Pharisaic interlocutor (see Daniel R. Schwartz, "MMT, Josephus, and the Pharisees," in *Reading 4QMMT: New Perspectives on Qumran Law and History*, ed. John Kampen and Moshe J. Bernstein, SBLSymS 2 [Atlanta: Scholars Press, 1996], 67–80). For a good survey of the positions of the various parties to the letter, see Reinhartz, "Boundary Language in 4QMMT," 89–95.

[84] For the "artificialization" of the law and its statutes as a strategy shared by diasporic Judaism as well as nonpriestly Judaism of Judea, including Paul, the Pharisees, and the Essenes, see Daniel R. Schwartz, "Someone Who Considers Something to Be Impure—For Him It is Impure (Rom 14:14): Good Manners or Law?" in Casey and Taylor, *Paul's Jewish Matrix*, 293–309, esp. 305–7. Awareness of such artificialization, in Paul's case, does not prevent him or his Alexandrian contemporary Philo from invoking naturalistic views of law as well.

sources and first-century sages sometimes stumble on the paucity of pre-70 names associated with the Pharisees (Hillel and Shammai, for instance, are not "explicitly connected with the Pharisees" until a fifth-century CE commentary by Jerome),[85] in Paul's case we have the distinct advantage of working with a self-professed Pharisee. While not everything in Paul that has Tannaitic resonance necessarily stems from Paul's Pharisaic education, in a case (like this one) where Essene and Alexandrian parallels are less compelling, probability leans in favor of Pharisaic provenance. This conclusion also helps position Paul "within" the matrix of later Judaism. In particular, his relationship to Scripture and Torah can now be seen as a part of the emerging hermeneutics of the Tannaim—a confirmation that there is a "bridge," however narrow, between the exegesis of the Pharisees and later rabbinic religion.[86]

The payoff for our portrait of Paul in his own day is equally important. Paul emerges, first, as a bridge between the inspired Jewish exegetes of Palestine and the early "sober" Tannaitic midrashists. In his apocalyptic and mystical portraiture, Paul also anticipates the transformation of Rabbi Ishmael and Rabbi Akiva into inspired exegetes and mystical "descenders" in developing rabbinic tradition and *hekhalot* texts.[87] The recognition of particularly Ishmaelian features in Galatians, moreover, provides a new heuristic for describing the contingency of Paul's theology and exegesis in that letter, over and against the harmonization of Scripture and tradition in 1 Corinthians, Romans, and 2 Thessalonians. In certain aspects of his scripturalism, charted above, the Paul of Galatians and 1 Timothy appears as an Ishmaelite *avant la lettre*.

---

[85] John P. Meier, "The Quest for the Historical Pharisee: A Review Essay on Roland Deines, *Die Pharisäer*," CBQ 61 (1999): 713-22.

[86] See the survey of positions in Meier, "Quest for the Historical Pharisee," esp. 714-15, 721. In stating my position this way, I intentionally situate myself somewhere between skeptics of the theory of a Pharisaic "bridge" to rabbinic Judaism, like Jacob Neusner and Morton Smith, on the one hand, and proponents like Martin Hengel and Roland Deines, on the other.

[87] Yadin-Israel, *Scripture and Tradition*, 103-18. On this transformation of Rabbi Akiva *within* Tannaitic tradition, see ibid., 119-40.

New and Recent Titles

FOUNDATIONS FOR SOCIORHETORICAL EXPLORATION
A Rhetoric of Religious Antiquity Reader
Vernon K. Robbins, Robert H. von Thaden Jr., and Bart B. Bruehler, editors
Paperback $65.95, 978-1-62837-142-0 Forthcoming, 2016 Code: 067103
Hardcover $85.95, 978-0-88414-169-3 E-book $65.95, 978-0-88414-168-6
Rhetoric of Religious Antiquity 4

EXPLORING PHILEMON
Freedom, Brotherhood, and Partnership in the New Society
Roy R. Jeal
Paper $30.95, 978-0-88414-091-7 262 pages, 2015 Code: 067101
Hardcover $45.95, 978-0-88414-093-1 E-book $30.95, 978-0-88414-092-4
Rhetoric of Religious Antiquity 2

LYDIA AS A RHETORICAL CONSTRUCT IN ACTS
Alexandra Gruca-Macaulay
Paperback $45.95, 978-1-62837-137-6 336 pages, 2016 Code: 064818
Hardcover $60.95, 978-0-88414-160-0 E-book $45.95, 978-0-88414-159-4
Emory Studies in Early Christianity 18

RELIGIOUS COMPETITION IN THE GRECO-ROMAN WORLD
Nathaniel DesRosiers and Lily C. Vuong, editors
Paperback $34.95, 978-1-62837-136-9 346 pages, 2016 Code: 064210
Hardcover $49.95, 978-0-88414-158-7 E-book $34.95, 978-0-88414-157-0
Writings from the Greco-Roman World Supplements 10

THE SBL HANDBOOK OF STYLE, SECOND EDITION
Hardcover $39.95, 978-1-58983-964-9 E-book $39.95, 978-1-58983-965-6

SBL Press • P.O. Box 2243 • Williston, VT 05495-2243
Phone: 877-725-3334 (toll-free) or 802-864-6185 • Fax: 802-864-7626
Order online at www.sbl-site.org/publications

Jesus's Testimony before Pilate in 1 Timothy 6:13

MICHEL GOURGUES
michel.gourgues@dominicanu.ca
Dominican University College/
Carleton University, Ottawa, ON K1R 7G3, Canada

Apart from the Gospels and the Acts, 1 Timothy is the only New Testament writing to mention Pontius Pilate. This article studies the context, structure, and content of 1 Tim 6:12-13, with its parallelism between Timothy's and Jesus's experiences. Thereafter it develops two major arguments in favor of viewing 1 Tim 6:12-13 as an echo of what was already or was to become part of the Johannine passion narrative. This would provide an additional indication of the late composition of 1 Timothy.

Apart from the four Gospels and three passages in the Acts of the Apostles, the First Letter to Timothy is the only New Testament writing to speak of Pontius Pilate.[1] This reference raises a number of questions: Why mention Pilate in the exhortation addressed to Timothy in the last section of the letter (6:11-16)? To what does the "good confession" (καλὴ ὁμολογία) made by Jesus (6:13) refer? Might the reference in 1 Timothy help to clarify the relationship between 1 Timothy and the Gospels, especially the Gospel of John, whose passion narrative is the only one to portray Jesus as "testifying" before Pilate? This article will pay special attention to the last question, which is not usually addressed by commentators, whose attention is often mobilized by other issues, such as the reference in 1 Tim 3:13 to a

---

[1] In the Gospels, almost all the references are in the passion narratives (nine times in Matt 27, ten in Mark 15, ten in Luke 23, and twenty in John 18-19). There are two other passages in Luke: (1) in 3:1 in the solemn introduction to John's ministry ("In the fifteenth year of the reign of Tiberius Caesar, *Pontius Pilate being governor of Judea*..."); (2) in 13:1, in reference to the tragic lot of a group of Galileans "whose blood Pilate had mingled with their sacrifices." In Acts, Pilate is mentioned three times: (1) in two speeches, that of Peter in Jerusalem (3:13) and that of Paul at Antioch in Pisidia (13:28); and (2) in the prayer of the Jerusalem community (4:27).

traditional confession of faith[2] and the specific occasion of Timothy's "nice confession."[3]

After examining the context of the exhortation (6:11–16) in the final chapter of 1 Timothy, and of verses 12 and 13 in particular within the exhortation, I will turn my attention to interpreting this passage and to answering the questions that have just been raised.

I. Context

"But as for you, man of God": these are the opening words of the exhortation addressed to Timothy that begins in 6:11 and continues with four singular imperatives.[4] This passage marks a new beginning with respect to what came earlier in chapter 6. A brief instruction to Timothy in verse 2b[5] is followed in verses 3–5 by a list of behaviors having to do with deviant or heterodox teaching (ἑτεροδιδασκαλεῖν), an issue that is one of the letter's main concerns and has already been addressed twice (1:3–11, 4:1–7).[6] Verses 6–10 elaborate on the theme of wealth and material goods.[7]

The exhortation to Timothy then follows (6:11–16). After the imperatives in verses 11 and 12, it continues in verses 13 and 14 with a solemn injunction that contains the reference to Pilate:

---

[2] See Martin Dibelius and Hans Conzelman, *The Pastoral Epistles: A Commentary on the Pastoral Epistles*, trans. Philip Buttolph and Adela Yarbro, Hermeneia (Philadelphia: Fortress, 1972), 88–89; Lorenz Oberlinner, *Die Pastorale Briefe, erste Folge: Kommentar zum ersten Timotheusbrief*, HTKNT 11.2 (Freiburg: Herder, 1988), 287–93; Jürgen Roloff, *Die erste Brief an Timotheus*, EKKNT 15 (Neukirchen-Vluyn: Neukirchener Verlag, 1998), 344; Klaus Wengst, *Christologische Formeln und Lieder des Urchristentums*, SNT 7 (Gütersloh: Mohn, 1973), 124–25.

[3] See I. Howard Marshall, *A Critical and Exegetical Commentary on the Pastoral Epistles*, ICC (Edinburgh: T&T Clark, 1999), 660–61; William D. Mounce, *Pastoral Epistles*, WBC 46 (Nashville: Nelson, 2000), 357–58.

[4] The imperatives are φεῦγε ("shun") and δίωκε ("aim") in v. 11 and ἀγωνίζου ("fight") and ἐπιλαβοῦ ("take hold") in v. 12.

[5] Ταῦτα δίδασκε καὶ παρακάλει, "teach and urge these things." In earlier exhortations, ταῦτα ("these things") referred to what had preceded (3:14; 4:6, 11; 5:21). If the same is true here, then "teach these things" would refer to the instructions in the section 5:1–6:2a, which successively address different categories of the faithful (people of different age groups, widows, presbyters, and slaves).

[6] Following the opening address (1:1–2), the letter begins (1:3) with the theme of heterodox teaching, forming an *inclusio* with 6:3–5, which confirms the importance of the theme while pointing out some complementary aspects.

[7] Verses 6–8 present a positive attitude to material goods, while vv. 9–10 adopt a negative attitude.

(v. 13) In the presence of God who gives life to all things, and of Christ Jesus who in his testimony before Pontius Pilate made the good confession,[8] (v. 14) I charge you to keep the commandment unstained and free from reproach until the appearing of our Lord Jesus Christ.[9]

The exhortation extends into verses 15–16 with a solemn doxology that has a liturgical ring to it, perhaps borrowed from Hellenistic Judaism.

The last part of the chapter (6:17–21) returns to considerations that are similar to those preceding the exhortation addressed to Timothy (vv. 3–10). The same themes that had appeared in the first section reappear here, but now in reverse order: wealth and material goods (vv. 17–19)[10] followed by heterodox teaching (vv. 20–21a).[11] Our passage (6:11–16) is therefore at the center of a section that has a chiastic structure of themes:

    A   6:2b–5: Heterodox teaching
      B   6:6–10: Wealth and material goods
        C   6:11–16: Exhortation to Timothy: stand firm in the faith
      B′ 6:17–19: Wealth and material goods
    A′ 6:20–21a: Heterodox teaching.

---

[8] Two major variant readings are attested in v. 13: (1) Instead of the rare verb ζωογονέω ("give life, quicken"), which is better attested here, certain manuscripts have the synonym ζωοποιέω ("make alive, give life"). This substitution may have been made in order to clarify the meaning by using a verb that was more common. See A. T. Hanson, *The Pastoral Epistles* (NCBC; Grand Rapids: Eerdmans, 1982), 111. (2) A good number of manuscripts, including Codex Sinaiticus, invert the word order ("Jesus Christ" instead of "Christ Jesus," frequently attested in 1 Timothy). See J. K. Elliott, *The Greek Text of the Epistles to Timothy and Titus*, Studies and Documents 36 (Salt Lake City: University of Utah Press, 1968), 201.

[9] In v. 14, some manuscripts have a double object following the verb παραγγέλλω ("to command"), "I charge you [σοι] … that you [σε] keep the commandment." See Bruce M. Metzger, *A Textual Commentary on the Greek New Testament: A Companion Volume to the United Bible Societies' Greek New Testament (Fourth rev. ed.)*, 2nd ed. (Stuttgart: Deutsche Bibelgesellschaft, 1994), 576.

[10] The doxology in vv. 15–16 might suggest the end of the letter, but vv. 17–19 unexpectedly return to the theme of wealth, viewing it in a far more positive light than vv. 6–10. The whole passage is a long phrase in which the end corresponds to the beginning; "good capital sum/future" in v. 19a echoes "rich/in this world's goods" in v. 17a.

[11] Even if this brief final passage makes no specific mention of διδασκαλία ("teaching") or of ἑτεροδιδασκαλεῖν (lit., "teach something else"), the use of terms that were previously employed in connection with the idea of heterodox teaching, in particular the verbs ἐκτρέπομαι ("avoid, turn aside"; cf. 1:4) and ἀστοχέω ("miss the mark"; cf. 1:6), along with the adjective βέβηλος ("profane, impious"; cf. 4:7), leave no doubt that the reference is to heterodox teaching.

Verses 11–16 appear to be an insertion that interrupts this thematic arrangement.[12] If the first words of the exhortation were missing (v. 11a: "But as for you, man of God, shun all this"), the passage would seem unconnected to the context and could just as easily fit anywhere else in the letter. Moreover, since it extends into a doxology that closes with "Amen" (v. 16), it would be a "logical chain of thinking"[13] to conclude that the exhortation would find its natural location at the end of the letter (as is the case with the doxology in Rom 16:25–27), just before the exhortation and closing salutation (6:20–21).

In its present location, however, the exhortation is not entirely unconnected with what immediately precedes. Whereas the earlier section (6:6–10) dealing with the Christian attitude toward wealth and material goods ended with the idea of wandering away from the faith (v. 10b), the exhortation addressed to Timothy takes up and develops the notion of preserving the faith. The passage mentions πίστις ("faith") twice (vv. 11b and 12a) and speaks of "the good confession" (vv. 12, 13). Similarly, in contrast to the notion of wandering away from the faith (v. 10b), both fidelity (v. 11b) and the steadfast observance of the demands flowing from faith (v. 14a) are affirmed. The "good confession" earlier made by Timothy (v. 12b) and the "good confession" once given by Jesus before Pilate (v. 13b) are both related to the experience and example of faith described in the immediate context (vv. 11–14) and are unrelated to the rest of chapter 6.

There are grounds, therefore, for making a distinction between the exhortation itself, which is addressed to Timothy (vv. 11–14), and the doxology into which it extends and with which it ends (vv. 15–16). The exhortation itself comprises two components. The first (v. 11b) makes general reference to a series of attitudes that are characteristic of those who believe,[14] while the second (vv. 12–14) describes the dynamic dimension of these attitudes with a specific reference to Timothy's own

---

[12] For example, Burton Scott Easton, *The Pastoral Epistles: Introduction, Translation, Commentary, and Word Studies* (London: SCM, 1948), 165; Norbert Brox, *Die Pastoralbriefe*, RNT 7.2 (Regensburg: Pustet, 1969), 212; Dibelius and Conzelmann, *Pastoral Epistles*, 87; J. L. Houlden, *The Pastoral Epistles: I and II Timothy, Titus*, PNTC (Harmondsworth: Penguin, 1976), 100; Karoline Läger, *Die Christologie der Pastoralbriefe*, HThSt 12 (Münster: Lit, 1996), 55; James D. Miller, *The Pastoral Letters as Composite Documents*, SNTSMS 93 (Cambridge: Cambridge University Press, 1997), 91.

[13] Ernst Käsemann, "La formule néotestamentaire d'une parénèse d'ordination," in *Essais exégétiques* (Neuchâtel: Delachaux et Niestlé, 1972), 111–19, here 111.

[14] "Follow after righteousness, godliness, faith, love, steadfastness, gentleness": this list is formulated in exactly the same way as that in 2 Tim 2:22 with the addition of three supplementary dispositions (godliness, steadfastness, gentleness). Here the words are addressed to Timothy as an individual, whereas in 2 Timothy they have a communal dimension. Timothy, however, is not addressed as an individual per se but as one who has a specific role within a community. See Michel Gourgues, *Les deux lettres à Timothée, la lettre à Tite*, Commentaire biblique: Nouveau Testament 14 (Paris: Cerf, 2009), 223, 300–301.

experience. It is in relation to Timothy's experience that one must place and understand the καλὴ ὁμολογία mentioned twice, in verses 12b and 13b.

II. From Timothy's "Good Confession" to Jesus's "Good Confession"

Having enjoined attitudes such as faith and love (6:11) in general terms, the exhortation then becomes more specific and personal, evoking Timothy's own experience (v. 12) and then relating it to God and Christ (v. 13). Verses 12 and 13 have corresponding themes:

6:12	6:13
Fight the good fight of the faith, take hold of the eternal **life** and **confess** (ὡμολόγησας) the **good confession** (τὴν καλὴν ὁμολογίαν) in the presence of many witnesses (μάρτυρες)	I charge you, before God who gives **life** to all things and Christ Jesus who in his **testimony** (μαρτυρήσας) before Pontius Pilate made the **good confession** (τὴν καλὴν ὁμολογίαν)

From a series of Christian attitudes that should be the object of one's efforts (v. 11b), the subject shifts to the basic drive of existence, represented in Pauline symbolism as a combat or sports competition that results in the acquisition of eternal life (cf. 1 Cor 9:25, Phil 1:30). From the call to eternal *life* received by Timothy, we are led back to the God who gives life; from the good *homologia* professed by Timothy before several *witnesses* we are led back to Christ, who witnessed with his good *homologia*. From Timothy's experience, we are led back to Christ's exemplary experience—but in what did these experiences consist?

1. *Timothy's experience.* The meaning of ὁμολογία, translated as "confession," needs to be clarified since it is designated as the means by which Jesus gave his testimony, τοῦ μαρτυρήσαντος τὴν καλὴν ὁμολογίαν. When it is the action of a community or of a group of people, ὁμολογία can mean an accord, a pact, or a common declaration. When it is the action of an individual, as is the case here (in regard both to Timothy [v. 12] and to Jesus [v. 13]), ὁμολογία means a declaration, admission, confession, or commitment. In a religious context, it could even denote a profession of faith that is shared with others.[15] In addition to noting Timothy's responsibility for the community, 1 Timothy deals with the ministries of bishop (3:1–7), deacon (3:8–13), and presbyter (5:17–22), as well as the laying on of hands

---

[15] These shades of meaning can be found in the Gospels and Acts, e.g., Matt 7:23, 10:32, 14:7, Luke 12:8, John 1:20, 9:22, 12:42, Acts 7:17. See Otto Michel, ὁμολογέω, *TWNT* 5:199–220; Ceslas Spicq, *Lexique théologique du Nouveau Testament* (Paris: Cerf, 1991), 1108–9, s.v. ὁμολογουμένως.

(5:22).¹⁶ This has led some scholars to think that Timothy's *good confession* refers to an "ordination ritual" or some form of commitment to serve that would have required a profession of faith.¹⁷ There is no evidence of such an institution during New Testament times, and in our passage (6:12) Timothy's *homologia* is mentioned only in connection with the call to eternal life he has received from God. The verse literally reads, "Conquer the eternal life, in view of which you have been called and (in view of which) you have confessed [aorist] the good confession." The call to eternal life, which is the goal of the combat of faith, concerns each and every believer. Thus, Timothy's *homologia* seems linked to the commitment of faith itself, to a basic receptivity to God and God's promises so that there is every reason to consider baptism—which, to the contrary, is well attested from the very beginnings—as the context within which this proclamation is made.¹⁸ The *homologia*,

---

¹⁶ For a further discussion of these elements in the context of 1 Timothy, see Michel Gourgues, "Les pouvoirs en voie d'institutionnalisation dans les épîtres pastorales," in *Le pouvoir: Enquêtes dans l'un et l'autre Testament,* ed. Didier Luciani and André Wénin, LD 248 (Paris: Cerf, 2012), 289–323, esp. 308–17.

¹⁷ See Käsemann, "La formule néotestamentaire," 115–17; Victor C. Pfitzner, *Paul and the Agon Motif: Traditional Athletic Imagery in the Pauline Literature,* NovTSup16 (Leiden: Brill, 1967), 180–81; and the several commentaries cited in Marshall, *Critical and Exegetical Commentary on the Pastoral Epistles,* 654 n. 62. See also Robert W. Wall with Richard B. Steele, *1 and 2 Timothy and Titus,* Two Horizons New Testament Commentary (Grand Rapids: Eerdmans, 2012), 145. For a critical appraisal of that position, see Hermann von Lips, *Glaube - Gemeinde - Amt: Zum Verständnis der Ordination in den Pastoralbriefen,* FRLANT 122 (Göttingen: Vandenhoeck & Ruprecht, 1975), 177–80; Helmut Merkel, *Die Pastoralbriefe,* NTD 9.1 (Göttingen: Vandenhoeck & Ruprecht, 1991), 49–50; and Philip H. Towner, *The Letters to Timothy and Titus,* NICNT (Grand Rapids: Eerdmans, 2006), 411–12.

¹⁸ For authors who hold this position, see Marshall, *Critical and Exegetical Commentary on the Pastoral Epistles,* 654 n. 61. Just as with the exhortation in vv. 11–12, the injunction then made to Timothy in vv. 13–14 ("I charge you to *keep the commandment*") must concern him as a believer and not as a leader of the community. Neither the noun ἐντολή ("commandment") nor its corresponding verb (ἐντέλλομαι) occurs elsewhere in 1 Timothy. The solemnity of the injunction (v. 13) indicates the decisive importance of the matter at hand. Moreover, reference in v. 12 to the life of faith as a whole and to Timothy's once and for all commitment invites us to assign the term ἐντολή a wide meaning. "Keep the commandment" (v. 14a) must be the equivalent of "Fight the good fight of the faith" (v. 12a), and we can deduce that ἐντολή refers to all the demands flowing from faith and receptivity to the gospel. This wide dimension of ἐντολή, designating in some sense "that which God expects of believers," is not unknown in Greek (see BDAG, s.v. ἐντολή) and is attested in certain late writings of the New Testament, in particular 2 Pet 2:21, 3:1. The word occurs a few times in Polycarp's letter to the Philippians and, in a particularly striking way, in a passage in which the bishop of Smyrna seems to be referring to 1 Tim 6:7. "The source of all evil is the love of money. Mindful, therefore, of the fact that, 'we brought nothing into the world, and we cannot take anything out of the world,' let us arm ourselves with the 'arms of justice' and let us first learn ourselves to walk in *the commandment of the Lord* [πορεύεσθαι ἐν τῇ ἐντολῇ τοῦ Κυρίου]" (*Phil.* 4.1; my translation). A little earlier on, in 2.2, Polycarp had used the expression "walk in his commandments" to designate overall Christian commitment in response to the gospel and in

therefore, refers to a precise event that involves a verbal proclamation—within *homologia* there is *logos*, word—undergone by Timothy, as by other believers, at a particular moment.

2. *Jesus's experience.* Verse 13 refers to an experience lived by Jesus ἐπὶ Ποντίου Πιλάτου. The preposition ἐπί followed by the genitive can mean "before, in front of."[19] It can also have a a temporal sense, such as "under Pontius Pilate" or "at the time of Pontius Pilate."[20] In that case, the experience in Jesus's life being referred to could extend beyond his appearance before the Roman prefect. The "testimony" he gives could encompass the whole of his existence or, if the term is to be taken literally, could refer only to his proclamation of the kingdom of God at the time when Pontius Pilate served as the representative of Roman power. In parallel with Timothy's experience, however, Jesus's experience must consist in a strictly verbal testimony like that given before Pilate rather than in a "testimony" understood in a more existential sense, such as the crucifixion or the earthly life of Jesus taken as a whole.[21] Just as Timothy uttered his *homologia* "in the presence of many witnesses," Jesus uttered his confession "before Pontius Pilate." The preposition ἐπί in verse 13 corresponds to the preposition ἐνώπιον ("before, in the presence of") in verse 12. On the basis of Jesus's bitter experience of adversity during his passion and appearance before Pilate, scholars suggested that the situation in which Timothy professed his faith was one of conflict or persecution.[22] In the context of the call to eternal life in verse 12, however, which suggests baptism, the implied difficulty or trials probably have to do with the "good fight" of the faith and the "conquest" of eternal life.

By recalling Jesus's trial before Pilate, 1 Tim 6:13 shows an interest in Jesus's lived experience and a particular incident within that experience. Other passages in 1 Timothy also refer to Jesus's human condition and his earthly life: 1:15 and 6:3 speak of Jesus's coming into the world and his words; 2:5 refers to "the man Christ Jesus"; and 3:16 tells of how he was "manifested in the flesh."

---

conformity to God's will. Again in 5.1: "Knowing therefore that, 'God will not be mocked,' we must walk in a way worthy of his commandment [ἄξιος τῆς ἐντολῆς αὐτοῦ]and of his glory."

[19] Cf., e.g., Mark 13:9: "you will stand before governors and kings [ἐπὶ ἡγεμόνων καὶ βασιλέων] for my sake"; Acts 23:30: "I sent him to you at once, ordering his accusers also to state before you [ἐπὶ σοῦ] what they have against him."

[20] Cf., e.g., Matt 1:11: "at the time of the deportation [ἐπὶ τῆς μετοικεσίας] to Babylon"; Mark 2:26: "when Abiathar was high priest [ἐπὶ Ἀβιαθὰρ ἀρχιερέως]"; Luke 3:2: "in the high priesthood [ἐπὶ ἀρχιερέως] of Annas and Caiaphas"; Luke 4:27: "there were many lepers in Israel in the time of the prophet Elisha [ἐπὶ Ἐλισαίου του προφήτου]."

[21] The parallelism noted above between vv. 12 and 13 indicates that the verbs ὁμολογέω and μαρτυρέω, both aorist participles, are synonymous.

[22] Similarly, Wall and Steele, *1 and 2 Timothy and Titus*, 145–46.

III. The Reference to Tradition

If the *homologia* in verse 12 is to be understood in the sense of a baptismal confession of faith, does this imply that the affirmation regarding Christ in verse 13 echoes a traditional formula, as is the case, for example, in the christological proclamations of 1 Tim 3:16?[23] Some think that this verse refers to the content of Timothy's faith confession of verse 12. This profession may have included an article analogous to "I believe in God who created all things and in Christ who testified before Pontius Pilate."[24]

If 1 Tim 6:13 refers to traditional formulas, they are well integrated into the context and it is difficult to detect the presence of a literal quotation of a formula.[25] The content of the exhortation in verse 12 would have had to be conceived and expressed in terms of the formula in verse 13. Would not the reverse, however, be more natural and probable, that, on the basis of the content of the exhortation in verse 12, the author formulated the attributes of God and Christ in verse 13? Could these be borrowed from existing formulas? Nowhere else in the New Testament is God designated as being "he who gives life to all things," and the reference to Jesus as appearing before Pilate is found in none of the traditional formulas. Formulas of this type—hymns or creeds—usually focus on the core of faith, Jesus's death and resurrection, rather than on any particular aspect of his earthly life.

Is there a reference to tradition here that takes a form other than a quotation or allusion to an existing formula? First Timothy 6:13 recalls Jesus's appearance before Pilate, and the Gospels depict the event in their passion narratives. The Gospel of John, however, offers the longest account of Jesus's witness before Pilate (18:29–38). The Synoptic narratives emphasize Jesus's silence after a simple recollection of his laconic response to the question, "Are you the king of the Jews?"[26] John recalls an exchange concerning Jesus's sovereignty (18:34–36) and his witness to the truth. Could 1 Tim 6:13 be alluding to John's version of the event? The fact that verse 13 uses the verb μαρτυρέω ("give testimony") for Jesus's witness is reason

---

[23] See Michel Gourgues, "Les formes pré-littéraires, ou l'Évangile avant l'écriture," in *Histoire de la littérature grecque chrétienne*, ed. Bernard Pouderon, 2 vols. (Paris: Cerf, 2008–2013), 2:265–82, esp. 266–68.

[24] Wengst, *Christologische Formeln und Lieder*, 124–25; Roloff, *Die erste Brief an Timotheus*, 344.

[25] Oberlinner, *Die Pastorale Briefe*, 1:287.

[26] The account is extremely laconic in Mark 15:2–5: "And Pilate asked him, 'Are you the king of the Jews?' And he answered him, 'You have said so.' And the chief priests accused him of many things. And Pilate again asked him, 'Have you no answer to make? See how many charges they bring against you.' But Jesus made no further answer, so that Pilate wondered" (par. Matt 27:11–14). Luke fits everything into a single verse: "And Pilate asked him, 'Are you the King of the Jews?' And he answered him, 'You have said so'" (23:3).

for raising the question. The verb is not part of the normal vocabulary of 1 Timothy; it appears only in 5:10, where it is used in connection with widows who are called to "give the testimony" of good works. This is the word used by Jesus in John 18:37 in response to Pilate's question, "So, you are a king?": "You say that I am a king. For this I was born, and for this I have *come into the world*, to *bear witness* [ἵνα μαρτυρήσω] to the truth. Everyone who is of the truth hears my voice."

Could 1 Tim 6:13 be echoing the Gospel of John? Is there any other evidence of this? In addition to the verb μαρτυρέω, the reply given by Jesus to Pilate in John 18:37 also contains the typically Johannine expression "come into the world" (ἐλήλυθα εἰς τὸν κόσμον). This phrase is also used in reference to Jesus in 1 Tim 1:15: "Christ Jesus *came into the world* [ἦλθεν εἰς τὸν κόσμον] to save sinners." The phrase "come into the world" has a very Johannine ring to it; the formula occurs often, scattered throughout the Fourth Gospel, beginning with 1:9 ("the true light that enlightens everyone was *coming into the world*") up to the statement before Pilate in 18:37 ("for this I have *come into the world*, to bear witness to the truth").[27] In 1 Timothy, however, the phrase seems out of place. The verb "to come" is used three times in the letter in both a literal (3:14, 4:13) and a figurative (2:4) sense, but it never has Jesus as its subject. The word *world* (κόσμος) appears only once elsewhere in the letter (3:16) in relation to Christ, in a passage that is clearly identifiable as a traditional formula. The expression "come into the world" is found nowhere else in 1 Timothy, nor does it occur in 2 Timothy or Titus. In the Pauline corpus it appears in Rom 5:12, but there it refers not to Christ but to sin.[28]

Finally, the proclamation concerning Christ in 1 Tim 1:15b is introduced in 1:15a by the solemn formula "The saying is sure" (πιστὸς ὁ λόγος). This affirmation of credibility is a typical expression of the Pastoral Epistles, distinguishing them from the rest of the Pauline correspondence. The formulation is found five times in the three letters, and three of the occurrences are in 1 Timothy.[29] In 2 Tim 2:11, the formula "the saying is sure" introduces the quotation of a traditional faith statement ("If we die with him..."). There is reason to think that the same is true of 1 Tim 1:15. In this instance the christological proclamation introduced would be the

---

[27] See also John 3:19, 6:14, 9:39, 11:27, 12:46, 16:28.

[28] The rest of the phrase in 1 Tim 3:15 is closer to the Synoptics. "Come to save sinners" recalls Jesus's words in Mark 2:17 par., in the passage narrating the call of Levi the publican: "I came not to call the righteous but sinners." In Luke 19:10, at the end of the Zacchaeus pericope, we find similar words spoken by Jesus in a passage that shares the same two verbs "come" and "save": "The Son of Man *came* [ἦλθεν] to seek and *save* [σῶσαι] the lost." The evidence suggests the use of borrowed formulas that echo Gospel passages where the Synoptic and Johannine traditions intersect.

[29] Four of the five times, the formula precedes (1 Tim 1:15, 4:9, 2 Tim 2:11) or immediately follows (Titus 3:8) passages called "faithful sayings" by commentators, in which it is a matter of God's salvation in Jesus Christ. The only exception is 1 Tim 3:1, where the formula precedes considerations regarding the office of bishop.

following: "Christ Jesus came into the world to save sinners." Hence, the introductory formula, "The saying is sure and worthy of full acceptance," is followed by the conjunction ὅτι, the equivalent of a colon preceding a quotation or a reference to a known fact.[30]

IV. Conclusion

The theological and literary evidence presented here suggests that 1 Tim 6:13 alludes to the Johannine version of Jesus's appearance before Pilate. If this is correct, this conclusion suggests a late date for 1 Timothy. It is important, of course, to distinguish between a reference to the Johannine narrative itself and a reference to the traditions on which it drew and which, especially in the case of the passion narrative, had previously circulated in oral form. Regardless of whether the reference is to oral or written accounts, however, the apparent allusion suggests that 1 Timothy must be associated in a particular way with the advanced theology manifested in John's account of Jesus's dialogue with Pilate.

---

[30] This occurs repeatedly in Paul, especially in known introductory formulas, for example, 1 Thess 4:14 ("we believe *that*…"); 1 Cor 15:3 ("I delivered to you as of first importance what I also received, *that*…"); Rom 10:8–9: "the word of faith" that we preach, *that* if you believe in your heart *that*…"); Phil 2:11: "and every tongue confess *that*…").

Emotional Physiology and Consolatory Etiquette: Reading the Present Indicative with Future Reference in the Eschatological Statement in 1 Peter 1:6

TROY W. MARTIN
martin@sxu.edu
Saint Xavier University, Chicago, IL 60655

Although present tense in form, the verb ἀγαλλιᾶσθε in 1 Pet 1:6 is read contextually with future reference by commentators and translators who distinguish between present grieving and future rejoicing. This interpretation of 1 Pet 1:6 dominated until the Reformation, when John Calvin and Conrad Horneius argued that the present tense form of ἀγαλλιᾶσθε takes precedence over the context. Their reading assumes that the recipients of this letter simultaneously experience rejoicing and grieving, and Calvin and Horneius appealed to the experience of their sixteenth-century readers for proof that humans can have such conflicting emotions. In this article, I evaluate this assumption by examining ancient discussions of the emotions that treat joy and grief as opposites, with the former as pleasurable and the latter as painful. I demonstrate that these emotions cannot be experienced simultaneously according to ancient physiology. I also evaluate the tendency to read ἀγαλλιᾶσθε with present reference by examining ancient consolatory etiquette and conclude that informing these grieving recipients at the beginning of the letter that they are rejoicing would be inappropriate and contrary to consolatory etiquette, theory, and practice. Even though almost all recent Petrine commentators follow Calvin and Horneius in reading ἀγαλλιᾶσθε in reference to present rejoicing, I demonstrate that ancient physiology and consolatory etiquette support the pre-Reformation reading of this verb in reference to future rejoicing.

In an article I published in 1992, I took sides in the exegetical debate over the temporal reference of the verb ἀγαλλιᾶσθε in 1 Pet 1:6, which reads: ἐν ᾧ ἀγαλλιᾶσθε, ὀλίγον ἄρτι εἰ δέον [ἐστὶν] λυπηθέντες ἐν ποικίλοις πειρασμοῖς ("at which [time] you [will] rejoice although now for a little while, if it is necessary, you are grieved by manifold trials").¹ This verb is clearly present tense in form, but I argued in that article for reading this verb in reference to future time.² Even though I considered my arguments to be compelling, some subsequent commentaries, including those by Paul J. Achtemeier, Mark Dubis, Karen H. Jobes, and Reinhard Feldmeier nevertheless continue to read ἀγαλλιᾶσθε in reference to present time.³ Rather than restating the arguments from my initial article, I present here a brief history of this debate and then critique two assumptions required by a present temporal reading of ἀγαλλιᾶσθε that are incompatible with ancient physiology and consolatory etiquette, theory, and practice.

---

[1] Troy W. Martin, "The Present Indicative in the Eschatological Statements of 1 Pet 1:6, 8," *JBL* 111 (1992): 307–12, http://dx.doi.org/10.2307/3267546. For a succinct summary of the issues in this debate, see Troy W. Martin, *Metaphor and Composition in First Peter*, SBLDS 131 (Atlanta: Scholars Press, 1992), 59–64; and Reinhard Feldmeier, *The First Letter of Peter: A Commentary on the Greek Text*, trans. Peter H. Davids (Waco, TX: Baylor University Press, 2008), 79–80.

[2] The strongest argument for those who read ἀγαλλιᾶσθε as present rejoicing is the present tense form of this verb itself. Both the grammarians and several classical and New Testament examples, however, indicate that in the Greek language a present tense verb can refer to future circumstances (e.g., Mark 9:31, 1 Cor 15:32; see Martin, "Present Indicative," 311; Martin, *Metaphor and Composition*, 63–64). Ernest de Witt Burton states that the present tense "used with reference to a fact still in the future is recognized by all grammarians," and he lists several of these nineteenth-century grammarians (*Syntax of the Moods and Tenses in New Testament Greek*, 3rd ed. [1898; repr., Edinburgh: T&T Clark, 1976], 10). His statement also pertains, however, to more recent twentieth-century grammarians, including among others Herbert Weir Smyth (*Greek Grammar*, rev. Gordon M. Messing [1956; repr., Cambridge: Harvard University Press, 1980; orig., 1916], §1879), Max Zerwick (*Biblical Greek: Illustrated by Examples*, SPIB 114 [Rome: Iura Editionis et Versionis Reservantur, 1963], §278), Stanley E. Porter (*Verbal Aspect in the Greek of the New Testament, with Reference to Tense and Mood*, Studies in Biblical Greek 1 [New York: Lang, 1989], 230–32), and K. L. McKay (*A New Syntax of the Verb in New Testament Greek: An Aspectual Approach*, Studies in Biblical Greek 5 [New York: Lang, 1994], §4.2.3).

[3] Paul J. Achtemeier, *1 Peter: A Commentary on First Peter*, Hermeneia (Minneapolis: Fortress, 1996), 99; Mark Dubis, *1 Peter: A Handbook on the Greek Text*, Baylor Handbook on the Greek New Testament (Waco, TX: Baylor University Press, 2010), 10; Karen H. Jobes, *1 Peter*, BECNT (Grand Rapids: Baker Academic, 2005), 92–93; and Feldmeier, *First Letter of Peter*, 79–80. For additional commentators who argue for a present tense reading, see Ernst Kühl, *Die Briefe Petri und Judae*, 6th ed., KEK 12 (Göttingen: Vandenhoeck & Ruprecht, 1897), 82–86; Rudolf Knopf, *Die Briefe Petri und Judä*, 7th ed., KEK 12 (Göttingen: Vandenhoeck & Ruprecht, 1912), 47–49; Edward Gordon Selwyn, *The First Epistle of St. Peter: The Greek Text with Introduction, Notes, and Essays*, 2nd ed., Thornapple Commentaries (1946; repr., Grand Rapids: Baker, 1981), 126, 258–59; J. N. D. Kelly, *A Commentary on the Epistles of Peter and Jude*, Thornapple Commentaries (1969; repr., Grand Rapids: Baker, 1981), 53; Peter H. Davids, *The First Epistle of Peter*, NICNT (Grand Rapids: Eerdmans, 1990), 54–55; and I. Howard Marshall, *1 Peter*, IVP New Testament Commentary Series (Downers Grove, IL: InterVarsity Press, 2003), 39–40.

I. History of the Debate

Ancient Greek interpreters consistently understand ἀγαλλιᾶσθε in 1 Pet 1:6 as future. In a passage where he proposes that the one who remains until the end will be saved, for example, Origen quotes 1 Pet 1:6–7 but uses the future ἀγαλλιάσεσθε ("you will rejoice") rather than the present (*Mart.* 39).[4] Origen's change in tense may mean that the manuscript he is using has the future. Since no surviving manuscript of 1 Peter has the future, however, it more likely means that Origen understands the present as a future, as do subsequent Greek commentators. Oecumenius and Theophylact comment, "'In the last time, you will rejoice [ἀγαλλιάσεσθε)]' the ἀγαλλιᾶσθε has been received for a future circumstance rather than a present circumstance."[5] To support their future reading of the present, these commentators cite John 17:11 and 16:33, where affliction is the lot of this world but affliction will be turned into rejoicing in the future.[6]

Similar to the Greek commentary tradition, Latin commentators also understand ἀγαλλιᾶσθε in reference to a future rejoicing. The Venerable Bede translates and comments, "In which you will exult [*exultabitis*].... When he [Peter] says, 'in which,' he refers to that time when a prepared salvation will be revealed and will be given to those who are worthy."[7] Didymus Alexandrinus, Eusebius Hieronymus, Pseudo-Hilarius, and Martinus all interpret ἀγαλλιᾶσθε with the Latin future verb *exultabitis* ("you will rejoice), as do almost all Latin commentators.[8] Explaining the Latin translations and quotations of 1 Pet 1:6, Walter Thiele notes, "The future in 1:6 is easily understood after 1:5."[9] Thus, the ancient Greek and Latin commentary traditions understand ἐν καιρῷ ἐσχάτῳ ("at the end time") at the end of 1 Pet 1:5 to

---

[4] See also Irenaeus, *Haer.* 4.9.2; 5.7.2. The Latin manuscripts of Irenaeus's work have the future *exultabitis* for ἀγαλλιᾶσθε in 1 Pet 1:8 and indicate that the original Greek *Vorlage* may have also had a future form of this verb. For a discussion, see Selwyn, *First Epistle of St. Peter*, 258–59.

[5] Oecumenius, *Commentarii in epistolas catholicas* (PG 119:517); Theophylact, *Expositio in Epistolam Primam S. Petri* (PG 125:1196). All translations of ancient texts are mine unless otherwise noted.

[6] Martin, *Metaphor and Composition*, 60.

[7] David Hurst, trans., *The Commentary on the Seven Catholic Epistles of Bede the Venerable*, CistSS 82 (Kalamazoo, MI: Cistercian Publications, 1985), 43.

[8] Didymus Alexandrinus, *Enarratio in Epistolas Catholicas* (PL 39:1756); Eusebius Hieronymus, *Divina bibliotheca* (PL 29:877); Ps.-Hilarius Arelatensis, *Expositio in Epistolas Catholicas* (PL Sup 3:85); Martinus Legionensis, *Expositio in epistolam I B. Petri Apostoli* (PL 209:219).

[9] Walter Thiele, *Die lateinischen Texte des 1. Petrusbriefes*, VL 5 (Freiburg: Herder, 1965), 84.

be the antecedent of ἐν ᾧ ("at which [end time]") at the beginning of 1 Pet 1:6 and then take the present ἀγαλλιᾶσθε as a reference to the future.[10]

This understanding of ἐν ᾧ designating the end-time and ἀγαλλιᾶσθε as having future reference dominates the interpretation of 1 Pet 1:6 until the Reformation, when John Calvin proposes a present tense reading of this verb.[11] Calvin's proposal is later defended by Conrad Horneius, who argues:

> The ancient translator *has the future tense*, "in which you will rejoice." ... But they translated it in that way primarily because they referred the phrase ἐν ᾧ, *in which*, taken independently, to the final day and secondarily because this phrase seemed to have some appearance of incompatibility; *you are rejoicing although you are grieved by sadness*.... But it is more correct that the present tense be retained, which has been received in the manuscripts, for the ἐν ᾧ refers to everything that precedes.[12]

Horneius acknowledges that the tradition he receives understands ἀγαλλιᾶσθε in 1 Pet 1:6 as a reference to the future. Nevertheless, he follows Calvin by taking exception to the ancient reading of a future reference for this verb. Instead, like Calvin, he reads the verb in reference to present rejoicing and thus occasions the debate that continues to divide subsequent commentators, some of whom read ἀγαλλιᾶσθε as present but others as future.[13]

---

[10] When a present tense verb is used with future reference, Blass and Debrunner (BDF §323) explain, "Ordinarily a temporal indication of the future is included." Thus, ἀγαλλιᾶσθε ("you will rejoice") in 1 Pet 1:6 is a textbook example of the present tense for the future that has ἐν ᾧ ("at which [end time]") as a temporal indication of the future followed by ἄρτι ("just now") as an antithesis to this future reference. Regarding the purpose for using a present tense with future reference, Smyth explains, "The present is used instead of the future in statements of what is immediate, likely, certain, or threatening" (*Greek Grammar*, §1879). Peter thus uses the present tense form rather than the future to emphasize that this rejoicing is not far away in the distant future but rather more immediate, likely, and certain. The present tense form with a future temporal reference rather than a future tense form better serves his attempts to console and encourage his recipients, when he says ἐν ᾧ ἀγαλλιᾶσθε ("at which end time, you will rejoice").

[11] John Calvin, *The Epistle of Paul the Apostle to the Hebrews and The First and Second Epistles of St Peter*, trans. William B. Johnston (Grand Rapids: Eerdmans, 1994), 234.

[12] Conrad Horneius, *In Epistolam Catholicam Sancti Apostoli Petri Priorem expositio litteralis* (Braunschweig: Andrea Duncker, 1654), 16.

[13] For the present reading, see the commentators cited in n. 3. For the future reading, see Hans Windisch, *Die Katholischen Briefe*, ed. Herbert Preisker, HNT 15 (Tübingen: Mohr Siebeck, 1951), 53; James Moffatt, *The General Epistles: James, Peter, and Judas*, MNTC (London: Hodder & Stoughton, 1947), 96; Leonhard Goppelt, *A Commentary on 1 Peter* (Grand Rapids: Eerdmans, 1993), 88–89; J. Ramsey Michaels, *1 Peter*, WBC 49 (Waco, TX: Word, 1988), 27; Martin, "Present Indicative," 307–12; Martin, *Metaphor and Composition*, 59–64; Philip L. Tite, *Compositional Transitions in 1 Peter: An Analysis of the Letter-Opening* (San Francisco: International Scholars, 1997), 78–79; and Barth L. Campbell, *Honor, Shame, and the Rhetoric of 1 Peter*, SBLDS 160 (Atlanta: Scholars Press, 1998), 47.

II. The Physiological Assumption

In reading ἀγαλλιᾶσθε as present, both Calvin and Horneius and those who follow their reading must make a crucial physiological assumption that a human being can rejoice and grieve simultaneously. Calvin states,

> It seems somewhat inconsistent when he [Peter] says that the faithful, who exult with joy, are at the same time sorrowful, for these are contrary feelings, but the faithful know by experience that these things can exist together much better than can be expressed in words.... Hence, they experience sorrow because of evils, but it is so mitigated by faith that they never cease at the same time to rejoice. Thus sorrow does not prevent their joy, but rather gives place to it.[14]

Similarly, Horneius asserts, "Neither is it incompatible for the same men to feel simultaneously both happy and sad since this happens for different reasons: for believers are grieved on account of present afflictions; but they rejoice on account of eternal hope of retribution.... And Paul says in 2 Cor 6:10, 'Being afflicted but always rejoicing'" (*In Epistolam Petri* 16).

Calvin and Horneius both recognize that their reading of ἀγαλλιᾶσθε in 1 Pet 1:6 in reference to the present rests on the crucial assumption that a human can simultaneously experience joy and grief. To support this assumption, they appeal to the experience of their fellow believers. To be valid, this experiential argument requires a consistent understanding of the emotions that does not change during the sixteen centuries separating Calvin and Horneius and their fellow believers from the author of 1 Peter and his readers. Significantly, neither Calvin nor Horneius cites any ancient author to substantiate the argument or the assumption that humans can rejoice and grieve at the same time.

Experiencing simultaneous joy and grief, however, is not only unsubstantiated by ancient understandings of the emotions but impossible.[15] For example, Aristotle (*Rhet.* 2.2–11 [1378a–1388b]) treats the emotions as pairs of opposites (ἐναντία).[16] Thus, anger is the opposite of settling down, and friendly feelings the opposite of enmity. Since these emotions move people to action, Aristotle advises the orator in how to engender or create (ἐμποιεῖν) these emotions in an audience. Aristotle's entire treatment rests on the understanding that experiencing one of these emotions necessarily replaces and excludes its contrary.

---

[14] Calvin, *Epistles of St Peter*, 234.

[15] Troy W. Martin, "The Voice of Emotion: Paul's Pathetic Persuasion (Gal 4:12–20)," in *Paul and Pathos*, ed. Thomas H. Olbricht and Jerry L. Sumney, SymS 16 (Atlanta: Society of Biblical Literature, 2001), 181–202; Martin, "Sorting the Syntax of Aristotle's Anger (*Rh.* 2.2.1 1378a30–32)," *Hermes* 129 (2001): 474–78; Olbricht and Sumney, *Paul and Pathos*, passim.

[16] David Konstan, *The Emotions of the Ancient Greeks: Studies in Aristotle and Classical Literature*, Robson Classical Lectures (Toronto: University of Toronto Press, 2006), 34.

Although Aristotle does not specifically treat grief and joy in his discussion of the emotions (*Rhet.* 2.2–11 [1378a–1388b]), he does mention them earlier and says, "For we do not render decisions similarly while we are grieving or distressed [λυπούμενοι] and while we are rejoicing [χαίροντες] or while we are loving and hating" (*Rhet.* 1.2.5 [1356a]; cf. Aristotle, *De an.* 1.1 [403a]). Since he specifically treats loving and hating as opposites in his discussion of the emotions, he clearly regards grief or distress and joy as opposite emotions as well, although he may have good reasons for not including them in his treatment of the emotions useful for an orator.[17]

As opposites, grief or distress and joy cannot be experienced simultaneously, as Socrates says, "How astonishing the relation it [pleasure] has with what is thought to be its opposite, namely pain! A man cannot have both at the same time" (Plato, *Phaed.* 60b).[18] Socrates proceeds to state that one almost always follows the other. Although pleasure and pain are not emotions but rather sensations that engender emotions, the thought that a painful emotion such as distress or grief and a pleasant emotion such as joy can be experienced simultaneously is precluded.[19] Aristotle even says that no one could account happy a person living a life of misery or misfortune except in philosophical discussions of a paradox (*Eth. nic.* 1.5.6 [1096a]).

Indeed, joy and grief exclude each other since these emotions are movements of the soul and the soul can move only in one direction or another but not in opposite directions at the same time (Aristotle, *De an.* 1.1 [403a–408b]). From the ancient physiological understanding, therefore, grief or distress and joy are opposites and cannot be present in a single person at the same time, and reading ἀγαλλιᾶσθε 1 Pet 1:6 as a present indicative informing the recipients that they are rejoicing now while simultaneously grieving or being distressed (λυπηθέντες) is not only highly improbable but impossible from ancient physiological perspectives on the emotions.

Calvin's and Horneius's assertion most likely represents a Christian physiological development from late antiquity that is based on a present tense reading of 1 Pet 1:6. In the seventh century, Maximus the Confessor quotes this verse and then asks how it is possible for someone to rejoice while grieving.[20] He answers by redefining grief as twofold. He distinguishes a hidden grief of the soul from a manifest grief of the senses. One can therefore be grieving outwardly while rejoicing inwardly and vice versa. In contrast, Aristotle (*De an.* 1.1 [403a]) states, "It is likely that all

---

[17] Ibid., 244–58.

[18] Translation by G. M. A. Grube, *Plato, Five Dialogues: Euthyphro, Apology, Crito, Meno, Phaedo* (Indianapolis: Hackett, 1981), 96.

[19] See Plato, *Tim.* 42a–b, where love or desire (ἔρως) is said to be mingled with pleasure and pain. This statement does not mean that pleasure and pain occur at the same time but that love or desire can occasion or cause either pleasure or pain—at different times, however.

[20] Maximus the Confessor, *Quaestiones ad Thalassium* 58. See C. Laga and C. Steel, *Maximi confessoris quaestiones ad Thalassium*, 2 vols., CCSG 7, 22 (Turnhout: Brepols, 1980–1990).

the affections of the soul are with the body ... for along with these affections of the soul, the body also suffers something." In addition to Aristotle, many ancient authors explain that movements of the soul are also linked to the action of a specific corresponding bodily member.[21] For example, Hippocrates (*De humoribus* 9) describes the emotions arising from external stimuli and then states that to each of these emotions the appropriate member of the body also responds. Hence, Maximus's separation of the soul from the physical senses departs from the ancient understanding of the soul as the mediator or facilitator of the bodily senses and marks a Christian physiological development that postdates 1 Peter. This physiological development required by the Reformation assertion about simultaneous joy and grief is simply unavailable to Peter and his recipients.

Calvin's and Horneius's experiential argument to support their assumption is also faulty. Their appeal to their fellow believers' experience of simultaneous joy and grief is not convincing because the understanding of the emotions and what the human body is capable of experiencing changed between the writing of 1 Peter and the Reformation. In contrast to these reformers, therefore, ancient commentators correctly perceive that joy and grief are incompatible emotions and understand ἀγαλλιᾶσθε ("you will rejoice") in reference to future rather than present rejoicing.

One other argument made by Horneius merits consideration. He tries to substantiate his assumption about the emotions and his present tense reading of ἀγαλλιᾶσθε ("you will rejoice") by citing 2 Cor 6:10, where Paul says, ὡς λυπούμενοι ἀεὶ δὲ χαίροντες ("as though grieving but always rejoicing").[22] At first sight, this verse appears to demonstrate that grieving and rejoicing can be simultaneous. This verse, however, occurs in a context (2 Cor 6:4–10) that C. K. Barrett describes as "an impassioned and almost lyrical passage, where precision in the interpretation ... is probably not possible."[23] Furthermore, the juxtaposition of grieving and rejoicing occurs in a series of paradoxical pairs in which the first is introduced by the adverbial adjunct ὡς ("as though"). This adverbial adjunct does not state a fact but rather "sets forth the ground of belief" or the mental "opinion ... pretense ... impression" that someone has "without implicating the speaker or writer."[24]

The first member of these paradoxical pairs describes the mental conception

---

[21] Beate Gundert, "Soma and Psyche in Hippocratic Medicine," in *Psyche and Soma: Physicians and Metaphysicians on the Mind-Body Problem from Antiquity to Enlightenment*, ed. John P. Wright and Paul Potter (Oxford: Clarendon, 2000), 29–30.

[22] Horneius, *In Epistolam Petri*, 16.

[23] C. K. Barrett, *The Second Epistle to the Corinthians*, HNTC (New York: Harper & Row, 1973), 185.

[24] Smyth, *Greek Grammar*, §2086. See also A. T. Robertson, *A Grammar of the Greek New Testament in the Light of Historical Research* (1914; repr., Nashville: Broadman, 1934), 966; Nigel Turner, *Syntax*, vol. 3 of *A Grammar of New Testament Greek* by James Hope Moulton (Edinburgh: T&T Clark, 1963), 158; and H. P. V. Nunn, *A Short Syntax of New Testament Greek* (Cambridge: Cambridge University Press, 1969), §229. Also see the discussion of the force of this adverbial

others hold of Paul and his ministry team without implicating Paul in this assessment.²⁵ Thus, others perceive Paul's team as though they are deceivers (ὡς πλάνοι, 2 Cor 6:8), as though unknown nobodies (ὡς ἀγνοούμενοι, 2 Cor 6:9), as though dying (ὡς ἀποθνῄσκοντες, 2 Cor 6:9), as though being divinely punished (ὡς παιδευόμενοι, 2 Cor 6:9), as though being grieved (ὡς λυπούμενοι, 2 Cor 6:10), as though poor (ὡς πτωχοί, 2 Cor 6:10), and as though having nothing (ὡς μηδέν ἔχοντες, 2 Cor 6:10). The adverbial adjunct ὡς ("as though") indicates that all these first members of each paradoxical pair express not reality but rather only the false and unreal perceptions that others have of Paul and his ministry team.

In paradoxical contrast, the second member of each pair states the reality that Paul and his group are actually genuine (ἀληθεῖς, 2 Cor 6:8), actually recognized by God (ἐπιγινωσκόμενοι, 2 Cor 6:9), actually alive (ζῶμεν, 2 Cor 6:9), actually not under sentence of death (μὴ θανατούμενοι, 2 Cor 6:9), actually always rejoicing (ἀεὶ χαίροντες, 2 Cor 6:10), actually having the means to enrich many (πολλοὺς πλουτίζοντες, 2 Cor 6:10), and actually possessing everything (πάντα κατέχοντες, 2 Cor 6:10). The phrase ὡς λυπούμενοι ἀεὶ δὲ χαίροντες ("as though being grieved but actually always rejoicing") in 2 Cor 6:10 thus proves the opposite of what Horneius tries to demonstrate by citing it. In this verse, Paul does not claim to experience the emotions of grief and joy simultaneously, and neither does this verse substantiate the impossible mixture of these emotions in 1 Pet 1:6.²⁶

Subsequent commentators who want to take ἀγαλλιᾶσθε in reference to

---

adjunct in 1 Pet 2:13–14 by Louis R. Donelson, *I & II Peter and Jude: A Commentary*, NTL (Louisville: Westminster John Knox, 2010), 72–73.

²⁵ John T. Fitzgerald, *Cracks in an Earthen Vessel: An Examination of the Catalogues of Hardships in the Corinthian Correspondence*, SBLDS 99 (Atlanta: Scholars Press, 1988), 195.

²⁶ Someone might cite 2 Cor 12:10 as an example of an impossible mixture of opposites in Paul's statement that when he is weak, then he is strong. This statement occurs at the end of the Fool's Speech (2 Cor 11:1–12:10) and is typically ironical and paradoxical. Only a fool can claim to be both weak and strong because such a claim is foolishly impossible. The Lord utters the truth that power is made perfect in weakness (2 Cor 12:9). Indeed, only in weakness does power attain its proper essence. When two forces of equal power meet, equilibrium ensues and neither power can exert itself. When one force encounters a weaker one, however, the powerful one conquers and obliterates the weaker force and attains its proper essence as power. In his Fool's Speech, Paul demonstrates to the Corinthians that God has inverted the world's conceptions of wisdom and foolishness and of weakness and power (cf. 1 Cor 1:18–25). See L. L. Welborn, *Paul, the Fool of Christ: A Study of 1 Corinthians 1–4 in the Comic-Philosophic Tradition*, JSNTSup 293 (London: T&T Clark, 2005), 117. The *Peristasenkatalog* that precedes Paul's paradoxical statement demonstrates his weakness according to the world's standards, but Paul is really strong and powerful because these circumstances are merely occasions for the power of Christ to be demonstrated in his life (Fitzgerald, *Cracks in an Earthen Vessel*, 205). Thus, Paul's foolish paradoxical statement in 2 Cor 12:10 does not demonstrate an impossible mixture of opposites, for although Paul appears weak by worldly standards, he is really strengthened by Christ's power in circumstances of weakness. Hence, Paul's statement does not support a reading of 1 Pet 1:6 in which the opposite emotions of joy and grief are concurrently experienced, since Paul's statement does not actually

present rejoicing also cite several other texts that express the theme of joy in suffering, such as Matt 5:11–12, Luke 6:22–23, Rom 5:3, Heb 10:32–36, Jas 1:2, and even 1 Pet 4:13.[27] None of these texts, however, is parallel to 1 Pet 1:6, for none speaks of the experience of joy and grief or distress at the same time but rather joy in suffering. Ancient physiology certainly allows for a human to experience joy in the midst of trying circumstances and suffering by a change of mind-set that engenders joy or apathy rather than grief or distress, and the Stoics in particular strive to master this strategy. First Peter 4:13, for example, calls for those suffering to rejoice by considering that they are partners in the sufferings of Christ. This verse calls upon the recipients not to experience the conflicting emotions of joy and grief or distress at the same time but to change their mind-set when suffering so that they experience joy rather than distress or grief. These additional texts cited by those who want to interpret ἀγαλλιᾶσθε in 1 Pet 1:6 as a reference to present joy while simultaneously experiencing grief do not actually support this interpretation.

In contrast, ancient Greek and Latin commentators interpret ἀγαλλιᾶσθε ("you will rejoice") in 1 Pet 1:6 from their own ancient physiological understanding, in which joy and grief or distress cannot be experienced simultaneously. These commentators therefore understand ἀγαλλιᾶσθε ("you will rejoice") as a present tense verb in reference to future rejoicing, since Peter's recipients are distressed in the present. Therefore, the crucial physiological assumption made by Calvin and Horneius to support their present reading of ἀγαλλιᾶσθε is simply impossible from an ancient perspective of what a human body is capable of feeling, and ἀγαλλιᾶσθε in 1 Pet 1:6 can be read only with a future reference by the ancients.

III. The Consolatory Assumption

In addition to their impossible physiological assumption in their reading the present in 1 Pet 1:6, Calvin and Horneius assume that Peter informs his readers that they are rejoicing as he attempts to console them in their grief. This assumption also encounters difficulties. The ancients are sensitive to appropriate and inappropriate ways to converse with the grief-stricken.[28] Plutarch writes to Apollonius, who is grieving over the untimely loss of his son, that to deal with grief (λύπη) is the hardest of all the emotions (πάντων παθῶν) (Cons. Apoll. 2 = Mor. 102c).

---

concern the emotions but rather weakness and power—and even these opposites do not really ever coexist.

[27] For example, see Wolfgang Nauck, "Freude im Leiden: Zum Problem einer urchristlichen Verfolgungstradition," ZNW 48 (1957): 68–80. See also Achtemeier, 1 Peter, 99–100.

[28] Paul A. Holloway, Consolation in Philippians: Philosophical Sources and Rhetorical Strategy, SNTSMS 112 (Cambridge: Cambridge University Press, 2001), passim, http://dx.doi.org/10.1017/CBO9780511487996; Holloway, Coping with Prejudice: 1 Peter in Social-Psychological Perspective, WUNT 244 (Tübingen: Mohr Siebeck, 2009), 76–112.

Plutarch explains that it would have been unsuitable (ἀνοίκειον) for him to urge Apollonius, immediately after the loss of his son, to bear his loss as a man (ibid.). He further explains that he needed to give Apollonius the time and the permission to grieve as well as to allow himself to share Apollonius's grief (συμπαθεῖν). Plutarch then quotes Aeschylus (*Prom.* 379): "Words are healers of an ailing soul whenever someone soothes the heart at an appropriate time." Plutarch demonstrates that οἰκείωσις ("taking as one's own") and συμπάθεια ("sympathy"), when expressed at the right time, are essential to consoling.

The word οἰκείωσις means that the one who consoles "takes an interest in what concerns another as though it were his or her own, up to the point of being as concerned for the other as one is for oneself."[29] The word συμπάθεια means that the consoler empathetically puts himself or herself in the shoes of the grieving. Demetrius illustrates both of these strategies in his sample letter of consolation that begins, "When I heard of the terrible things that you met at the hands of thankless Fate, I felt the deepest grief, considering that what had happened to you had not happened to you more than to me … all that day long, I cried over them" (*Formae epistolicae* 5).[30] After identifying with the grief-stricken, this sample letter then offers words to alleviate the grief.

The second-century CE letter of Irene to Taonnophris and Philo, who have just lost a child, illustrates these two consoling strategies of identifying with and empathetically sharing the grief of another in an actual letter.[31] Irene writes, "I grieve and weep over the deceased as I wept for Didymas." Previously, Irene has lost a husband or, more likely, a child and thus identifies with Taonnophris and Philo's grief by naming her own lost loved one. Irene then informs them that she and all her household have done what is fitting (καθήκοντα). Ancient consolatory etiquette stipulates that empathy and sensitivity are of utmost importance when consoling and conversing with someone in grief, and Paul Holloway affirms, "It was not uncommon … for consolers to begin with words of sympathy acknowledging the depth of the other's suffering."[32]

If Peter were writing to his grieving recipients and informing them that they are rejoicing while grieving, he would be violating consolatory etiquette and demonstrating his insensitivity and lack of empathy. This etiquette allows for the use of an imperative at the appropriate time to exhort the grieving to replace their grief or distress with rejoicing, as Peter does later in his letter in 4:13. Etiquette, however,

---

[29] Ilaria Ramelli, *Hierocles the Stoic: Elements of Ethics, Fragments, and Excerpts*, ed. and trans. David Konstan, WGRW 28 (Atlanta: Society of Biblical Literature, 2009), 123.

[30] Translation by Abraham J. Malherbe, "Ancient Epistolary Theorists," *OJRS* 5 (1977): 33; reprinted in *Ancient Epistolary Theorists*, SBLSBS 19 (Atlanta: Scholars Press, 1988).

[31] Adolf Deissmann, *Light from the Ancient East: The New Testament Illustrated by Recently Discovered Texts of the Graeco-Roman World* (1910; repr., Grand Rapids: Baker, 1978), 176–77.

[32] Holloway, *Coping with Prejudice*, 80. Holloway also notes that the first task of Job's friends was to join him in his mourning rites and grief (89–90).

does not sanction the use of an indicative to inform the grieving that they are rejoicing especially before treating or addressing their grief. Peter's use of the indicative in this way to tell these exiles that they are rejoicing would be highly insensitive to the emotion of grief they are feeling and would neither demonstrate his identification with (οἰκείωσις) nor his sharing of (συμπάθεια) this vexing emotion, as Plutarch does with Apollonius and Irene with Taonnophris and Philo.

If Peter had begun his letter by informing his recipients that they are rejoicing while grieving, then his letter would furthermore be *sui generis* and without analogy in ancient consolatory theory or literature. Demetrius "broadly defines the consolatory letter as one written to those grieving 'because something unpleasant has happened to them'" (*Formae epistolicae* 5).[33] He does not even hint that such a letter could be written to someone who is rejoicing and grieving at the same time. His definition is confirmed by the preserved corpus of such letters from antiquity, since these letters do not address anyone who is concurrently rejoicing and grieving. Indeed, such letters urge recipients to replace their grief with a different emotion such as joy or no emotion at all, and such letters, the purpose of which is to alleviate grief, are not needed if the recipient has already found a way to rejoice while grieving. Neither those who write about consolation nor those who practice the art envision the need to console someone who is both rejoicing and grieving because they consider the experience of simultaneous joy and grief impossible.

Reading ἀγαλλιᾶσθε in 1 Pet 1:6 in reference to present rejoicing while the recipients are grieving, as Calvin and Horneius do, makes this letter most unusual and even unique when it is compared to ancient consolatory etiquette, theory, and practice. Their assumption that Peter writes to console those rejoicing while grieving, therefore, conforms neither to the theory nor to the practice of ancient consolations. If ἀγαλλιᾶσθε refers to future rejoicing, however, then 1 Peter conforms quite nicely, as Peter holds out the prospect, and indeed even the certainty, of future rejoicing for his grieving recipients.

IV. Conclusion

Both the physiological and consolatory assumptions necessary for reading ἀγαλλιᾶσθε in 1 Pet 1:6 with present reference are not only improbable but also impossible from ancient perspectives. Although Calvin and Horneius and those who follow them read ἀγαλλιᾶσθε in reference to present rejoicing, the original author and readers of 1 Peter could not have. For them, experiencing joy and grief at the same time exceeds the ability of the human body or at least their understanding of the body and how it works. Furthermore, Peter's telling his grieving recipients that they are presently rejoicing would more likely disturb rather than console

[33] Ibid., 79.

them. The ancients' understanding of physiology and their sensitivities of how to console the grieving can be respected and retained only by reading ἀγαλλιᾶσθε with a future reference, as did the ancient commentators and interpreters of 1 Pet 1:6. Even though the article that I published in 1992 failed to persuade all subsequent commentators, perhaps these additional considerations may at last lead to some consensus in the debate about how to read ἀγαλλιᾶσθε in 1 Pet 1:6 as well as this same verb in 1 Pet 1:8.

Of course, reading ἀγαλλιᾶσθε in 1 Pet 1:6 with future reference indicates that this same verb in verse 8 also relates to future rejoicing. Since verse 8 does not mention grief or distress, however, the physiological arguments pertaining to verse 6 cannot be made for verse 8. Nevertheless, the argument from consolatory etiquette, theory, and practice does have some bearing on how to read ἀγαλλιᾶσθε in 1 Pet 1:8, since mentioning rejoicing before treating the grief is inappropriate. In both verses, this verb refers to future rejoicing, as I initially argued in my 1992 article.[34]

A final observation about ἀγαλλιᾶσθε is that this verb does not occur in secular Greek but is developed in biblical Greek to express a rejoicing occasioned by the divine presence. This verb is formed from the nominal stem of ἀγαλλία ("joy"), which is a combination of the root ἀγαλ- with an *iota* suffixed. This noun names a joy to which the ἄγαλμα ("cult statue") belongs or pertains in some way.[35] Thus, the joy expressed in this word group arises from being in the presence of the divine image. The cult image for Christians is not some statue made from gold, silver, stone, or wood but their living, resurrected Lord. When he is revealed at the last time, Christians will rejoice exuberantly as they see their Lord face to face, although they do not see him at present (1 Pet 1:8) and are grieved by manifold trials (1 Pet 1:6). The present tense verb ἀγαλλιᾶσθε is therefore the appropriate word in both 1 Pet 1:6 and 1:8 to express this future exuberant joy at the revelation of Jesus Christ and to emphasize the nearness and certainty of this joy for those who are grieving at present.

---

[34] Martin, "Present Indicative," 307–12.
[35] Smyth, *Greek Grammar*, §858.2.

New Releases from WJK

Jesus and the Gospels
An Introduction

John T. Carroll
Paper • $40.00

The Genesis of Liberation
Biblical Interpretation in the Antebellum Narratives of the Enslaved

Emerson B. Powery
and Rodney S. Sadler Jr.
Paper • $35.00

Acts
A Commentary
NEW TESTAMENT LIBRARY

Carl R. Holladay
Hardback • $75.00

Money and Possessions
INTERPRETATION: RESOURCES FOR THE USE OF SCRIPTURE IN THE CHURCH

Walter Brueggemann
Hardback • $40.00

WJK WESTMINSTER JOHN KNOX PRESS
www.wjkbooks.com | 1.800.523.1631

New and Recent Titles

SBL PRESS

TRANSGENDER, INTERSEX, AND BIBLICAL INTERPRETATION
Teresa J. Hornsby and Deryn Guest
Paperback $27.95, 978-1-62837-135-2 132 pages, 2016 Code: 060686
Hardcover $42.95, 978-0-88414-156-3 E-book $27.95, 978-0-88414-155-6
Semeia Studies 83

EMPIRICAL MODELS CHALLENGING BIBLICAL CRITICISM
Raymond F. Person Jr. and Robert Rezetko, editors
Paperback $51.95, 978-1-62837-132-1 Forthcoming, 2016 Code: 062628
Hardcover $71.95, 978-0-88414-150-1 E-book $51.95, 978-0-88414-149-5
Ancient Israel and Its Literature 25

THE VISION OF THE PRIESTLY NARRATIVE
Its Genre and Hermeneutics of Time
Suzanne Boorer
Paperback $89.95, 978-0-88414-062-7 Forthcoming, 2016 Code: 062627
Hardcover $109.95, 978-0-88414-064-1 E-book $89.95, 978-0-88414-063-4
Ancient Israel and Its Literature 27

XV CONGRESS OF THE INTERNATIONAL ORGANIZATION FOR SEPTUAGINT AND COGNATE STUDIES
Munich, 2013
Wolfgang Kraus, Michaël N. van der Meer, and Martin Meiser, editors
Paperback $99.95, 978-1-62837-138-3 Forthcoming, 2016 Code: 060464
Hardcover $119.95, 978-0-88414-162-4 E-book $99.95, 978-0-88414-161-7
Septuagint and Cognate Studies 64

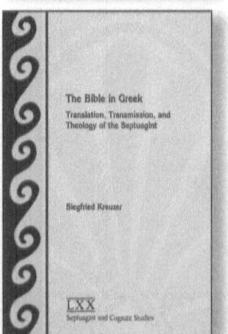

THE BIBLE IN GREEK
Translation, Transmission, and Theology of the Septuagint
Siegfried Kreuzer
Paperback $44.95, 978-0-88414-094-8 332 pages, 2015 Code: 060463
Hardcover $59.95, 978-0-88414-096-2 E-book $44.95, 978-0-88414-095-5
Septuagint and Cognate Studies 63

SBL Press • P.O. Box 2243 • Williston, VT 05495-2243
Phone: 877-725-3334 (toll-free) or 802-864-6185 • Fax: 802-864-7626
Order online at www.sbl-site.org/publications

New and Recent Titles

SBL PRESS

THE LIFE OF ADAM AND EVE IN GREEK
A Critical Edition
Johannes Tromp, editor
Paperback $31.95, 978-1-62837-143-7 214 pages, 2016 Code: 069576
PVTG 6, Brill Reprints 76

ENOCH AND THE SYNOPTIC GOSPELS
Reminiscences, Allusions, Intertextuality
Loren T. Stuckenbruck and Gabriele Boccaccini, editors
Paperback $62.95, 978-0-88414-117-4 Forthcoming, 2016 Code: 063544
Hardcover $82.95, 978-0-88414-119-8 E-book $62.95, 978-0-88414-118-1
Early Judaism and Its Literature 44

ONE TEXT, A THOUSAND METHODS
Studies in Memory of Sjef van Tilborg
Patrick Chatelion Counet and Ulrich Berges, editors
Paperback $56.95, 978-1-62837-146-8 376 pages, 2016 Code: 069577
BibInt 71, Brill Reprints 77

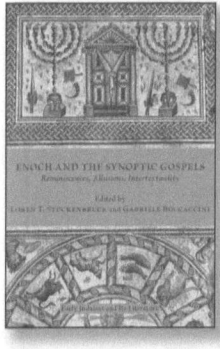

HANDBOOK OF UGARITIC STUDIES
Wilfred G. E. Watson and Nicolas Wyatt, editors
Paperback $99.95, 978-1-62837-036-2 908 pages, 2015 Code: 069558
HdO 39, Bril Reprints 58

HOW JOHN WORKS
Storytelling in the Fourth Gospel
Douglas Estes and Ruth Sheridan, editors
Paperback $46.95, 978-1-62837-131-4 Forthcoming, 2016 Code: 060392
Hardcover $61.95, 978-0-88414-148-8 E-book, $46.95, 978-0-88414-147-1
Resources for Biblical Study 86

THE PEOPLE BESIDE PAUL
The Philippian Assembly and History from Below
Edited by Joseph A. Marchal
Paper $43.95, 978-1-62837-096-6 354 pages, 2015 Code: 064517
Hardcover $58.95, 978-1-62837-097-3 E-book $43.95, 978-1-62837-098-0
Early Christianity and Its Literature 17

SBL Press • P.O. Box 2243 • Williston, VT 05495-2243
Phone: 877-725-3334 (toll-free) or 802-864-6185 • Fax: 802-864-7626
Order online at www.sbl-site.org/publications

www.ingramcontent.com/pod-product-compliance
Lightning Source LLC
Chambersburg PA
CBHW021353300426
44114CB00012B/1214